CULTURAL DIVERSITY
AND
SOCIAL WORK PRACTICE

CULTURAL DIVERSITY
AND
SOCIAL WORK PRACTICE
Second Edition

By

DIANNE F. HARRISON, Ph.D.
BRUCE A. THYER, Ph.D.
JOHN S. WODARSKI, Ph.D.

CHARLES C THOMAS • PUBLISHER, LTD.
Springfield • Illinois • U.S.A.

Published and Distributed Throughout the World by

CHARLES C THOMAS • PUBLISHER, LTD.
2600 South First Street
Springfield, Illinois 62794-9265

© *1996 by* CHARLES C THOMAS • PUBLISHER, LTD.
ISBN 0-398-06606-X (cloth)
ISBN 0-398-06607-8 (paper)
Library of Congress Catalog Card Number: 96-1038

Printed in the United States of America
SC-R-3

Library of Congress Cataloging-in-Publication Data

Cultural diversity and social work practice / edited by Dianne F.
 Harrison, John S. Wodarski, Bruce A. Thyer. — 2nd ed.
  p.   cm.
 Includes bibliographical references and index.
 ISBN 0-398-06606-X. — ISBN 0-398-06607-8 (pbk.)
 1. Social work with minorities—United States. 2. Social service—
United States. I. Harrison, Dianne F. II. Wodarski, John S.
III. Thyer, Bruce A.
HV3176.C85   1996
362.84′00973—dc20   96-1038
                                                        CIP

CONTRIBUTORS

Mary Blount, MSW
Apalachicola Band of Creek Indians
Doctoral Student
School of Social Work
Florida State University
Tallahassee, FL 32306

Karolin E. Davis Meggett, MSW
Doctoral Student
University at Buffalo
School of Social Work
360 Baldy Hall
Buffalo, NY 14260

Kevin L. DeWeaver, Ph.D.
Professor
School of Social Work
University of Georgia
Athens, GA 30602

Cheryl Davenport Dozier, Ph.D.
Assistant Professor
School of Social Work
University of Georgia
Athens, GA 30602

Sophia F. Dziegielewski, Ph.D.
Associate Professor
School of Social Work
University of Alabama
Tuscaloosa, AL 35487-0314

Alicia K. Isaac, D.P.A.
Assistant Professor
School of Social Work
University of Georgia
Athens, GA 30602

Nancy P. Kropf, Ph.D.
Associate Professor
School of Social Work
University of Georgia
Athens, GA 30602

Dianne F. Harrison, Ph.D.
Dean and Professor
School of Social Work
Florida State University
Tallahassee, FL 32306

Donald Leslie, Ph.D.
Assistant Professor
School of Social Work
University of Windsor
Windsor, Ontario, N9B 3P4 Canada

Laura L. Myers, MSW
Doctoral Student
School of Social Work
University of Georgia
Athens, GA 30602

Larry Nackerud, Ph.D.
Assistant Professor
School of Social Work
University of Georgia
Athens, GA 30602

Manuel Nakanishi, Ph.D.
Associate Professor
School of Social Work
Barry University
Miami Shores, FL 33161

Barbara Rittner, Ph.D.
Assistant Professor
School of Social Work
State University of New York
Buffalo, NY 14260

Kathryn Wambach, Ph.D.
Assistant Professor
School of Social Work
1925 San Jacinto
University of Texas
Austin, TX 78712-1203

Hilary Weaver, DSW
Assistant Professor
School of Social Work
State University of New York
Buffalo, NY 14260

John S. Wodarski, Ph.D.
Janet Wattles Professor of Social Work
University at Buffalo
School of Social Work
360 Baldy Hall
Buffalo, NY 14260

PREFACE

We are pleased that the favorable reception accorded to the First Edition of *Cultural Diversity and Social Work Practice* has generated sufficient demand for a revised and expanded Second Edition. Each previously included chapter is newly written and updated, and we were fortunate to be able to recruit authors for two additional chapters dealing with client groups we were unable to include the earlier edition, chapters on persons with developmental disabilities, and persons with adult-onset physical disabilities. Each of these groups possesses significantly distinct attributes to warrant inclusion in a text on culturally diverse practice. There is precedent for this. Mary Richmond's (1917) class text, *Social Diagnosis,* contained chapters on practice with the "feebleminded" and blind individuals, as well as more traditional client groups such as women.

The reader will note that we have taken a largely atheoretical orientation to conceptualizing culturally diverse practice in social work in favor of a more broadly based empirical approach. In part, this is because we believe that the existing theoretical approaches are insufficiently developed to encompass the many aspects of diversity seen among social work clients, and in part we have found that the empirical research itself is derived from such a plethora of orientations that reconciling them in review chapters would be an insurmountable task.

The concept of cultural diversity is receiving considerable press lately, much of it controversial. In part, this is because the term itself is not well defined. For our purposes, we have adopted the point of view suggested by Marsella and Kameoka (1989): "Culture is shared learned behavior that is transmitted from one generation to another for purposes of human adjustment, adaptation, and growth" (p. 233).

Cultural diversity refers to shared, not idiosyncratic, ways of behaving transmitted to one by family and peers. Culture is *learned,* and such learned behavior is capable of being understood in terms of its past adaptive significance to the client and to the survival of his/her culture.

All of us, social workers and clients alike, are immersed in a cultural milieu which affects our ways of seeing, believing, acting and reacting. When there is disparity between social worker and client, the potential exists for misunderstandings to arise and for a less than optimal helping relationship to develop. By understanding certain aspects of the culture experienced by a client, a social worker is better equipped to be of service, to assess, to plan, to cooperate, and to intervene.

The profession of social work has a long history of concern for individuals and groups who are oppressed or disenfranchised in our society. As is true today, much of early social work practice dealt with immigrant groups. Professional organizations such as the National Association of Social Workers and the Council on Social Work Education have adopted formal policies which mandate social workers to be knowledgeable about cultural diversity, including the characteristics of racial and ethnic minorities and other so-called special populations, such as women. This book was written to provide social work practitioners and students with increased knowledge and sensitivity toward cultural diversity in social work practice.

As social work educators, practitioners, and researchers, we have been aware of the need for current, research-based information about client characteristics and special issues associated with race/ethnicity, sexual orientation, age and gender. While such information is available, it is typically scattered throughout the literature from several disciplines. Further, this knowledge is only infrequently made directly relevant to social work practice, policy, research, and educational concerns. *Cultural Diversity and Social Work Practice, Second Edition* is intended to bridge these gaps and to present to readers, in one source, a wealth of practice-relevant information about African Americans, Asian Americans, Hispanic Americans, Native Americans, gay, lesbian, and bisexual individuals, women, the aged, the developmentally disabled, and those with adult-onset physical disabilities. It is designed for both undergraduate and graduate students, as well as for practitioners who desire to enhance their skills in working with culturally diverse clients.

As editors and authors, the contributors to this second edition reflect the diverse makeup of the profession and society at large. We are men and women, coming from White, Black, Hispanic, Native American, and Asian backgrounds. Some of us are elderly, others comparatively young; our sexuality is expressed in differing ways; and some of us possess various physical disabilities. We believe that this diversity has enabled us to produce a book with greater integrity and credibility than a work any one of us could have authored alone. This reflects a fundamental fact of contemporary life: In diversity there is strength.

A central theme of this book is that knowledge about cultural diversity should encompass both historical information and current knowledge that is applicable to direct practice, human behavior, social policy, research, and education in social work. We are deeply committed to the advancement of effective, ethical, and culturally sensitive social work practice. We hope that this book contributes toward that goal.

As with the first edition, the editors would like to gratefully acknowledge the marvelous contributions of the individual chapter authors and to our culturally diverse students, friends, colleagues, and clients, who have so enriched our lives.

Dianne F. Harrison
Bruce A. Thyer
John S. Wodarski

REFERENCES

Marsella, A.J., & Kameoka, V.A. (1989). Ethnocultural issues in the assessment of psychopathology. In S. Wetzler (Ed.), *Measuring mental illness: Psychometric assessment for clinicians* (pp. 231–256). Washington, D.C.: American Psychiatric Press.
Richmond, M. (1917). *Social diagnosis.* New York: Russell Sage Foundation.

CONTENTS

Preface   vii

Chapter

  1. Culturally Diverse Social Work Practice:
      An Overview . . . . *Nancy P. Kropf*

                                 Alicia K. Isaac   3

  2. Social Work Practice with
      African Americans . . . . *John S. Wodarski*

                    Karolin E. Davis Meggett   14

  3. Social Work Practice with Latinos . . . . *Hilary Weaver*

                            John S. Wodarski   52

  4. Social Work Practice with
      Asian Americans . . . . *Manuel Nakanishi*

                            Barbara Rittner   87

  5. Social Work Practice with Women . . . . . *Kathryn G. Wambach*

                         Dianne F. Harrison   112

  6. Social Work Practice with the Aged . . . . . *Sophia Dziegielewski*

                         Dianne F. Harrison   138

  7. Social Practice with Persons with
      Developmental Disabilities . . . . *Nancy P. Kropf*

                         Kevin L. DeWeaver   176

  8. Social Work Practice with Persons with
      Adult-Onset Disabilities . . . . *Donald R. Leslie*

                           Laura L. Myers   201

  9. Social Work Practice with
      Gay Men, Lesbian Women,
      and Bisexual Individuals . . . . *Sophia F. Dziegielewski*

                         Dianne F. Harrison   232

10. Social Work Practice with Native Americans . . . . *Mary Blount*   257

11. Cultural Diversity: Future Directions
     for Practice, Research and Education . . . . *Cheryl Dozier*
                                              Larry Nackerud   299

Index   331

CULTURAL DIVERSITY
AND
SOCIAL WORK PRACTICE

Chapter 1

CULTURAL DIVERSITY AND SOCIAL WORK PRACTICE: AN OVERVIEW

NANCY P. KROPF AND ALICIA R. ISAAC

During the 1960s, the Civil Rights Movement was instrumental in beginning to identify and eradicate forms of discrimination. Subsequent initiatives such as desegregation, fair housing legislation, and affirmative action laws had goals of instituting a more equal and just society. The impetus for change spearheaded other disenfranchised groups to demand increased political and social power. Groups of gay/lesbian/bisexual individuals, the elderly, and the physically challenged formed political organizations and lobbies to address their concerns. With the increased awareness of diversity within society, the ensuing years could have been times of increased tolerance and acceptance for cultural pluralism.

Prejudice, discrimination, and violence continues to persist against individuals based upon personal characteristics, however. Hate crimes, defined by Barnes and Ephross (1994) as "crimes directed against persons, families, groups, or organizations because of their racial, ethnic, religious, or sexual identities or their sexual orientation or condition of disability" (p. 247), are common occurrences. Hate groups such as Neo-Nazis, the Ku Klux Klan, and other racially based supremist groups, continue to attract recruits. These events indicate that intolerance against many different groups continues to exist. While some progress has been made in eradicating prejudice and discrimination, much additional work has yet to be done.

An Historical Overview of Social Work and Diversity

As a profession invested in social justice, social work has a long history of intervention with culturally diverse client groups. Though the characteristics of these individuals have changed and broadened through the

3

years, the mandate to provide services to an array of client groups has remained intact. When Mary Richmond (1899) wrote *Friendly Visiting Among the Poor: A Handbook for Charity Workers,* she could not have envisioned such a spectrum of social work practice with people of color, immigrants from other countries, the aged, the physically challenged, women, gay/lesbian and bisexual individuals. The "friendly visitors" of these times were female workers assisting poor and/or sick women and children. During this period, the recognizable poor and chronically ill constituted a culturally diverse population in the midst of a larger, less tolerable society.

The settlement house movement, initially for immigrants, was one of the earliest formalized interventive efforts specifically focused on culturally diverse clients. Two of the most famous settlement houses in the United States were the Neighborhood Guild on the Lower East Side of New York and Hull House in Chicago. Settlements quickly spread to other large and middle-sized cities in the country. Despite language barriers, poverty, scarce resources, and discrimination, the planned focus and efforts to provide specialized services to a diverse population made the settlement house movement effective. Social workers actually lived in the impoverished neighborhoods and attempted to understand the values, traditions, and feelings of immigrants who were trying to integrate into American society. These early residents and staff of settlement houses became champions of social reform.

Since the early days of social work, a great deal of change has occurred in society and the profession. The roles and contexts of social work practice have expanded dramatically, as social workers practice in situations as diverse as private therapy and within elected political office. Equally diverse are the clients with whom social workers practice. The expansion of professional roles and contexts has allowed our profession to have influence on multiple levels—from working with individual clients to improve or maintain functioning, to creating more humane and socially just programs and policies.

Recently, the profession has been chastised for losing perspective of our historical mission to social justice (Specht & Courtney, 1994). The profession has also been accused of paying inadequate attention to clients of diverse racial and ethnic backgrounds, prompting the question of whether social work is a racist profession (McMahon & Allen-Meares, 1992). Into the next century, the profession of social work must embrace with a new enthusiasm the concepts and models for effective intervention with culturally diverse client systems. Homelessness, problems of aging in an increasingly complex and technological society, discrimination in employment against gay and lesbian individuals, treatment of family systems affected by HIV/AIDS, and the dramatic increase in Hispanic population are some examples of the continuing need for cultural sensitivity.

Culturally Sensitive Practice

Since the clients with whom social workers practice have become a more heterogenous group, sensitivity to issues of cultural diversity has increased in all areas of practice. It is not enough to have an intellectual understanding of particular characteristics of clients, but the ability to acknowledge their different perceptions and experiences must be incorporated into practice applications. This information must then be translated into appropriate and culturally congruent interventions and practice roles (Henderson, 1994). As stated by Greene (1994), "effective multicultural practice requires the simultaneously simple and complex activity of putting the client—with all that implies about the particular aspects of the client's life experience and meaning system—at the center of the helping process" (p. 17).

Unfortunately, racism, sexism, ageism, ableism and heterosexism are deeply interwoven into the social fabric of our culture. Examples of institutional discrimination include the feminization of poverty, employment discrimination against older workers and adults with disabilities, and economic and social discrimination against same-sex households. Effective social work practice involves a commitment to eradication of these social inequalities as well as promoting optimal functioning with individual clients who experience problems as a result of oppression and discrimination.

Culturally Sensitive Research

Practice evaluations with diverse client systems need to determine effective treatment and service delivery models. The importance of empirically based interventions is becoming more appreciated and acknowledged in social work. For example, the NASW National Committee on Lesbian and Gay Issues (1992) issued a policy statement that condemned as unethical the use of reparative therapy for people who are gay/lesbian, in part based upon the lack of empirical support for these so-called reparative treatments. One wonders how many other psychosocial treatments employed by social workers similarly lack credible evidence of efficacy, particularly those used with various cultural/racial/ethnic clientele. Clearly it is essential that well-crafted empirical research studies be conducted to test the usefulness of various social work interventions on diverse groups.

A major criticism leveled at traditional research on culturally diverse groups is related to samples which are included in the studies. Researchers have routinely used white middle-class standards as comparative norms (cf. Tidwell, 1990). A second criticism has been the use of sample sizes which are too small or otherwise unrepresentative of various groups. These unrepresentative samples are frequently used to make generalizations about large diverse populations (cf. Engram, 1982).

Different methods of inquiry need to be incorporated into research on different client groups. The use of ethnographic studies provides a view of culturally diverse populations as compared to themselves. This methodology promotes a greater awareness of differences that exist among subgroups of the population. For example, the life situations of elderly African American farm women, a relatively invisible segment of our population, was studied through the use of an oral history process (Carlton-LaNey, 1993). Likewise, the lives of older deinstitutionalized adults with developmental disabilities were researched through an ethnographic method (Edgerton & Gaston, 1991). Alternatives to traditional research methods can explore life experiences, perceptions, and identify the resources available to diverse individuals and groups.

Social work research also needs to focus on strengths and resources within culturally diverse populations (cf. Myers, 1982). Attention to well-functioning aspects of clients provides a basis for future interventions. Traditionally, research has been instrumental in problem identification. For effective practice with culturally diverse clients, however, research must be instrumental in problem solving.

Culturally Sensitive Education

On a policy level, the Council on Social Work Education (1992) mandates that the curriculum incorporate multiculturalism in BSW and MSW instruction. The classroom instructor has a significant impact on preparing practitioners to work with culturally diverse populations. An essential ingredient in effective social work practice is understanding the racial and ethnic characteristics of clients (Jacobs & Bowles, 1988). Logan, Freeman, and McRoy (1990) assert that the triad of social work curriculum in terms of policy, practice, and research must be made more relevant to cultural diversity. This process must begin with social work educators having a clear philosophy on multiculturalism and the ability to impart this information to beginning practitioners.

In addition to teaching skills, educators must be prepared to assess changes in students as a result of their learning experiences. Carrillo, Holzhalb and Thyer (1993) provide an overview of rapid assessment instruments that can be used in the classroom to evaluate change in students. These authors provide a summary of instruments that measure attitudinal change toward individuals of racial/ethnic groups, by gender roles, people with physical disabilities, the aged, and general acceptance of others.

Another curriculum area which requires additional emphasis is the development of practice skills relevant to culturally diverse populations. There is a need to develop, refine, and teach multi-level skills such as brokerage, advocacy, confrontation, manipulation of systems, bargaining, and negotiation, that allow practitioners to promote both individual and social change. On a macro level, social workers must be taught how policy affects culturally diverse populations. These skills include lobbying and coalition-building.

Organization of This Text

As previously stated, the profession of social work has a rich history working with groups that have experienced oppression and discrimination. The material contained in this volume has the goal of providing students with information about the norms, practices, and special issues associated with various groups of our society. Although the topic of cultural diversity could be approached in a number of different ways, this text employs a group-oriented format. Social work practice and policy issues related to race/ethnicity, sexual orientation, age, gender, and disability are discussed separately. Additionally, issues related to sensitivity in research and education are explored.

Race/Ethnicity

Four racial/ethnic groups are included in this text. These are: African Americans, Asian Americans, Hispanic Americans, and Native Americans. A brief summary of issues relating to each of these groups is provided.

A contributing consequence of ongoing patterns of prejudice and discrimination is a disproportionate number of African Americans living in impoverished conditions. Many of the African American clients with whom social workers practice experience multiple correlates of poverty, including addictions, unemployment, violence, mental illness, and poor physical health. Myths about social welfare participation of African Americans, including welfare dependency and defrauding the system, are widespread in our society. In addition to constructing policies and social programs to eradicate these inequalities, social workers need to construct practice models that are built upon strengths of the African American family and community (Daly, Jennings, Beckett, & Leashore, 1995; Williams & Wright, 1992).

Asian Americans also suffer from societal myths. This ethnic group is often viewed as the "model minority," implying a smooth assimilation into the dominant culture. This stereotype tends to minimize the problems faced by members of this group. Many Asian Americans arrive in this country as refugees in need of numerous social services. Additionally, problems with the language and underemployment may negatively impact Asian Americans' adjustment (Nah, 1993). Other issues which need to be explored with Asian Americans include differential social welfare needs by age and gender (Fong & Mokuau, 1994).

Hispanic Americans are the fastest-growing ethnic group in our country. Increases in this group are a result of a high birth and immigration rates. While many Hispanics are bilingual, others speak only Spanish. Due to the diversity of the group who are identified as Hispanic or Latino, many social workers are uncertain about the most effective way to provide services to these clients (Castex, 1994). Additional social workers will be needed who are culturally sensitive and can communicate with the increasing number of Hispanic clients.

Historically, Native Americans have suffered injustices by our government. Today, conditions on many reservations include high rates of substance abuse, poverty, and substandard housing. Yet as a profession, social work has paid little attention to the concerns of this client group.

Members of all of these racial/ethnic groups experience subtle and overt forms of prejudice and discrimination. Social workers who are involved with clients from diverse racial backgrounds need to be sensitive to the unique issues facing these individuals. Practitioners also need to be aware of ways social forces contribute to the problems experienced by African American, Asian, Hispanic, and Native American clients.

Sexual Orientation

Unlike the traits of race/ethnicity, age, and gender, sexual orientation is not an observable characteristic. Although stereotypes of effeminate men and masculine women are prevalent, these images do not accurately discriminate between gay/lesbian/bisexual and heterosexual groups. Identity development and management with gay men and lesbian women are important issues in social work practice with these clients. Identity issues in work with gay and lesbian adolescents are extremely critical since confusion, self-depreciation, and a lack of available role models may cause serious psychosocial and adjustment problems for these youths (Morrow, 1993; Proctor & Groze, 1994).

As adults, gay men and lesbian women experience economic, legal, and social discrimination. Even in committed relationships, same-sex households do not enjoy the tax advantages, health care options, or social rituals which are part of heterosexual marriages. These forms of discrimination against gay and lesbian clients must be addressed by our profession which is committed to social change.

Gender

The past few decades have included increased opportunities for women. Women have experienced additional employment, family and social role choices with different options available to young women from those of their mothers and grandmothers. The unfortunate consequence for many women is role overload or stress as they attempt to juggle roles of heads of households and caregivers in addition to other responsibilities in the labor force.

Although choices have increased, women continue to experience discrimination, oppression, and brutality in contemporary society. Although the rate of poverty for women exceeds that of men, many women also have economic responsibility for others including their children, grandchildren or aging family members. The incidence of domestic violence and rape continues at unacceptably high levels. Practitioners in all service settings will encounter gender issues, since women comprise the majority of social work clients.

Age

The number of older people in society has increased dramatically since the early 1900s. Additionally, this demographic shift is predicted to continue into the next century which forecasts a society of greater numbers of older people who are living longer lives. Unfortunately, social work practice approaches rarely distinguish between needs of the younger cohorts of the older adults and those who are in latest life. In coming years, it will be more common to have older people who live into their 90s and 100s which necessitates additional investigation of the life experiences and social welfare needs of the oldest of the old (Kropf & Pugh, 1995).

These demographic changes have implications for the current structure of the social welfare system. One change is in the present health care system which does not adequately address the chronic medical needs of older people. In the mental health system, additional attention to the needs of the elderly, including working with the depressed elderly and people with organic impairments, is necessary. Assistance in retirement, leisure planning, and income security can be provided by social workers to enhance social functioning of older adults. Additionally, attention to financial security of our older population is necessary. Although income security programs are available to older adults (e.g., Social Security, private pension funds), many older adults, especially single women of color, live in poverty. Income disparity is greatest among strata in the older population, and there are more extremely poor individuals in later life than any other age groups (Ozawa, 1995).

Disability Status

Two disability chapters have been included in the second edition of this text. People with disabilities have not traditionally been included in multicultural education, yet there are several reasons why these clients should be understood in this context. Many problems in functioning experienced by individuals with a disability are a result of social barriers, limited opportunities and stigma. The rising social activism on the part of people with disabilities is another reason why they should be included in diversity courses (cf. Shapiro, 1993). The community of people with disabilities was instrumental in achieving swift passage of the Americans with Disabilities Act of 1990 (ADA) which prohibits discrimination on the basis of disability in employment, state and local government services, public accommodations, and telecommunications. The ADA has dramatic consequences for social work clients who have disabilities and provides a source of protection for the agencies that serve the disabled community (Orlin, 1995).

Numerous practice issues emerge in working with people who have disabilities. An important one is the time of onset, as adults who acquire disabilities through an accident, illness or progressive condition will need support and assistance in adjustment to their new roles and conditions. People with lifelong disabilities, such as mental retardation, hearing impairment, and cerebral palsy, may have other practice issues such as educational needs, family adjustment issues, and support across the life span. Due to changes in service systems for people with disabilities, greater numbers of these clients are living in community and family based settings than in previous years. Social workers may practice in specialized service systems for people with disabilities such as vocational rehabilitation and developmental disabilities. However, practitioners in diverse service settings such as medical social work, aging services, and educational contexts will also have clients on their case loads who have a disabling condition.

Limitations of the Group-Oriented Approach to Cultural Diversity

Certain problems are inherent when using a group-oriented approach to cultural diversity. One difficulty is in aggregating the data from a number of subgroups to represent a typical profile of the total group. For example, a 65-year-old and a 105-year-old are both called "elderly" although their life situations are probably dissimilar. Likewise, an "Asian American" could be a refugee from a war-battered country or a college professor. While categories are used to provide a framework for understanding different cultural distinctions, within-group differences need to be kept in mind.

A second problem is the dilemma about which groups to include. Unfortunately, this text does not exhaustively discuss all cultural groups. The decision to restrict the information to certain groups was solely based upon space limitations, not upon a belief that the issues facing other groups are less important.

A third and extremely important issue is that these groups are not mutually exclusive. For example, a practitioner may work with a client who is an elderly African American woman with a developmental disability. This person faces prejudice and discrimination based upon race, gender, age, and her disability condition. Individuals with whom social workers will practice will likely hold multiple memberships in the various groups.

The importance of a text on diversity arises from the cultural pluralism present in contemporary society. While social work has historic roots in working with socially devalued populations, the diversity in the client groups has increased since our professional beginnings. Social workers are not immune from their membership in a racist, sexist, ageist, and heterosexist society. In order to be effective practitioners, part of social work education is raising the level of sensitivity to issues of cultural diversity in all areas of social work practice. As authors of the second edition of this textbook, we hope that the contents contribute to this process.

REFERENCES

Barnes, A., & Ephross, P.H. (1994). The impact of hate violence on victims: Emotional and behavioral responses to attacks. *Social Work, 39,* 241–336.

Carlton-LaNey, I. (1993). Elderly black farm women: A population at risk. *Social Work, 37,* 517–526.

Carrillo, D., Holzhalb, C.M., & Thyer, B.A. (1993). Assessing social work students' attitudes related to cultural diversity: A review of selected measures. *Journal of Social Work Education, 29,* 263–268.

Castex, G.M. (1994). Providing services to Hispanic/Latino populations: Profiles in diversity. *Social Work, 39,* 288–297.

Council on Social Work Education. (1992). *Curriculum policy for the master's degree and baccalaureate degree programs in social work education.* Alexandria, VA: Author.

Daly, A., Jennings, J., Beckett, J.O., & Leashore, B.R. (1995). Effective coping strategies of African Americans. *Social Work, 40,* 240–249.

Edgerton, R.B., & Gaston, M.A. (Ed.). (1991). *"I've seen it all!" Lives of older persons with mental retardation living in the community.* Baltimore: Paul H. Brookes.

Engram, E. (1982). *Science, myth, reality: The black family in one-half century of research.* Westport, CT: Greenwood.

Fong, R., & Mokuau, N. (1994). Not simply "Asian Americans": Periodical literature review on Asians and Pacific Islanders. *Social Work, 39,* 298–306.

Greene, R.R. (Ed.). (1994). *Human behavior theory: A diversity framework.* New York: Aldine DeGruyter.

Henderson, G. (1994). *Social work interventions: Helping people of color.* Westport, CT: Bergin & Garvey.

Jacobs, C., & Bowles, D. (1988). *Ethnicity and race: Critical concepts in social work.* Silver Spring, MD: National Association of Social Workers.

Kropf, N.P., & Pugh, K. (1995). Beyond life expectancy: Social work with centenarians. *Journal of Gerontological Social Work, 23*(3/4).

Logan, S., Freeman, E., & McRoy, R. (Eds.). (1990). *Social work practice with black families.* New York: Longman.

McMahon, A., & Allen-Meares, P. (1992). Is social work racist? A content analysis of recent literature. *Social Work, 37,* 533–539.

Morrow, D.F. (1993). Social work with gay and lesbian adolescents. *Social Work, 38,* 655–660.

Myers, H.F. (1982). Research on the African American: A critical review. In B.A. Bass, G.E. Wyatt, & G.J. Powell (Eds.), *The African American family: Assessment, treatment and research issues* (pp. 35–68). New York: Grune & Stratton.

Nah, K. (1993). Perceived problems and service delivery for Korean immigrants. *Social Work, 38,* 289–297.

NASW National Committee on Lesbian and Gay Issues. (1992). *"Reparative" or "conversion" therapies for lesbian women and gay men.* NASW Position Statement. Washington, D.C.: Author.

Orlin, M. (1995). The Americans with Disabilities Act: Implications for social services. *Social Work, 40,* 233–240.

Ozawa, M.N. (1995). The economic status of vulnerable older women. *Social Work, 40,* 323–333.

Proctor, C.D., & Groze, V.K. (1994). Risk factors for suicide among gay, lesbian, and bisexual youths. *Social Work, 39,* 504–514.

Richmond, M.E. (1899). *Friendly visiting among the poor. A handbook for charity workers.* New York: Macmillan.

Shapiro, J.P. (1993). *No pity: People with disabilities forging a new civil rights movement.* New York: Times Books.

Specht, H., & Courtney, M.E. (1994). *Unfaithful angels: How social work has abandoned its mission.* New York: Free Press.

Tidwell, B. (1990). Research on black families. In S. Logan, E. Freeman, & R. McRoy (Eds.), *Social work practice with black families* (pp. 259–272). New York: Longman.

Williams, S.E., & Wright, D.F. (1992). Empowerment: The strengths of black families revisited. *Journal of Multicultural Social Work, 2*(4), 23–36.

Chapter 2

SOCIAL WORK PRACTICE
WITH AFRICAN AMERICANS

JOHN S. WODARSKI AND KAROLIN E. DAVIS MEGGETT

Historical Background

"The expatriation of millions of Africans in less than four centuries constitutes one of the most far-reaching and drastic social revolutions in the annals of history" (Franklin & Moss, 1988). Human bondage for African Americans in this country began in August of 1619, when a Dutch ship landed in Jamestown, Virginia, with "twenty Negras" as cargo (Sloan, 1971). Thus began one of the most unconscionable periods of human suffering ever executed in the history of America by one group over another and signaled the structuralization of "the peculiar institution," of that period known as plantation slavery. Captured Africans were sold to the highest bidder as chattel and were primarily utilized for cheap agricultural labor and as "breeders" for increasing the slave population which in turn increased laborers for the plantations. The women were exploited as sexual commodities, nannies, etc. In essence, the Africans were presumed to be less than human, devoid of intelligence.

This was a collective effort by Euro-Americans to eradicate all remnants of the traditional African life, including the cohesiveness of the family unit. The family unit was not a consideration when selling the Africans. Husbands and wives, sisters and brothers, both in Africa and America, were separated, most never to reunite again (Mays, 1986). While slavery officially ended on December 18, 1865 with the ratification of the Thirteenth Amendment, psychological slavery, prejudice, discrimination, and overt and covert racism continue. African Americans in the South became sharecroppers and cotton pickers who made only about forty cents a day and lived in substandard housing. Terrorist groups such as the Ku Klux Klan intimidated Blacks and prevented them from voting, from getting a quality education, or becoming profitable in business. As Blacks became less valued for physical labor, murders, beatings, and lynchings increased; between 1882 and 1935, approximately three thousand Blacks were lynched (Mays, 1986). The stigma of racism was an overpowering factor in not allowing the former slaves the same rights extended to other citizens of this country. The continued mistreatment and denial of citizenship rights to the Africans, and the continuance of "Jim Crow" laws and practices ultimately became the catalyst for what is known as "The American Civil Rights Movement."

The underlying principle of the Civil Rights Movement (1950s–1960s) was a refusal by Blacks to accept the White power structure's rationalizations for the continued mistreatment of them (Mays, 1986). A period of reconstruction was set in motion by the landmark United States Supreme court case, *Brown vs. Board of Education,* which declared that racial segregation in public schools was unconstitutional. Additionally, one of the most poignant and significant demonstrations of Blacks' fight for freedom and equality in this country began by the refusal of an African American woman, Rosa Parks, to give up her seat and move to the back of the bus. Under Jim Crowism, Blacks had to continuously submit themselves to the whims of Whites, including giving up their seats on public transportation if Whites ordered them to do so. The refusal of Rosa Parks to obey these laws and surrender her seat facilitated the Montgomery Bus Boycott by Blacks.

Bus boycotts began in an attempt to integrate public transportation, and sit-ins were organized to protest discrimination in public accommodations such as restaurants. On August 29, 1963, Dr. Martin Luther King, Jr. organized the largest civil rights demonstration in history when 250,000 people marched for racial equality between the Lincoln and Washington Memorials in Washington, D.C.

In the early 1970s, the Black Power Movement began and the ideology of many African Americans shifted from integration to segregation (Mays, 1986). Continuous riots demonstrated Blacks' feelings of frustration and anger toward Whites. Blacks were concerned with the "nation-building" of their people and with asserting a positive self-image, which was vocalized through the slogan "Black is beautiful" (Mays, 1986).

With the election of Jimmy Carter to the presidency in 1976, the Black population gained a speaker in the executive branch of government. Human rights and integration became a central issue of the four-year Carter presidency. However, with the election of Ronald Reagan in 1980, Americans became more concerned with foreign policy and millions of dollars were redirected from social services defense.

Using the pretense of "The New Federalism," Reaganomics chose private interests over the public good. The Black community suffered as a result. For example, cuts were made in programs that helped make college more affordable and, as a result, Blacks' prospects for attending college were dimmed. A study by Gary and Leashore (1984) revealed that limited educational opportunity and attainment among Black men invariably led to restricted employment and income, which in turn made it difficult to meet basic needs, including meeting the basic needs of caring for their families. The pillages of public policies and its consequences are still painfully obvious.

In the 1980s and early 1990s, many African Americans struggled to define what being an African American means after stereotypes are discarded. They continue to wrestle with questions concerning their identity—an identity that has been defined by White America. Should they continue to model Whites' behavior and adapt to Whites' societal institutions, or should they base their identity on their African cultural heritage and traditions? (Mays, 1986). The preferred use of the term African American by many individuals, instead of "Black," illustrates the increased identity with the African cultural heritage. The legacy of plantation slavery continues to haunt the African American race in myriad ways: psychologically, economically, socially, and physically.

Current Characteristics

More than three-quarters of the African American population in the U.S. live in metropolitan areas. At least four major American cities now have Black majorities: Washington, D.C., Atlanta, GA, Newark, NJ and Gary, IN. The millions of Blacks who migrated from the South to the North between 1915 and 1970 ended up in the central zones of cities and have remained there (Blackwell, 1975). New York, Chicago, Philadelphia, and Detroit house more than one-quarter of the nation's inner-city poor (Yeakey, 1992).

Most of the families in the U.S. are composed of a married couple, or by one parent, and one or more of the parents' children. Over 85 percent of Black families in 1980 were of these two types, and the corresponding proportions for all families without regard to race was 93 percent (U.S. Bureau of the Census, 1980). Although the vast majority of families consist of one of these types, twice as large a proportion of Black families as other families (as defined by the Census Bureau) were not of these types (14% vs. 7%). Many of the families of the latter type consist of grandparents providing homes for grandchildren whose parents live elsewhere (e.g., they are incarcerated, in rehabilitation programs for substance abuse, have died as a result of Black-on-Black homicide, or consist of combinations such as brothers and sisters living together apart from their families) (Glick, 1981).

African American families continue to be more likely than other families to include young children. By 1980, 62 percent of the Black families, compared to 52 percent of the families of all races, included one or more sons and/or daughters under the age of 18 in the home. In 1980, one-half of the Black families with children present were one-parent families (31%) and one-half were married couples (31%). At the same time, less than one-fifth of the families (20%) of all races with children were maintained by one parent. By 1984, approximately 60 percent of Black children lived in a family situation other than with both parents (Bane, 1986). In 1980, 14.6 percent of all families of all races in the U.S. were female-headed households; whereas, the percentage for Black families was 40.2 percent, up from 28.3 percent in 1970. More recently compiled data revealed in 1992, only 72 percent of American children lived in two-parent families in 1990, compared to 85 percent in 1970. According to Carol Yeakey, 59 percent of African American children were in two-parent families in 1970, yet only 36 percent remained in this familial structure in 1990.

One explanation for this dramatic difference between Black and other families is that there is a great deal of misreporting in census reports and surveys on the subject of the absence of the husband from the household. Most likely many poor couples, regardless of race, report that the husband is absent if they believe that doing so will improve their chances of receiving welfare benefits. White families are less likely to separate during hard times because of the prospects of their economic situation improving. If such reporting is more likely to occur among Black families, it could be in part because a larger proportion of Black families than other families are poor. Also, Black husbands are more likely than other husbands to live apart from their wives, because larger proportions of them are serving in the armed forces or are residing in an institution (Glick, 1981). Overall, poverty is an overriding factor and stressor in the breakup of African American families.

Another explanation for the dramatic rise in the proportion of female-headed Black families is the "economic motivation" theory, which posits that the attractiveness of welfare is an inducement to Black women to "choose" to remain unmarried. A study by Darity and Myers (1984) examined this explanation and found no statistical relationship between the growth of female-headed Black families and the attractiveness of welfare. Rather, the statistical driving force behind the increase appeared to be the *decline* in the number of Black males. A recent report in *Emerge Magazine* by Linda Faye Williams indicates that African American women do choose welfare over other alternatives. However, one of the mitigating factors of this choice is that because of a lack of education, the only jobs available are low paying and do not allow them to meet their family's basic needs such as medical benefits. Another reason that some African American women choose welfare do so because it's generational; it's the only way of life they have ever known.

Bane (1986) suggests the argument for economic motivation is difficult to support when welfare benefit levels were going down at the same time Black female-headed households were rising. Extensive research regarding the relationship of AFDC levels to family structure changes suggests that welfare has very small effects on divorce and separation rates and little discernible effects on birth rates of unmarried women. Welfare benefits do have a substantial effect on poverty rates among single-parent families. However, blaming the increasing dependency of Black American children on the increase in welfare benefits is not tenable when, in fact, welfare benefits were cut by a third during the 1970s.

Feminization of Poverty and Black Female-Headed Families

During the past several decades, there has been an increased awareness of the status of single-parent families, most notably Black female-headed households. The "feminization of poverty" has been delineated as one of the most severe economic and social problems in America (Nichols-Casebolt, 1988).

Notwithstanding the implementation and enforcement of affirmative action programs, anti-discrimination laws, and an increase in social welfare benefits, African American families appear to have severely regressed economically (Nichols-Casebolt, 1988). Data retrieved from census reports indicate that although there was phenomenal growth in the number of African American female-headed households during the 10-year span from 1969–1979, there was not a significant increase in the income of the Black family. The median family income for African

American families was 61 percent that of Whites; by 1979 it had decreased to 59 percent. Statistically, there was a 73 percent increase in the numbers of African American female-headed households with children during this 10-year span. Single mothers with children accounted for more than 48 percent of all African American children by 1980; in conjunction, 56 percent of African American single mothers with children lived below the official poverty threshold (U.S. Bureau of the Census, 1970a, 1970b, 1980a, 1980b). In 1980, the median family income for all families of all races in the U.S. was $21,521; whereas, for Black families it was $11,648, and for Black female-headed households, $6,907. A study by Cotton (1988) found that when skills are fairly comparable, the Black female earns an average wage nearly 21 percent lower than the White male average.

Economic trends concerning the Black population are disheartening. The poverty rate among Blacks is reportedly 50 percent. The poverty rate for Black children under the age of 15 is reported as 48 percent, and for ages 15 and up it has reached an unprecedented 51.1 percent. An African American child is three times more likely to be born into poverty than a White child (Graham, 1987; National Commission on Children, 1991). An analysis by the Congressional Research Service found that one poor child in seven stays poor at least 10–15 years and is considered "persistently" poor.

Among persistently poor children, 90 percent are African American and 61 percent lack a father in the home (Moynihan, 1986). For African American men, the unemployment rate is nearly double that of White men, over 40 percent of African American teenagers are without jobs, and African Americans comprise almost half the federal and state prison population. Even more disheartening is the fact that over 60 percent of African American families are headed by women. Approximately half of those are considered poor and living in poverty.

Research indicates that relative to the rest of the population, the living standards of Black families have declined (Moon, 1986). This is a result of the trend toward a less equal distribution of income from 1980–1984 and the escalation of deindustrialization—the loss of industrial jobs in the steel, automobile, rubber, and textile industries from the inner cities and relocating to the suburbs, thereby denying many African Americans access due to lack of transportation. The general conditions of the United States partially explain this downward move; however, specific federal tax and expenditure policy changes have aggravated the situation. From 1980–1984, Black families had lower absolute and relative disposable incomes; family income after taxes and inflation adjustments dropped 2 percent for Blacks but rose 4 percent for families as a whole (Moon, 1986). Forty-three percent of Black families are highly represented in the lowest income quintile. This high percentage may be caused by a higher proportion of female-headed families, but if adjusted for these differences, Black families still have lower incomes than other families in the U.S. Bureau of the Census reports for 1984 revealed that 31 percent of all Black families (2.1 million) had incomes below the poverty level. Black female-headed households accounted for 73 percent of all poor Black families.

Exacerbating the income problem is the fact that policy changes during 1980–1984 negatively affected the poor. Specifically, the value of welfare declined and the income tax law revisions of 1981 overlooked the needs of low-income workers. In the revisions, the standard deduction and personal exemption remained the same, causing many low-income working families to experience higher taxes over time (Moon, 1986). Though it did not affect the poverty rates, this was an added burden for low-income families.

Since 1969, unemployment rates for Blacks have been consistently double those for Whites. In 1984, the jobless rate for the entire Black population was 15.9 percent vs. 6.5 percent for Whites. Among all groups, both Black and White, the rates for Black teenagers were the highest, with the sharpest increases. In 1984, Black teenage unemployment was 40 percent. Part of this large unemployment rate among Blacks is related to the structural shifts from low-skilled jobs to technological job opportunities. In our new age of science and technology, there appears to be little place for a population that remains disproportionately without the technical skills needed for the new era (Darity & Myer, 1984). This situation points to the increasing need for job training and education. Farley (1987) found that Black male unemployment was higher relative to that of Whites where jobs were most suburbanized and the minority population least so. This supports the view that housing segregation (separating minorities from job locations) elevates minority unemployment. Among the findings of a study by Stafford (1985) were that Blacks did not benefit from the growth.

According to McAdoo (1981), there has been a steady erosion of the proportion of Blacks who are preparing for and being employed in traditional professional careers. There has been a loss of earning power per family unit, in relation to all other families in the U.S. More families are being forced to "double up" with other family members as a result of the high unemployment rate and growing inflation. The growing underclass entrapment of African Americans, including the working poor, prevents any consideration of upward mobility (Glasgow, 1980). Extensive research indicates that in spite of an increase in jobs following the 1975 recession, and despite the increasing numbers of Black college graduates, African Americans were poorly represented in professional jobs. This lack of African Americans in professional jobs has produced the so-called African American "underclass," and "cyclical poverty."

The cycle of poverty among African Americans and the so-called "underclass" can not be attributed to welfare, nor an unwillingness to work. Conversely, cyclical poverty is attributed to the loss of jobs in the inner city and chronic unemployment. According to Wilson (1989), "African Americans have borne the brunt of the destruction and devastation wrought by deindustrialization." There is a greater disparity between the incomes of middle-class White Americans and that of middle-class African Americans more so now than in the 1970s. African Americans have yet to recover from the last recession. African Americans, in increasing numbers, are becoming this nation's population of "disposable workers."

The home health care industry is becoming a significant employer of low-income and minority women in the United States. There appears to be an escalating trend and demand for "disposable workers." These temporary workers often provide the hands and mental brainpower that companies are not willing to hire as permanent employees. As a result, there are no pensions, no paid vacations, no paid health care plans, no promotions, and more significantly, no more legal actions for wrongful termination. According to Donovan (1987), many of the new non-professional jobs, such as home attendant and home health care aide, are structured within subemployment systems that keep wages low and benefits few or nonexistent. It is suggested that the current conditions have historical roots in U.S. slavery and the persistent segregation of Black women in work roles as domestic servants in private households.

Becker and Hills (1980) researched the effects of unemployment on Black and White youth. They found that while White teenage unemployment among White out-of-school youth is a productive experience, teenage unemployment can have a negative effect on the future wages of

Black teens. Indirect evidence was provided that public training programs can partially offset added costs of long-term unemployment.

According to developmental theory, adolescents' efforts toward achieving emotional, functional, and financial independence from their parents are natural and predictable. However, for many unemployed Black teenagers, this natural striving for independence may be blocked. Freeman and McCoy (1986) described a group counseling program for Black teenagers that not only helped them identify and cope with separation issues but also helped to increase their qualifications for employment and their job search skills.

Family

There is a familial tradition in the ethos of the African American culture which extends beyond the structural boundaries of "blood kin" to the extended family network. This tradition is known as "the helping tradition" and clearly has indigenous roots in the African diaspora. In Africa, tenacious kinship bonds facilitated the inclusion of smaller family units who would join larger units, creating clans and sometimes entire communities (Martin & Martin, 1985). African American family life varies by types of marriage, authority structure, household patterns, family functions, and degree of stability. The following discussion is based upon Blackwell's (1975) study of "The Black Family in American Society," from *The Black Community: Diversity and Unity.*

Monogamy is the norm among Black families in America; that is, almost all Black people conform to the law permitting one spouse at a time. Serial monogamy (a series of marriages of relatively short duration) occurs among Black Americans but is found predominately in the low socioeconomic groups. Common law marriages and various forms of boyfriend-girlfriend living arrangements are other patterns found within the Black community; however, almost all Black people who marry are united through some kind of formal and legitimate channel. African American family life and kinship bonds differ significantly from mainstream America in that there is a sense of "we" rather than "I." Traditionally, they live, work, and socialize as a collective unit rather than as an individual "I." What affects one member of the clan affects all. Even today to a certain degree this holds true. When one African American is discriminated against, it is perceived as discrimination against the entire group. It is imperative to recognize that although this African world view has been greatly modified by African Americans, the tradition of helping has been passed on from generation to generation and is the underpinning of African American society today (Harvey, 1985).

While Black families in America are characteristically stereotyped as matriarchal, the equalitarian family pattern is actually the most common authority pattern found. Even at low-income levels, equalitarianism (both husband and wife sharing responsibilities equally) exceeds in importance both in matriarchy and patriarchy as dominant family types (Billingsley, 1968). Family patterns among Black Americans vary in terms of household composition. Billingsley (1968) identified three primary family types: (1) basic, characterized by the presence of husband and wife only; (2) nuclear, consisting of husband, wife, and children; and (3) attenuated nuclear families, characterized by the absence of one of the marital partners. He subdivided these primary types into extended families, subfamilies, and augmented families.

Extended families are comprised of one or more relatives as members of the nuclear or basic families. Subfamilies consist of relatives who join another family as a basic family unit. These persons may be boarders, roomers, or extended guests. Thus, there is tremendous diversity in types and composition of Black family structures (Blackwell, 1975). The apparent heterogeneity among Black family structures is an adaptation developed to survive what has been an alien and hostile experience for a sizeable portion of the Black population in America (Billingsley, 1968).

According to Billingsley (1968), the Black family has two basic functions: instrumental and expressive. Instrumental functions include such activities as providing for the economic well-being of family members and for physical and social sustenance. Instrumental functions contribute to the stability of the family when meeting the basic needs of food, clothing, housing, and health care. Given the disadvantaged income and occupational structure in the Black community, Black families are predictably less effective in instrumental function performance (Blackwell, 1975). Expressive functions are largely internal to the family system and depend upon the quality of reciprocal relationships among individual family members.

Hill (1971) demonstrated how exchanges may occur between husbands and wives in terms of traditional role expectations. These changes may be essentially role reversals structured by the social situation in order to get the job done. Thus, husbands may change diapers or cook or do heavy housework and wives may mow the lawn and repair things around the house (Blackwell, 1975).

According to Staples (1981), these more equalitarian roles among Black couples have their roots in the slavery system, which did not permit Black males to assume the superordinate role in the family, since the female was not economically dependent on him. In the post-slavery era, the economic parity of Black men and women continued. Due to the low wages of most Black males, women were forced to work and contribute to the household and thus developed attitudes of equality and freedom unknown to most women in the nineteenth century.

There are five critical elements of African American family life that distinguish it from the family structure of other ethnic/racial groups. The traditional African American family is a unique cultural form enjoying its own inherent resources. It is comprised of several individual households, with the channels of authority reaching beyond the household units that compose it. In periods of crisis and at times of ceremony, the extended family is most visible and provides needed emotional support for its members. The family may (and often does) perform many ritual, social, and psychological functions, including the education of its young and the adjudication of the family's internal conflicts. Even though some features of the African American family can be explained situationally (as adaptive responses to certain pressures of the moment), the underlying structure of the African American extended family is ultimately traceable to Africa (Nobels, 1981).

The African American family has been seen by some as a sanctuary that protects individuals from the pervasiveness of White racism and provides needed support systems that are unavailable from other majority group institutions. Thus the family maintains the emotional well-being of its individual members in spite of the wider society (Nobels, 1981).

A study by Nobels (1976) found that African American parent-child interactions were characterized by an atmosphere that emphasized strong family ties, unconditional love, respect for self and others, and the assumed natural goodness of the child. Child-rearing techniques associated with the parent-child bond centered on the unconditional expression of love.

Low academic performance of Blacks has been a persistent educational problem in the U.S. Ogby (1981) observed that this problem is partly the result of the inferior education Blacks have received in U.S.

schools and is also due to negative teacher attitudes and low expectations, biased testing, classification, and an inferior curriculum. It has been contended that the public school sector has held true to its task; that being to select individuals for opportunities according to their social hierarchy. This social hierarchy is juxtaposed with social class status.

Religion

The Black church has been the foundation, the mainstay of Black families and communities, a support network sustaining African Americans during some of the most oppressive periods in American history. Black churches have performed the functions of sustaining Black identity, incorporating social groupings and support, and nurturing religious values that have impacted the quality of life (Jones, 1982). Apart from the theological aspects, several prominent religious leaders have preached in favor of social action for racial justice and equality. The goals of Martin Luther King, Jr., were to break down the educational, legislative, and physical barriers to integration. The Reverend Jesse Jackson focused on the plight of the poor and minorities in this country during his 1988 campaign for the presidency. The Southern Christian Leadership Conference and the National Association for the Advancement of Colored People joined together to strengthen the spiritual and cultural identity of the Black community.

The Black community church can be the catalyst for social action, family enrichment, and cultural awareness (Black Family Summit, 1984). Some scholars assert that too often, the churches leave the responsibility for education to other sectors of society that are less visible. They say that though the church has typically existed for the purpose of reconciliation and personal healing, this reconciliation and healing cannot be fully accomplished without social changes, family restructuring, and a positive sense of community pride and individual self-worth (Jones, 1971). Within the African American religious community, other factions of spirituality exist that espouse a belief in cultural, ethnic, and racial pride, self-help, and separatism. For example, Elijah Muhammad was the founder of the Nation of Islam, or Black Muslims. This group is competing for religious allegiance from the Black community and denounces Christianity as a White man's strategy to deceive and subjugate Blacks (Jones, 1983). The Muslims emphasize social and economic ideology rather than theology. They are conscientious objectors, believing in pacifism.

Crime

In 1982, African Americans constituted only 12 percent of the total population; in that same year, they comprised 48 percent of the overall prison population (Bridges & Crutchfield, 1986). One in four Black men in their twenties is either in jail, in prison, on parole, or on probation (Flesher, 1990). In 1986, the National Urban League published an article titled "The State of Black America." According to the statistics quoted in this article, although the Black population constituted only 12 percent of the total population in the U.S., they comprised 46.6 percent of the arrests for violent crime, they represented 48.8 percent of all arrests for murders, 46.6 percent arrests for all rapes, 62 percent of all arrests for robbery, 39.8 percent of all arrests for assault, 29.5 percent of all arrests for burglary, 30.1 percent of all arrests for theft, and 34.7 percent of all arrests in 1986 for auto theft (The National Urban League, 1988). In fact, the Black and Hispanic population in the federal prison system has increased at a rate five times faster than that of the White population in U.S. prisons during the last decade (Staples, 1984).

Another method of assessing the relationship of crime to African Americans is to research the number of African Americans in prison relative to the number in the general population. In December, 1984 there were a total of 462,422 prisoners in state and federal institutions. Blacks accounted for 45 percent or 209,673 of this population. Additionally, 10,786 of the federal prison population were Black out of a total of 34,263 which constitutes 31 percent. With respect to the state prison population, the total population was 428,179; of this number, 198,887 were African Americans. Blacks constituted 46 percent of the state prison population. Blacks represented 40 percent of the total prison population nationwide as of June of 1984. The statistics for African American youth are just as daunting. The National Urban League reports that as of February 1, 1985, there were a total of 29,969 juveniles held in public facilities. Of this number, 18,269 or 61 percent were African American.

When attempting to ferret out a reason why Blacks seem to be at such an alarming risk for incarceration, several theories come to the forefront. First, some suggest that minorities, especially Black males, are more heavily involved in crime than are whites (Hill, 1985). However, though numerous empirical studies show minority race and incarceration rates to be positively correlated, these same studies show the relationship between race and crime to be a purely spurious one (Staples, 1984; Nagel, 1975; Nagel, 1977). In an attempt to theoretically isolate factors of criminality, Eysenck (1964) identified what he called the "criminal personality." Though this paradigm gained sociologic popularity, scholars have since found it to be poorly delineated and empirically unsound (Hill, 1985). In other attempts to identify the causation of crime, conservatives point to a supposed moral decay inherent within Black individuals and to poor family conditions within the Black culture. These theoretical propositions have also proven to be erroneous (Hill, 1985).

Crime obviously has some of its roots in economic issues and Nagel (1975) noted a strong positive correlation between unemployment and crime. Hill (1985) argued that the correlation between unemployment and crime is weaker than what Nagel proposed, but agreed that a contingent relationship does exist. Since Black men have been chronically unemployed (Becker & Hills, 1980), this theory does help to partially explain the high incarceration rate. Two other theories presented in the literature are also relevant to the treatment that Blacks experience in the American criminal justice system: labeling and conflict theories.

According to labeling theory, discrete behaviors that are exhibited by individuals (in this case, Blacks) are labeled as deviant. As behaviors are inaccurately labeled, response to the labels becomes inaccurate and unfair (Wodarski, 1985). Research has identified the practice of labeling in America's judicial system. Specifically, a sample of criminal justice personnel identified a stereotypical portrait of lower-class Black homicide defendants. Called "normal primitives," these defendants were identified as dangerous by virtue of their membership in the lower-class Black subculture (Swigert & Farrell, 1977).

Conflict theory suggests that coercion is used by the dominant class to maintain power through the legal enforcement system (Hill, 1985). Evidence of the conflict theory's veracity is found in research indicating that a disproportionate number of Blacks are arrested, tried, convicted, and returned to prison, compared to Whites who commit comparable crimes (Jacobs, 1976; Wolfgang et al., 1962; Wolfgang & Reidel, 1973). Also, a survey of American cities showed a positive correlation between the percentage of Black population within a city and the average number of complaints of police brutality (Staples, 1984).

The concepts of labeling and conflict then may be seen as components of institutional racism—the denial of equal treatment by major social and economic institutions in society (Bridges & Crutchfield, 1986). Additional research has established that racial disparities exist throughout the criminal justice system: at the pre-sentencing, sentencing, and post-sentencing phases (Dike, 1982; Pannick, 1982; Bowers, 1983; Bowers et al., 1984; Baldus et al., 1983; Gross & Mauro, 1984).

CONCERNS RELEVANT TO PRACTICE

Health Care

Since the first crude tabulations of vital statistics, the fact that Black Americans are not as healthy as Whites has been apparent (Krieger & Bassett, 1986). From birth onward, Blacks have a higher death rate than do Whites. Historically, Blacks have been dependent and relied on self-diagnosis and self-help health care. This dependency of self-reliance was fostered by a segregated society which circuitously fostered segregated health care and a dual health care system, one for the upper and middle-class and one for the poor and underclass.

One theory that has been used to explain the higher occurrence of death in the African American group is the genetic model. The genetic model characterized Blacks as being genetically more susceptible to disease. Despite overwhelming contradictory evidence, this theory continues to exert substantial influence on both professional thinking and popular ideology. Krieger and Bassett (1986) refute this theory; they assert that the health of the Black community reflects the social forces that create radically oppressed communities. They propose that skin color consistently correlates with health because race is a powerful determinant of the location and life destinies of individuals within the U.S. class structure. The health of Whites is not due to their genetic structure but to their economic advantages.

The environmental model also attempts to explain racial differences in the area of health. There are two approaches to this theory: liberal and conservative. The liberal approach blames unfortunate social conditions (poverty) for poor mental and physical health in the Black community. This version does not include the underlying structures of racial oppression and class exploitation as possibilities for explaining poor health.

The conservative version of the environmental model views the Black "life-style," not poverty, as being the source of poor health among Blacks. The faulty life-style approach shifts responsibility for the problem directly to the minority population (Krieger & Bassett, 1986).

Statistically, African Americans constitute 12 percent of the population. Longevity, mortality, and other variables are causes for distress. Any major medical problem or disease in America is intensified and magnified many times over in the African American community. According to King (1987), America pays a terrible price for its lack of a national health care system: An infant mortality rate that is higher than in 16 other industrialized nations. Black infants in the U.S. are less likely to be covered by private health insurance and their mortality rate is twice that of White infants. The proportion of births to Black teens outnumbers births to White teens by about 2 to 1 (Washington, 1982). In 1979, there were 104.9 live births per 1,000 Black adolescents between the ages of 15 to 19, and 44.5 live births per 1,000 White females of the same age group. Hogan and Kitagawa (1985) found, in a random sample of 1,000 Black females ages 13–19 living in the city of Chicago, that the chance of becoming pregnant was much greater for teenagers from high-risk social environments. The following are characteristics of a high-risk environment: lower class, resident in a ghetto neighborhood, non-intact family, five or more siblings, a sister who became a teenage mother, and lax parental control on dating. It was found that teenagers from such environments have rates of pregnancy that are 8.3 times higher than girls from low-risk environments.

The life expectancy of African American women is at least 5.5 years less than that of their White counterparts; for African American males their numbers are even more significant and cause for distress. White males are expected to outlive African American males by 7.4 years. There are approximately 100,000 more deaths per year in the African American community comparatively speaking when reviewing the average death rate of America collectively.

A study by Gabriel and McAnarney (1983) examined the effect that cultural values have on the decisions made by Black, low-income adolescents, and White, middle-class couples to become parents. They found that in the Black community, high cultural values are placed on motherhood relative to other social roles, most likely because these other roles are perceived by Black adolescents as unavailable or inaccessible. Motherhood is viewed as a passage into adulthood; marriage, schooling, and economic security need not precede parenthood. In contrast, White, middle-class women see adult roles other than motherhood as equally accessible and important. The authors suggested that health care programs aimed at preventing pregnancy among Black adolescents may be ineffectual because White, middle-class professionals do not understand their patients' values. According to Goodwin (1986), health care programs for pregnant adolescents should provide the following services: (1) counseling concerning available alternatives; (2) facilitation of contact with agencies that are appropriate for various alternatives; (3) provision of sensitive, highly qualified, ongoing, comprehensive prenatal care, including parenting and education skills for those who elect to become parents; and (4) programs that include completion of education, training, job placement and suitable day-care services to promote and support mature and productive adulthood for young parents.

A study by Mays and Cochran (1987) focused on special psychosocial issues relating to AIDS in the Black population. Although African Americans comprise only 12 percent of the total population, they represent 30 percent of the AIDS population. According to Staples (1990), in 1984, there was an increase from 25 percent to 29 percent in the number of African Americans diagnosed with AIDS in 1988 relative to all AIDS cases. For children under the age of 13, Blacks comprise approximately 55 percent of this population. It is estimated that roughly three times as many Blacks as Whites may be infected with the HIV virus. Workers must be sensitive to ethnically relevant issues in the provision of medical care to Blacks with AIDS, as well as to cultural factors that may affect health education efforts.

It has been noted that America's "War on Drugs" may in effect be a war on African Americans (Staples, 1990). According to the U.S. Department of Health, Education, and Welfare (1980), Blacks utilize drug abuse facilities more often and are much more likely to be institutionalized for drug addiction than any other racial or ethnic group. Substance abuse seems to be so much a part of the "Black scene" that it appears normal to the Black community (McMillan, 1981). According to Coggins (1982), 90 percent of minority youth are using one or more substances, while only 5 percent receive exposure to any type of prevention or education program. As the government's attempt to curtail and eradicate the consumption and distribution of illegal drugs has escalated, the arrest and imprisonment of African Americans involved in illicit drug activity has also increased from 30 percent in 1984 to 38 percent in 1988.

Alcohol abuse is a major health issue among African Americans. According to a report by the Task Force on Black and Minority Health, established by the Secretary of Health and Human Services in 1984, medical problems associated with heavy drinking have increased dramatically in the Black population: (1) the mortality rate from cirrhosis of the liver among Blacks is almost twice that for non-minorities; (2) the incidence of esophageal cancer among Black males aged 35–44 was 10 times that of Whites; and (3) the prevalence of fetal alcohol syndrome may be higher in the Black population than in the White population (Ronan, 1986–1987). Alcohol clearly contributes to the health disparity that exists between Black and White Americans.

Caetano (1984) has identified three predictors of heavy drinking: having a liberal attitude toward alcohol use, being male, and being unemployed. Watts and Wright (1985) suggested that reducing the high unemployment rate could be an important prevention strategy. Caetano (1984) found certain beliefs to be prominent in the Black community: (1) Black males are nonsupportive of drunkenness in women; (2) Black males highly support the notion that a "real man" can hold his liquor; and (3) Blacks tend to view people who drink as having more fun and friends.

A study by Gary and Berry (1985) found significant associations between substance use and attitudes, religious affiliation, gender, and age. Men were found to be more tolerant than women and young men more tolerant than old. The issue of racial consciousness was of central importance in determining substance use attitudes. Racial consciousness is defined as the extent to which the individual has a positive view of Black people and an awareness of racial oppression in the U.S. Racially conscious individuals were found to be less tolerant of substance abuse. Marriage and education were also found to be associated with more liberal attitudes towards substance abuse.

According to Watts and Wright (1985), in focusing on the prevention of alcohol abuse among Black Americans, the following issues need to be examined: the availability of alcohol in Black communities; this should be inclusive of the marketing strategies employed in Black communities, unemployment among Black youth, and the high school dropout rate. A comprehensive, coordinated federal (and state) commitment to reducing alcoholism among Black people is needed. A survey revealed that there is more billboard advertising in the Black community of alcohol and tobacco products than in other communities (*The New York Times*, 1989).

Mental Health

According to Gary (1985), the percentage of non-White people comprising case loads in community mental health centers increased from 15.5 percent in 1972 to 19.4 percent in 1977. Also, the percentage of White persons added to centers' case loads has declined as the percentage of non-White persons has risen (National Institute of Mental Health, 1980). Non-White recipients of services from community mental health centers tend to be younger and less well educated than White patients using such facilities.

According to a study by Neighbors and Taylor (1985), a strong relationship exists between level of family income and use of social services. When the effects of education, gender, and age are taken into account, low-income Blacks are more than twice as likely as high-income Blacks to use social services. Low-income Blacks are significantly more likely to use social services for all types of personal problems, not just for difficulties related to their low income. For many Blacks, social service agencies operate as primary sources of care or as a primary referral source (Neighbors & Taylor, 1985).

Research indicates that African Americans and other minority groups have limited access to quality mental health services because of their low socioeconomic class status (Rosenthal & Carty, 1988). Lack of advocacy resources, inability to understand accessibility, and lack of understanding services available are all contributing factors.

Though one of the main goals of mental health programs is to be responsive to the needs of a local community, research indicates that mental health centers that are located in areas having high concentrations of ethnic minorities do not provide non-White persons with the same type and/or quality of services that they do Whites (Cockerhan, 1981). Specifically, when mental health staffs plan and deliver services to Blacks, they often fail to consider the need for culturally sensitive services or for educating Blacks regarding the availability of community mental health services (Parker & McDavis, 1983).

African Americans seek counseling and mental health services less frequently than the general population, relying instead on informal networks within their communities; for example, the church, kinship networks, and their circle of friends. A study conducted by Dawkins and Terry (1979) identified some personality and life-style differences between Blacks receiving and Blacks not receiving services. This study indicates that the most crucial factors in predicting who seeks services are feelings of independence and a sense of pride about being Black. The study by Gary (1985) found that Blacks who were very conscious of racial issues had more positive attitudes toward these centers than those who were less conscious.

Several studies have found that clients who do not have characteristics similar to their counselors are more likely to terminate counseling than clients who are similar (Baekeland & Lundwall, 1975). More specifically, it has been found that Black clients who have been assigned to a White counselor are more likely to terminate counseling prematurely than White clients who have been seen by a White counselor (Terrell & Terrell, 1984). Blacks' mistrust of Whites is one explanation for this early termination. A study by Terrell and Terrell (1984) examined whether the combined variable of counselor's race and cultural mistrust level were related to early drop out from counseling. They found that Black clients with a high level of mistrust who were seen by a White counselor had a higher rate of premature termination from counseling than did highly mistrustful Black clients seen by a Black counselor.

According to Hollingshead and Redlick (1958), Black clients are less likely than Whites to be offered psychotherapy; most often, Blacks are offered custodial care and medication. If a minority client does receive therapy, he/she will probably see a paraprofessional staff member at intake and during therapy (Sue, 1976), while Whites will see professionals. When a Black client does become involved in psychotherapy as a treatment process, many therapist/client problems can occur. The majority of therapists are White and in order to be empathic and helpful, they must be able to deal with their own conflicts about racial prejudice or bias (Cohen, 1974). Research also indicates that problems may exist when Black therapists work with Black clients. A Black therapist may tend to either over-identify with the client or deny appropriate racial identification.

Data indicate that these two types of reactions in the therapeutic situation are often derived from racist attitudes in society (Calnek, 1970). Society has seen an African heritage as synonymous with evil (Brantly, 1983). Some scholars assert that negative images are presented to Blacks throughout their lives and become a part of their self-perception.

Mosby (1972) contended that Black persons develop within a culture that teaches that all their behaviors, beliefs, and characteristics are inferior, maladjusted, and inadequate. Thus, Blacks internalize a sense of inadequacy (Mays, 1986). Clients must learn to develop new skills to cope with these negative images and feelings of inadequacy in order to attain a more positive sense of self. It is the responsibility of the therapist to help the client explore his/her own coping mechanism and to develop more productive ways of dealing with anxiety brought on by racism.

In developing these coping skills, it is crucial that the therapist not minimize the significance of the racial issue. According to Brantly (1983), if the therapist avoids dealing with these issues, the patient will also avoid actively investigating the racial conflicts. Also, if the therapist tries to deny the existence of racism, then the client may interpret this as the therapist's inability or unwillingness to hear and understand the messages being communicated. However, if the client and the therapist develop a productive relationship and the client is helped to develop positive coping styles, the therapist should try to not allow the racism issue to become the dominate controlling force in the Black patient's life (Brantly, 1983).

It is imperative for the social worker to be cognizant of how environmental factors influence the psyche of African Americans. Another aspect that should be considered in dealing with Black clients in therapeutic situations is that they tend to be non-disclosing in clinical treatment. Psychotherapy, also known as the talking cure, requires highly verbal and articulate clients for successful outcomes. In most cases, clients' non-disclosure is a barrier to the therapeutic process and often is interpreted by therapists as an indicator of individual pathology (Jourard, 1969). Given the history of the mistreatment of African Americans in this country, therapists should be aware of the fact that the socialization of Blacks in America has resulted in a reluctance by them to expose their inner selves and psychological world (Ventress, 1969). Instead, their methods of self-expression include playing it cool and exhibiting a healthy "cultural paranoia" (Grier & Cobbs, 1968). The expression of emotions in public is strongly discouraged; tears are often seen as a sign of weakness, and such phrases as "breaking down," "coming apart," and "losing it" are often used to describe weeping (Boyd-Franklin, 1987). Every White person may be viewed as a potential enemy and every social system as an opponent (Grier & Cobbs, 1968). Blacks view their situations as hopeless and unchanging (Triandis, 1976). According to Boyd-

Franklin (1987), while this mechanism of "cultural paranoia" may be helpful to Blacks in coping with a racist outer world, it is counterproductive to developing close, intimate relationships. Ridley (1984) illustrates the therapeutic paradox: By not disclosing, Black clients protect their self-esteem; however, non-disclosure means forfeiting the opportunity to engage in therapeutic exploration.

Ridley (1984) suggested that the social worker should try to determine whether the Black client's nondisclosure is the result of cultural or functional paranoia. While cultural paranoia is a healthy psychological reaction to racism, functional paranoia is considered to be an illness. In treating clients, possible pathology should be dealt with first and foremost, followed by concern over racial problems. A sensitized social worker confronts and encourages discussion of cultural paranoia early in treatment; this type of early confrontation increases potential benefits of therapy and future interracial experiences could be less inhibited.

Another technique that is thought to facilitate client disclosure is that of social worker self-disclosure. Rubin (1973) suggested that when the dyadic effect occurs, individuals disclose because the therapist disclosed to them first. Self-disclosure appears to be most beneficial when it conveys accurate empathy. If the social worker is perceived by the client as an open, approachable person, then the client may be likely to engage in risk-taking (Ridley, 1984).

Since Blacks have been seen by some mental health professionals as having limited abilities and as being excessively suspicious and hostile, they have been less likely to qualify for psychodynamic treatment and have been overrepresented in crisis intervention, medication, and inpatient treatment clinics (Wood & Sherrets, 1976). The social control theory of mental illness proposes that powerless and culturally marginal individuals are more likely to be diagnosed as having psychiatric disorders (Horowitz, 1982). In a study by Rosenfeld (1984), Blacks were much more likely to be hospitalized for mental illness than more powerful Whites. It was also found that Blacks are more likely to experience coercive, involuntary hospitalization. Additionally, Blacks and other minorities are more apt to be misdiagnosed with schizophrenia than other racial groups (Rosenthal & Carty, 1988).

Gove (1970) found that the higher involuntary hospitalization rates among non-Whites are due to more serious psychiatric conditions existing among non-Whites. This can be attributed to the environmental conditions that exists for these groups, institutionalized and endemic racism, oppression, and bias (Pinderhughes, 1989).

Labeling theory suggests that non-Whites are viewed as powerless and this perception causes others to view their behavior as negative or deviant (Rosenfeld, 1984). According to Scheff (1966), the social distance between non-White clients and their White workers is responsible for the more serious diagnoses of illness in non-White clients. As a result of labeling, there is a greater chance of police intervention in dealing with deviance in non-Whites (Brody, 1967). Police intervention often results in severely distorted perceptions by mental health workers; therefore, decisions about the client's entry into treatment may be biased (Rosenfeld, 1984).

In the area of stress and mental health, a number of studies have shown that being poor, Black, female, and a single parent, together form a chronic source of stress (Brown & Harris, 1978; Dohrenwend, 1973b; Gerstein et al., 1977) and that chronic stress may be more detrimental than non-continuous, distinct stressful events. In a study by Lindblad-Goldberg, Dukes and Lasley (1988), stressful life events and the effects of demographic and social network variables were explored in 126 urban, Black, low-income, single-parent families. Seventy of the families were classified as functional and 56 as dysfunctional. The dysfunctional families were found to evidence greater stress, and social network characteristics were not shown to be significant mediators. The authors suggested that the family's internal resources may, therefore, be the most important buffer against stress.

In a study by Neighbors, Jackson and Bowman (1983), a research approach was used that considered not only rates of psychological distress but also stressors and the various coping strategies used to adapt to them among Blacks. Findings indicated that prayer was an important coping response, especially among those making less than $10,000 a year, those above age 55, and women. The informal social network was used extensively as a means of coping with problems in all social demographic groups studies. Those between the ages of 18 and 34 were less likely than those age 35 and above to seek professional help, and women were more likely than men to seek such assistance. Hospital emergency rooms, private physicians, and ministers were relied on more frequently as sources of professional help.

A study by Lewis (1985) focused on the relationship between reliance on extended kin, current partner, children, friends, and religious community support networks and Black mothers' reports of role strain in economic, parental, and household maintenance areas. Economic role strain was found to be negatively related to the respondent's age and household income and to the absence of a supportive current partner. Parental role strain was positively related to the number of minor children in the home and to residence in the Northeast and was negatively related to the proximity of extended kin networks and the presence of a supportive current partner.

According to Boyd-Franklin (1987), many Black women, particularly in large urban areas, feel very isolated and alone in their struggles. They sorely miss and express a need for a feeling of sisterhood with other Black women. Thus an important development in the psychological literature is the model of group treatment for Black women, which, in addition to promoting therapeutic change on a psychological and behavioral level, provides a network support system for this population as well.

Among the elderly Black in America, patterns of social support include family, friend, neighbors, and the church. In a study by Taylor and Chatters (1986) that drew on data from the National Survey of Black Americans, findings indicated that eight out of ten respondents received support from either a best or close friend, about six out of ten from church members, and more than half from extended family members. Petchers and Milligan (1987) reported on results of a community survey on the size, interaction, availability, and adequacy of support and roles of kin and non-kin networks among the Black urban elderly. The findings revealed frequent contact among family, relatives, friends, and neighbors.

In a study by Smith (1986), it was hypothesized that the communal properties of churches (1) are highly effective mechanisms for integrating aged people into the church and for raising their morale, (2) provide resources for personal crises, and (3) offer prestigious positions for individuals with relatively low status in the larger society. The study's hypotheses were empirically tested using a 1978 sample of rural, Southern Blacks, aged 55 and older. Survey data demonstrated that women and other people who reported being "better off" than others were generally more likely to attend church services.

In a study of the informal support system of rural Black families around the event of childbirth, Beckley (1986) found that respondents depended heavily on maternal kin, on the prospective fathers of their babies, and on the father's families, for both material and emotional support. Household arrangements were flexible in that the subjects and members of the extended family moved freely into one another's homes according to need.

Socialization

According to Jackson, McCullough and Gurin (1981), much of the social and psychological literature over the last 40 years on African Americans has dealt, directly or indirectly, with issues of group identification and consciousness. With any minority group experiencing discrimination, a central issue becomes how individual group members relate to the group and to the group's history of discrimination. This relationship forms the individual's group identity, which has been viewed as a critical determinant of the individual's psychic health and functioning.

Before the Civil Rights Movement, the literature on Black identification and personal functioning focused almost exclusively on supposedly negative effects of Black identification. Identifying as Black was seen as a "problem," because it meant identifying with an oppressed group and internalizing the negative group image from the dominant White society. The emphasis of literature published after the Civil Rights Movement is on the positive psychic effects of Black identification. Like the older studies that tied negative group identity to self-rejection and other negative psychological consequences, the newer studies tie positive identity to high self-esteem and other positive psychological consequences. Both assume a simple, direct relationship between group identity and psychological outcomes (Jackson, McCullough & Gurin, 1981).

Research by Spencer et al. (1985) indicated that children whose parents encouraged pro-Black attitudes and taught them about Black history, culture, and the Civil Rights Movement developed a more positive group identity. Research also suggested that Black parents who attempt to take a neutral stance regarding racial group orientation may put their children at risk for the development of diffuse, less secure group identification (Gray-Little, 1986).

While the development of group identity is no doubt important, Mays (1986) contended that organizations or groups that strive only to enhance racial/ethnic identification leave the individual developed only to the level of collective identity. The individual does not know him/herself in any other context than that of the group. The individual is able to develop and interact only as far as the boundaries of the group have progressed. Thus the search for a definitive experience of one's individual self is essential. Mosby (1972) contended that "identity has to be more personally based. . . . It is not forced identification with the dominant White culture, nor is it submissive advocacy of an alien African cultural heritage which bears no immediate relevancy to one's contemporary life" (p. 135). Chestang (1984) suggested that the maintenance of dignity is at the center of a Black person's quest for identity and that two elements are involved in the process: achieving success and developing a sense of both personal and racial identity. A study by Sawyer (1986) investigated the impact of perception of life chances among 318 single, Black working-class mothers on their orientations regarding child rearing and their children's racial socialization. Findings revealed that both middle-class and working-class mothers perceived individual efforts, rather than their membership in a racial group, to be more important regarding their perception of life changes. The practice of the mothers regarding child rearing and racial socialization were not significantly influenced by the life perceptions of the mothers or their socioeconomic status.

The Family

The dehumanizing effects of slavery, oppression, segregation, and racism distinguish African-American culture from any other racial or ethnic group in our society. How Black families have adapted to these atrocities is the point on which theoretical perspectives on the Black family diverge. For example, while Moynihan (1965) and Hill (1973) analyzed the same U.S. census data, their conclusions as to the nature of Black family life differed. Moynihan saw the Black family as deteriorating and recommended social policies that would encourage changes in the Black family structure and values. Hill, on the other hand, observed the resilience of Black families and recommended social policies that could build on the strengths of Black family values and structure (Johnson, 1981).

Dodson (1981) identified two basic schools of thought among the conceptualizations of Black families in social science research: the cultural ethnocentric view and the cultural relativity view. The cultural ethnocentric approach views Black families as primarily pathological, dysfunctional, disorganized, and unable to provide family members with the social and psychological support and development needed to assimilate fully into American society (Dodson, 1981). This perspective recognizes qualities that differentiate Black and White families and gives negative meaning to Black family traits. E. Franklin Frazier (1894–1962) was the leading proponent of this school of thought. He believed that Black families and family patterns, customs, and structure are the consequences of slavery and American culture, not African cultural transfers (Dodson, 1981).

Later, Moynihan (1965) repeatedly cited Frazier in a report for the Office of Planning and Research of the U.S. Department of Labor. The report concluded that the Black community is characterized by broken families, illegitimacy, matriarchy, economic dependency, failure to pass armed forces entrance tests, delinquency, and crime. Moynihan stated that the cause of these problems is the broken and unstable Black family. The report portrays Black men as irresponsible, weak, and unable to care for a family properly. Therefore, as Minuchin (1986) points out, poverty becomes merged with family disorganization and disorganization becomes merged with female-headed families.

The cultural relativity approach depicts Black American culture and family patterns as possessing a degree of cultural integrity that is neither related to nor molded on White American norms. The origin of these cultural differences is traced back to Black Americans' African cultural heritage and the focus is on the strengths of Black families (Dodson, 1981). While not all proponents of this view agree on the degree to which African culture influenced the culture of Black Americans, they do agree that Black Americans' cultural orientation encourages family patterns that are instrumental in combating the oppressive racial conditions of American society (Dodson, 1981). In contrast to the view of the Black male as weak and failing to perform the role of father/provider, writers from this school of thought point out that Black men are often denied educational and economic opportunities (Thompson, 1974; Billingsley, 1968). Blassingame (1979) asserted that ever since African American men were uprooted from their native land, they have had to struggle in their efforts to build a stable family. In slave times, the Black father's authority was restricted by his master. Families were often torn apart when members were sold separately. Husbands were powerless to protect their wives and daughters from the sexual advances of masters.

During the approximately 120 years since emancipation, the Black man has not regained the respect allotted him in his native country. Cazenave (1981) acknowledged that most of the research on position and roles constituting Black families has been concerned with matriarchy and father-absence theory. The Black father, then, qualifies as a "phantom" of Black American family structure. Cazenave pointed to Merton's work (1968) to help understand what happens when the Black male tries to measure up to unattainable standards of masculinity. Merton's theory of anomie argues that socially deviant or unacceptable behavior results when certain groups, while sharing the basic goals of society, do not share the means for achieving these goals. Thus, the very structure of society actually encourages individuals to function deviantly to obtain their cultural goals. Merton's theory is seen as one way of explaining the high mortality and suicide rate among Black men, the half-million Black men in prison, the one-third of urban Black men who are saddled with drug problems, and the 25 to 30 percent who do not have steady employment.

Regardless of the problems associated with being Black in a predominately White, middle-class society, proponents of the cultural relativity school view the Black family as a strong, resilient force, able to overcome the negative pulls of the larger society (Hill, 1971; Stack, 1974; Billingsley, 1968). The family's strength and endurance is seen as evolving from an African cultural heritage of extended families or a system of kinship ties that exist not only of conjugal and blood relatives, but of non-relatives as well.

In Stack's (1974) account of how the Black urban poor adapt to poverty, she reported that domestic functions are carried out by clusters of kin who may or may not live together. While Stack associated these networks with cooperation required to survive under the dire conditions of urban poverty, McAdoo (1970) extended these kinships to include middle-class Black families. Her interviews with 88 urban and 90 suburban middle-class Black domestic families revealed they also engaged in interaction and mutual helping activities with kin. All those interviewed said they had received aid from their kin that helped them achieve middle-class status.

The kin network is also viewed as a source of economic and emotional support for children and other family members as well as a protection from isolation in the larger society (Hill, 1971). Billingsley (1968) stated that Black families cope by banding together to form a network of intimate mutual aid and social interaction. Other theorists (Wilson, 1978; Mutran, 1985) viewed the extended family as a fertile source of security and love for children where a value system of respect for other family members, especially the elderly, is taught. Blassingame (1972) believed, like many other theorists in the school of cultural relativity, that the Black family kinship pattern was derived from African cultures. In addition, he asserted that not only did African cultural patterns survive American slavery, but new patterns were created. Therefore, as Aschenbrenner (1973) suggested, Blacks are far from being the passive victims of society that they are sometimes pictured; they have developed a life-style in their family system that offers a high degree of security while giving scope for individual needs for independence and management.

IMPLICATIONS FOR PRACTICE

Discrimination, institutionalized racism, and class exploitation are intrinsic components of society and the most salient forms of oppression in the contemporary world. African Americans reside in a country which devalues and labels those "different" from mainstream America. This denigration has resulted in a class of people economically, psychologically, and socially impoverished. It is well recognized that poverty is a complex issue and one that cannot be resolved overnight. A long-term commitment is needed to help the United States's poor break the cycle of poverty. Real progress against poverty can only come when efforts are focused on helping families become self-sufficient and ensuring that men and women have sufficient earning opportunities to enable them to maintain families (Bane, 1986).

Human service organizations must develop strategies for educating their workers about cultural diversity and ethnic consciousness (Gary, 1985). When agencies begin developing prevention programs, the workers within the agency must possess a working knowledge of the range of attitudes existing in the Black community. Workers must be willing to adapt their skills to effectively serve the client population.

The study of alcohol abuse in the African American community is relatively novel. Yet, past research studies identified it as one of the most daunting problems in the African American community (Logan, Freeman, & McRoy, 1990). Alcohol abuse is perceived as the primary health and social problem in the Black community (Logan, Freeman, & McRoy, 1990). The excessive use and abuse of alcohol is a way of medicating the self; it is an escape from the harsh realities of racism towards African Americans in this society. Therefore, any treatment plan must take into consideration the quantitative and qualitative differences as they relate to the Black client.

The key element in prevention strategies for the problem of substance abuse is to clearly define the target population and to identify various groups within the population that need immediate education or intervention (Gary & Berry, 1985). Ultimately, culturally sensitive intervention is needed. According to McCulloch (1980), prevention planning should look beyond age, gender, and education variables; the individual person, the social group or organization, the community, the culture, and the interaction of these forces should be investigated. Workers in prevention programs must involve the church as well as social and civic organizations to reach and be effective with the target population.

Family therapy is intended to increase the strengths and coping skills of family members. However, as McAdoo (1977) pointed out, the very premises upon which family therapy is built, as it pertains to Black families, may be faulty. Major criticisms of therapy for Black families is that it does not consider the Black experience and Black culture in totality (McAdoo, 1977; Pinderhughes, 1982) and that basic treatment hypotheses are dependent on the stereotyped Black family—poor, disorganized, and fatherless. As a result of these misinterpretations and value judgments, Blacks often perceive community agencies as insensitive and unhelpful (McAdoo, 1979; Pinderhughes, 1982). Therefore, instead of seeking aid from these agencies, they turn to family, friends, members of clergy, and others in their extended network for help.

Pinderhughes (1989) coined the phrase "cultural belonging." Wholistic in its approach, the concept of cultural belonging facilitates a positive, psychological, well-integrated psyche which is an integral factor in practice for the African American family. There is a distinctive uniqueness in the cultural ethos of African Americans. This uniqueness is characterized by common bonds of sharing, beliefs, religion, ethnic origins, and race. It incorporates interactions of social processes, interrelationships, and mutual acceptance of self and others, which are critical to the survival of the individual and the group collectively, both conscious and unconscious. Cultural belonging satiates an innermost psychological need. This psychological need is a need for historical continuity which aids in development of a self-identity and security. According to Pinderhughes (1990), cultural belonging permits one to feel connected and linked in a world that can be perceived as both vertical and horizontal, external, and internal. Vertical connectedness satisfies this need as it alludes to continuity with time, history, and a "pre-conscious" recognition of traditionally held patterns of thinking, feeling, and behaving. Horizontal linkage intimates present linkage to others who share these same ways of thinking and belonging in the world. Horizontal linkage and vertical connectedness traverse all else, connecting the individual to the external, thereby validating his/her reason for being, making some sense of a nonsensical existence.

Since the kinship structure is a vital part of Black culture, treatment should be directed at strengthening the family structure and reinforcing the extended family network to give the family more effective support (Pinderhughes, 1982). Another goal should be to help them constructively cope with the stresses related to racism and oppression inherent in society.

McAdoo (1977) saw two large hurdles faced by social workers who work with Black families: being White and coming from the middle class. One solution to this problem would be to have Black workers in community agencies that work with Black families. Another suggestion is to provide a link by means of a Black paraprofessional who would work with the White social worker. The paraprofessional could provide valuable practical knowledge of the people and their experiences. However, in an ever-changing society, all social workers need to learn how to work with all clients. White therapists should avail themselves of any pertinent knowledge regarding the cultural ethos of African Americans.

The importance of kinship ties should be kept in mind and incorporated into family planning and sex education programs for Black teens. In doing so, it would seem logical to work not only with the adolescent but also with parents and other important members of the extended family network whose support would lend credence to the programs.

Finally, social workers must be clear about issues involved in racial and personal identity. These issues have major consequences for problems associated with the development of adolescents, their achievement in school, and their romantic relationships and marriages. Social workers and teachers should view individuality as a strength and a positive step. Black youths should be encouraged to express their uniqueness, which can serve as a control on the negative influences of peer groups.

REFERENCES

Aschenbrenner, J. (1973). Extended families among black Americans. *Journal of Comparative Studies, 4,* 257–268.

Baekeland, F., & Lundwall, L. (1975). Dropping out of treatment: A critical review. *Psychological Bulletin, 82,* 738–783.

Baldus, D.C., Woodworth, G., & Pulaski, C. (1983). *Discrimination in Georgia's capital charging and sentencing system: A preliminary report.* Unpublished report submitted by petitioner in McClesky vs. Kemp, 753F 2nd 877 (1985).

Bane, M.J. (1986). *Poverty and hunger in the black family.* (Hearing before the Select Committee on Hunger, House of Representatives, Serial No. 99-107.) Washington, D.C.: U.S. Government Printing Office.

Bane, M.J. (1983a). Household composition and poverty. In S.H. Danzinger & D.H. Weingberg (Eds.), *Fighting poverty* (pp. 209–231). Cambridge, MA: Harvard University Press.

Becker, B.E., & Hills, S.M. (1980). Teenage unemployment: Some evidence of the long-run effects on wages. *Journal of Human Resources, 15,* 354–372.

Beckley, G.D. (1986, May). *Informal support systems in rural black families around the event of childbirth.* Unpublished doctoral dissertation, Columbia University, New York.

Bell, P., & Evans, J. (1983). Counseling the black alcoholic client. In T.D. Watts & R. Wright (Eds.), *Black alcoholism: Toward a comprehensive understanding* (pp. 100–121). Springfield, IL: Charles C Thomas.

Billingsley, A. (1968). *Black families in white America.* Englewood Cliffs, NJ: Prentice-Hall.

Billingsley, A., & Giovannoni, J.M. (1972). *Children of the storm: Black children and American welfare.* New York: Harcourt Brace Jovanovich.

Blackwell, J.E. (1975). *The Black community: Diversity and unity.* New York: Dodd, Mead.

Blassingame, J.W. (1979). *The slave community.* New York: Oxford Press.

Bowers, W.J. (1983). The pervasiveness of arbitrariness and discrimination under post-Furman capital statutes. *Journal of Criminal Law and Criminology, 74,* 1067.

Bowers, W.J., Pierce, G.L., & McDevitt, J.F. (1984). *Legal homicide, death and punishment in America.* Boston: Northeastern University Press.

Boyd-Franklin, N. (1987). Group therapy for black women: A therapeutic support model. *American Journal of Psychiatry, 140,* 1605–1608.

Boyd-Franklin, N. (1990). *Black families in therapy.* New York: Guilford Press.

Brantly, T. (1983). Racism and its impact on psychotherapy. *American Journal of Psychiatry, 140,* 1605–1608.

Brown, Lee. (1988). *The state of black America.* New York: National Urban League.

Brown, S., & Harris, T. (1978). The social origins of depression. New York: Free Press.

Caetano, R. (1984). Ethnicity and drinking in northern California: A comparison among whites, blacks, and Hispanics. *Alcohol and Alcoholism, 19,* 31–44.

Calnek, M. (1970). Racial factors in countertransference: The black client. *American Journal of Orthopsychiatry, 40,* 39–46.

Cazenave, N.A. (1981). Black American men in America: The quest for manhood. In H.P. McAdoo (Ed.), *Black families* (pp. 176–185). Beverly Hills, CA: Sage.

Chestang, L.W. (1984). Racial and personal identity in the black experience. In B. White (Ed.), *Color in a white society* (pp. 83–94). Silver Spring, MD: National Association of Social Workers.

Children's Defense Fund. (1992). *The state of America's children.* Washington, D.C.: Children's Defense Fund.

Coggins, P.C. (1982). *Policy imperatives on alcohol and drug use prevention with racial minorities in the state of Georgia.* A position paper developed by the Executive Committee and the Advisory Council of the Statewide Minority Advocacy Group for Alcohol and Drug Prevention.

Cohen, A.I. (1974). Treating the black patient: Transference questions. *American Journal of Psychotherapy, 28,* 137–143.

Cotton, J. (1988). Discrimination and favoritism in the U.S. labor market. The cost to wage earner of being female and black and the benefit of being male and white. *American Journal of Economics and Sociology, 47,* 15–28.

Cooper, Helene. (1991, 15 May). Health care networks' attempts to cut costs are trimming patients' options. *The Wall Street Journal.*

Danzinger, S., & Gottschalk, P. (1985). *The poverty of losing ground. Challenge, 28,* 32–38.

Danzinger, S., & Moss, C.M. (1984). *Poverty and minorities.* Unpublished manuscript, Institute for Research on Poverty, University of Wisconsin-Madison.

Darity, W.A., Jr., & Myers, S.L., Jr. (1984). Does welfare dependency cause female Headship? The case of the black family. *Journal of Marriage and the Family, 46,* 765–779.

Dawkins, M., & Terry, J.A. (1979). Personality and lifestyle characteristics of uses and non-users of mental health services in an urban black community. *The Western Journal of Black Studies, 3,* 43–52.

Dike, S.T. (1982). *Capital punishment in the U.S.* Hackensack, NJ: National Council on Crime and Delinquency.

Dodson, J. (1981). Conceptualizations of black families. In McAdoo, H.P. (Ed.), *Black families.* Beverly Hills, CA: Sage.

Dohrenwend, B. (1973). Social status and stressful life events. *Journal of Personality and Social Psychology, 28,* 225–235.

Donovan, R. (1987). Home care work: A legacy of slavery in U.S. health care. *Affilia, 2,* 33–44.

Ellwood, D.T., & Summers, M.L. (1986). Poverty in America: Is welfare the answer of the problem? In S.H. Danziger & D.H. Weinberg (Eds.), *Fighting poverty* (pp. 78–105). Cambridge, MA: Harvard University Press.

Eysenck, H. (1964). *Crime and personality.* London: Pergamon.

Farley, J.E. (1987). Disproportionate black and Hispanic unemployment in U.S. metropolitan areas: The roles of racial inequality, segregation, and discrimination in joblessness. *The American Journal of Economics and Sociology, 46,* 129–150.

Farley, R. (1984). *Blacks and whites: Narrowing the gap?* Cambridge, MA: Harvard University Press.

Freeman, E.M., & McRoy, R. (1986). Group counseling program for unemployed black teenagers. *Social Work with Groups, 9*(1), 73–89.

Freeman, E.M., Logan, M.L., & McRoy, R.G. (1990). *Social work practice with black families: A culturally specific perspective.* White Plains, NY: Longman.

Gabriel, A., & McAnarney, E.R. (1983). Parenthood in two subcultures: White, middle-class couples and black, low-income adolescents in Rochester, New York. *Adolescence, 18,* 595.

Gary, L. (1985). Attitudes toward human service organizations: Perspectives from an urban black community. *Journal of Applied Behavioral Sciences, 21,* 445–458.

Gary, L.E., & Berry, G.L. (1985). Predicting attitudes toward substance use in a black community: Implications for prevention. *Community Mental Health Journal, 21,* 42–51.

Gary, L.E., & Leashore, B.R. (1984). Black men in white America: Critical issues. In B. White (Ed.), *Color in a white society* (pp. 115–125). Silver Spring, MD: National Association of Social Workers.

Gary, L.E. (1981). *Black men.* Beverly Hills, CA: Sage.

Gerstein, J., Langner, T., Eisenburg, J., & Semch-Fagan, O. (1977). An evaluation of the etiologic role of stressful life change events in psychological disorders. *Journal of Health and Social Behavior, 18,* 228–244.

Glasgow, D. (1980). *The black underclass, poverty, unemployment, and entrapment of ghetto youth.* San Francisco, CA: Jossey-Bass.

Glick, P.C. (1981). A demographic picture of black families. In H.P. McAdoo (Ed.), *Black families* (pp. 106–126). Beverly Hills, CA: Sage.

Goodwin, N.J. (Ed.). (1986). Black adolescent pregnancy: Prevention and management [Special issue]. *Journal of Community, 11*(1).

Gove, W. (1970). Societal reaction as an explanation of mental illness. *American Sociological Review, 35,* 873–884.

Gray-Little, B. (1986). The development and socialization of black children. *Contemporary Psychology, 31,* 956–958.

Green, J.W. (1982). *Cultural awareness in the human services.* Englewood Cliffs, NJ: Prentice-Hall.

Grier, W., & Cobbs, P. (1968). *Black rage.* New York: Bantam.

Gross, S.R., & Mauro, R. (1984). Patterns of death: An analysis of racial disparities in criminal sentencing and homicide victimization. *Stanford Law Review, 37.*

Harvey, A. (1985). Traditional African culture as the basis for the Afro-American church in America: The foundation of the black family in America. In A.R. Harvey (Ed.), *The black family: An Afro-centric perspective.* New York: United Church of Christ Commission for Racial Justice.

Hill, R. (1971). *The strengths of black families.* New York: Emerson Stall.

Hill, R. (1973). Health conditions of black Americans. *Urban League News, 3*(5), 5.

Hill, R. (1986, December). The future of black families. *Currents in Modern Thought,* 573–586.

Hill, R. (1987). *Building the future for black families. American Vision,* pp. 16–25.

Hill, W. (1985). A reassessment of blacks in crime. *Western Journal of Black Studies, 8*(2), 62–72.

Hogan, D.P., & Kitagawa, E.M. (1985). The impact of social status, family structure and neighborhood on the fertility of black adolescents. *American Journal of Sociology, 90,* 825–853.

Hollingshead, A., & Redlick, F. (1958). *Social class and mental illness.* New York: Wiley.

Horowitz, A.V. (1982). *The social control of mental illness.* New York: Academic Press.

Jackson, J.S., McCullough, W.R., & Gurin, G. (1981). Group identity development with black families. In H.P. McAdoo (Ed.), *Black families.* Beverly Hills, CA: Sage.

Jacobs, H. (Ed.). (1967). *Law, politics, and the federal courts.* Boston, MA: Little-Brown.

Johnson, L.B. (1981). Perspective on black family empirical research: 1965–1978. In McAdoo, H.P. (Ed.), *Black families* (pp. 87–102). Beverly Hills, CA: Sage.

Jones, L. (1982). Urban black churches: Conservators of value and sustainer of community. *Journal of Religious Thought, 39*(2), 41–50.

Jones, M. (1971). *Black awareness: A theology of hope.* New York: Abington.

Jones, O. (1983). The black Muslim movement and the American constitutional system. *Journal of Black Studies, 13,* 417–437.

Jourard, S. (1969). Self-disclosure and other cathexis. *Journal of Abnormal and Social Psychology, 59,* 428–431.

King, C.S. (1987, January). America pays a terrible price for lack of a health-care program. *Atlanta Journal and Constitution,* p. 8C.

Krieger, N., & Bassett, M. (1986). The health of black folk: Disease, class, and ideology in science. *Monthly Review, 38,* 74–85.

Lewis, E.A. (1985, May). *Role strain in black women: The efficacy of support network utilization.* Unpublished doctoral dissertation, University of Wisconsin, Madison, WI.

Lindblad-Goldberg, M., Dukes, J.L., & Lasley, J. (1988). Stress in black, low-income, single-parent families: Normative and dysfunctional patterns. *American Journal of Orthopsychiatry, 58,* 104–120.

McAdoo, H.P. (1977). Family therapy in the black community. *American Journal of Orthopsychiatry, 47,* 75–79.

McAdoo, H.P. (1979). Black kinship. *Psychology Today,* pp. 67–71.

McAdoo, H.P. (1980). Black mothers and the extended family support network. In L. Rogers-Rose (Ed.), *The Black woman.* Beverly Hills, CA: Sage.

McAdoo, H.P. (1981). Patterns of upward mobility in black families. In H.P. McAdoo (Ed.), *Black families.* Beverly Hills, CA: Sage.

McCulloch, P.C. (1980). The ecological model: A framework for operationalizing prevention. *Journal of Prevention, 1,* 35–43.

McMillan, D.R. (1981). Alcohol: A weapon of black genocide. *Urban Research Review, 7*(4), 1–3.

Martin, J.E., & Martin, E.P. (1985). *The helping tradition in the black family and community.* Silver Spring, MD: National Association of Social Workers.

Mays, V.M. (1986). Identity development of black Americans: The role of history and the importance of ethnicity. *American Journal of Psychotherapy, 40,* 582–593.

Mays, V.M., & Cochran, S.D. (1987). Acquired immunodeficiency syndrome and black Americans: Special psychosocial issues. *Public Health Reports, 102,* 224–231.

Merton, R.K. (1968). *Social theory and social structure.* New York: Free Press.

Minuchin, S. (1986). Beyond benign neglect. Review of Family and Nation by D.P. Moynihan. *Readings: A Journal of Mental Health, 1*(4), 4–6.

Moon, M. (1986). *Poverty and hunger in the black family.* (Hearing before the Select Committee on Hunger, House of Representatives, Serial No. 99-107.) Washington, D.C.: U.S. Government Printing Office.

Mosby, D.P. (1972). Toward a theory of the unique personality of blacks: A psychocultural assessment. In R.L. Jones (Ed.), *Black psychology.* New York: Harper and Row.

Moynihan, D.P. (1965). *The Negro: A case for social action.* Washington, D.C.: U.S. Department of Labor, Office of Planning Research.

Mutran, E. (1965). Intergenerational family support among blacks and whites: Response to culture and the socioeconomic differences. *Journal of Gerontology, 40,* 382–389.

Nagel, J.H. (1977). *Crime and incarceration: A reanalysis.* Philadelphia, PA: University of Pennsylvania, Center of Government School of Public and Urban Policy.

Nagel, W.G. (1975, Winter). For a moratorium on prison construction. *Crime and delinquency,* 154–172.

National Institute of Mental Health. (1980). *Provisional data on federally funded community mental health centers, 1977–1978.* Rockville, MD: National Institute of Mental Health.

Neighbors, H.W., Jackson, J.S., & Bowman, P.J. (1983). Stress, coping and black mental health: Preliminary findings from a national survey. *Prevention in Human Services, 2*(3), 5–29.

Neighbors, H.W., & Taylor, R.J. (1985). The use of social service agencies by black Americans. *Social Service Review, 59,* 259–268.

Nichols-Casebolt, A.M. (1986). Black families headed by single mothers: Growing numbers and increasing poverty. *Social Work, 33,* 306–313.

Nichols-Casebolt, A.M. (1986). The economic impact of child support reform on the poverty status of custodial and noncustodial families. *Journal of Marriage and Family, 46,* 875–880.

Nobels, W.W. et al. (1981). African-American family life. In McAdoo, H.P. (Ed.), *Black families* (pp. 77–86). Beverly Hills, CA: Sage.

Nobels, W.W. (1976). *A formulative and empirical study of black families.* Washington, D.C.: U.S. Department of Health, Education and Welfare.

Nobels, W.W. et al. (1981). African-American family life. In McAdoo, H.P. (Ed.). *Black families* (pp. 77–86). Beverly Hills, CA: Sage.

Ogby, J.U. (1981). Black education: A cultural-ecological perspective. In H.P. McAdoo (Ed.), *Black families* (pp. 139–154). Beverly Hills, CA: Sage.

Oliver, W. (1989). Black males and social problems: Prevention through Afrocentric socialization. *Journal of Black Studies, 20,* 1.

Pannick, D. (1982). *Judicial review of the death penalty.* London: Duckworth.

Parker, W.M., & McDavis, R.J. (1983). Attitudes toward mental health agencies and counselors. *Journal of Non-White Concerns, 11,* 89–98.

Petchers, M.K., & Milligan, S.W. (1987). Social networks and social support among black urban elderly: A health care resource. *Social Work in Health Care, 12*(4), 103–117.

Pinderhughes, E.B. (1982). Family functioning of African-Americans. *Social Work, 27*, 91–96.

Pinderhughes, E. (1989). *Understanding race, ethnicity, and power: The key efficacy in clinical practice.* New York: Free Press.

Ridley, C.R. (1984). Clinical treatment of the non-disclosing black client: A therapeutic paradox. *American Psychologist, 39*, 1234–1244.

Ronan, L. (1986/1987). Alcohol-related health risks among black Americans: Highlights of the Secretary's Task Force Report on Black and Minority Health. *Alcohol Health and Research World, 11*(2), 36–39, 65.

Rosenfeld, S. (1984). Race differences in involuntary hospitalization: Psychiatric vs. labeling perspectives. *Journal of Health and Social Behavior, 25*, 25, 14–23.

Rosenthal, E., & Carty, L.A. (1988, June). Impediments to services and advocacy for black and hispanic people with mental illness.

Rubin, Z. (1973). *Linking and loving: An invitation to social psychology.* New York: Holt, Rinehart & Winston.

Sawyer, M.B. (1986). *A study of single black mothers: Their perception of life changes and its influence on their children's racial socialization.* Unpublished doctoral dissertation, Howard University, Washington, D.C.

Scheff, T. (1966). *Being mentally ill: A sociological theory.* Chicago, IL: Aldine.

Sloan, I. (1971). *Blacks in America, 1492–1970: A chronology and fact book.* New York: Praeger.

Smith, J.M. (1986, May). *Church participation and morale of the rural, southern, black aged: The effects of socioeconomic status, gender, and the organizational properties of churches.* Unpublished doctoral dissertation, University of Michigan, Ann Arbor, MI.

Spencer, M.B., Brookins, G.K., & Allen, W.R. (Eds.). (1985). *Beginnings: The social and affective development of black children.* Hillsdale, NJ: Erlbaum.

Stack, C. (1974). *All our kin: Strategies for surviving in a black community.* New York: Community Service Society of New York.

Stafford, W.W. (1985, January). *Closed labor markets: Underrepresentation of blacks, Hispanics, and women in New York City's core industries and jobs.* New York: Community Service Society of New York.

Staples, R. (1981). Race and marital status: An overview. In H.P. McAdoo (Ed.), *Black families* (pp. 173–175). Beverly Hills, CA: Sage.

Staples, R. (1984). American racism and high crime rates: The inextricable connection. *The American Journal of Black Studies, 8*(2), 62–72.

Sue, S. (1976). Clients; demographic characteristics and therapeutic treatment: Differences that make a difference. *Journal of Consulting and Clinical Psychology, 44*, 864.

Swigert, V.L., & Farrell, R.A. (1977). Normal homicides and the law. *American Sociological Review, 42*(16), 38–47.

Taylor, R.J., & Chatters, L.M. (1986). Patterns of informal support to elderly black adults: Family, friends, and church members. *Social Work, 31*, 432–438.

Terrell, R., & Terrell, S. (1984). Race of counselor, client sex, cultural mistrust level and premature termination from counseling among black clients. *Journal of Counseling Psychology, 11*, 371–375.

Thompson, D.C. (1974). *Sociology of the black experience.* Westport, CT: Greenwood Press.

Triandis, H. (1976). *Variations in black and white perceptions of the social environment.* Urbana, IL: University of Illinois Press.

U.S. Department of Health, Education & Welfare. (1980). *The Alcohol, Drug Abuse and Mental Health National Data Book.* Washington, D.C.: U.S. Government Printing Office.

Ventress, C. (1969). Cultural barriers in the counseling relationship. *Personnel and Guidance Journal, 48,* 11–17.

Washington, A.C. (1982). A cultural and historical perspective on pregnancy-related activity among U.S. teenagers. *Journal of Black Psychology, 9,* 1–28.

Watts, T.D., & Wright, R. (Eds.). (1985). *Prevention of black alcoholism: Issues and strategies.* Springfield, IL: Charles C Thomas.

Wilson, W.J. (1978). *The declining significance of race: Blacks and changing American institutions.* Chicago, IL: University of Chicago Press.

Wodarski, J.S. (1985). *Introduction to human behavior.* Austin, TX: Pro-Ed.

Wolfgang, M.E., Kelly, A., & Nolde, H. (1962). Comparisons of the executed and committed among admissions to death row. *Journal of Criminal Law, Criminology, and Police Science, 12*(5), 26–39.

Wolfgang, M.E., & Riedel, M. (1973). Race and judicial discretion and the death penalty. *Annals of the American Academy of Political and Social Science, 53,* 301.

Wood, P., & Sherrets, T. (1976). A program to train operators of board and care homes in behavioral management. *Hospital and Community Psychiatry, 27,* 767–770.

Young, V.H. (1974). A black American socialization pattern. *American Ethnologist, 1,* 405–413.

Chapter 3

SOCIAL WORK PRACTICE WITH LATINOS

HILARY N. WEAVER AND JOHN S. WODARSKI

HISTORICAL BACKGROUND

Latinos or Hispanics make up both one of the oldest and one of the most recent groups to settle in the United States. Although Spanish speakers came to parts of the Southwestern United States before the Pilgrims arrived in New England, the majority of Latinos settled in the United States after World War II (Gann & Duignan, 1986).

The terms Latino and Hispanic refer to persons of Spanish origin or descent and include those who classify themselves as Chicano/Mexican American, Puerto Rican, Cuban, and those who come from Central America, South America, and the Caribbean. Generally, when a sense of panethnic identity develops it is because of a sense of a common collective experience. However, although groups that fall under the labels Hispanic or Latino are considered together as an ethnic group, they differ in terms of historical experiences, socioeconomic status, and identity (Calderon, 1992). Thus, blanket terms such as Hispanic and Latino, although frequently used, can be misleading. For example, Puerto Ricans, Chicanos, Peruvians, Guatemalans, and all other Latino cultures have distinctive backgrounds. An Argentinean is as different from a Puerto Rican as an English person is from a Jamaican. The first two speak Spanish; the second pair speak English; but all of them have a separate historical tradition (Gann & Duignan, 1986).

The categorization of various groups under the term Hispanic arose from external forces such as the media, government agencies, the Census Bureau, and U.S. foreign policy (Castex, 1994; Calderon, 1992; Gomez, 1992). While some Spanish speakers use the label Hispanic, other Spanish speakers view this as an imposed label used by those who are more assimilated and less politically active (Calderon, 1992). Thus, many Spanish-speaking Americans reject the general term Hispanic because they believe it obscures their diversity and because they perceive it as a negative, derogatory term. Instead, they prefer to identify themselves according to their specific national origin (Castex, 1994; Oboler, 1992). In instances in which a sense of commonality and panethnic identity has developed in response to external forces, the term Latino is generally preferred over Hispanic (Calderon, 1992).

Latino identity is situation-specific and exists when Spanish-speaking people unite around common issues and concerns. Panethnic unity under a label such as Latino and a separate ethnic identity linked to national origin are not mutually exclusive. More general (Latino) or specific (e.g., Puerto Rican) labels are often used as the situation dictates. Gomez (1992) found that people of Spanish-speaking origin use more than one term to refer to themselves and that the choice of term depends on the situational context.

The earliest Spanish speakers to settle in the Southwestern United States are sometimes called Hispanos (Jaffe, Cullen, & Boswell, 1980). They are also sometimes referred to as Mexican settlers. The Hispanos or early Mexicans are those whose ancestors were a collection of poor Spanish peasants, Indians and mixed population, and some religious and aristocratic Spanish conquistadors. This group migrated to New Mexico from Mexico (then called New Spain) from the sixteenth through the nineteenth centuries. The culture of the Hispanos was basically seventeenth and eighteenth century Spanish mixed with some Native American influences of the same period. Hispanos today are largely concentrated in New Mexico, Colorado, and California.

Although Mexicans are the largest Latino immigrant group in the United States, the first Mexicans did not come to the U.S. as immigrants but were incorporated into the United States through military conquest and annexation of California, Arizona, New Mexico, Colorado, and Texas in the 1840s (Melendez, Rodriquez, & Figueroa, 1991). The Treaty of Guadalupe Hidalgo, which ended the war between the United States and Mexico, resulted in Mexico ceding approximately half its territory to the United States. This territory included 75,000 Mexicans, only 2000 of whom chose to leave their homes and move South when the Mexican border changed (Gomez, 1992).

After the turn of the century, economic expansion in the United States and political instability in Mexico led to more Mexicans arriving in the U.S. These immigrants largely supplied cheap labor for agricultural production. The first large modern wave of Mexican immigration began at the turn of the century and lasted until the mid-1960s. This wave is characterized by extreme fluctuations in population flows, which peaked during periods of high labor demand in the U.S. and ebbed during mandatory repatriation programs (Morales & Bonilla, 1993). The majority of the Mexican population in the United States is a product of twentieth century immigration from Mexico. These Mexican Americans are largely concentrated in Texas, Arizona, California and are also found in Colorado, New Mexico, and Illinois (Jaffe, Cullen, & Boswell, 1980).

Puerto Ricans constitute the second largest Latino group in the United States. Puerto Rico became a U.S. possession in 1898, Puerto Ricans were granted U.S. citizenship in 1917, and Puerto Rico became a semiautonomous commonwealth in 1952. The dependent relationship between the United States and Puerto Rico resulted in citizenship for Puerto Ricans, yet they have no national representation in the U.S. Congress and cannot vote for the presidency (Morales & Bonilla, 1993).

After World War II, many Puerto Ricans migrated to the mainland U.S. Migration slowed down in the 1950s, and since that time large numbers of Puerto Ricans have returned to their homeland, bringing cultural influences from New York City with them. There have been vast movements from the island to the mainland and back. No restrictions exist on these migrations since Puerto Ricans are citizens of the United States. Thus, the mainland culture has both been influenced by, and had an influence on, the island's original Spanish culture. Puerto Ricans are found mostly in New York City, parts of New Jersey, Illinois, and California.

Cubans began to arrive in the U.S. after the Cuban revolution of 1959. The first wave of Cubans were predominantly middle-class, had professional skills, and spoke English. These factors helped them adjust to life in the United States relatively easily, and today these Cuban Americans tend to have more socioeconomic characteristics in common with non-Latino White Americans than other Latino groups (Melendez et al., 1993). The second wave of political refugees from Cuba arrived in the early 1980s. These refugees were generally poorer and less skilled than their predecessors (Morales & Bonilla, 1991). Although Cubans were more likely to receive resettlement assistance from the government than other Latino groups (Morales & Bonilla, 1991), there was a significant public outcry and fear that this second wave of Cuban immigrants consisted largely of mental patients and prisoners who Castro had expelled from Cuba. Cuban Americans are concentrated in Florida and to a lesser extent in New York City and California (Jaffe et al., 1980).

People from the Caribbean, Central American, and South America have been coming to the United States since about 1960. This group includes Guatemalans, Colombians, Nicaraguans, Chileans, Dominicans, and Argentineans. As civil strife in Central America increased, so did the number of immigrants to the United States. Between 1961 and 1978, a total of 38,000 El Salvadorans, 35,700 Panamanians, 35,500 Guatemalans, and 28,000 Hondurans legally entered the U.S. By the early 1980s almost 200,000 Nicaraguans had left their country, and by 1983, officials estimated that the number of El Salvadorans in the U.S. amounted to as many as 500,000 (Gann & Duignan, 1986). Many Latinos from the Caribbean come as economic refugees, many from Central America come as political refugees, and those from the rest of Latin America come as immigrants (Morales & Bonilla, 1993). South American immigrants such as Chileans and Argentineans resemble the first wave of Cuban immigrants in that they are from the middle and upper classes, are well educated and skilled in urban occupations. The Central and South Americans are found largely in New York and California (Jaffe et al., 1980).

The history of Latino groups in the United States reflects the impact of territorial expansion, its sphere of political influence, and American economic interdependencies (Melendez et al., 1991). While there are some commonalities found among Latino groups such as a historical connection to Spain and the Spanish language, there is tremendous diversity among Latino people. Class differences are apparent between many South Americans and Central Americans. Racial differences also exist among Latino people. Latin American heritage includes descent from Spaniards and other Europeans, as well as descent from indigenous American populations and Africans that were brought to the new world as slaves. This mixture is present in varying degrees in the different Latino populations.

Characteristics and Demographics

During the first decade of this century, the Latino population numbered less than a quarter of a million. Now they are the fastest-growing population in the United States (Gann & Duignan, 1986). The growth of the Latino population is due to both above average immigration and above-average reproduction (Morales & Bonilla, 1993). In March of 1993 the Latino population was estimated to be 22.8 million or 8.9% of the total population in the United States. Out of the general Latino population, 64.3% are Mexican, 13.4% are Central or South American, 10.6% are Puerto Rican, 4.7% are Cuban, and 7% are other Latino (Montgomery, 1994).

The median age of the Latino population as a whole is less than that of the non-Latino White population. The median age of the Latino population in 1993 was 26.7 years as compared to 35.5 years for non-Latino Whites. In spite of this difference, the median age of the Latino population has increased over the last decade, up from 24.3 years in 1983 (Montgomery, 1994). The impact of the Latinos' younger median age is apparent in the enrollment figures of elementary schools where Latino children are overrepresented in the lower grades and will soon be overrepresented through the tenth grade (Estrada, 1985).

Substantial variation exists in the median age of the various groups that fall under the Latino label. The Mexican American population has the lowest median age at 24.6 years, followed by the Puerto Ricans at 26.9, the Central and South Americans at 28.6, and other Latino populations at 32.5 years. The Cuban American population has the highest median age at 43.6 years (Montgomery, 1994).

While educational achievement of Latinos has increased over the last decade, it still remains substantially below that of non-Latinos. In 1993 11.8% of Latinos age 25 or over had less than a fifth grade education as compared to 15.6% in 1983. In 1993 only 1.3% of the non-Latino population had less than a fifth grade education. Latinos age 25 or over who had completed four years of high school or more in 1993 was 53.1%, which is up from 45.7% in 1983. Of the non-Latino population who had completed four years of high school or more in 1993, this figure was 82.4%. Substantial variation in educational achievement exists among the various Latino groups. Mexican American young adults are the least likely to have a high school diploma and Cuban American young adults are the most likely to have a college degree (Montgomery, 1994). The school dropout rate for Latino students is twice that of African Americans and nearly three times that of White youth (DeFreitas, 1991).

The gender gap in labor force participation has narrowed over the last decade for both Latinos and non-Latinos. In March of 1993 the labor force participation of Latino females was 51.9% and for Latino males was 79.2%. Latinos were more likely to be unemployed in March of 1993 than their non-Latino counterparts (11.9% as compared to 7.3%). Employed Latino males are more likely to be in operator, fabricator, and laborer positions than in any other occupational group (28.4%), while their White counterparts are most likely to be in managerial and professional positions (29.2%). Both Latino and non-Latino White females are most likely to work in technical, sales, and administrative support jobs, although Latino females are more likely than their White counterparts to be in service jobs and White females are more likely than their Latino counterparts to hold managerial and professional jobs (Montgomery, 1994).

Farley (1987) outlined two possible reasons for the differences between Latino and White labor market statistics. One hypothesis, the "residential segregation and job decentralization explanation," argues that racial segregation has restricted Latinos (and African Americans) to the central city at a time when industrial plants are moving to the suburbs. This has created a geographic separation between the populations of color and job opportunities. The second explanation is that the economic disadvantages among Latinos are due to disadvantages associated with class, including such factors as education, income, and occupation. In addition to structural barriers and human capitol theories, Morales and Bonilla (1993) suggest that institutional constraints, such as the failures of the educational system and the safety net of social programs, lead to a growing and persistent inequality in opportunities in spite of increasing numbers.

The poverty rate for Latino people was 29.3% in 1992, which, despite variation over the decade, was not substantially different from the 1982 rate of 29.9%. The poverty rate for non-Latino Whites in 1992 was 9.6%. The median earnings for Latino males in 1992 was 63% of non-Latino males. The median earnings for Latino women in 1992 was 78% that of non-Latino women (Montgomery, 1994).

About 80% of Latino households in March 1993 were family households compared with 69.6% of non-Latino White households. In Latino households, 55.4% were maintained by married couples as compared to 58.1% of non-Latino Whites. Of the Latino households, 6.1% were single-parent households headed by men and 18.7% were single-parent households headed by women. This compares with 2.7% single-parent households headed by men and 8.9% single-parent households headed by women in the non-Latino White population. The average number of people in a Latino household was 3.41 in 1993 which is virtually unchanged from 3.48 in 1983. The average number of people in a non-Latino White household was 2.57 in 1993 as compared with 2.69 in 1983 (Montgomery, 1994).

While great variation exists among Latino groups, in general, the Latino population can be characterized by high rates of immigration and reproduction, low education, high urbanization, concentration in low-paying jobs, and poverty (Morales & Bonilla, 1993).

Concerns for Social Work Practice

When working with Latino clients, social workers must keep in mind cultural issues as well as competently applying generic social work skills. It is important that social workers recognize the unique cultural traits of each Latino group as well as cultural variations within groups. Culture is fluid and not static, therefore, there must be a readiness to constantly assess and to maintain a flexible view of culture in relationship to the therapeutic process. Clients must be viewed as individuals with a variety of influences on their lives in addition to culture. Social workers must be aware of the meanings of the differences in ethnicity, race, and culture. This may need to be explored as part of the therapeutic process.

While cultural awareness and knowledge are important, it is not possible for the social worker to know everything about every culture. Rather, it is important that the worker express a willingness to learn about different cultures, and in particular demonstrate a willingness to listen to and learn from the client. Theories of human behavior based on European models may not be adequate for understanding the behavior of all clients. Interventions which take into account the social dynamics and parameters inherent in a specific culture are likely to be more effective in resolving problems. It is important to understand the client's beliefs about the nature and origin of the problem and incorporate this in the work. Social workers must recognize that a client's use of symbols and words may differ from those used in the dominant society even though the same words may be used.

Some Latino clients may be reluctant to seek help from a social worker. It is important to recognize and appreciate that an element of distrust may be manifested by Latino clients. Social workers should be sensitive to any conflicts that may exist between the worker's ethnic group and Latino groups (Burgest, 1985).

Social workers, agency administrators, and policymakers must all become sensitive to, and knowledgeable about the history, heritage, culture, and life-styles of members of the various Latino groups. It is important that those working with Latino clients examine their own stereotypes and biases as well as institutional biases found within professional educational systems, assessment criteria, and the society as a whole if they are to be effective in their work with Latino clients.

Since a significant percentage of the Latino population in the United States are immigrants and refugees, it is important that social workers have an understanding of issues particular to this population. Vargas-Willis and Cervantes (1987) state that a host of psychosocial stressors affect the mental health status of Latino immigrants. These include loss of family members and friends, language difficulties, lowered socioeconomic status and concerns over children's welfare and education. These stressors must be thoroughly assessed as part of the treatment process and at times must become the major focus of the therapeutic intervention.

There are several general issues which should be considered in work with Latino clients. Social workers should become familiar with issues related to cultural identity, values, family, religion, and language. It is also important that the social worker be aware of relevant social policies and their impact on Latino clients. The issues discussed below have greater or lesser meaning, depending on the Latino group in question. These issues should be kept in mind when assessing and working with Latino clients, however, the social worker must be careful to recognize the individuality of each client rather than to make stereotypical assumptions about values, life-style, and other issues.

Cultural Identity

As stated above, the term Latino includes people from many different historical backgrounds, classes, and races. No assumptions can be made about the cultural identity of any given Latino client. Early assimilation theories asserted that ethnic and cultural groups would blend together in a melting pot to form an American culture while abandoning the traits and customs of the culture of origin. In spite of such theories, ethnic identities have persisted. Two important processes must be understood when looking at ethnic or cultural identity of Latino people. Enculturation, or the process of ethnic socialization, is learned from families, peers, and the ethnic community. Acculturation is the process of ethnic group members learning the dominant culture. Cultural identification is a result of both enculturation and acculturation processes.

Culture consists of the beliefs, values, and world view that are learned and integrated into an individual's identity. In a pluralistic society people are exposed to more than one culture, and it is not uncommon for people to identify with more than one culture (Weaver, in press). Early theories suggested that identification with the ethnic culture of origin while residing within the United States, or even a bicultural identification, which includes identification with the culture of origin and the dominant society, were stressful and had negative implications. It was believed that people would be torn between two cultures and not really feel that they fit anywhere (Colman, Gerton, & La Fromboise, 1993). More recently research has found that cultural identification, including identification with more than one culture, can have positive implications for social functioning (Oetting & Beauvais, 1991).

Several factors can influence why some members of one culture become completely absorbed within another while others remain completely identified with their culture of origin and still others develop multicultural identifications. Among these influential factors are the initial attitudes the individual has about the culture; if they have left their cultural community or society of origin, their reasons for doing so; the amount of prejudice and discrimination encountered; and the nature of the cultural customs. Some cultural patterns such as competitiveness as opposed to cooperative life-styles and nuclear versus extended family ties may be mutually exclusive. Acquiring one may mean excluding the other (Mendoza & Martinez, 1981).

Most theorists agree that before problem solving can be initiated in the Latino individual or community a clear understanding of the acculturation level or cultural identification must be assessed. It is possible to provide services that incorporate multicultural training components that reduce stress, so that shifts from one cultural context to another can occur easily without the loss of one's cultural tradition. The ability to function appropriately in more than one cultural context can be a source of strength rather than a source of stress and confusion.

Definitions of race must be considered in examining issues related to Latino cultural identification. Race has been defined differently in the United States than in many Latin American cultures. In the U.S., race is an ascribed characteristic that does not change after birth. It is, at least theoretically, based on genetics and biological inheritance. For many Latinos, the concept of race is fused with learned characteristics that are generally associated with culture in the U.S. In some Latin American countries race can change over time. It is a cultural, social, and a political concept. In the 1980 census, 40% of Latinos identified their race as "other." Rodriquez (1992) studied this phenomenon and found that it was not due to misunderstanding or the presence of multiracial individuals in the census, but was due to the fact that Latinos have a more continuous and culturally defined concept of race than is found in the dominant society.

Values

The attitudes and value systems that exist in Latino cultures should be considered in planning interventions. The value systems of many Latinos are rooted in Catholicism. Values such as devotion to God, family, and work transcend organized religion and serve as a source of influence.

For some Latinos, attitudes toward planning may be diametrically opposed to majority U.S. attitudes. The present is a stronger reality than the future. The use of time, planning, and organization are not held in esteem as in the dominant culture. There is little obsession with being "on time," planning, and trying to control the future. It is not uncommon for Latinos to resign themselves to the way things are rather than to value and strive for change. Fatalism (perceived lack of control over environmental outcomes), extended familism, and present time orientation are values which have been presumed to be antithetical to those held by the dominant society.

Interpersonal behaviors are often more important than task achievements. An individual who is *simpatia* behaves with dignity and respect toward others and strives for harmony in interpersonal relations; conflicts are always avoided (Triandis, Lisansky, Marin, & Betancourt, 1984). Social workers who focus their work on tasks rather than relationships are likely to have misunderstandings with their Latino clients.

Clients from Latino cultures may differ from mainstream society in the value placed on activity. "Being" is often emphasized over "doing." This does not imply that the Latino has necessarily accomplished less, but accomplishment may be defined in terms of a sense of belonging and worth as a family member rather than acquiring prestige and status in the workplace (Inclan, 1985).

Family

The family has been defined by sociologists as a social group characterized by common residence, economic cooperation, and reproduction (Mizio, 1974). Such a core definition allows for the various configurations that exist among family units in society. The importance of understanding the ethnic differences in family systems cannot be overemphasized, but to truly understand a family, one must review it within the context of the external environment in which it exists.

Emphasis is usually placed on the family rather than the individual, and an extended kinship network may be available to provide practical and emotional support (Cox & Monk, 1993). It has been theorized that the family plays an important role in alleviating personal distress and that the level of reliance on traditional family structure is related to the level of acculturation. The reasoning is that traditional culture exerts social controls by way of religious, family, and interpersonal sanctions to deter socially disruptive behaviors. In a study by Taylor, Hurley, and Riley (1986) differences were found in the family support systems of more and less acculturated Latinos. Less acculturated Latinos rely upon family support more so than the more acculturated. Because the family support system may lessen the impact of stress on being from a single-parent family, the children of less acculturated Latinos are not likely to be detrimentally affected by living in a single-parent family.

The nuclear family has been idealized within the dominant society. Typically a nuclear family consists of a husband, wife and offspring. Kin are generally excluded from the family's decision making.

In Latino cultures, ties to family are in no way considered pathological. Contrasted to the idealized American family, Latino family bonds extend beyond the nuclear family. This extended network may include grandparents, aunts, and uncles, as well as more distant relatives. This intimate kinship system is highly valued and serves as a source of pride and security. The extended family unit may be viewed as a composite form of the nuclear family where relationships are intense and frequent. There are important mutual obligations that exist and each individual's worth is guaranteed by the fulfillment of these responsibilities (Mizio, 1974).

Results of a study conducted by Sabogal, Marin, Otero-Sabogal, Van Oss Marin, and Perez-Stable (1987) suggest that the most essential dimension of Latino familism is the high level of perceived family support and that this perception remains constant even as the level of acculturation changes. Families with extended family networks generally have a greater expectation of involvement among members than do Anglo-American families (Hepworth & Larsen, 1986). For example, De Anda (1984) states that in the mainstream culture, a young adult displays his or her maturity and responsibility by physically separating from the family and establishing an independent living situation. In Latino communities, such behavior would be viewed as a selfish disregard of familial responsibility. Instead, maturity and responsibility would be demonstrated by the young adult remaining at home and contributing to the support of the family. According to Galan (1985), in Latino cultures, the value of honoring one's mother and father takes precedence over other considerations. Since the family is the strongest social unit among Latinos, the group's welfare becomes the responsibility of each family member and actions by any member are designed to bring honor to the culture and to the family. A decision to act in a particular way is weighed against the principal of family unity, because any action that could potentially disrupt the family is one that would bring dishonor to the parents.

Another characteristic that generally exists in the Latino family is the system of paternal authority, which emphasizes the absolute authority of the male, deference of the female, and obedience of children (Hepworth & Larsen, 1986). The concept of masculine superiority and dominance of the family still remains a part of Latino cultures. Clear sex-role distinctions and divisions of labor according to sex exist in varying degrees in the different Latino populations. In a study by Davis and Chavez (1985), 22 Latino men who assumed roles within their families that emphasized household maintenance and emotional family support were found to view their role reversals as brought about by economic circumstances and as temporary. The authors suggest that the perceived short-term role reversal may have long-term effects on sex-role statuses and social order in Latino communities.

Machismo is the label given to the ideal male characteristics valued in Latino societies. Macho ideals such as courage, fearlessness, pride, honor, charisma, and leadership abilities are prized within Latino cultures, yet *machismo* is usually interpreted exclusively as aggressiveness and sexual prowess by non-Latinos. A distinction must be made between the ideals of *machismo* and the way these ideals are sometimes distorted into a hypermasculine behavior which parodies these ideals (Panitz, McConchie, Sauber, & Fonseca, 1983).

Marianismo is the value that women should be pure like the Virgin Mary. Latino women are expected to subordinate their own needs to the needs of their husbands and children. Puerto Rican women on the island are more likely to display depressive symptomatology than Puerto Rican women on the mainland. This has been attributed to the more patriarchal social context found in Puerto Rico (Amaro & Russo, 1987). Older women continue assisting their children and grandchildren in caregiving responsibilities and they carry the responsibility for sustaining the ties between generations. The cultural expectation that women will be caregivers is still generally accepted in Latino communities, but fulfilling this role may be particularly difficult when caring for elderly parents with Alzheimers (Cox & Monk, 1993).

In Latino families, deep respect is accorded to the aged (Cox & Monk, 1993). The elderly are greatly respected in many Latino cultures and positions of authority are assigned to them regardless of their gender. The special regard for the elders' place in the family and for what they have accomplished in their lives, for the sacrifices they have made for the family, all are embraced in the value of respect (Galan, 1985).

Latino cultures emphasize respect and responsibility to family members, therefore, elderly adults are often cared for within the family rather than through formal social services. However, reliance on family support for the elderly may result in such side effects as depression and overwhelming the caregiving capacity of the family (Cox & Monk, 1993; Purdy & Arguello, 1992).

The Latino family not only includes those related by blood and marriage but also those tied to it through custom. These "adopted" relatives fulfill either formal or informal functions within the extended family. The words *como familia,* meaning like family, are often used to describe these individuals (Delgado & Humm-Delgado, 1982). The members of these kinship groups usually are close family friends and special neighbors, who have proven through the years their willingness to engage in important family matters and events (Delgado & Humm-Delgado, 1982). This kinship network encompasses a deep sense of obligation by its members to each other for economic assistance, encouragement, support, and even personal correction.

Compadrazgo is the ritual kinship process that serves to widen and enhance the individual's primary group by transforming outsiders into family members, or more distant relatives into closer associates (Delgado & Humm-Delgado, 1982). This kinship process is generally achieved by participation as sponsors in such ceremonies as a child's baptism, confirmation and first communion, and serving as witnesses at a marriage. In those ceremonies that involve children, the participants become known as "companion parents" or *compadres.* With some variation among Latino groups, this practice involves assuming responsibility for the child if the biological parents are unable and raising the child as one's own. There is no stigma attached to the parent who surrenders the child or the child who is given up (Mizio, 1974). This arrangement may be either temporary or permanent.

In the U.S., such arrangements may present legal problems for the families involved, as legal documents for the child may not be easily produced. The traditional family structure found within Latino cultures is placed in jeopardy by the strains placed upon it by the external environment that is geared toward the nuclear family. For example, housing authority regulations may not allow the dweller to extend the traditional hospitality of an open door to extended "relatives" during times when it would be mutually supportive to do so. However, in the face of such constraints, many Latino families continue to hold on to their traditions.

As in the wider society, the family is very important to Latinos; this is the place one first learns socialization skills, to trust and love, and where one's identity is formed. Again, just as in the wider society, the Latino family serves as a source of comfort, a place to retreat from the users and abuses of the outside world. Although Latino families share some of the basic attributes of Anglo families, there exist culturally based characteristics that are exclusive to Latino cultures. Rothman, Gant, and Hnat (1985) found that Latinos prefer to rely on family members for support in times of crisis, rather than seek out external resources. In many cases it may be appropriate for social workers to help facilitate the resolution of problems through family channels rather than rely on outside resources.

One of the integral parts of Latino cultures is the importance placed on preserving the family unit through respect and loyalty. Latino males often view themselves as protective of women and young family and community members. According to a market survey conducted in 1981, 55% of Latinos share the view that the husband's role as a good provider is a token of his masculinity (Gann & Duignan, 1986).

Within Latino cultures the whole community can be viewed as a cohesive family. The extended family network in Latino communities often serves to help community members through problem solving.

Much emphasis is put on personal dignity and on respect of the community and its members. Although the literature does not often discuss the use of family therapy with Latinos, family therapy can be an effective intervention if Latino values and family structure are incorporated into the work (Hardy-Fanta & MacMahon-Herrera, 1981).

Religion

According to Ramirez (1985), the historical roots of Latino spirituality can be traced to two distinct cultural groups: the indigenous of the Americas and Iberian Europe. When the Spaniards came to the New World in the fifteenth and sixteenth centuries, they encountered indigenous philosophical and theological systems with complex religious thinking, rituals, and a profusion of symbolic objects and places. They also had brought over centuries of Christian thought and practice, which emphasized a mystical and intensely subjective approach to spirituality. Thus, many Latino religious values that have become institutionalized have foundations in both Native American cosmology and Christianity. Latino spirituality is an essential component in the process of motivation, decision making, priority setting, and value formation that in turn influences the values of Latinos (Ramirez, 1985). In addition, African belief systems have blended with Catholicism and Native beliefs to form a basis for Latino spirituality. This is apparent in religions such as *santeria* (Castex, 1994).

The Latino ideology of Catholicism centers around the concepts of life and death. One assumption of many Latino Catholics is that God will provide. The crucifix, the suffering of Christ, and the Sacred Heart are often highlighted in Latino's homes and as jewelry to testify to their personal identification with the religion. According to Galan (1985), blessed objects are more than lucky or magic charms that bring desired results. They are reminders and symbols of the ever-abiding presence of God, of His protection and providential care. They represent the transcendent, the world of the spirit, God's world and scheme of things. These objects also reflect Latino's acceptance of the hardships of life as the will of God. There is a pervading sense that much of what happens is beyond one's control. This can be seen in the language structure. Future events are often planned with the thought *"Si Dios quiere"* or "only if God wills it."

Traditional Catholic rituals are used during times of need by many Latinos. These means are employed before going to a priest to discuss personal problems. For many Latinos, a counselor is often the last resort. These devotions may include going to many Catholic churches and making promises, making novenas, lighting candles, and praying to a Patron Saint. A Patron Saint is the saint after which one is named, or one may adopt a Patron Saint. Also there are Patron Saints for specific needs. For example, one prays to Saint Jude to do the impossible, and to Saint Anthony to find what is lost. Catholics are devoted to Jesus' mother, the Virgin Mary. She will help one with life because she is an understanding mother. Latinos' emphasis on both faith and practice is part of a long-standing tradition in Spanish and Latin American cate-chism (oral instruction in religious doctrine) on how ritual behavior serves as proof of one's faith (Ramirez, 1985).

In many Latino communities the priest is a source of help. Expecta-tions of and participation in mental health services may be influenced by Latinos' understanding of the helping process as defined in a religious context. For example, through the process of confessing sins, priests are able to provide absolution (in the name of God) for penitent believers. Some Catholic, Latino clients may perceive the mental health practi-tioner in a role similar to that of a priest.

Latinos currently account for nearly one-third (some 15 million) of U.S. Catholics, although 30% to 40% of Latinos are not involved in parish life. According to Gann and Duignan (1986), Latino Catholics, especially the poor among them, are more apt to emphasize personal belief and folk religion over duty to the church and parish. The bulk of Latinos, at least in New York, do not know much about many church beliefs; 60% could not name a single one of the seven sacraments. Erosion of beliefs and practices increases with the second-generation Latinos.

Among the poor in Puerto Rico and Cuba, the Indian and African legacies have contributed to the creation of syncretic creeds such as *espiritismo* among Puerto Ricans and *santeria* among Cubans. Many adherents of these belief systems still regard themselves as Catholics (Gann & Duignan, 1986). The term "Catholic" is strongly associated with traditional devotions and customs. Perhaps that is one reason why Latinos will insist they are Catholic even though they do not participate frequently in the official rituals of the church (Ramirez, 1985).

Religious groups offer many social and psychological support services to members and may, in effect, serve as multiservice organizations situated in a Latino community with bilingual, bicultural staff members.

Religions such as *espiritismo, santeria,* and Catholicism must be examined from a social service perspective as well as from a religious one in order to assess the nature and extent of social support in Latino communities. Research has documented that Puerto Ricans in the mainland U.S. use *espiritismo* as a major source of emotional assistance (Comas-Diaz, 1981).

Folk healers play valuable roles in many Latino communities. Among the various Latino groups folk healers may be called *espiritista, santero,* herbalist, *santiguador,* or *curandero.* These folk healers address particular needs experienced by individuals who are in distress and use unique culture-specific methods to assess and treat ailments. The *santero* and *espiritista* focus primarily on emotional and interpersonal problems, the herbalist and *santiguador* focus on physical ailments, and the *curandero* maintains a balance between the physical and mental spheres.

Espiritismo is the belief that the visible world is permeated by an invisible world inhabited by both good and evil spirits (Delgado & Humm-Delgado, 1982). The *espiritista* diagnoses the presenting problem and makes an appropriate treatment plan. The plan may vary and can range from a referral to medical authorities to a ritualistic plan. Comas-Diaz (1981) suggests that *espiritismo* is an adaptive mechanism which helps individuals to cope with alien environments and as such is a more important factor for Puerto Ricans in the mainland United States than those who have remained on the island.

Santeria is a syncretism of African and Roman Catholic religious beliefs. The syncretism is manifested through the representation of Yoruba deities in the form of Roman Catholic saints (Delgado & Humm-Delgado, 1982). The *santero* uses the African methods to diagnose the presenting symptoms. These methods may include songs, music, and the sacrificing of animals. They are highly ritualistic and may last for several days. The *santero* also prescribes an appropriate treatment plan. *Santeria* is used primarily for dealing with personal spiritual and emotional problems. *Santeria* may be used more in the United States than in Cuba. *Santeria* rituals help Cubans of all classes deal with the stresses of relocation to a foreign environment (Queralt, 1984).

Many Latinos use herbs for medicinal purposes. According to a naturalistic belief system, there are certain diseases, herbs, foods, and medicines that are classified as having either "hot" or "cold" origins and properties. Once a disease has been categorized as being either "hot" or "cold," medication is prescribed to reestablish the individual's balance or equilibrium. "Hot" illnesses require "cold" remedies and vice versa.

Santiguadores specialize in treating chronic and intestinal diseases, as well as in setting dislocated bones and curing various forms of muscle and body aches. The beliefs of the *santiguadores* have a naturalistic foundation, although they also consider the possibility that supernatural forces may be involved in an individual's problem. A cure must enlist the will of God (Delgado & Humm-Delgado, 1982). *Santiguadores* use various methods for treatment. These may include the laying on of hands, as well as massages, herbs, prayers, changes in daily routine, and various dietary recommendations.

Curanderismo is based on the premise that illness and bad luck are brought about by weakening ties with the Roman Catholic church, the family, and the culture. The theme of Christ permeates much of the *curandero*'s thinking about illness and misfortune. *Curanderos* see their work as harmonious with orthodox religion and do not view themselves as being in conflict with Catholicism (Delgado & Humm-Delgado, 1982). Culturally, symbolic techniques are used by *curanderos* to return individuals to harmony with the culture and with God.

Folk beliefs and practices serve very distinctive functions for many Latinos. Syncretic religions often function as mental health systems. Social work practitioners must be sensitive to clients' belief systems and not automatically assume that belief in such systems is a sign of psychological disturbance (Comas-Diaz, 1981; Queralt, 1984).

Language

Language barriers often exist between Latinos and non-Latino institutions and systems for receiving social services. In addition to racial and cultural stereotyping, Latinos often face harassment and abuse for not speaking English. Effective mastery of the English language is often associated with intelligence and superiority which leads to condescension toward non-English-speaking clients. Devaluing the language results in devaluing the client. It is difficult to separate the language of a people from the culture and way of life of a people. The language is an integral part of who they are, since language reflects culture and culture reflects language.

Spanish is the most frequently spoken non-English language in the United States. Two-thirds of those who speak Spanish report that they speak English "well" or "very well," which is indicative of the bilingual nature of the majority of Latinos who live in the United States (Estrada, 1987). While the majority of Latinos are bilingual, it should be acknowledged that some of the more vulnerable segments of the Latino population, such as the elderly and new immigrants, are likely to speak only Spanish; therefore, they have the most need of bilingual services. Also, Queralt (1984) found that among Cubans who spoke both English and Spanish, there was a tendency to use a hybrid language mixing Spanish and English together rather than to communicate solely in one language.

Not surprisingly, English fluency has been repeatedly linked to academic achievement (Rothman, Gant, & Hnat, 1985). As the number of years of bilingual instruction increases, so does grade point average and the probability of retention (Curiel, Rosenthal, & Richek, 1986). Mexican American students who primarily speak Spanish have been shown to do better in bilingual programs than Mexican American students who primarily speak English do in English-only programs in grades one through three (Garza & Medina, 1985).

Although language barriers can be significant for Latino clients, it would be inappropriate to assume that all Latinos are fluent and literate in Spanish. Latino clients may speak a number of regional Spanish dialects or may not speak Spanish at all. In the 1980 census over three million Latinos in the U.S. indicated that they did not speak Spanish in the home. Latinos in the United States speak five major European languages (Spanish, Portuguese, French, Dutch, and English) and major Native American languages such as Quecha, Maya, Aymara, and Guarani, as well as creole dialects.

Lambert, Goldfield, Chamot, and Cahir (1981) have shown that an accent can stereotype individuals and provoke an image of a less dependable, less socially attractive, less likely to succeed person than if the same person did not have an accent. This reflects one of many pressures put on ethnolinguistic minority groups to shed all traces of their native cultures. This puts adults as well as children in a psychological limbo that contributes both to the trouble they have with English and the difficulties they have at school and at work. Linguistic policies which either promote or inhibit bilingualism also have an effect on psychosocial well-being and cognitive growth (Grosjean, 1982).

Social Work Service Delivery

In order to adequately provide services to Latino clients, social workers must have some knowledge and appreciation of Latino cultures. Provision of a wide range of services by bilingual, bicultural staff in neighborhood-based services that have been planned with community input are recommended. Social workers must be aware of environmental factors and the influence they have on intrapsychic conflicts. The role of the family within Latino cultures and the valuable functions filled by folk therapists must be considered in the delivery of culturally competent services (Delgado & Scott, 1979).

It is important to consider cultural concerns when working with Latino clients, but other issues are often relevant as well. As people of color, Latinos often face racism and discrimination. Issues of class and gender must also be considered. The foundation for culturally competent social work practice will always be competent social work practice. The social worker must consider a variety of variables in assessing and intervening with the client including variables within the client, variables within the environment, and the relationship between these sets of variables. While this chapter discusses many characteristics of work with Latino clients, not all the values and characteristics apply equally to all clients. It is important to recognize diversity within Latino groups and not to stereotype Latino clients.

Principles for Practice

When working with Latino clients the writers suggest the following considerations:

1. Family is the primary source of support. Be aware that seeking services may be perceived as an admission of failure within the family.
2. Latino clients may not know what to expect from a social worker. They may be reluctant to discuss problems with a stranger, and if disappointed in the social work process may simply not return rather than voicing disagreement with an authority figure.
3. Seeking help is a family affair and members of the extended family may come to the interview.
4. Religion, including Catholicism and syncretic blends of Native American and African religions, plays an important role in the lives of many Latinos.
5. Interdependency among family members is valued within many Latino cultures and should not be viewed as pathological.

6. Socioeconomic concerns may present pressing issues for many Latinos. Concrete services such as food and shelter may be more pressing concerns than inter- or intrapsychic issues.
7. There may be an expectation that the social worker be directive and solve all the client's problems rather than working together on the client's concerns.
8. Given the value placed on personal relationships, the social worker may be expected to be a friend and go beyond the typical bounds of a social work relationship.

Policy Issues

While many social policies relate to Latino people, probably the most significant policy areas that have implications for social workers are those of immigration and education.

Immigration. Immigration status has many implications for access to social services. Citizens, resident aliens, refugees, asylum seekers, and undocumented people all vary in the type of services that are available to them. Legal status has implications for mobility, employment, entitlements, and ability to plan for the future (Castex, 1994). Latino citizens qualify for all the rights and entitlements of non-Latino citizens (with the exceptions noted earlier of the political rights of people in Puerto Rico). Resident aliens are legally able to work and live in this country but may not be entitled to certain social welfare programs for their first several years in the U.S. Refugees and asylees are usually entitled to the full range of social benefits available to citizens and may have special programs such as relocation assistance available to them. Even undocumented people have certain rights, such as access to basic medical care, due process, and public education. However, at the time of this writing, legal challenges such as Proposition 187 in California are being initiated regarding the right of undocumented children to a public school education.

Immigration policies have been shaped according to the need for cheap farm labor and the fear of losing control over U.S. borders and being overwhelmed by Latino immigrants. The fear has often been expressed that Latino immigration, both documented and undocumented, will depress wage levels and cause U.S. born workers to lose jobs, yet empirical data reveal that positive economic effects of immigration outweigh any negative consequences (DeFreitas, 1991).

In 1986 the Immigration Reform and Control Act (IRCA) was passed. The most well known component of the act offered amnesty to undocumented people who had resided continuously in the United States since January 1, 1982. Approximately 1.8 million people sought amnesty under this provision which was well below the anticipated number (Gelfand & Bialik-Giland, 1989). The law also contained provisions for continued importation of farm laborers, mostly from Mexico, and it sanctioned employers for hiring undocumented workers. The provision for employer sanctions caused much confusion and led to employers firing or refusing to hire workers who looked or sounded as if they might be foreign, rather than to risk hiring an undocumented worker and facing penalties. IRCA led to widespread discrimination against many people of color and people with accents (General Accounting Office, 1990). Many of the people who experience discrimination due to IRCA are Latino.

Education

More than 1.3 million students whose primary language is not English are enrolled in federal, state, or local study programs that provide instruction in their native languages. These programs have their roots in the Federal Bilingual Education Act of 1968. This act's original aim was to generate optimal instruction that would help immigrant youngsters and native born Latino children learn English quickly. Meanwhile, they were to move ahead in their schoolwork by using their own language as much as necessary (Bowen, 1985). The amended Bilingual Education Act of 1978 limited the number of English-speaking children in the program to no more than 40%, involved parents more, and required bilingual proficiency in both languages. The voting bloc represented by their parents has generated congressional support for expanding bilingualism into cultural maintenance (Bowen, 1985). The Bilingual Education Act of 1968 allows for teaching of primary subjects in both English and the native language when a substantial number of children which speak the same language attend the same school (Grosjean, 1982).

The Latino National Political Survey found that more than 80% of Latinos were in favor of bilingual education. Ninety percent of those surveyed believed that citizens and residents of the United States should learn English (De La Garza, DeSipio, Garcia, Garcia, & Falcon, 1992).

CONCERNS FOR SOCIAL WORK RESEARCH

Research related to Latinos covers a wide range of issues such as effectiveness of services, political opinions, and health status. Since research informs practice, many research studies have already been cited. This section will examine the results of studies on self-esteem as it relates to cultural identity. Studies on service delivery and overarching methodological issues in research involving Latinos will also be discussed.

Self-Esteem and Cultural Identity

The research on self-esteem in Latino people generally focuses on ethnic identity, behavioral adjustment, and level of acculturation. While much research has been done in these areas, the results vary substantially. In a study conducted by Gomez (1987), significant correlations were found to exist between biculturality and the subjective mental health measures in a sample of 151 Cuban Americans. Results of a study by Grossman, Wirt, and Davis (1985) supported the notion that there is a relationship between being Latino and having low self-esteem and lower behavioral adjustment, but higher ethnic self-esteem. A significant difference was found between the test scores of Anglos and Latinos in West Texas on several measures of self-esteem. Anglos scored higher than Latinos on behavioral adjustment. Results of a study conducted by Martinez and Dukes (1987) showed that minorities tend to have lower levels of self-esteem in the area of intelligence than do whites, but higher levels in the area of satisfaction with self.

The ecological theory may explain why lower self-esteem is prevalent among Latinos. Its premise states that an individual learns from the outcome of interactions between self and environment, and can explain the lack of self-worth experienced by Latinos and all people of color as a result of discrimination and prejudice. The assumption is made that members of the dominant society experience greater harmony with the environment and, therefore, adjust to it more easily. This theory presents the idea that the adjustment is less a function of self-esteem than of one's place within society.

Evidence provided by the Cuban Americans who came to the United States in the late 1950s and early 1960s further supports the ecological theory. Most of these Cubans possessed above average education and skills as well as class backgrounds and values which were compatible with those of mainstream U.S. citizens. Therefore, they were able to make remarkable progress in adjusting to the U.S. and in establishing a sufficient economic base to ease the difficulties of adjustment. A study conducted by Frasier and DeBlassie (1982) examined self-concepts in the areas of academic success of 49 Mexican Americans and 80 non-Mexican American students. Given equal levels of ability, no differences in self-concept in regard to academic success emerged between the two groups. Data suggested that Mexican American students and non-Mexican American students, whose abilities are equal, are likely to achieve equally in college.

Mena, Padilla, and Maldonado (1987) explored the relationship of acculturative stress to self-esteem, locus of control, and loyalty to American culture among a multicultural group of college undergraduates. Results revealed that students who immigrated after age 12 had higher acculturative stress than those who immigrated before age 12 or who were second- or third-generation immigrants. Also, late immigrants coped with stress more often by taking a direct, individualistic approach, while second- and third-generation immigrants coped more often by using a social network approach, that is, by talking to others about the problem. The authors state that for immigrants, the most stressful part of the acculturation process is the reevaluation of their role within the new culture and their sense of not belonging. The more strongly immigrants cling to their ethnic identity, the greater the stress they report and the lower their self-esteem.

Results of a study conducted by Salgado de Snyder (1987) showed that Mexican women immigrants who remained highly loyal to Mexican culture had significantly lower levels of self-esteem and satisfaction and higher levels of acculturative stress than their counterparts who remain less loyal to Mexican culture. Leon, Mazur, Montalvo, and Rodriguez (1984) suggest that a successful model for assisting Latino mothers with the problems that arise when faced with conflicting cultural systems and values is a self-help group based in facilities that provide children and family services such as counseling, therapy, health care information, and referral. The self-help group approach strengthens the self-esteem of Latino parents and provides Latino mothers with an opportunity to build personal relationships and mutual support systems, thereby reducing social isolation.

Not all literature suggests that maintaining a strong connection to Latino cultures is unhealthy or has negative implications for self-esteem. Work done at the Tri-Ethnic Center for Prevention Research has found that identification with a culture has positive implications for social well-being (Oetting & Beauvais, 1991). Additionally, much research indicates that Latinos can successfully function in more than one cultural context (Domino, 1992).

Many Latinos in the U.S. face harsh socioeconomic realities, language barriers, and discrimination. While cultural adjustment may be one explanation for low self-esteem it is certainly not the only one. Social workers must carefully assess the source of problems such as low self-esteem before choosing and intervention. It may well be that interventions on a macro level could be more effective than those on a micro level.

Although much has been published on ethnic identity and acculturation there is little discussion on the difficulty of operationalizing these terms. Typically language use, where the individual was born, and type of community where the individual resides have been used to measure cultural identity and level of acculturation. More recently the validity of such measures has been questioned (Domino, 1992; Marin, 1992; Oetting & Beauvais, 1991). There is little correspondence between the various models of acculturation and the ways in which acculturation is measured. Earlier models did not always have operational definitions and even current models generally do not have more complex scales. Domino (1992) suggests that some acculturation scales are appropriate for some Latino groups and not for others, yet overall these scales have received little study and there is little evidence for their generalizability. Most acculturation scales for Latinos have been designed for use with Mexican Americans and Cuban Americans and have not been applied to other groups (Marin, 1992).

Measures of acculturation tend to measure variables that are easy to measure such as language preference and patterns in food consumption. These are the more superficial aspects of acculturation. More significant factors such as changes in values and norms are much more difficult to measure yet would be more meaningful (Marin, 1992).

Service Delivery

Various human service systems and providers have not always been effective in meeting the needs of Latino clients. Human service providers who work with Latinos do not always understand cultural differences, especially those pertaining to low socioeconomic status. A study by Ghali (1985) examined the extent to which a sample of 40 psychiatrists, psychologists, and social workers recognized three Puerto Rican cultural values (the primacy of family loyalty and obligation, the concept of *personalismo,* and the primacy of the spiritual) and how they made use of these values in the treatment process. Interview data revealed that the Puerto Rican practitioners (50% of the sample) recognized the three cultural values, used them in the treatment process, and modified their techniques with Puerto Rican clients more often than did the non-Puerto Rican practitioners.

Latinos often do not take their problems to mental health agencies. In part this may be due to lack of familiarity with mainstream social agencies. Cultural and institutional barriers may exist which prevent people from seeking help. It may also be because family members, the church, or folk healers can effectively help clients while working within their own cultural norms and therefore people do not need to seek out additional help.

In an evaluation of folk therapies by de la Cancela and Martinez (1983), two different views are presented. One view sees folk therapy as a dangerous reliance on primitive defense mechanisms; the other is that folk practitioners are appropriate within their cultural context and refer to them as ethnotherapists. Indeed, a host of similarities exist between Western psychotherapy and folk healing. The salient ones include the admission of unacceptable impulses and emotions and their displacement to culturally acceptable outlets, acceptance and tolerance of deviance by the practitioners who instill introspection and identification with others, and a long process of training undertaken by practitioners to perfect their craft. Authors such as Comas-Diaz (1981) point out that practices such as *espiritismo* and psychotherapy need not be mutually exclusive.

In a study by Gomez (1985) conducted at two community mental health centers serving primarily Chicanos, a model of psychosocial casework was evaluated. The study used the Hollis conceptualization of person-in-the-situation gestalt, which involves awareness of culture-oriented behavior. The two issues addressed were the following: the effects of psychosocial casework with Chicanos and the behaviors that workers exhibit that clients associate with service satisfaction. The unique quality of both the centers is their history of selecting staff guided by principals of cultural compatibility in service delivery. This general attention to the role of culture led to the belief that there would be a high worker/client congruence. Sixty-two percent of the caseworkers were Chicano and used Spanish in the delivery of service. The result was positive changes in client outcomes after treatment. There were several behaviors performed by the caseworkers that were correlated with service satisfaction; the highest of these was the reinforcing of positive concepts of self as Mexican Americans. Other behaviors were communicating honestly, showing respect, and developing client motivation, all of which were supported by Hollis. The cultural aspects associated with client satisfaction were inquiring about clients' beliefs as they relate to problems being addressed, allowing clients to use language of preference or need, and exploring natural helping systems.

Arroyo and Lopez (1984) constructed a model for service delivery to the Chicano community. They hypothesized that the task of making an agency's services visible to the community is made easier if an agency is located in the barrio. At the same time, staff at such an agency will be able to maintain a higher degree of community awareness. This awareness will, in turn, lead to a heightened sensitivity to the language and cultural uniqueness of the Chicano people.

Gomez (1985) compared the perceptions of human service workers and Latino clients. Because each was coming from his or her own particular frame of reference there was a difference in worker/client perceptions in both initial assessments and assessments of change in problem severity. Even though the therapists were familiar with the culture, there still tended to be a discrepancy between their perceptions.

A study by Garcia (1984) tested the effectiveness of an undergraduate training program designed to increase the pool of service providers who are sensitive to the needs of Latino communities. Results indicated that because of their need to balance their own ethnicity while functioning within the dominant culture, bilingual and bicultural workers were sensitive to the needs of clients and they maximized efforts to facilitate positive outcome of service.

However, in a study by Lynskey (1987), which examined the impact that an ethnic background of a helper might have on congruence or dissonance of perception with a group of Puerto Rican teenagers, findings indicated that the ethnic background of helpers, although important especially in initial encounters, was not of overriding importance in the helping process. A helper's competence and ability to empathize are also important.

According to Rothman, Gant, and Hnat (1985), knowledge of cultural variables alone does not lead to effective service provision for populations of color. Social class factors also need to be recognized, the effects of racism and discrimination must be understood, and generic aspects of psychosocial functioning must be grasped. Efforts must be aimed at going beyond sensitivity and establishing definite culturally infused intervention models and techniques.

Melendez et al. (1991) discuss some of the problems inherent in conducting research on Latinos, particularly Puerto Ricans in the labor force. Much of the research conducted is derivative of research on other ethnic populations; therefore, the questions asked, the methodology, and the statistical models used may not be a good fit. Since the Puerto Rican population is small, limited data is available for analysis. Additionally, since Puerto Ricans are citizens, it is not possible to trace their migratory patterns as easily as foreigners. Diversity exists among Latino groups, yet many studies which only identify participants by this broad category obscure the in-group diversity and generate misleading data. The literature on Latino inequality is filled with significant gaps between theory and empirical testing which in turn hamper further research and policy analysis (Melendez, 1991).

It is often difficult to get a sample size large enough to clearly see differentials between various Latino groups (DeFreitas, 1991). Good research must appreciate the heterogeneity within Latinos. The validity and reliability of measurement instruments can be judged only when this within-group diversity is considered (Padilla, 1992).

The multiracial character of Latino populations may pose questions for the researcher, given the strong racial dichotomy found within the continental U.S. The assumption that Latinos are primarily immigrants is problematic for researchers. Some Latinos have been here for seven or eight generations. This group may be significantly different from new immigrants. Additionally, those who do not have legal status in the United States are likely to be mistrustful and reluctant to participate in research, thereby leaving a major gap in the research on the Latino population as a whole.

The trend toward quantification and methodological abstraction has led toward a significant gap between the researchers and the practitioners. This gap has led many in the Puerto Rican community to believe that the research on Puerto Ricans does not accurately reflect or represent the Puerto Rican community. The research is criticized for lacking insight and understanding and for pointing out the obvious (Melendez, 1991). Current research on Puerto Rican disadvantage is criticized for not building on past research and for having little input from Puerto Ricans. Research driven by outside agendas may not reflect the needs and concerns of the Puerto Rican community.

Historical misuse of tests and research with Latino populations has led to a climate of mistrust (Padilla, 1992). Researchers wishing to work in Latino communities must be prepared to work to establish trust before they will be allowed to begin any work. As part of establishing trust researchers should be prepared to demonstrate that their measurement instruments are valid for this population and that the research will benefit the community. Many communities of color are justifiably wary of outside researchers who want something (data, knowledge, etc.) and never give anything back to the community. Research that is not used to improve service delivery or the conditions in the community is often exploitative and is likely to cause resentment and fear of future research projects.

Cultural and linguistic concerns must be taken into account in research studies (Padilla, 1992). Studies that do not take into account cultural values are not likely to yield meaningful results. If the study participants cannot understand research questions either because of language barriers or because the research questions are not posed in a way that has meaning for the Latino subjects, the data collected will be inherently flawed.

Principles for Research

In planning research projects with Latino clients or Latino communities the writers suggest the following considerations:

1. Diversity among Latino groups must be considered in planning the sample. If comparisons between Latino groups (i.e.: Cuban Americans and Mexican Americans) are desired, the number of participants of each group must be sufficiently large. Data collected on the Latino population in general may not be very meaningful because it obscures variation between groups.
2. The multiracial nature of the Latino population must be considered when attempting to make comparisons between Latinos and other groups such as Whites or African Americans.
3. Measurement instruments normed for other groups may not be

applicable to Latinos. Measurement instruments normed for one Latino group may not be appropriate for another Latino group.

4. There is disagreement about how to operationalize and measure concepts such as cultural identity and acculturation. Many instruments commonly used to measure cultural identity and acculturation have questionable validity.

5. Language barriers and different cultural norms may lead to unreliable research results.

6. Variations in immigration status may effect research. Substantial differences may exist between new immigrants and those who have been in the U.S. for generations. Additionally, those who do not have a legal immigration status may be reluctant to participate in research, leading to a significant gap in the knowledge base.

7. Researchers interested in working in Latino communities must establish trust and alleviate fears about exploitation caused by past research in order to gain access to this population. This is particularly true if the researcher is from outside the community.

CONCERNS FOR SOCIAL WORK EDUCATION

The Latino population in the United States is rapidly expanding. Social work education must acknowledge this population and begin to prepare social workers to be culturally competent in working with Latinos.

Social work education should include content on Latino populations both in diversity courses and integrated throughout the curriculum. Social work students need to learn about the history and cultures of the various Latino populations in the United States. Content specific to work with immigrants and refugees must also include information on Latinos.

In order to train culturally competent social workers, schools of social work need to teach students to reflect on their own values and biases and the way in which these will have an impact on their work with clients. Social work students must be aware of their own feelings and stereotypes that they hold about Latino people. Interactive learning experiences which involve going into Latino communities and interacting with Latino people are good learning tools. Exposure to literature and the arts of various Latino cultures can also help students begin to understand Latino communities on an affective level.

Schools of social work must include accurate information on Latino communities, issues in the delivery of social services, and relevant policies. Texts that include Latino case examples can be used in the classroom. Articles that reflect the state of social work knowledge with Latino clients should be used. However, it is important to note the limitations of the research and possible biases within studies that may conclude with inaccurate information.

Theories and models discussed in schools of social work must be critiqued for their relevance to Latino populations. It should be clearly stated that assessments and interventions must be tailored to the needs of various populations and that includes consideration of variables such as culture, class, sexual preference, disability, gender, etc. Schools of social work must not perpetuate myths and stereotypes about Latino clients nor ignore the diversity within Latino groups.

Schools of social work must expand their efforts to recruit and retain Latino students. Efforts to recruit and retain Latino faculty and to incorporate Latino issues throughout the curriculum will help to insure that a climate exists in which all social work students can develop skills in cultural competence. Schools of social work must take the lead in encouraging diversity in all aspects of the school rather than simply tolerating diversity in marginalized areas.

FUTURE DIRECTIONS

The Latino population in the United States is rapidly expanding. Social workers, whether involved in research, teaching, administration, policy development, or practice, must all become knowledgeable about work with Latino populations. Theories and models of practice must be evaluated in terms of their relevance for Latinos. The quality of research and publication on social work and Latino populations must increase. Research and practice which do not take into account cultural considerations may lead to misinformation which reinforces stereotypes and can harm clients.

Social work education must include more content on Latino populations. Quality research should be used to inform social work education and to train culturally competent social workers. Without such competence, social workers will not effectively be able to serve their Latino clients.

The authors make the following recommendations:

1. Existing research must be critiqued for its level of bias and relevance to various Latino groups.
2. Quality research must be conducted in Latino communities which takes into consideration diversity within this group and various cultural considerations.
3. Schools of social work must make use of quality research on Latino populations by integrating it throughout the curriculum as well as highlighting it in diversity courses.
4. Social work theories, models, assessment instruments, and methods of interventions must be critiqued for relevance to Latino populations.
5. Schools of social work must create a climate which respects diversity through methods such as recruiting and retaining students and faculty of color and students and faculty who are interested in issues of diversity.
6. Social work practitioners must become culturally competent through obtaining knowledge of the culture and history of various groups, becoming aware of their own biases and institutionalized biases, and developing the skills to apply this knowledge and awareness in the context of social work practice.

REFERENCES

Amaro, H., & Russo, N.F. (1987). Hispanic women and mental health: An overview of contemporary issues in research and practice. *Psychology of Women Quarterly, 11,* 393–407.

Arroyo, R., & Lopez, S. (1984). Being responsive to the Chicano community: A model for service delivery. In B.W. White (Ed.), *Color in a white society* (pp. 66–73). Silver Spring, MD: National Association of Social Workers.

Bernal, M.E., & Knight, G.P. (1993). Introduction. In M.E. Bernal & G.P. Knight (Eds.), *Ethnic identity: Formation and transmission among Hispanics and other minorities* (pp. 1–7). Albany, NY: State University of New York Press.

Burgest, D.R. (1985). *Casework intervention with people of color.* Lanham, MD: University Press of America.

Calderon, J. (1992). "Hispanic" and "Latino": The viability of categories for panethnic unity. *Latin American Perspectives, 19*(4), 37–44.

Castex, G.M. (1994). Providing services to Hispanic/Latino populations: Profiles in diversity. *Social Work, 39,* 288–296.

Coleman, H.L.K., Gerton, J., & La Fromboise, T. (1993). Psychological impact of biculturalism: Evidence and theory. *Psychological Bulletin, 114,* 395–412.

Comas-Diaz, L. (1981). Puerto Rican Espiritismo and psychotherapy. *American Journal of Orthopsychiatry, 51,* 636–645.

Cox, C., & Monk, A. (1993). Hispanic culture and family care of Alzheimer's patients. *Health and Social Work, 18,* 92–100.

Curiel, H., Rosenthal, J.A., & Richek, H.G. (1986). Impacts of bilingual education on secondary school grades, attendance, retention and dropout. *Hispanic Journal of Behavioral Sciences, 8,* 357–367.

Davis, S.K., & Chavez, V. (1985). Hispanic househusbands. *Hispanic Journal of Behavioral Sciences, 7,* 317–332.

De Anda, D. (1984). Bicultural socialization: Factors affecting the minority experience. *Social Work, 29,* 101–107.

De Freitas, G. (1991). *Inequality at Work: Hispanics in the U.S. Labor Force.* New York: Oxford University Press.

De la Cancela, V., & Martinez, I.Z. (1983). An analysis of culturalism in Latino mental health: Folk medicine as a case in point. *Hispanic Journal of Behavioral Sciences, 5,* 251–274.

De la Garza, R.O., DeSepio, L., Garcia, F.C., Garcia, J., & Falcon, A. (1992). *Latino voices: Mexican, Puerto Rican, and Cuban perspectives on American politics.* Boulder, CO: Westview Press.

Delgado, M., & Humm-Delgado, D. (1982). Natural support systems: Source of strength in Hispanic communities. *Social Work, 27,* 83–85.

Domino, G. (1992). Acculturation of Hispanics. In S.B. Knause, P. Rosenfeld, & A. Culbertson (Eds.), *Hispanics in the workplace* (pp. 56–74). Newbury Park, CA: Sage Publications.

Estrada, L.F. (1985). The dynamics of Hispanic populations: A description and comparison. *Social Thought, 11*(3), 23–39.

Farley, J.E. (1987). Disproportionate black and Hispanic unemployment in U.S. metropolitan areas. *The American Journal of Economics and Sociology, 46,* 129–149.

Frazier, D.J., & DeBlassie, R.R. (1982). A comparison of self-concept in Mexican-American and non-Mexican-American late adolescents. *Adolescence, 17,* 327–334.

Galan, J. (1985). Traditional values about family behavior: The case of the Chicano client. *Social Thought, 11*(3), 14–22.

Gann, L.H., & Duignan, P.G. (1986). *The Hispanics in the United States: A history.* Boulder, CO: Westview.

Garza, J.V., & Medina, M. (1985). Academic achievement as influenced by bilingual instruction for Spanish-dominant Mexican-American children. *Hispanic Journal of Behavioral Sciences, 7,* 247–259.

Gelfand, D.E., & Bialik-Giland, R. (1989). Immigration reform and social work. *Social Work, 34,* 23–27.

General Accounting Office. (1990). *Immigration reform.* Washington D.C.: Author.

Ghali, B.B. (1985). *The recognition and use of Puerto Rican cultural values in treatment: A look at what is happening in the field and what can be learned from this.* Unpublished doctoral dissertation, New York University, New York.

Gomez, E. (1985). Guest editorial. *Social thought, 11*(3), 2–4.

Gomez, L.E. (1992). The birth of the "Hispanic" generation: Attitudes of Mexican-

American political elites toward the Hispanic label. *Latin American Perspectives*, *19*(4), 45–58.

Grosjean, F. (1982). *Life with two languages: An introduction to bilingualism.* Cambridge, MA: Harvard University Press.

Grossman, B., Wirt, R., & Davis, A. (1985). Self-esteem, ethnic identity, and behavioral adjustment among Anglo and Chicano adolescents in West Texas. *Journal of Adolescence, 8,* 57–58.

Hardy-Fanta, C., & MacMahon-Herrera, E. (1981). Adapting family therapy to the Hispanic family. *Social Casework, 62,* 138–148.

Hepworth, D.H., & Larsen, J.A. (1986). *Direct social work practice: Theory and skills.* Homewood, IL: Dorsey Press.

Inclan, J. (1985). Variations in value orientations in mental health work with Puerto Ricans. *Psychotherapy, 22,* 324–334.

Jaffe, J.A., Cullen, R.M., & Boswell, T.D. (1980). *The changing demography of Spanish Americans.* New York: Academic Press.

Lambert, W.E., Goldfield, B.A., Chamot, A.U., & Cahir, S.R. (1981). *Facts and facets of bilingualism.* Washington, D.C.: National Clearinghouse for Bilingual Education.

Leon, A.M., Mazur, R., Montalvo, E., & Rodriguez, M. (1984). Self-help support groups for Hispanic mothers. *Child Welfare, 63,* 261–268.

Lynskey, J.A. (1987). *Puerto Rican adolescents and helper view the helping experience: A comparison of the populations and their perspectives.* Unpublished doctoral dissertation, Columbia University, New York.

Marin, G. (1992). Issues in the measurement of acculturation among Hispanics. In K.K. Geisinger (Ed.), *Psychological testing of Hispanics.* Washington, D.C.: American Psychological Association.

Mendoza, R.H., & Martinez, J.L. (1981). The measurement of acculturation. In A. Baron, Jr. (Ed.), *Explorations in Chicano psychology* (pp. 71–82). New York: Praeger.

Melendez, E., Rodriguez, C., & Figueroa, J.B. (Eds.). (1991). *Hispanics in the labor force: Issues and policies.* New York: Plenum Press.

Mena, E.J., Padilla, A.M., & Maldonado, M. (1987). Acculturative stress and specific coping strategies among immigrant and later generation college students. *Hispanic Journal of Behavioral Sciences, 9,* 207–225.

Mizio, E. (1974). Impact of external systems on the Puerto Rican family. *Social Casework, 55,* 76–83.

Montgomery, P.A. (1994). The Hispanic population in the United States: March 1993. *Current Population Reports: Population Characteristics.* Series P20-475. U.S. Department of Commerce, Economics and Statistics Administration, Bureau of the Census.

Morales, R., & Bonilla, F. (Eds.). (1993). *Latinos in a changing U.S. economy: Comparative perspectives on growing inequality.* Newbury Park: Sage.

Obolcr, S. (1992). The politics of labeling: Latino/accultural identities of self and others. *Latin American Perspectives, 19*(4), 18–36.

Oetting, E.R., & Beauvais, F. (1991). Orthogonal cultural identification theory: The cultural identification of minority adolescents. *International Journal of the Addictions, 25,* 655–685.

Padilla, A.M. (1992). Reflections on testing: Emerging trends and new possibilities. In

K.F. Geisinger (Ed.), *Psychological testing of Hispanics* (pp. 273–283). Washington, D.C.: American Psychological Association.

Panitz, D.R., McConchie, S., Sauber, R., & Fonseca, J.A. (1983). The role of machismo and the Hispanic family in the etiology and treatment of alcoholism in Hispanic American males. *American Journal of Family Therapy, 11,* 31–44.

Purdy, J.K., & Arguello, D. (1992). Hispanic familism in caretaking of older adults: Is it functional? *Journal of Gerontological Social Work, 19,* 29–43.

Ramirez, R. (1985). Hispanic spirituality. *Social Thought, 11*(3), 6–13.

Rodriguez, C.E. (1992). Race, culture, and Latino "otherness" in the 1980 census. *Social Science Quarterly, 73,* 930–937.

Rothman, J., Gant, L.M., & Hnat, S.A. (1985). Mexican-American family culture. *Social Service Review, 59,* 197–215.

Sabogal, F., Marin, G., Otero-Sabogal, R., Van Oss Marin, B., & Perez-Stable, E.J. (1987). Hispanic familism and acculturation: What changes and what doesn't? *Hispanic Journal of Behavioral Sciences, 9,* 397–412.

Salgado de Snyder, V.N. (1987). The role of ethnic loyalty among Mexican-American immigrant women. *Hispanic Journal of Behavioral Sciences, 9,* 287–298.

Taylor, V.L., Hurley, E.C., & Riley, M.T. (1986). The influence of acculturation upon the adjustment of preschool Mexican-American children of single-parent families. *Family Therapy, 13,* 249–256.

Triandis, H.C., Lisanky, J., Marin, G., & Betancourt, H. (1984). Simpatia as a cultural script of Hispanics. *Journal of Personality and Social Psychology, 47,* 1363–1375.

Vargas-Willis, G., & Cervantes, R.C. (1987). Consideration of psychosocial stress in the treatment of the Latina immigrant. *Hispanic Journal of Behavioral Sciences, 9,* 315–330.

Weaver, H.N. (in press). Cultural identification: Implications for social work with Native people. *Families in Society.*

Chapter 4

SOCIAL WORK PRACTICE WITH ASIAN AMERICANS

MANUEL NAKANISHI AND BARBARA RITTNER

Historical Background

Culture subtly shapes our expectations of self or others and our perceptions of environmental realities (Nakanishi & Rittner, 1992). The ease with which new immigrants integrate into host cultures is influenced by many factors, including ethnicity, religion, economic status, cultural milieu, and environmental experiences that predate as well as follow immigration. Further, cultural identities may mutate as individuals inhabit and interact with new environments, assimilating or adopting the cultural features of those environments. Among factors most likely to elevate levels of stress are isolation from those with shared cultural or ethnic backgrounds, changes in the size and intensity of extended family networks, changes in socioeconomic status, religious or political reasons for emigration, expectations about returning to countries of origin, and adjustments to dramatic environmental differences (rural versus urban, non-technological versus technological, tropical versus more polar).

Among recent arrivals, Asians comprise the most ethnically and culturally diverse minority group in the United States. The global term "Asian" can encompass such divergent groups of peoples as those from the Indian subcontinent, Mongolians from northern China, and Ainus from the island of Hokkaido in northern Japan.

Because it is impractical to deal with all potential subgroups in a single chapter, we will focus primarily on recently settled immigrants from the East and Southeast Asian countries of China (mainland and island), Japan, Korea, the Philippines, and Southeast Asia. The effects of out-group marriages, adoption of Asian children by non-Asian families, and children of bi-racial unions will not be addressed. Chao (1992)

87

captured the complexity of Asian cultures when he stated that "we do not even eat rice the same" (p. 158).

Chinese

Like the United States, China is a country of diverse populations. Mongolians live in a culture that is quite different from that of Tibetans, or of Jewish Chinese along the Yalu River, or of people from the dominant culture in Beijing. The earliest Chinese emigration to the United States was triggered by catastrophic social and political upheavals in the 1800s that included widespread famine, flooding, crop failures, overcrowding, and war. Those forces coincided with economic opportunities in America ensuing from the gold rush and the expansion of the railroads (Dunn, 1975; Kim, 1973; Melendy, 1984).

After the first transcontinental railroad was completed in 1869, there was extensive unemployment among all groups dependent on its development. An epidemic of anti-Chinese sentiments led to the passage of the Chinese Exclusion Act in 1882, suspending immigration of Chinese laborers for ten years. This act was continuously renewed until 1943 (Dunn, 1975; Kim, 1973; Kung, 1962; Melendy, 1984; Miller, 1969; Tsai, 1983). When the U.S. joined China against Japan in World War II, the treatment of Chinese Americans improved somewhat. After World War II, the Communists in mainland China closed their borders, and emigration of Chinese shifted to those from Taiwan and Hong Kong. Historic political differences between mainland Chinese and those from the islands often result in friction among Chinese subgroups in this country, as old hostilities and distrusts resurface.

Japanese

Japanese immigration to the U.S. began in the early 1890s. Most of the early immigrants were young, poorly paid males with limited educations working as unskilled laborers (Kitano & Kikumura, 1980). Treated with the same distrust that greeted the Chinese, Japanese immigrants were vilified by the majority culture as immoral, vulgar, filthy, vicious, and cruel. Like the response to the Chinese, laws were passed that denied them entry and blocked access to farmlands or middle-rank occupations (Kitano & Kikumura, 1980).

Prejudice against Japanese Americans reached extreme proportions during World War II, when they were evacuated en masse to "relocation camps" in remote western areas following the bombing of Pearl Harbor. Without compensation or transfers of titles, properties and businesses belonging to Japanese Americans were confiscated and sold to non-Asians. In an act rationalized as military necessity, established and stable communities were disrupted and largely destroyed as families were herded together and placed in barbed-wire encampments guarded by soldiers. While lingering resentments and occasional open hostilities still exist, overt anti-Asian policies officially ended with the repeal of all restriction/exclusion legislation in 1943 (Wong, 1985).

Southeast Asians (Cambodians, Vietnamese, and Laotians)

Since 1975, approximately 1,111,000 Southeast Asian refugees have settled in the United States (Boucher, 1988; U.S. Census, 1990). They include those fleeing war-ravaged regions of Cambodia, Laos, and Vietnam following the collapse of U.S.-supported governments. Finding few intergenerational Southeast Asian communities that could offer social, religious, or economic supports, they experienced high levels of family estrangement, social isolation, racial tensions, and unemployment (Owan, 1985). Stresses associated with settling in a country so dramatically different in culture and level of technology from their places of origin exacerbated recurrent themes of trauma and loss (Bromley, 1987; Rumbaut, 1985; Westermeyer, 1985). There is a high prevalence of chronic depression and chronic psychosocial maladjustment among Southeast Asian refugees. It is associated with a variety of problems, including illiteracy, unemployment, cultural isolation, loss of religious practice and personal meaning in life, ignorance of American society, widowhood or singlehood, solo parenting, untreated major depression, and related or similar psychiatric and psychosocial ills (Westermeyer, 1985).

The Vietnamese are the most visible Asian immigrants in the last 20 years because they arrived in such large numbers following the collapse of the South Vietnamese government in 1975. Vietnam was a French colony until 1946, when the Vietnamese rose up to regain their autonomy from the French (which they accomplished in 1954) (Henkin & Nguyen, 1981). Western influences in Vietnamese life-styles can be observed in their education, dress, cuisine, and religion. These influences, first introduced by the French, were continued by Americans when they became involved in the Vietnamese civil war in the 1960s.

The first wave of Vietnamese refugees to enter this country in 1975 were U.S. government employees and agents, military leaders and soldiers, and members of the professional class, particularly journalists, medical personnel, and lawyers. Like early Cuban refugees, they were generally well educated, financially prosperous, familiar with Western culture, and comfortable speaking English and French. The second wave of Vietnamese refugees comprised less well-educated, less affluent immigrants, mainly from the agrarian class, who had suffered under the Communist regime.

Cambodia was also liberated from French rule in 1954. Initially Cambodia attempted to remain neutral during the Vietnamese civil war, but that ended in 1969 when North Vietnamese troops invaded border areas and were attacked by U.S. and South Vietnamese troops (Kinzie, 1985). Cambodia eventually fell to the Communists in 1975 and became isolated from other nations under the radical Marxist regime led by Pol Pot. The purges of the Pol Pot regime are among the most notorious and brutal perpetrated during the post-war era in Southeast Asia. Thousands died of starvation and disease, while others survived in constant states of torture, terror, and horror. Estimates of the number who died between 1975 and 1979 range from several hundred thousand to over two million. Over five hundred thousand Cambodians fled their country, and by 1985 approximately 130,000 had arrived in North America (Bromley, 1987; Kinzie, Sack, Angell, Manson, & Rath, 1986).

After Laos gained its independence from France in 1954, it gradually became enmeshed in the Southeast Asian conflict and was invaded by both U.S. and North Vietnamese troops (Rynearson & DeVoe, 1984). The American air war inflicted heavy civilian losses, causing massive dislocations of Laotian people (Branfman, 1970). When the Communists took over in 1975, large numbers of refugees fled the country. Hundreds of thousands of Laotians entered Thailand and were kept in refugee camps. The plight of the Laotian boat people was much like that of the Vietnamese and Cambodians. By the end of 1982, about 120,000 Laotian refugees had been admitted to the U.S.; there were an estimated 149,000 living in this country at the time of the 1990 U.S. census.

Refugee workers have called the resettlement of the agrarian Hmong people from Laos a worst-case condition (Sherman, 1988). Most Hmong experienced inclusive environmental displacement, of climate, topography, life-style, work, language, and food. Many were also separated from family, kin, and community during resettlements to cities presenting stark contrasts to the agriculture-centered lives of their past (Westermeyer,

1985). In his work with Hmong refugees, Westermeyer observed suspiciousness, depressive mood, high rates of psychophysiological symptoms, family problems, social withdrawal, social disorganization, apathy and inactivity.

Filipinos

Filipino immigration is closely coupled to the political relationship between the Philippines and the United States. The first wave of Filipino immigrants followed an 1899 invasion by the U.S. to expel the Spaniards. The invasion was allegedly to ensure the development of a civilian democratic government.

Students (*pensionados*) were recruited in 1903 and educated in America in democratic self-governance. Most *pensionados* returned to the Philippines. However, approximately 119,000 Filipinos immigrated during this time to Hawaii to work on plantations and, subsequently, settled on the mainland to replace laborers lost as a result of the Chinese Exclusion Act. They were eventually subjected to open discrimination, as evidenced by acts of violence against them and the passage of the California anti-miscegenation law, which targeted all Asian groups, including Malay-Polynesians (California Statutes, Section 60 of the Civil Code). Like the Chinese and Japanese, Malay-Polynesians were excluded from further immigration to the U.S. (Cordasco, 1990).

During World War II, Filipinos joined U.S. armed forces to fight in the Pacific, becoming eligible for naturalization. In addition, a number of Filipino women married American servicemen stationed in the Philippines and returned with them after the war. After quota laws were repealed in 1965, an additional 30,000 Filipinos had immigrated to the U.S. by 1968. At the time of the 1990 census, the number of Filipinos estimated to be living in this country was 1,407,000.

Koreans

Koreans, like Filipinos, first migrated to this country through Hawaii, where they were hired as laborers on sugar plantations. In addition to emigrating for economic reasons, Koreans left following the occupation of their peninsula by Japan at the turn of the century. The immigration experiences of Koreans were similar to those of the Chinese. During the first four decades of this century, they were excluded; but following

World War II and the Korean War, women who married servicemen began entering this country in substantial numbers. In addition, many Korean and Amerasian children were adopted by American families, and many students who entered the country to study remained. The passage of the 1965 Immigration Law precipitated a 400% increase in Korean arrivals from 1970 to 1980. The most recent Korean immigrants have generally been college graduates and professionals.

CURRENT CHARACTERISTICS

World View

Asians and Euro-Americans view their place in the world in fundamentally different ways. Most Asians are "environment-centered while Euro-Americans tend to be individual-centered" (Chung, 1992, p. 29). This difference shapes how Asians view social roles, relationships, and obligations. While mainstream Americans feel pressured to attain personal potentials, Asians feel responsible for seeking harmony with their group and environment. This complex epistemology requires attention to ordinate and subordinate roles, parent-child interactions, husband-wife relationships, sibling hierarchies and responsibilities, and friend and community associations, all within the context of nature and metaphysical forces. Their world view tends to foster a greater collective orientation marked by substantive commitments to others, with greater emphasis on teamwork and group process and with little inherent value assigned to egalitarian relationships.

Religion

While many Asians, particularly Filipinos, are practicing Christians or Moslems, the impact of ancient traditional religions should not be underestimated. Three major philosophical and religious forces shape Asian families: Confucianism, Taoism, and Buddhism. Based on a rigid social order, Confucian thought explains man's place in the universe and defines the nature of filial piety, loyalty, chastity, heroism, selfless friendship, and service to country and family (Dunn, 1975). Harmony resides in the balance of conflict between man and nature (Melendy, 1984). Over time, Confucian beliefs have become intertwined with the religions of

Buddhism and Taoism, each acting as counterpoints or complements to the other (Melendy, 1984).

Taoism challenged some rigid social order precepts of Confucianism (Melendy, 1984), stressing detachment and avoidance of conventional social obligations through a simple life and harmony with nature. Dunn (1975) suggests that some Chinese Americans' reaction to mistreatment with passivity derives from their philosophical perspective.

The largest of the religions in East Asia, Buddhism stresses attaining Nirvana, a blissful afterlife, through ideals of good work, philanthropy, and enlightenment (Dunn, 1975; Melendy, 1984). Buddhism established a morality that was consistent with Taoism and Confucian thought and frustrated Western missionary efforts (Fairbank, 1958; Melendy, 1984).

The Japanese share a composite of beliefs grouped under Shinto, or "Way of the Gods," and a number of foreign ideologies of which Confucianism and Buddhism are the most significant. Shinto, the native religion, and Taoism, an ideological import from China, have given the Japanese a deep and reverent feeling for nature. The mingling of Shinto and Buddhism has stimulated the holding of many festivals, such as the flower festival, the moon festival, and the New Year's festival, among many others (Welty, 1976).

Among Cambodians, the single most important religious institution is the Wat, the Buddhist temple complex. More than a place of worship, the Wat serves as a gathering place for agrarian communities. Observances and celebrations of holy days and festivals provide social and religious supports through communal activities that unite village members. In the Cambodian Khmer community, money assumes importance only as a means for achieving respect and prestige through religious donations. Although good character traits (selfless compassion, temperance, noncombativeness, honesty, and generosity) are essential to high status, a person cannot rise to an exalted position if he does not possess exceptional religious piety.

Family

One of the most universal cultural values in Asian families is the virtue of filial piety. Unquestioning loyalty and devotion to parents is fundamental to family structure (Chung, 1992; Henkin & Nguyen, 1981; Melendy, 1984). Originating in the demands of an agrarian society, individuals are expected to comply with familial and social authority, even to the point of sacrificing individual desires and ambitions for the good of the whole (Dunn, 1975; Ho, 1976; Hsu, 1971). It has been suggested that, among Chinese, Filipinos, and Japanese, agrarian society has helped foster the principle that joined effort, more than innate ability, leads to success (Uba, 1994).

The father is traditionally the dominant figure in Asian families, and marital partners do not share equal status. Parents are responsible for elucidating for their children the societal rules they must obey and the expectations they are expected to fulfill. Parent-child interactions are clearly defined and delimited, consisting primarily of one-way communication, from parent to child. Children are not encouraged or allowed to become independent at as early an age as are American children. Parents' centrality to all decision making involving their children can cause conflict when, for example, social workers encourage young Asian Americans to strive for greater independence (Chung, 1992; Ryan, 1985). Education is highly valued, and children are taught to conform to regulations imposed by society, especially in schools (Melendy, 1984).

Historically, Cambodian families have been large. Family relationships are the basis for all social relations in rural Khmer communities. The Khmer view families as units, or wholes, and links to the community through intermarriage and kinship are binding. The mother's domestic authority is at least as powerful as that of the father, who is considered the head of the family. She occupies a key position in the household, with the well-being, prosperity, and reputation of the family revolving around her. Strong friendships are paramount, while outsiders are viewed with mistrust.

Relations between genders appear to be quite egalitarian among Laotians, when compared with the better known patrilineal societies of Asia (Rynearson & DeVoe, 1984). Families of lowland Laotians and highland Hmong are large and extended, rather than nuclear (Rynearson & DeVoe), endowing them with maximum flexibility in adjusting to life within their households and within U.S. society in general. Research indicates that the lack of extended community and naturally occurring support systems in the U.S. is a harmful deficit in the life of immigrant Southeast Asians and has resulted in adjustment problems characterized by depression and self-destruction (Gordon, Matousek & Lang, 1980; Rynearson & DeVoe, 1984).

Immigrant Filipino families have not been the subject of substantial empirical studies. However, findings from the limited studies conducted suggest that they highly value strong social commitments and positive social interactions. Families forcefully pressure children to get along with others, to be sensitive and considerate of others, to reciprocate favors, to be circumspect about criticisms, and to avoid behaviors which could be interpreted as hostile or aggressive (Uba, 1994).

The Elderly

Adjusting to life in America poses special problems for Asian and Southeast Asian elderly. Many lack formal education and find learning the English language very difficult. Though they are held in great esteem in their native cultures, they find that in Western culture they are not especially appreciated. They see themselves becoming less central to their families as their children become more assimilated. At the time of resettlement, some are even separated from their children. Feelings of alienation, loneliness and fear are pervasive (Bliatout, Ben, Do, Keopraseuth, Bliatout & Lee, 1985).

A study by Wong and Reker (1985) compared the stress levels, perceived well-being, and coping behaviors of a group of immigrant Chinese elderly to a group of Euro-American elderly. Findings revealed that the Chinese subjects experienced more stress growing old than did the Euro-Americans. They also reported a lower level of psychological well-being, had a greater dependency on external coping strategies, and felt less effective in coping than did the Euro-American group. In an earlier study, Wong (1984) found that immigrant Asian elderly suffer greater disadvantages than do Euro-American elderly, despite being more socioeconomically prosperous than other minority groups.

Elderly Asians' roles change significantly after immigration, often dislodging them from their prior status as authorities and counselors. Bliatout et al. (1985) suggested engaging elders in community centers with a focus on social and language skills enhancement, together with recreational activities. Elders can be valuable resources in implementing mental health prevention programs, and their services as teachers and consultants should be solicited.

Social Expectations

Protecting and preserving family honor is a core social value among Asians. Children are taught that improper behavior brings injury and shame to parents, to the family, and to the community. Both parents and the community reinforce conformist behavior (DeVos, 1982). Socially deviant behavior, in addition to illegal or immoral behavior, reflects poorly on the family and is to be strenuously avoided. Children are taught early and consistently not to disrupt family harmony, not to engage in activities which might shame the family, and to use self-control and self-restraint (Ho, 1976).

Avoiding shame is an important social control mechanism in Asian families. Shame, rather than guilt, occurs when individual behaviors conflict with traditional concepts of respect for political, familial, social, or religious authority. Chinese American and Japanese American women, for example, may experience increased social disequilibrium when they adopt more flexible and independent roles consistent with American cultural norms because such behavior is likely to be perceived as disrespectful of parental or spousal authority (Melendy, 1984; Ryan, 1985). The potential consequences are cultural disjunction from expected submissive roles for women demanded by tradition and admonishment by parents or spouses for dishonorable behavior (Ryan, 1985).

There are greater cultural pressures on Japanese Americans to show loyalty to organizations and respect for authority than on their Euro-American counterparts. They are taught that it is important to conform to the group and to refrain from expressing disagreement, which leads to indirect and ambiguous ways of interacting. For the Japanese, *enryo* establishes norms of deference and submissiveness by inferiors to superiors, leading to hesitancy about appearing aggressive or demanding, reluctance to speak out about needs or desires, lack of verbal participation, and refusal to ask questions (Kitano & Kikumura, 1980).

Differences in communication styles between Asian Americans and Euro-Americans are typified by Japanese reluctance to engage in personal disclosures. A person who talks a lot is viewed as insincere. Many Asians value implicit, nonverbal, intuitive communication over explicit, verbal, and rational exchanges of information (Chung, 1992; Hsu, Tseng, Ashton, McDermott, & Char, 1985). Among important nonverbal cues are distances between conversants, signalling the nature and importance of the conversation. The tighter the space, the more intimate the topic. Non-subjective information is delivered at considerable distance, while very private communications require that participants be less than a foot apart. Further, among many Asian groups, eye contact is often avoided, consistent with the submissive role appropriate for help seeking (Chung). In some groups, expansive emotional expressiveness is discouraged while in others it is encouraged (Uba, 1994). Generally the Chinese and Japanese value those who can control their emotions, while the Koreans tend toward tolerating less control.

The differences between Asian Americans and Euro-Americans are particularly apparent in Vietnamese refugees. Like most Asians, they avoid confrontation and are not likely to express their feelings publicly for fear of hurting another's feelings, appearing assertive or self-centered, or acting selfishly and without regard for the group as a whole. Sensitivity to others is a highly valued trait among Vietnamese (Henkin & Nguyen, 1981).

For Laotian Hmong, such self-help groups as the Lao Family Community Association in Orange County, California serve as safety nets, teaching them living skills. Utilizing the community model, this organization resembles the typical Hmong clan structure in Laos. Activities such as outreach centers, child care services, English classes, and newsletters serve some of the basic needs of the Laotian community (Owan, 1985).

SOCIOECONOMIC STATUS

As a whole, Asian Americans have achieved higher socioeconomic status in this country than have other recent immigrant groups, though there has been a tendency in the media to exaggerate their successes (Ross-Sheriff, 1992). It has been argued that Asian immigrants have benefitted from the myth of the "model minority," contributing to their reputation as intelligent and hardworking employees and making them less discriminated against than other recent immigrant groups (Ross-Sheriff).

Based on analyses of select Asian groups, factors associated with greater economic power are high educational levels, higher concentrations in professional occupations, and combined family incomes earned as professionals or small business owners (Cabezas & Kawaguchi, 1988). Of course, variations are likely to be accounted for by community determinants and resources, educational levels, cultural differences, length of residence, English proficiency, and other environmental factors (Tran & Wright, 1986).

The educational levels of Asian Americans have been improving and may contribute significantly to their emerging near socioeconomic parity with Euro-Americans (Hirschman & Wong, 1981). Most older Asian Americans arrived with little formal education, but by 1976 young Asian immigrants averaged 14–16 years of formal schooling (higher than the average of 13 years for White males). American-born Asians were educated at an average level 10–20 percent above Euro-Americans, and 90 percent of young Chinese American and Japanese American men had some college education (Hirschman & Wong). Chinese Americans were disproportionately well represented in white-collar positions and in "self-employed manager" categories and underrepresented in blue-collar positions, suggesting that American-born Chinese had achieved a high degree of assimilation in mainstream economic life (Hirschman & Wong).

Nee and Sanders (1985) found that Chinese Americans and Japanese Americans reported higher average incomes than Euro-Americans in California cities. Uba (1994), among others, suggests that this may be a reflection of the economic status of some recent immigrants, many of whom originated in privileged classes where servants were the norm and professional achievement was standard. In a comparative study of the socioeconomic status of Asian Americans, African Americans and Hispanics from 1960 to 1976, Wong and Hirschman (1983) found that Asian Americans had earnings slightly higher than the majority population. Asian American women were more likely to participate in the labor force than Euro-American women and to have above-average earnings (Hirschman & Wong, 1981). Moon (1985) suggested that, in addition to educational factors, length of residence is positively related to Asian American socioeconomic success.

Recent studies suggest that some Asian groups feel intense pressure to be "super" achievers (Uba, 1994). Korean American parents have been shown to be unsympathetic to their children's fears and anxieties, expecting them to succeed in school, regardless of their talents and inclinations. This problem is also seen in Chinese American and Japanese American families, with evidence that pressures to achieve start early.

Stein (1979) reported that, while Vietnamese refugees are represented at all socioeconomic levels, there is evidence they are generally at lower socioeconomic levels than Chinese Americans or Japanese Americans.

More recent arrivals, they are pressured to take menial jobs because government and refugee resettlement agencies want them to become self-sufficient quickly. In a three-year follow up, the Vietnamese were still worse off than other Asian American groups, although they had made some gains. Male unemployment had dropped from 32 percent to 4.9 percent, and the percentage of families earning less than $400 a month had dropped from 52.4 percent to 22.4 percent. However, 60.0 percent of white-collar refugees remained in blue-collar jobs. Stein suggests that the barriers Vietnamese professionals faced include great disparity in culture between original and host societies, lack of an established ethnic community here to assist refugees, and the relatively poor U.S. economy at the time of heaviest Vietnamese immigration.

Theories that attempt to explain the economic success of Asian Americans can be examined both from the cultural and the structural perspective. The most common cultural explanation is that Asian Americans possess "middle-class" cultural values such as thrift, perseverance and commitment to work, which facilitate socioeconomic success. A more complex variation of cultural theory posits that kinship networks, ethnic institutions, and a high degree of ethnic solidarity are more significant factors. These cultural factors include religion, strong family ties, and strong ties to ethnic groups (Hirschman & Wong, 1981).

Bonacich (1980) describes Asian American immigrants as a "sojourner community." Many Asian Americans originally had the long-term goal of returning to their homeland; they deferred gratification and accumulated savings and investment in human capital in order to realize this goal. Another theoretical exposition of Asian Americans' socioeconomic position is that of the "middleman" minority, somewhere between the majority and other minority groups in a multi-ethnic society. This theory suggests that Asian Americans are allowed to occupy certain niches within the economy that are not competitive with dominant groups. The middleman position allows somewhat higher status than is associated with other minority groups but nonetheless prevents achievement of real power (Hirschman & Wong, 1981). Disadvantage theory suggests that Asian American immigrants are disadvantaged in the labor market and are underemployed due to language problems and discrimination. As a result, they turn to self-employment as an economic outlet (Hirschman & Wong, 1981).

Self-employment has been a significant factor in Asian American socioeconomic success. Historically, the Chinese and Japanese have turned to self-employment, sidestepping economic barriers and developing ethnic alcove communities such as Chinatown and Little Tokyo. They have depended on family ties and ethnic relations for generating commercial enterprise, and ethnic labor has been an important factor in their success in small businesses. Rotating credit and extended kinship ties have also helped Chinese American and Japanese American family businesses.

Ecological succession in ghetto areas is another factor to be considered. As African Americans populated inner cities, White-owned businesses fled, opening up new opportunities for other minorities. In recent years, Asian Americans often filled business vacuums in these areas because potential African American entrepreneurs lacked sufficient capital (Jaret & Min, 1985).

ELEMENTS OF PROVIDING SERVICES

Help-seeking behaviors are culturally determined (Broman, 1987; Nakanishi & Rittner, 1992). Among immigrant groups, a willingness to use professional help is often associated with assimilation, acculturation, and length of residence (Atkinson & Gim, 1989; Connor, 1974; Szaposnick & Kurtines, 1987). Studies of the utilization of mental health services by Asian Americans in California, Hawaii, Boston, and Seattle have shown that they are more reluctant to use those services than are Euro-Americans (Nguyen, 1985). In addition, conditions which precipitated emigration and post-immigration experiences often predict the extent to which Asian Americans are comfortable seeking and using outside help. Mokuau (1987) suggests that low utilization and early termination rates of mental health services by Asian Americans raise serious concerns about the failure of cross-cultural counseling to meet their needs.

Several explanations, addressing client-centered and social worker-centered problems, have been offered for why Asian Americans refuse or prematurely terminate counseling. Their concerns include hesitancy about seeking services, communication obstacles to identifying the nature of difficulties, different expectations about what constitutes help, and lack of knowledge about and access to services. Social workers, on the other hand, may fail to understand cultural issues in help-seeking behaviors, may rely too strongly on Western psychological constructs in diagnoses and treatment, and may engage in stereotyping of individuals based on expected "recipes" of behavior which preclude effective engagement with individual clients (Nakanishi & Rittner, 1992).

Decisions to use formal counseling services are serious matters for most Asian Americans. Traditions favor dependence on family and maintenance of family privacy. In the words of Confucius: "The father conceals the misconduct of the son and the son conceals the misconduct of the father. Uprightness is found in this" (Shon & Davis, 1982, p. 221). Going to a professional, particularly an outsider, for help increases the potential for social stigmatization and ostracism. Asian Americans expect to receive help from family members as legitimate attributes of the instrumental roles established for elders and parents. To seek help from non-family or non-group members may be perceived to dishonor family and community. Unless members are overtly psychotic, families will seek outside help only as a last resort (Sue & Sue, 1973).

Southeast Asians may find it particularly stressful to use professional services. After decades of war, they emigrated to places with neither existing Southeast Asian support networks nor social support mechanisms through which to seek outside help (True, 1985). Yet, they are beset with a variety of stresses and problems that tax their coping resources. Even when Asian Americans consider using professionals to help solve problems, they may not know what resources are available or how to gain access to them. When informed about services, they may encounter communication barriers, if professionals or front-desk support staff do not speak their language. According to Tung (1985), very few refugees know what community resources are available to them nor how to go about obtaining such information. If they do know, they most likely confront transportation difficulties.

When Asian Americans do accept outside help, they expect it to embody the holistic approaches with which they are familiar, incorporating interactive and environmentally contextual perspectives on assessing and treating problems. The integration of social, familial, psychological, physical, and cultural aspects in treatment is essential for Asian Americans to feel they have found a balance between health and behavior. To restore harmony, they may need to involve the entire family and significant members of the community (Lee, 1982). Practitioners may resist this because of concerns about potential violations of confidentiality.

Language difficulties extend beyond the challenge of getting an initial appointment. Even when translators are available, they may lack skills in interpreting concepts into English that adequately express concerns or feelings (Tung, 1985). Concepts in one language may have no corresponding phrases or ideas in the other. Therapists should be aware of such differences and recognize that interpreters must also serve as cultural consultants for effective work with Asian Americans (Ishisaka, Nguyen, & Okimoto, 1985).

Unconscious intrusion of practitioners' world views into professional relationships is almost certainly a barrier to effective engagement and treatment. Often practitioners are unaware that they have imported their values and norms, but do so by how they define problems or how they expect people to behave (Nakanishi & Rittner, 1992). For example, a Western social worker taught to value personal autonomy and independence may fail to recognize and support interdependence and family networks in Asian Americans. Worse, relationships with family members may be inappropriately diagnosed as enmeshed, or individuals may be incorrectly assessed as dependent personalities or passive-aggressive. Failure to understand how families and their members are connected and interdependent may result in mistaking behaviors which are culturally syntonic and socially necessary as manifestations of pathology (Carlin & Sokoloff, 1985).

Most Western social workers have no equivalent framework of experiences for their Asian American clients. Among Cambodian refugees, symptoms of post-traumatic stress disorder are common. Treatment usually includes reviewing the traumatic experience. Most Cambodians are culturally constrained from discussion of traumatic events and may be inaccurately labelled as evidencing avoidance behavior.

Cultural stereotyping, another factor associated with barriers to engagement and premature termination of services (Tsui & Schultz, 1985), may be defined as rigid preconceptions of expected attitudes, beliefs, and behaviors applied to all members of a group, regardless of individual variations (Atkinson, Morten & Sue, 1979). Failure to adopt culturally competent perspectives in assessment, diagnosis, and treatment of complex human problems can result in formulaic evaluations and impositions of solutions that do not appreciate and account for subtle mixes of individual and group characteristics (Mokuau, 1987; Nakanishi & Rittner, 1992).

As Ishisaka, Nguyen and Okimoto (1985) pointed out, some practitioners, in an attempt to be culturally sensitive, rely on simplistic cultural models for assessment and intervention. They select interventions based on stereotypic recipes of expected ethnic/cultural characteristics and predetermined sets of traits. Problems surface when these practitioners work with individuals who differ from such formulaic expectations, exhibiting strictly personal characteristics, dominant family idiosyncratic patterns, or unique syntheses of cultural and individual traits evolved from exposure to specific circumstances. Individuals' particularities may be overlooked, or subsumed as pathology.

Additional barriers are erected by misinterpretations of behaviors and mind-sets when receiving help. Western-trained mental health practitioners are familiar with clients who are psychologically minded, accustomed to the jargon associated with that construct, willing to explore the past in order to control the future, and aware of possible hostile or ambivalent feelings harbored toward family members (Kinzie, 1981). For some Asian Americans, the construct and jargon of psychology are unknown, and the idea of attempting to control the future or "attacking" family members is inconceivable and incompatible with their world view. It is culturally dystonic for the Vietnamese refugees to live for the future, focus on doing rather than being, or attack and conquer nature/problems, rather than to master tolerance and acceptance of the present situation (Tran, 1985).

Non-Asian therapists unfamiliar with how symptoms are likely to be presented may find assessments difficult to conduct. Asian Americans generally avoid directly discussing emotional content and focus instead on somatic complaints. For example, somatization to Chinese Americans is an acceptable way of expressing inner conflicts without having to deal directly with overt expressions of feelings. Asian Americans, generally, are likely to circle emotional issues with lengthy discussions about bodily functions (Ryan, 1985).

Asian Americans may become confused when clinicians initiate history taking by gathering information about previous periods of emotional difficulties, prior mental health treatments, family psychiatric histories, attainment of developmental milestones, and current and past psychosocial stressors, while failing to explore physical symptoms and past medical or folk medicine treatments. Attempting to guide their therapists, they may turn to discussions of physical symptoms. Their attempts to obtain straightforward, directive advice about physical symptom reduction may be misinterpreted as resistance and defensiveness.

According to Murase, Egawa and Tashima (1985), building rapport with Asian Americans is dependent on social workers' establishing themselves as "helping persons." Trust is more likely to occur if the initial focus is on concrete services, such as obtaining financial assistance, intervening with other agencies, connecting clients to language programs, facilitating housing applications, or expediting acceptance into job training programs. These activities set the stage for later discussions about psychological distress.

Bromley (1987) suggests using crisis intervention approaches with refugees from war-torn areas because they focus on enhancing indigenous coping mechanisms, which may include strong reliance on family and ethnic group support and willingness to accept one's fate. Emotional suppression joins with avoidant behavior to yield a coping style that seems to minimize symptoms and the social consequences of symptoms (Kinzie et al., 1986). Crisis intervention modalities need to be adjusted to accommodate continued concentration by patients on their physical rather than psychological symptoms, including collaborations with medical support systems. This allows therapists to build credibility and trust with patients (Kinzie, 1981).

Probably the least successful modes of intervention with Asian Americans are insight or psychoanalytically oriented therapies, including existentialism or gestalt. They are more likely to respond to structured, short-term, goal-directed and problem-oriented therapies, such as crisis intervention, task-centered therapy and cognitive-behavioral therapy with appropriate family involvement (Ho, 1976).

Family Therapy

Decisions about goals for families must be culturally appropriate. Hsu et al. (1985) compared family interaction patterns of Japanese American and Euro-American families in Hawaii. Differences in levels of expression about emotional or affectionate concerns were found, with Japanese American families appearing more restrictive. The differences in family interactional patterns indicate that profiles of healthy families differ between distinct cultures. Without culturally relevant family interaction profiles, normal behaviors in families outside the mainstream could be misinterpreted as pathological.

Treatment of Asian American clients may not be possible without involving their families, including various kin. In fact, family therapy is very often the most appropriate mode of intervention when working with Asian Americans (Tsui & Schultz, 1985). That approach diminishes the likelihood that therapy will be perceived as threatening to the family and increases the viability of agreed-upon objectives of interventions (Lee, 1982).

The primary role of therapists in early stages of family work is to act as knowledgeable experts. Families expect therapists to provide information or strategies that will successfully resolve some of their problems. In so doing, the therapists' worth is assured. In early stages, families are unlikely to disagree or express negative feelings toward practitioners, avoiding shows of disrespect. When therapists are from different cultural backgrounds than the families with which they are working, they should move very slowly and frequently check the families' understanding of suggestions and the feasibility of those suggestions. Often, family members give subtle nonverbal cues about problems latent in what therapists have said, including simple communication failures or conflicts between suggestions and family norms. In most cases, insensitivity to such problems and to the need for reopening broken lines of communication will lead to premature, family initiated termination of treatment (Shon & Davis, 1982).

An important facet of establishing initial rapport is therapists' willingness to disclose personal information. If families sense that therapists are uncomfortable sharing educational, family, and work backgrounds, they will in turn feel uncomfortable (Shon & Davis, 1982). According to Tsui and Schultz (1985), personal disclosure and an appropriate level of emotional expressiveness are often the most effective ways to put Asian Americans at ease. Since Asian Americans are restricted about discussion of personal matters with strangers, they often attempt to draw therapists closer to their families by seeking to learn personal information.

It is important for therapists to recognize and understand traditional family roles and show proper respect for them. Fathers, for instance, may be easily offended if any aspect of treatment or decision making fails to involve them (Shon & Davis, 1982). Moreover, Asian Americans abide by hierarchical roles that determine who expresses what to whom within their families. Lower-status members (children) are likely to repress negative feelings toward higher-status members (parents); to encourage such expressions would violate family norms. Such feelings are often internalized as somatic symptoms or self-recrimination and self-criticism, socially acceptable ways of expressing negative emotions (Ryan, 1985). Social workers must engage in extensive education and delicate restructuring before all family members feel free to express their feelings openly (Shon & Davis, 1982).

Kim (1985) proposes a strategic-structural model for working with Asian American families, including stratagems such as recharacterization of help-seeking behaviors from "shameful" to "courageous." How families define problems that lead them to seek services often imposes the boundaries of changes they are willing to accept. Asian parents can "save face" by focusing directly on their children's problems. They can then address marital or environmental problems indirectly as part of the acculturation process, balanced against their need to preserve past traditions. This requires careful and sensitive timing on the part of social workers, who must help families define changes they want to make, provide them with the means to do so, and respect their strengths and cultural integrity in the process.

As much information as possible should be gathered before initial interviews, so therapists can give information rather than simply ask questions. The directive approach to therapy is compatible with the values and beliefs of Asians, who expect that specific advice will be given about how to conduct their lives. Family members should be addressed in their order of social and power hierarchy in their culture. Goals should be defined in terms of solving problems or relieving symptoms (Kim, 1985).

Marital Counseling

Marital counseling should address mutually identified instrumental roles consistent with couples' cultural norms (AAMHTC, 1983). This may necessitate meeting with each member separately in order to determine how individuals understand their current and traditional roles and how they perceive their marital problems.

Consistent with the experience of family therapists, marital counselors need to adopt a variety of roles. Frequently, presenting problems will be concrete, requiring that information or referral services be provided, with therapists functioning as case advocates in the management of those services. Couples are unlikely to discuss role or personal conflicts until they perceive their counselors as trustworthy and able to help (Shepard, 1992).

Often, counselors continue to meet with members of the marital dyad separately (AAMHTC, 1983). In those cases, they are perceived as mediators, separately advising each person. Only with the acquiescence of each spouse are couples counseled jointly to formalize agreements.

This form of counseling is compatible with the cultural style of Laotians, in which village headmen were called upon to judge cases when problems became too intractable to handle within families.

IMPLICATIONS FOR SOCIAL WORK PRACTICE

Social workers must be innovative in bridging Western and Eastern values to successfully serve Asian Americans. They must be knowledgeable about and sensitive to cultural practices and medical beliefs and customs, since these considerations play significant roles in attitudes toward healing resources. Psychosocial interventions should strive to conform to patient value systems.

Tung (1985) suggests that interventions should be time limited, focused in problems identified by the patient, goal directed, and active rather than passive on the part of therapists. Counselors are more effective when they use such techniques as role modeling, persuasion, and pressure. Direct services should be concrete, with tangible manifestations of power (advocacy, material assistance). In general, interventions should be supportive and encouraging and focus on the present and immediate future. Asian Americans are likely not to initiate, not to benefit from, or to prematurely terminate mental health services they perceive to be unresponsive to their needs, values, expectations, and life-styles (Nguyen, 1985).

REFERENCES

Asian-American Mental Health Training Center (AAMHTC). (1983). *Bridging cultures: Social work with Southeast Asian refugees.* Los Angeles, CA: Special Services for Groups.

Atkinson, D., & Gim, R. (1989). Asian American cultural identity and attitudes toward mental health services. *Journal of Counseling Psychology, 36,* 209–212.

Atkinson, D., Morten, G., & Sue, D. (1979). *Counseling American minorities: A cross-cultural perspective.* Dubuque, IA: W.C. Brown.

Bliatout, B.T., Ben, R., Do, V.T., Keopraseuth, K.O., Bliatout, H.P., & Lee, D.T.T. (1985). Mental health and prevention activities targeted to Southeast Asian Refugees. In T.C. Owan (Ed.), *Southeast Asian mental health* (pp. 183–208). Washington, D.C.: U.S. Department of Health and Human Services.

Bonacich, E. (1980). Small business and Japanese-American solidarity. In R. Endo, T. Sue, & N. Wagner (Eds.), *Asian Americans: Social and psychological perspectives II* (pp. 122–131). Palo Alto, CA: Science and Behavior Books.

Boucher, N. (1988, September). The struggle goes on. *The Boston Globe Magazine,* p. 18.

Branfman, F. (1970). Presidential war in Laos, 1964–1970. In N.S. Adams & A.W. McCoy (Eds.), *Laos: War and revolution* (pp. 213–283). New York: Harper and Row.

Broman, C.L. (1987). Race differences in professional help seeking. *American Journal of Community Psychology, 15,* 473–489.

Bromley, M. (1987). New beginnings for Cambodian refugees—or further disruptions? *Social Work, 32,* 236–239.

Cabezas, A., & Kawaguchi, G. (1988). Empirical evidence for continuing Asian American income inequity: The human capital model and labor market segregation. In G.Y. Okihiro et al. (Eds.), *Reflections on shattered windows: Promises and prospects for Asian American Studies* (pp. 148–154). Pullman, WA: Washington State University Press.

Carlin, J.E., & Sokoloff, B.Z. (1985). Mental health treatment issues for Southeast Asian refugees. In T.C. Owan (Ed.), *Southeast Asian mental health* (pp. 91–112). Washington, D.C.: U.S. Department of Health and Human Services.

Chao, C.M. (1992). The inner heart: Therapy with Southeast Asian families. In L.A. Vargas & J. Koss-Chioino (Eds.), *Working with culture: Psychotherapeutic interventions with ethnic minority children and adolescents* (pp. 157–181). San Francisco, CA: Jossey-Bass.

Chung, D.K. (1992). Asian cultural commonalities. In S.M. Furuto, R. Biswas, D.K. Chung, K. Murase, & F. Ross-Sheriff (Eds.), *Social work practice with Asian Americans* (pp. 27–44). Newbury Park, CA: Sage.

Cordasco, F. (1990). Filipinos. In F. Cordasco (Ed.), *Dictionary of American immigration history* (pp. 216–223). Metuchen, NJ: The Scarecrow Press.

Connor, J. (1974). Acculturation and family continuities in three generations of Japanese-Americans. *Journal of Marriage and the Family, 36,* 159–165.

DeVos, G. (1982). Ethnic pluralism: Conflict and accommodation. In G. Devos and L. Romanucci-Ross (Eds.), *Ethnic identity* (pp. 5–41). Chicago, IL: University of Chicago Press.

Dunn, L.P. (1975). *Asian Americans: A study guide and source book.* Laguna Beach, CA: Reed.

Fairbank, J.K. (1958). *The United States and China.* New York: Viking.

Gordon, V., Matousek, I., & Lang, T. (1980). Southeast Asian refugees: Life in America. *American Journal of Nursing, 37,* 447.

Greeley, A. (1969). *Why can't they be like us?* New York: Institute of Human Relations Press.

Henkin, A.B., & Nguyen, L.T. (1981). *Between two cultures: The Vietnamese in America.* Saratoga, CA: Century Twenty-One.

Hirschman, C., & Wong, M. (1981). Trends in socioeconomic achievement among immigrant and native born Asian Americans, 1960–1976. *The Sociological Quarterly, 22,* 495–513.

Ho, M.K. (1976). Social work with Asian Americans. *Social Casework, 57,* 195–201.

Hsu, F.L. (1971). *The challenge of the American dream: The Chinese in the United States.* Belmont, CA: Wadsworth.

Ishisaka, H.A., Nguyen, Q.T., & Okimoto, J.T. (1985). The role of culture in the mental health treatment of Indochinese refugees. In T.C. Owan (Ed.), *Southeast Asian mental health* (pp. 441–463). Washington, D.C.: U.S. Department of Health and Human Services.

Jaret, C., & Min, P. (1985). Ethnic business success: The case of Korean small business in Atlanta. *Sociology and Social Research, 69,* 412–432.

Kim, B.L.C. (1973). Asian Americans: No model minority. *Social Work, 18,* 44–53.

Kim, S.C. (1985). Family therapy for Asian Americans: A strategic-structural framework. *Psychotherapy, 22,* 342–348.

Kinzie, J.D. (1981). Evaluation and psychotherapy of Indochinese refugee patients. *American Journal of Psychotherapy, 35,* 251–261.

Kinzie, J.D. (1985). Overview of clinical issues in the treatment of Southeast Asian refugees. In T.C. Owan (Ed.), *Southeast Asian mental health* (pp. 113–135). Washington, D.C.: U.S. Department of Health and Human Services.

Kinzie, J.D., Sack, W., Angell, R.H., Manson, S., & Rath, B. (1986). The psychiatric effects of massive trauma on Cambodian children. *Journal of the American Academy of Child Psychiatry, 25,* 370–376.

Kitano, H.H.L., & Kikumura, A. (1980). The Japanese American family. In R. Endo, S. Sue, and N.N. Wagner (Eds.), *Asian Americans: Social and psychological perspectives II.* Palo Alto, CA: Science and Behavior Books.

Kung, S.W. (1962). *Chinese in American life.* Seattle, WA: University of Washington Press.

Lee, E. (1982). A social systems approach to assessment and treatment for Chinese-American families. In M. McGoldrick, J. Pearce, and J. Giordano (Eds.), *Ethnicity and family therapy* (pp. 527–551). New York: Guilford Press.

Melendy, H.G. (1984). *Chinese and Japanese Americans.* New York: Hippocrene.

Miller, S.C. (1969). *The unwelcome immigrant: The American image of the Chinese, 1785–1882.* Berkeley, CA: University of California Press.

Mokuau, N. (1987). Social workers' perceptions of counseling effectiveness for Asian-American clients. *Social Work, 32,* 331–335.

Moon, C. (1985). Year of immigration and socioeconomic status: A comparative study of three Asian populations in California. *Social Indicators Research, 18,* 129–152.

Murase, K., Egawa, J., & Tashima, N. (1985). Alternative mental health services models in Asian/Pacific communities. In T.C. Owan (Ed.), *Southeast Asian mental health* (pp. 229–259). Washington, D.C.: U.S. Department of Health and Human Services.

Nakanishi, M., & Rittner, B. (1992). The inclusionary cultural model. *Journal of Social Work Education, 28,* 27–35.

Nee, V., & Sanders, J. (1985). The road to parity: Determinants of the socioeconomic achievements of Asian-Americans. *Ethnic and Racial Studies, 8,* 75–91.

Nguyen, S.D. (1985). Mental health services for refugees and immigrants in Canada. In T.C. Owan (Ed.), *Southeast Asian mental health* (pp. 261–281). Washington, D.C.: U.S. Department of Health and Human Services.

Owan, T.C. (1985). *Southeast Asian mental health.* Washington, D.C.: U.S. Department of Health and Human Services.

Ross-Sheriff, F. (1992). Adaptation and integration into American society: Major issues affecting Asian Americans. In S.M. Furuto, R. Biswas, D.K. Chung, K. Murase, & F. Ross-Sheriff (Eds.), *Social work practice with Asian Americans* (pp. 45–64). Newbury Park, CA: Sage.

Rumbaut, R.G. (1985). Mental health and the refugee experience. In T.C. Owan (Ed.), *Southeast Asian mental health* (pp. 433–485). Washington, D.C.: U.S. Department of Health and Human Services.

Ryan, A.S. (1985). Cultural factors in casework with Chinese Americans. *Social Casework, 66*, 333–340.

Rynearson, A.M., & DeVoe, P.A. (1984). Refugee women in a vertical village: Lowland Laotians in St. Louis. *Social Thought, 10*, 33–47.

Shepard, J. (1992). The Vietnamese women immigrants and refugees in the United States: Historical perspectives on casework. In S.M. Furuto, R. Biswas, D.K. Chung, K. Murase, & F. Ross-Sheriff (Eds.), *Social work practice with Asian Americans* (pp. 85–120). Newbury Park, CA: Sage.

Sherman, S. (1988, October). The Hmong in America. *National Geographic,* pp. 586–610.

Shon, S.P., & Davis, Y.J. (1982). Asian families. In M. McGoldrick, J. Pearce, and J. Giordano (Eds.), *Ethnicity and family therapy* (pp. 208–228). New York: Guilford Press.

Stein, B. (1979). Occupational adjustment of refugees: The Vietnamese in the United States. *International Migration Review, 13*(1), 25–45.

Szaposnick, J., & Kurtines, W. (1980). Acculturation, biculturalism and adjustment among Cuban Americans. In A.M. Padilla (Ed.), *Acculturation: Theory models and some new findings* (pp. 139–159). Boulder, CO: Westview Press.

Tran, T.V. (1985). *Social support and alienation among Vietnamese Americans: Implications for refugee policy making and resettlement.* Unpublished doctoral dissertation, University of Texas at Arlington.

Tran, T.V., & Wright, R. (1986). Social support and subjective well-being among Vietnamese refugees. *Social Service Review, 60*, 449–457.

True, R.H. (1985). An Indochinese mental health service model in San Francisco. In T.C. Owan (Ed.), *Southeast Asian mental health* (pp. 329–341). Washington, D.C.: U.S. Department of Health and Human Services.

Tsai, S.S.H. (1983). *China and the overseas Chinese in the United States, 1868–1911.* Little Rock, AR: University of Arkansas Press.

Tsui, P., & Schultz, G. (1985). Failure of rapport: Why psychotherapeutic engagement fails in the treatment of Asian clients. *American Journal of Orthopsychiatry, 55*, 561–569.

Tung, T.M. (1985). Psychiatric care for Southeast Asians: How different is different? In T.C. Owan (Ed.), *Southeast-Asian mental health* (pp. 5–39). Washington, D.C.: U.S. Department of Health and Human Services.

Tung, W.L. (1974). *The Chinese in America, 1820–1973.* New York: Ocean Publications.

Uba, L. (1994). *Asian Americans: Personality patterns, identity, and mental health.* New York: Guilford Press.

Welty, P.T. (1976). *The Asians: Their heritage and destiny.* Philadelphia, PA: Lippincott.

Westermeyer, J. (1985). Mental health of Southeast Asian refugees: Observations over two decades from Laos and the U.S. In T.C. Owan (Ed.), *Southeast Asian mental health* (pp. 65–89). Washington, D.C.: U.S. Department of Health and Human Services.

Wong, E.F. (1985). Asian American middleman minority theory: The framework of an American myth. *Journal of Ethnic Studies, 13,* 51–79.

Wong, M.G. (1984). Economic survival: The case of Asian-American elderly. *Sociological Perspectives, 27,* 197–217.

Wong, M.D., & Hirschman, C. (1983). Labor force participation and socioeconomic attainment of Asian American women. *Sociological Perspectives, 26,* 423–446.

Wong, P.T., & Reker, G.T. (1985). Stress, coping and well-being in Anglo-Chinese elderly. *Canadian Journal on Aging, 4,* 29–37.

Chapter 5

SOCIAL WORK PRACTICE WITH WOMEN

Kathryn G. Wambach and Dianne F. Harrison

This chapter focuses on women in our society, including historical trends and current issues relevant for social work practice. Before we discuss women as a special population, it should be acknowledged that women do not comprise a homogenous group. While sex is certainly a major (if not the primary) "categorizing" force in modern society, other factors (including race/ethnicity and socioeconomic status) play critical roles in shaping the social realities of individual women. Throughout this chapter, an attempt has been made to reflect this range of experience within the context of highlighting the commonalities shared by all women.

HISTORICAL PERSPECTIVE

The oppression of women, or more precisely, social stratification based on gender, became a predominant social form of advanced horticulturist societies (Blumberg, 1978) roughly seven thousand years ago. While a complete recitation of such an immense history is beyond the scope of this chapter, the duration itself suggests several overriding considerations. First, for a power arrangement to remain intact for 70 centuries, one may assume that all social institutions, ideologies, norms, values, and stereotypes are involved in its maintenance (see Lipman-Blumen, 1984, for an excellent discussion on the dynamics of oppression). Second, the duration of women's oppression obscures its reality, creating the illusion of a "natural order" and making it difficult even to imagine a non-gendered society (Lorber, 1986). Finally, minority group status influences the course of individual lives as well as the resources (both internal and external) available for the journey (Lott, 1985; Parlee, 1981; Smith, 1985). Thus, the psychology of individual women today reflects

112

centuries of subjugation and insidiously supports its continuation (Miller & Mothner, 1981).

The focus of the present historical discussion is the United States in the twentieth century. By the turn of the century, women had emerged into the public spheres of American life via "moral" movements such as abolition, temperance, and settlement houses. Approximately one in five women worked outside the home (Evans, 1987). Among these, a small number of white, middle-class, college-educated women generally entered "female" professions (e.g., nursing, teaching, and social work) for a period of time prior to marriage. Working-class, immigrant, and black women, on the other hand, were forced by economic necessity to migrate to cities where more employment opportunities could be found. Once there, they faced limited employment options (usually domestic or factory work), low wages, and harsh working conditions. Only urban, black women, however, typically remained in the work force after marriage.

The leaders of the National American Woman Suffrage Association, the most visible of the early feminist organizations, came from among the white, middle-class women mentioned earlier (Strom, 1975). During the same time period, the Black Women's Club Movement (Davis, 1981) and the National Women's Trade Union League (Wertheimer & Nelson, 1989) were emerging. Through effective alliances among these divergent women's groups, the Nineteenth Amendment to the Constitution was ratified in 1920 (Scott & Scott, 1975). Having won the right to vote, these coalitions dissolved into separate purposes, unable to unite (even years later) behind the Equal Rights Amendment.

The Great Depression of the 1930s provided special hardships for women. Although men and women rarely competed for the same jobs, women were driven out of the labor force through social sanction and legislative restriction (Evans, 1987). Married and professional women were primary targets and, as an example, the proportion of men in the teaching profession rose from 16 percent to 24 percent during the Depression decade (Scharf, 1980). The union reforms of the same time period generally encouraged job segregation and supported separate, lower, pay scales for female employees (Milkman, 1980). While employment opportunities for poor women were generally restricted to domestic service, manufacturing, and agriculture, the proportion of clerical and sales workers who were women increased from 8 percent in 1900 to 29 percent in 1940 (Anderson, 1988). As white, single, native-born, middle-class women became concentrated in these fields, the status and salary associated with such positions declined (Davies, 1982).

World War II reordered these trends. Severe labor shortages motivated both government and industry to recruit women (regardless of race, class, or marital status) into the work force. A rapidly expanding national media depicted such participation as a patriotic contribution to the war effort. Six million women who had never before engaged in work outside the home entered the labor force during the war years (Evans, 1987). Nearly 15 percent of those employed prior to the war (1,500,000) changed occupational roles by March, 1944 (Wool & Pearlman, 1947). Women entered skilled industries and subsequently increased their union membership fourfold (Evans, 1987). Significant legislative reform (e.g., removal of laws barring married women teachers and adoption of equal pay standards in some states) occurred during the war years as well (Hartmann, 1982).

With the return of men to the labor force following World War II, women's status was once again reversed. Millions of women left the work force voluntarily and involuntarily (Evans, 1987). Segregation of women into devalued service sector jobs returned in force. For the first time in the past 150 years in this country, the birthrate rose substantially during the 1950s, reflecting the media-driven return to "domesticity" which occurred (Cherlin, 1987). Despite the conservative tone of the immediate post-war years, women's labor force participation never receded to pre-World War II levels and, in fact, has increased systematically ever since (Lipman-Blumen, 1984).

The three decades since the post-war conservative era have included dramatic demographic, social, economic, and political upheaval. The U.S. Census Bureau (1980) documented clear increases in "the postponement of marriage, the proportion of young adults remaining single, divorced adults living alone, unmarried couples (living together), families maintained by adults with no spouse present, and children living with only one parent" (p. 200). In sum, the "typical American family" with an employed male, a housebound female, and 2.5 children is no longer a majority experience; the majority are being forced to form new social structures and roles with which to confront an adjusted reality (Lipman-Blumen, 1984).

Numerous factors fueled changes in the pattern of female labor force participation. As has been indicated, married women who worked typically had husbands whose earning potential was limited. Through the

1950s and 1960s, married women entered the labor force regardless of their husband's earnings (Weiner, 1985). The values of consumer capitalism provided early incentives for this move as assessments of an "adequate" standard of living burgeoned (Evans, 1987). As middle-class married women entered the work force in unprecedented numbers, the general economic prosperity of the post-war years allowed more working-class women to remain at home (Rubin, 1976). However, the economic slowdown of the 1970s and downturn of the 1980s, coupled with demographic changes and work force demands, have drawn increasingly more women into the job market regardless of marital status and/or social class (Lipman-Blumen, 1984).

The revitalization of women as a political force emerged from other mass movements (i.e., civil rights and anti-war movements) (Evans, 1987). Beginning with the National Organization for Women (NOW) in 1966, a loosely organized feminist political community comprised of mass-based feminist organizations (e.g., NOW and the National Women's Political Caucus), single-issue groups (e.g., National Women's Health Network and National Abortion Rights Action League), litigation and educational organizations (e.g., National Council of Negro Women and Women's Legal Defense Fund), and research groups (e.g., Center for Women's Policy Studies) was established on the American political landscape (Palley, 1987). This community, in sporadic coalitions with more traditional women's groups, accomplished significant legislative reform during the 1970s (e.g., Title IX of the Education Amendments of 1972 which prohibited federal funding of educational institutions which discriminated against women and the Equal Credit Opportunity Act of 1975). Further, abortion rights (another highly visible feminist goal) seemed assured by the landmark 1973 Supreme Court decision *Roe vs. Wade.* The lack of consensus among the feminist political community as well as the influence of conservative coalitions were demonstrated in the inability to ratify the Equal Rights Amendment, passed by Congress in 1972. Despite judicial erosion of hard-won legislative gains and a general conservative backlash during the 1980s (see Faludi, 1992, for in-depth discussion), continued patterns of female voting, officeholding and social activism do not support the myth that the so-called Second Wave of feminism has ended (Palley, 1987).

CURRENT CHARACTERISTICS

This section will review current trends and issues related to women's socioeconomic, sociopolitical, health and mental health status. As noted previously, experiences of individual women and groups of women may vary considerably based on factors of race, ethnicity, social class, age, physical ability, and sexual preference.

Socioeconomic Status

Education, occupation, and income are the major components which indicate an individual's socioeconomic status. While women have gained entry into virtually every arena in the American power structure, achieving equality with men in terms of economic power remains an elusive goal. "Women are 50 percent of the global population; . . . one third of the paid labour force; . . . work two thirds of all working hours; . . . receive one tenth of the world's income; . . . [and] own less than one percent of the world's property" (Hanmer & Statham, 1989, p. 27).

Educationally, women now achieve nearly the same overall levels as men in the United States. Specifically, the median educational level for white women age 18 and over is 12.8 years compared to 13.0 years for white men, while among both men and women who are Black and other races, the median year of school completed is 12.7 (U.S. Dept. of Education, 1994). Closer examination reveals the deceptiveness of these statistics. While women earned roughly 50 percent of the bachelor's and master's degrees awarded in 1991–92, they earned only 42.7 percent of law degrees, 35.7 percent of medical degrees, and 32.3 percent of dental degrees (U.S. Department of Education, 1994). Further, examination of the fields in which bachelor's and master's degrees were earned indicates that considerable segregation continues, with most women concentrated in traditionally female fields (e.g., social work, nursing, home economics, library science, and education). Even within these areas, women earn a smaller share of doctorates than of lower degrees. For example in 1991–92, women received 86.6 percent of the BSW's, 83.1 percent of the MSSW's, and 66.1 percent of social work doctoral degrees (U.S. Department of Education, 1994).

This subtle pattern of inequality/segregation is more pronounced in occupational distribution in this country; most people work in jobs in which the clear majority of their coworkers are of the same sex (Sapiro,

1990). The most "female" jobs tend to be clerical and personal service while the most "male" job categories are blue-collar jobs (U.S. Department of Labor, 1989). Job segregation is evident by level within fields as well as by fields. For example, among school teachers (a traditionally female field) in 1994, women constituted 97.2 percent of prekindergarten and kindergarten teachers, 85.8 percent of the elementary school educators, 54.7 percent of secondary school teachers, and 36.4 percent of teachers at the college and university level (U.S. Department of Labor, 1995). Similarly, in 1987, among white-collar federal government employees, 75 percent of the workers in the lowest-paid jobs (i.e., GS 1–6) were women compared to 7 percent of those in the highest-paid jobs (i.e., GS 16–18) (U.S. Bureau of the Census, 1989).

Socioeconomic inequality is most evident when income is examined. The median annual earnings of full-time women employees was 65 percent that of men in 1987 (Blau & Winkler, 1989) and 76.4 percent that of men in 1994 (U.S. Dept. of Labor, 1995). Such discrepancies remain evident even when age, education, and occupation are controlled. For example, in 1990, the average dollar earnings for a woman with a college degree ($20,376) were comparable to those of a man with a high school diploma ($22,236) (U.S. Bureau of the Census, 1994). Similarly, within occupational categories, the median earnings of full-time, year-round employed women in 1992 was 64.7 percent of their male counterparts for executive, administrators, and managerial workers; 74.7 percent for administrative-support workers; 62.7 percent for service positions; 65.8 percent for precision production, craft, and repair; and 57.2 percent for sales workers (U.S. Bureau of the Census, 1994). Further, the above figures include all women and therefore represent overestimation of earnings by women of ethnic and racial minorities (see Smith & Tienda, 1988, for a thorough discussion of the dual oppression of race and gender).

While women have made some economic progress, during the same time period, they have increasingly become the sole supporters of themselves and their children. In 1993, 26 percent of all U.S. families with dependent children were headed by women including 20 percent of white families, 58 percent of black families, and 30 percent of Hispanic families (U.S. Bureau of the Census, 1994). The consequence of this demographic phenomenon coupled with socioeconomic inequality has dramatically increased the number of women and children living in poverty. Specifically, in 1992, the poverty rate for all families with children under 6 years old was 24 percent while 58.9 percent of female-headed households were below the federal poverty line (U.S. Bureau of the Census, 1994). Again, the impact of dual oppression was starkly evident. For families with children under 6 years old headed by white women, the poverty rate was 46.2 percent while 69.2 percent of those headed by black women and 68.6 percent of those headed by Hispanic women fell below the poverty level (U.S. Bureau of the Census, 1994).

Elderly women are also particularly vulnerable to poverty. More women are outliving their husbands and are faced with reduced benefits available upon his demise (O'Grady-LeShane, 1990). In 1991, the poverty rate for elderly women was 15.5 percent, compared to a 7.9 percent poverty rate for elderly men (U.S. Bureau of the Census, 1993). Rapidly increasing numbers of these two groups (i.e., female-headed families with dependent children and elderly women), coupled with economic inequality, have produced the phenomenon known as the feminization of poverty.

In summary, structural changes in the economy and antidiscrimination legislation have coincided with demographic upheaval and social change. In an attempt to estimate the relative economic well-being (i.e., access to goods, services, and leisure) of women in 1959 compared with 1983, Fuchs (1986) considered hours of work, money income, the imputed value of housework, the size and structure of households, and income sharing within households. The estimated net result ranged from a decrease of 15 percent to an increase of 4 percent, depending on assumptions of income sharing within households. The best scenario (i.e., a 4 percent increase) was based on the assumption that adult members of a household evenly divided their cumulative income and did not reflect any consideration of relative contribution.

Sociopolitical Status

Although women have gained access to institutional power positions, they remain distinctly in the minority. On the federal level, following the 1992 elections, there were 6 women in the U.S. Senate and 47 women in the U.S. House of Representatives ("U.S. Elections," 1993). As has been indicated, women are concentrated in the lower levels of the federal bureaucracy. In terms of publicly elected officials, women hold approximately 13 percent of municipal offices, 25 percent of county level offices, 16 percent of state legislative positions, and 4 percent of state governor posts (Sapiro, 1990). Following the 1992 elections, women had increased their percentage of statewide-elected legislative offices to 21.9 percent and held roughly one-fourth of governorships (Women in the States, 1994).

Highly visible legislative and judicial reforms do not seem to have achieved appreciable equality between the sexes and, further, have not benefited all women equally. As discussed earlier, judicial and legislative reform regarding equal pay and affirmative action have clearly not equalized earnings or ended job segregation. As the feminization of poverty progresses, public welfare policies more clearly become statements regarding the value of women and children. In 1987, Alaska was the only state in the country which provided AFDC payments sufficient to raise the recipients above the poverty level; the range among the remaining states was 16 percent (Alabama) to 85 percent (California) of the federal poverty level (Burke, 1987).

The 1973 Supreme Court decision in *Roe vs. Wade,* in effect, legalized abortion. However, since 1976, the Hyde Amendment has placed restrictions on the use of federal funds to pay for abortions. The 1989 *Webster vs. Missouri* decision allowed states to formulate more restrictive abortion policies and further eroded the constitutionally protected right to abortion established in *Roe vs. Wade.* The effect of these policies does not impact equally on all women; specifically, they serve to decrease the likelihood that poor women and younger women will receive safe abortions (Sapiro, 1990).

In the country's legal system, one woman, Sandra Day O'Connor (the first in history), is now one of two women serving as U.S. Supreme Court judges while women fill less than 10 percent of federal and state judiciary positions (Rix, 1987). In 1986–88, women were 11 percent of non-supervisory police and detectives, 5 percent of police and detective supervisors, 8 percent of FBI agents, and 6 percent of the Secret Service (McGuinness & Donahue, 1988). Women constitute a small percentage of persons arrested and/or convicted of crimes (Sapiro, 1990). They tend to commit property crimes rather than crimes against people (Parisi, 1982a), yet receive longer prison sentences and serve higher proportions of their sentences (Parisi, 1982b; Rix, 1988).

Women constitute only a small percentage of leaders in industry and labor. In 1982, women owned about 24 percent of all businesses but generated only about 10 percent of business receipts (Rix, 1987). In 1987, women were 35 percent of all union members but held few positions in the national union leadership (U.S. Department of Labor, 1989). While it is clear that inequality continues in women's socioeconomic and sociopolitical experiences, there appears to be little momentum behind proposed strategies to address the problems.

Pay equity or comparable worth are terms describing reform strategies that address the traditional devaluation of women's work through readjusting pay scales to reward equally work of similar value to society. The pressure from women's organizations and labor unions has resulted in some change in state and local governmental policies but has not been successful with the federal government or private industry (Harkess, 1988). Moreover, labor unions have demonstrated an unwillingness to include pay equity as an issue in collective bargaining. Similarly, unions have failed to support the inclusion of child care benefits in standard employee benefits programs (Christensen, 1988). In 1987, only about 5 percent of U.S. employers provided child care benefits (Sapiro, 1990).

The impact of other major societal institutions and their policies, while less direct, is more insidious as they serve to maintain attitudes which devalue and restrain women. Feminists have leveled strong criticisms against organized religion on these grounds (e.g., Daly, 1975; Heschel, 1983; Sanford & Donovan, 1984). In terms of current religious leadership, the ordination of women has been a focal issue. Roman Catholics, Orthodox Jews, and approximately 50 percent of current Protestant denominations in this country do not allow the ordination of women. In the 84 denominations ordaining women among members of the National Council of Churches in 1989, women constituted about 8 percent of active clergy (Sapiro, 1990).

Women's involvement in American mass media is likewise limited. In 1987, 36 of the 239 network new correspondents were female (Sanders & Rock, 1988). In the same study, stories reported by women were aired primarily on weekends (considered less desirable slots), and the top six men on network news commanded more air time than all the women combined. In commercial media and advertisement, women are now portrayed outside the home more frequently and in a wider range of occupations (Ferrante, Haynes & Kingsley, 1988). Again, the same study found that, overall, media images remain gender-typed, with women characterized as generally less competent.

As America's microcosmic social institution, the traditional family, while declining numerically, remains ideologically prominent. In 1993, 70 percent of American children lived with two parents present, while

26 percent lived with their mothers, and 4 percent with only their fathers (U.S. Bureau of the Census, 1994). Race and ethnicity are major factors in determining a child's living situation. While 76 percent of white children live in a two-parent household, the same is true of 65 percent of Hispanic and 37 percent of black children (U.S. Bureau of the Census, 1994). Fifty-three percent of black children, 30 percent of Hispanic, and 20 percent of white children live with only their mothers. The majority of women with children under the age of six are employed regardless of marital status (Blau & Winkler, 1989). Among preschoolers with employed mothers, 28 percent attend a day-care center or preschool; another 24 percent are cared for in the child's home; and the largest percentage (42%) are cared for in someone else's home (U.S. Bureau of the Census, 1989).

Among people 18 years and older, 63 percent of men and 59 percent of women were currently married (U.S. Bureau of the Census, 1994). Approximately half of all new marriages will end in divorce (Cherlin, 1987). Following divorce, women's standard of living typically declines steeply, especially when they have children (Weiss, 1984; Weitzman, 1985, 1988). Less than half of the women awarded child support in divorce settlements receive the full payment; 26 percent were not receiving any of the money owed (Rix, 1988).

Findings from Blumstein and Schwartz's (1983) research on couples have suggested that little change has occurred in the division of labor and power in heterosexual relationships. Women did most of the housework regardless of their marital or employment status, although cohabiting couples were somewhat more egalitarian in their division of domestic labor. With married couples, the more housework the husband performed, the more conflict the couple reported. Money clearly established the balance of power in terms of consumer decision-making in heterosexual relationships; increased earning power did not, however, result in appreciable shifts in domestic responsibilities for women (for a review of literature on division of domestic labor, see Coverman & Shelley, 1986). The caregiving provided by women within the home is not restricted to children and housework. Women incur major responsibility, compared to men, for the increasingly heavy burden of caring for the elderly (Walker, 1983), the disabled (Baldwin & Glendinning, 1983), and the mentally ill (Scheyett, 1990).

Wife battery and rape are two forms of criminal violence against women which have received a great deal of attention. Both rape and wife battery seem to be the products, at least in part, of gender-role socialization patterns (Hyde, 1990). In the last decade, significant reforms of statutory law regarding rape as well as law enforcement procedure in cases of sexual assault have been accomplished (Smith & Chapman, 1987). The result has been an improvement in the percent of rape arrests leading to convictions from 10 percent in 1975 to 19 percent in 1985 (Herman, 1989).

The number of reported rapes has continued to rise so that in 1987, 73 out of every 100,000 females in the United States reported that they were victims of rape or attempted rape (U.S. Department of Justice, 1987). Stated in terms of lifetime likelihood of this type of victimization, American women face a one-in-twelve chance of being assaulted in any twenty-five-year period, higher if she lives in an urban area (Gordon & Riger, 1989). Similarly, Koss (1988) estimated that 20 percent of adult women and 12 percent of adolescent girls have experienced sexual abuse and assault during their lifetimes.

Russell (1982) estimated that 12–14 percent of women who have been married have been raped by their husbands or ex-husbands, often accompanied by other types of physical violence. Prevalence data have suggested that 20–30 percent of all women will be physically assaulted by a partner or ex-partner during their lifetime (Frieze & Browne, 1989) and 4–20 percent of pregnant women will be assaulted during their pregnancy (Stewart & Cecutti, 1993). The FBI's *Uniform Crime Reports* do not single out wife beating as a specific category of crime, although the agency estimates its occurrence is three times that of rape. Beyond outright violence in marital relationships, instances of threats, harassment, breaches of fiduciary trust, and other forms of psychological abuse and/or intimidation are believed to be even more commonplace and less reported (Charney & Russell, 1994).

Sexual harassment, or unwanted sexual advances or coercion that can occur in the work place or academic settings (Kelly, 1990), is another issue faced by many women and one that reflects the continuing low sociopolitical status of women in our society. Examples of sexual harassment include verbal sexual suggestions or jokes, constant leering, a friendly pat, squeeze or pinch, indecent propositions backed by threats of job loss, and forced sexual relations (Hyde, 1990). In a study of over 20,000 members of the federal work force, 42 percent of the women and 15 percent of the men reported having been sexually harassed at work within the preceding two years (Tangri, Burt & Johnson, 1982); a 1987 survey of 8,500 government workers essentially duplicated these results. Following the highly publicized Senate hearings on the Anita Hill-Clarence Thomas harassment allegations, the number of sexual harassment complaints filed with the Equal Employment Opportunity Commission rose by 60 percent in 6 months (Reynolds, 1992). Although many colleges, government agencies, corporations, and branches of the military now have specific policies defining sexual harassment and procedures for handling cases, resolution of such cases is difficult, at best. It is not uncommon for such situations to become a test of one person's word versus another's (Kelly, 1990). Because there is usually an imbalance of power through which the offender has tried to take advantage of the victim, victims, who are typically female, have been known to either let the matter go unreported, quit their jobs, or leave school to avoid continuing sexual harassment.

Health and Mental Health Status

Although the life expectancy of women has exceeded that of men throughout this century, women visit doctors and hospitals more frequently than men. In 1986, the average woman visited a doctor 6.2 times and a dentist 2.2 times, while the average man saw a doctor 4.5 times and the dentist 1.9 times (Sapiro, 1990). In terms of hospitalization, women received 1053 days of inpatient care per 1000 population compared to 849 days for men (U.S. Bureau of the Census, 1987). Feminists have suggested that a substantial portion of these differences is explained by the medicalization of reproduction and childbirth (e.g., McCrea, 1983; Rothman, 1982; Sanford & Donovan, 1984).

Women are more likely to receive psychoactive drugs as a result of their contact with the medical profession (Gomberg, 1982). Doctors acknowledge they consider emotional factors more important in diagnosing women's problems than men's (Bernstein & Kane, 1981). Women are particularly overrepresented as consumers of mental health services (Russo & Sobel, 1981; Tavris, 1988). Among the 10 to 15 million participants in the proliferating self-help movement in this country (Goldsmith, 1989), women outnumber men more than three to one.

Research has consistently indicated that mental health practitioners generally hold different mental health standards for men and women and see traditional male behavior as healthier than traditional female behavior (Hampton, Lambert & Snell, 1986; Kabacoff, Marwit, &

Orlofsky, 1985; Kravetz & Jones, 1981). Undoubtedly, most currently identified psychological constructs have been examined for its potential differential distribution between the sexes. Many of these examinations have revealed statistically significant differences, some on a quite consistent basis (e.g., locus of control). However, in examining the meta-analytic reviews (i.e., additional reviews of studies) of this research, Deaux (1984) noted that "5% may approximate the upper boundary for the explanatory power of subject-sex main effects in specific social and cognitive behaviors" (p. 108). In other words, 95 percent of the variance was not explained by sex differences. As is typically the case, males and females display much more similarity than dissimilarity when considering the distribution of individual attributes.

Research has also demonstrated gender differences in the patterns of psychopathology (American Psychiatric Association, 1994; Myers et al., 1984; Robins et al., 1984; Tavris, 1988). Specifically, women's rates of depression and of anxiety (including panic disorders, phobias and obsessive-compulsive disorders) are found to be two to three times higher than men, while men's rates of alcoholism, drug dependence, and personality disorders are five to six times those of women. Women attempt suicide at a rate 2.3 times that of men, but men kill themselves 2.3 times more than women (Steffensmeier, 1984). Women are also more likely than men to suffer from eating disorders (including obesity) (Attie & Brooks-Gunn, 1987).

CONCERNS FOR PRACTICE

Feminism refers to a collection of theories and frameworks which share certain assumptions: (1) Gender is viewed as one of the most important bases of social structure and organization. Specifically, in most known societies, women occupy a position of lower status and value with more limited access to resources and less opportunity for personal autonomy than men. (2) Gender inequality is rooted in the social construction of human experience rather than a biological imperative. The implication is that gender inequality is subject to change. (3) Feminism maintains that these inequities should be eradicated and that united action is needed to accomplish such change.

Social work was among the first professions to formally acknowledge and confront sexism (see *Social Work*, Special Issue on Women, 1976). The profession has long claimed its uniqueness based on its values and the convergence of feminism, and social work in this regard has been acknowledged (Berlin & Kravetz, 1981). Several authors have suggested integration of feminism and social work (Bricker-Jenkins & Hooyman, 1986; Collins, 1986; Hanmer & Statham, 1989). Just as women are not a homogenous group, neither feminism or social work are monolithic. Our discussion of implications for practice is intended to be suggestive, rather than prescriptive or exhaustive, and is made from a feminist perspective.

Feminist therapy, like feminism itself, is a summary term describing therapeutic approaches which share the common assumption that ideology, social structure, and behavior are inextricably interwoven (Gilbert, 1980). While this perspective may be incorporated into any practice method, the present discussion assumes an empirical clinical practice approach (see Ivanoff, Robinson, & Blythe, 1987 or Davis & Proctor, 1989) and is organized around principles which have been consistent and predominant in the evolution of feminist therapy.

Feminist therapy maintains a focus on structural causation. Specifically, client awareness/knowledge regarding the sociocultural causes of their personal distress (Glidden & Tracey, 1989) is an assumed goal. Here, knowledge refers to an intellectual understanding of how behavior is currently influenced and it is part of the worker's responsibility to expand the client's base of information (Gambrill, 1983). Also, intellectual knowledge (i.e., awareness of contingencies) facilitates learning (Bandura, 1969) while new conceptual sets suggest and motivate change.

The power relations within the therapeutic context are particularly important to the feminist approach as the therapeutic relationship should provide a model for egalitarian behavior. Acknowledging the inherent asymmetry in a therapeutic contact, client assessment and treatment planning should be a cooperative venture. Contracting, however formal, enhances client power and autonomy (Ivanoff, Robinson & Blythe, 1987). Feminist therapy minimizes power differentials; feminist social work practice should be committed to empowerment (see Pinderhughes, 1983). In seeking structures conducive to client growth and learning, referrals to political, self-help and/or consciousness-raising groups as either primary or collateral intervention are a hallmark of feminist practice (Tavris, 1988).

Improved adjustment to an oppressive situation in the absence of effort to affect change in the oppressive situation is considered an inadequate therapeutic outcome by feminists. The goal of improvement in environmental conditions has received particular attention in family therapy (see Avis, 1987, for overview) and is consistent with the empowerment perspective important to a feminist approach. Another implication for practitioners is that feminist social work practice should be particularly concerned with certain areas which pertain uniquely to women (e.g., rape, assertiveness, body image, and issues of physical power) (Gilbert, 1980; Stock, Graubert & Birns, 1982). Practitioners who are using a feminist approach, then, would take into account not only issues of particular relevance to individual women but also would involve themselves on a macro level with changes in the status of women and women's rights, in general.

Finally, social work practitioners, when dealing with clients at any level, must be attentive to the special and unique concerns of women regardless of their presenting problem(s) or the gender of the worker. Without such sensitivity, social workers only contribute to the continued oppression of women. By acknowledging and acting upon the unique circumstances of women in our society, we further the goals and values of a rich professional heritage.

Beyond these general remarks, it should be noted that a growing body of literature has become available which provides more concrete guidance in incorporating feminism and direct practice. Some of these texts are broadly based and applicable across a wide range of practice situations (e.g., Bricker-Jenkins, Hooyman & Gottlieb, 1991; Comas-Diaz & Greene, 1994; Hall, 1992; Mirkin, 1994) while others are focused on more specific issues such as family therapy (Leeder, 1994), addiction (Bepko, 1991; Gomberg & Nirenberg, 1993), juvenile delinquency (Chesney-Lind & Shelden, 1992), and health care (Olson, 1994).

While all social policies should be examined for their potential effects on vulnerable groups, certain areas of policy are of particular concern for women. Decisions regarding reproductive rights, however intended or motivated, set parameters of social control and regulation on individual women. Regardless of one's stance on the abortion issue, current policies make access to abortion services an economic privilege. As advocates for the disadvantaged with goals of social justice, the social work profession must question this stance. Similarly, the profession's commitment to client self-determination would seem at odds with any limitations in access to contraceptive information or reproductive health care.

Numerous strategies have been suggested for addressing the socioeconomic inequality of women (including the feminization of poverty as its most extreme manifestation). One set of strategies aims at altering the structure of jobs and occupations and includes issues such as affirmative action, equal pay, comparable worth, and employee benefits (e.g., maternity leave and child care) (Pearce & McAdoo, 1981). Another approach involves expanding and reforming social welfare programs. Specific suggestions include increasing AFDC benefits to levels above the poverty line, augmenting other existing benefits programs (e.g., Medicaid, food stamp, and school lunch programs), and making housewives eligible for Social Security and unemployment compensation (Ehrenreich & Piven, 1984). A final set of strategies utilizes divorce law reform (particularly property and income allocation) and child support enforcement (Weitzman, 1988). While the relative merit of each of these strategies is debatable, accomplishing any of these initiatives would have a positive impact on the status of women.

The various deinstitutionalization initiatives have moved the burden of caring for the disabled and dependent from the public sector to the private sector without compensation (Cox, Parson, & Kimboko, 1988), where the burden has fallen disproportionately on women. Remedial strategies include direct monetary compensation (Briar & Ryan, 1986), the provision of supportive services (Scheyett, 1990), and the inclusion of elder care in employee benefits (Anastas, Gibeau, & Larson, 1990).

Enacting any of the proposed social policies would require massive expenditures. Consequently, funding mechanisms sufficient to ensure access, especially to disadvantaged groups, should be developed with any policy initiative. Further, these fiscal considerations will play a crucial role in determining the success of the initiative (Austin, 1983). The federal fiscal policies of the last decade have reduced the availability of social services (Hopps, 1989) and reflect a significant shift away from the country's historical commitment to the welfare state (Atherton, 1990a, 1990b). This climate poses a serious threat to any of the policy initiatives suggested above (Frumkin, Martin, & Page, 1987). Therefore, combating the erosion of American commitment to social welfare should be a primary goal in feminist social work practice.

Organizations may be viewed as microcosms reflective of their social environment. These policy issues are, then, directly relevant to social work administration; eradicating gender inequality at any level in any system benefits women. Administrators transform public policy into social reality and, in the process, may exercise considerable latitude (Lerner & Wanat, 1983). In a feminist practice, this responsibility should be performed with the goal of minimizing deleterious impact on women. Lipsky (1980) contended that practitioners at all levels of bureaucracy are actively engaged in turning policy into practice. Social workers at any organizational level should resist the "agentic state" in which a person relinquishes moral responsibility for his or her actions to authority figures who supervise their behavior (Milgram, 1974).

Again, a growing body of literature provides more detail regarding feminist practice in policy and administration. Perlmutter (1994) has taken an international perspective in examining social, cultural and economic issues in the growth of women's alternative organizations. Iannello (1992) has reviewed traditional organizational theory and challenged many basic assumptions in this area. Barusch (1994) has focused on the specific issues of older women and poverty.

CONCERNS FOR SOCIAL WORK EDUCATION

The Council on Social Work Education's Curriculum Policy Statement specifically stated that social work curriculum must provide content on women but did not require a separate course. This decision makes it difficult to monitor compliance. In a survey of 427 social work educators, Freeman (1990) found 33 percent had a strong feminist orientation; 18 percent were non-feminist or neutral; and 49 percent had weak to moderate feminist identification. While attitudes do not necessarily correspond with course content, these findings raise some concern regarding implementation. Further, in a survey of undergraduate social work majors, those who had taken a separate course on women knew more about women's history, biological processes, and current social status than those who had not (Vinton, 1992). While not denying the reality of an already crowded curriculum, inclusion of a separate course on women should be reconsidered.

Davis (1994), summarizing the efforts of numerous social work scholars, has attempted to provide a basic text for the purpose of forming a women's agenda in social work for the future. Overall, she suggests that a complete deconstruction/revision of the profession's knowledge base is a necessary first step in formulating an agenda for the twenty-first century. On a more practical note, a collection of course outlines on women in social work has recently become available through the CSWE (Graber, Halseth, & Korr, 1995).

CONCERNS FOR SOCIAL WORK RESEARCH

Some feminists have challenged science on epistemological and methodological grounds (e.g., Bleier, 1986; Hawkesworth, 1989; Rose, 1986) while related debate has raged in the social work literature (e.g., Brekke, 1986; Heineman, 1981; Hudson, 1982; Piper, 1985; Witkin & Gottschalk, 1988). While even a summary of these issues is beyond the scope of this chapter (see Stanley & Wise, 1993, for a thorough overview), several points regarding research in a feminist social work practice are pertinent.

Research methods should be non-sexist; achieving this goal will require removing problems which are imbedded in traditional methods. Eichler (1988) identified four primary, interrelated problem areas: (1) Androcentricity is viewing the world from a male perspective and includes female invisibility (gynopia), preference of male over female interests and assigning blame to women as a class. (2) Overgeneralization occurs when results from a study of one sex are applied to both sexes. Men are commonly used as an appropriate basis for generalization about virtually anything except the family. (3) Gender insensitivity refers to ignoring sex as a significant variable in social interactions. Finally, (4) a double standard is used when identical behaviors or situations are evaluated differently depending on the sex of the subject. These problems permeate language, concepts, methods, interpretation of data, and conclusions in both overt and subtle ways (see Eichler, 1988, for a comprehensive analysis).

Research on issues pertaining to women is given a priority in a feminist approach. Berlin and Kravetz (1981) asserted that social work had an obligation "to design, evaluate, disseminate, and implement powerful responses to eliminating the oppression of women" (p. 449). An important implication is that applied research is of particular value to an agenda aimed at social change. Feminist social workers are encouraged to view program evaluation as an opportunity to pursue such goals relatively free from the caprices of funding sources.

Finally, qualitative research methods have frequently been identified as feminist (although, as indicated in the above discussion, quantitative approaches need not be excluded). Reinharz (1992) has attempted to grapple with the basic questions regarding feminist research along with providing thorough discussions of various methodologies, consistently highlighting the contributions of women.

FUTURE DIRECTIONS

As has been indicated, the social work profession was quick to respond to the challenges of modern feminism. The compatibility between social work and feminist values and goals is evident. The profession's formal documents speak strongly against discrimination of any kind and clearly advocate social change. In the reflexive spirit of feminism, progress toward such lofty goals should be monitored. This discussion of women and social work concludes, therefore, by raising an issue of concern.

A final issue to be raised involves the profession's pursuit of licensure. Social work practice is legally regulated in over 44 states and territories, and third-party vendorship privileges have been awarded to clinical social workers in over 23 states (Thyer & Biggerstaff, 1989). Between 1975 and 1985, the number of social workers whose primary employment was private practice doubled to 7.6 percent; an additional 40.9 percent listed private practice as a secondary job (NASW, 1985). Whatever gain in power the profession has achieved in this venture, the immediate effect, access to the private market, offers no visible benefit to social work's traditional clientele, the disadvantaged.

During the same time period, the profession failed to mount an effective effort to block declassification of social work positions in public welfare systems. As a result, in many states public sector "social workers" are comprised of individuals who have little or no formal social work education. Wagner's (1989) recent analysis of the fate of idealism in the profession suggests detachment from ideals results from upward mobility as well as from burnout. From a feminist perspective, the compatibility of today's social work profession with its own traditional values may be the crucial question.

Women, however diverse, share the common theme of oppression weaved subtly and pervasively through our society. Even though women constitute the majority of our profession and our clientele, it is easy to lose sight of this fact. To fail to recognize oppression is to contribute to its continuation. We must not overlook the importance of gender in our practice and in our profession as we face the future.

REFERENCES

American Psychiatric Association. (1994). *Diagnostic and statistical manual of mental disorders* (4th ed.). Washington, D.C.: Author.

Anastas, J.W., Gibeau, J.L., & Larson, P.J. (1990). Working families and eldercare: A national perspective in an aging America. *Social Work, 35,* 405–411.

Anderson, K. (1988). A history of women's work in the United States. In A.H. Stromberg & S. Harkess (Eds.), *Women working: Theories and facts in perspective* (2nd ed., pp. 25–41). Mountain View, CA: Mayfield.

Atherton, C.R. (1990a). A pragmatic defense of the welfare state against the ideological challenge from the right. *Social Work, 35,* 41–45.

Atherton, C.R. (1990b). Liberalism's decline and the threat to the welfare state. *Social Work, 35,* 163–167.

Attie, I., & Brooks-Gunn, J. (1987). Weight concerns as chronic stressors in women. In R.C. Barnett, L. Biener, & G.K. Baruch (Eds.), *Gender and stress* (pp. 218-254). New York: Free Press.

Austin, D.M. (1983). The political economy of human services. *Policy and Politics, 11,* 343–359.

Avis, J.M. (1987). Deepening awareness: A private study guide to feminism and family therapy. *Journal of Psychotherapy and the Family, 3*(4), 15–46.

Baldwin, S., & Glendinning, C. (1983). Employment, women, and their disabled children. In J. Finch & D. Groves (Eds.), *A labour of love: Women, work and caring* (pp. 53–71). London: Routledge & Kegan Paul.

Bandura, A. (1969). *Principles of behavior modification.* New York: Holt, Rinehart & Winston.

Barusch, A.S. (1994). *Older women in poverty: Private lives and public policies.* New York: Haworth.

Bepko, C. (Ed.). (1991). *Feminism and addiction.* New York: Haworth Press.

Berlin, S., & Kravetz, D. (1981). Women as victims: A feminist social work perspective (Guest Editorial). *Social Work, 36,* 447.

Bernstein, B., & Kane, R. (1981). Physicians' attitudes toward female patients. *Medical Care, 19,* 600–608.

Blau, R.D., & Winkler, A.E. (1989). Women in the labor force: An overview. In J. Freeman (Ed.), *Women: A feminist perspective* (pp. 265–286, 4th ed.). Mountain View, CA: Mayfield.

Bleier, R. (1986). *Science and gender: A critique of biology and its theories on women.* New York: Pergamon.

Blumberg, R.L. (1978). *Stratification: Socioeconomic and sexual inequality.* Dubuque, IA: William C. Brown.

Blumstein, P.W., & Schwartz, P. (1983). *American couples: Money, work, sex.* New York: William Morrow.

Brekke, J.S. (1986). Scientific imperatives in social work research: Pluralism is not skepticism. *Social Service Review, 60,* 538–554.

Briar, K.H., & Ryan, R. (1986). The anti-institution movement and women caregivers. *Affilia, 1,* 20–31.

Bricker-Jenkins, M., & Hooyman, N.R. (Eds.). (1986). *Not for women only: Social work practice for a feminist future.* Silver Springs, MD: National Association of Social Workers.

Bricker-Jenkins, M., Hooyman, N.R., & Gottlieb, N. (Eds.). (1991). *Feminist social work practice in clinical settings.* Newbury Park, CA: Sage.

Burke, V. (1987, July). Welfare and poverty among children. *Congressional Research Service Review, 5.*

Charney, D.A., & Russell, R.C. (1994). An overview of sexual harassment. *American Journal of Psychiatry, 151,* 10–17.

Cherlin, A. (1987). Women and the family. In S.E. Rix (Ed.), *The American women 1987–88: A report in depth* (pp. 67–99). New York: W.W. Norton.

Chesney-Lind, M., & Shelden, R.G. (1992). *Girls, delinquency, and juvenile justice.* Pacific Grove, CA: Brooks/Cole.

Christensen, A.S. (1988). Sex discrimination and the law. In A.H. Stromberg & S. Harkess (Eds.), *Women working. Theories and facts in perspective* (2nd ed., pp. 329–347). Mountain View, CA: Mayfield.

Collins, B.G. (1986). Defining feminist social work. *Social Work, 41,* 214–219.

Comas-Diaz, L., & Greene, B. (1994). *Women of color: Integrating ethnic and gender identities in psychotherapy.* New York: Guilford.

Coverman, S., & Shelley, J. (1986). Changes in men's housework and child care time. *Journal of Marriage and the Family, 48,* 413–422.

Cox, E.O., Parsons, R.J., & Kimboko, P.J. (1988). Social services and intergenerational caregivers: Issues for social work. *Social Work, 33,* 430–434.

Daly, M. (1975). *The church and the second sex.* New York: Harper & Row.

Davies, M.W. (1982). *Woman's place is at the typewriter: Office work and office workers, 1870–1930.* Philadelphia, PA: Temple University Press.

Davis, A. (1981). *Women, race, and class.* New York: Random House.

Davis, L.E., & Proctor, E.K. (1989). *Race, gender and class: Guidelines for practice with individuals, families, and groups.* Englewood Cliffs, NJ: Prentice-Hall.

Davis, L.V. (Ed.). (1994). *Building on women's strengths: A social work agenda for the twenty-first century.* New York: Haworth.

Deaux, K. (1984). From individual differences to social categories: Analysis of a decade's research on gender. *American Psychologist, 39,* 105–116.

Eichler, M. (1988). *Non-sexist research methods: A practical guide.* Boston, MA: Allen & Unwin.

Ehrenreich, B., & Piven, F.F. (1984). The feminization of poverty: When the family wage system breaks down. *Dissent, 31,* 162–170.

Evans, S.M. (1987). Women in twentieth century America: An overview. In S.E. Rix (Ed.), *The American woman 1987–88: A report in depth* (pp. 33–66). New York: W.W. Norton.

Faludi, S. (1992). *Backlash: The undeclared war against American women.* New York: Crown.

Ferrante, C.L., Haynes, A.M., & Kingsley, S.M. (1988). Images of women in television advertising. *Journal of Broadcasting and Electronic Media, 32,* 231–237.

Freeman, M.L. (1990). Beyond women's issues: Feminism and social work. *Affilia, 5,* 72–89.

Frieze, I.H., & Browne, A. (1989). Violence in marriage. In L. Ohlin & M. Tonry (Eds.), *Family violence: Crime and justice: A review of research* (pp. 163–218). Chicago, IL: University of Chicago Press.

Frumkin, M., Martin, P.Y., & Page, W.J. (1987). The future of large public human service organizations. *New England Journal of Human Services, 7*(3), 15–23.

Fuchs, V.R. (1986). Sex differences in economic well-being. *Science, 232,* 459–464.

Gambrill, E. (1983). *Casework: A competency-based approach.* Englewood Cliffs, NJ: Prentice-Hall.

Gilbert, L.A. (1980). Feminist therapy. In A.M. Brodsky & R.T. Hare-Mustin (Eds.), *Women and psychotherapy* (pp. 245–265). New York: Guilford.

Glidden, C.E., & Tracey, T.J. (1989). Women's perceptions of personal versus sociocultural counseling interventions. *Journal of Counseling Psychology, 36,* 54–62.

Goldsmith, M.F. (1989). Proliferating "self-help" groups offer wide range of support, seek physician rapport. *Journal of the American Medical Association, 261,* 2474–2475.

Gomberg, E.S.L. (1982). Historical and political perspective: Women and drug use. *Journal of Social Issues, 38,* 9–23.

Gomberg, E.S.L., & Nirenberg, T.D. (Eds.). (1993). *Women and substance abuse.* Norwood, NJ: Ablex.

Gordon, M.T., & Riger, S. (1989). *The female fear.* New York: Free Press.

Graber, H., Halseth, J., & Korr, W. (1995). *Women working together II: A collection of course outlines on women in social work.* Alexandria, VA: Council on Social Work Education.

Hall, C.M. (1992). *Women and empowerment: Strategies for increasing autonomy.* Bristol, PA: Hemisphere.

Hampton, B., Lambert, F.B., & Snell, W.R. (1986). Therapists' judgments of mentally healthy beliefs for women and men. *Journal of Rational-Emotive Therapy, 4,* 169–179.

Hanmer, J., & Statham, D. (1989). *Women and social work.* Chicago: Lyceum.

Harkess, S. (1988). Directions for the future. In A.H. Stromberg and S. Harkess (Eds.), *Women working: Theories and facts in perspective* (2nd ed., pp. 348–360). Mountain View, CA: Mayfield.

Hartmann, S. (1982). *The home front and beyond: American women in the 1940s.* Boston: Twayne.

Hawkesworth, M.E. (1989). Knowers, knowing, known: Feminist theory and claims of truth. *Signs, 14,* 533–557.

Heinemann, M.B. (1981). The obsolete scientific imperative in social work research. *Social Service Review, 55,* 371–397.

Herman, D. (1989). The rape culture. In J. Freeman (Ed.), *Women: A feminist perspective* (2nd ed., pp. 20–44). Mountain View, CA: Mayfield.

Heschel, S. (Ed.). (1983). *On being a Jewish feminist.* New York: Schocken.

Hopps, J.G. (1989). Securing the future—What will we risk. (Editorial.) *Social Work, 34,* 291–292.

Hudson, W.W. (1982). Scientific imperatives in social work research and practice. *Social Service Review, 56,* 246–258.

Hyde, J.S. (1990). *Understanding human sexuality* (4th ed.). New York: McGraw-Hill.

Ianello, K.P. (1992). *Decisions without hierarchy.* New York: Routledge.

Ivanoff, A., Robinson, E.A.R., & Blythe, B.J. (1987). Empirical clinical practice from a feminist perspective. *Social Work, 32,* 417–423.

Kabacoff, R.I., Marwit, S.J., & Orlofsky, J.L. (1985). Correlates of sex role stereotyping among mental health professionals. *Professional Psychology: Research and Practice, 16,* 98–105.

Kelly, G.F. (1990). *Sexuality today: The human perspective* (2nd ed.). Guilford, CN: Dushkin.

Koss, M.P. (1988). Hidden rape: Sexual aggression and victimization in a national sample of students in higher education. In A.W. Burgess (Ed.), *Rape and sexual assault* (pp. 3–25). New York: Garland.

Kravetz, D., & Jones, L.E. (1981). Androgyny as a standard of mental health. *American Journal of Orthopsychiatry, 51,* 502–509.

Leeder, E. (1994). *Feminist therapy with abuse in families: Bringing in the community.* New York: Springer.

Lerner, A.W., & Wanat, J. (1983). Fuzziness and bureaucracy. *Public Administration Review, 43,* 500–509.

Lipman-Blumen, J. (1984). *Gender roles and power.* Englewood Cliffs, NJ: Prentice-Hall.

Lipsky, M. (1980). *Street-level bureaucracy: Dilemmas of the individual in public services.* New York: Russell Sage Foundation.

Lorber, J. (1986). Dismantling Noah's Ark. *Sex Roles, 14,* 567–580.

Lott, B. (1985). The potential enrichment of social/personality psychology through feminist research and vice versa. *American Psychologist, 40,* 155–164.

McCrea, F.B. (1983). The politics of menopause: The "discovery" of a deficiency disease. *Social Problems, 31,* 111–123.

McGuinness, K., & Donahue, T. (1988). Women in law enforcement. In S.E. Rix (Ed.), *The American woman, 1988–89: A status report.* New York: W.W. Norton.

Milgram, S. (1974). *Obedience to authority: An experimental view.* New York: Harper & Row.

Milkman, R. (1980). Organizing the sexual division of labor: Historical perspectives on "women's work" and the American labor movement. *Socialist Review, 10,* 95–150.

Miller, J.B., & Mothner, I. (1981). Psychological consequences of sexual inequality. In E. Howell & M. Bayes (Eds.), *Women and mental health* (pp. 41–50). New York: Basic Books.

Mirkin, M.P. (1994). *Women in context: Toward a feminist reconstruction of psychotherapy.* New York: Guilford.

Myers, J.K., Weissman, M.M., Tischler, G.L., Holzer, C.E., Leaf, P.J., Orvaschel, H., Anthony, J.C., Boyd, J.H., Burke, J.D., Kramer, M., & Stoltzman, R. (1984). Six-month prevalence of psychiatric disorders in three communities. *Archives of General Psychiatry, 41,* 959–967.

National Association of Social Workers. (1985). *NASW data bank.* Silver Springs, MD: Author.

O'Grady-LeShane, R. (1990). Older women and poverty. *Social Work, 35,* 422–424.

Olson, M.M. (Ed.). (1994). *Women's health and social work: Feminist perspectives.* Binghamton, NY: Haworth.

Palley, M.L. (1987). The women's movement in recent American politics. In S.E. Rix (Ed.), *The American women 1987–88: A report in depth* (pp. 150–181). New York: W.W. Norton.

Parisi, N. (1982a). Exploring female crime patterns: Problems and prospects. In N.H. Rafter & E.A. Stanko (Eds.), *Judge, lawyer, victim, thief: Women, gender roles, and criminal justice* (pp. 111–129). Boston, MA: Northeastern University Press.

Parisi, N. (1982b). Are females treated differently? A review of the theories and evidence on sentencing and parole decisions. In N.H. Rafter & E.A. Stanko (Eds.), *Judge, lawyer, victim, thief: Women, gender roles, and criminal justice* (pp. 205–220). Boston, MA: Northeastern University Press.

Parlee, M.B. (1981). Appropriate control groups in feminist research. *Psychology of Women Quarterly, 7,* 18–31.

Pearce, D., & McAdoo, H. (1981). *Women and children in poverty.* Washington, D.C.: National Advisory Council on Economic Opportunity.

Perlmutter, F.D. (Ed.). (1994). *Women and social change: Nonprofits and social policy.* Washington, D.C.: NASW Press.

Pinderhughes, E. (1983). Empowering for clients and for ourselves. *Social Casework, 64,* 331–338.

Piper, M.H. (1985). The future of social work research. *Social Work Research & Abstracts, 21*(4), 3–11.

Reinharz, S. (1992). *Feminist methods in social research.* New York: Oxford University Press.

Reynolds, L. (1992). As expected, job discrimination claims up sharply. *HR Focus, 69*(10), 1–2.

Rix, S.E. (Ed.). (1987). *The American woman 1987–88: A report in depth.* New York: W.W. Norton.

Rix, S.E. (Ed.). (1988). *The American woman 1988–89: A status report.* New York: W.W. Norton.

Robins, L.N., Helzer, J.E., Weissman, M.M., Orvaschel, H., Gruenberg, E., Burke, J.D., & Regier, D.A. (1984). Lifetime prevalence of specific psychiatric disorders in three sites. *Archives of General Psychiatry, 41,* 949–958.

Rose, H. (1986). Beyond masculinist realities: A feminist epistemology for the sciences. In R. Bleier (Ed.), *Feminist approaches to science* (pp. 57–76). New York: Pergamon.

Rothman, B.K. (1982). *In labor: Women and power in the birthplace.* New York: W.W. Norton.

Rubin, L. (1976). *Worlds of pain: Life in the working class community.* New York: Basic Books.

Russell, D.E. (1982). *Rape in marriage.* Riverside, NJ: Macmillan.

Russo, N.F., & Sobel, S.B. (1981). Sex differences in the utilization of mental health facilities. *Professional Psychology, 12,* 7–19.

Sanders, M., & Rock, M. (1988). *Waiting for prime time: The women of television news.* Urbana, IL: University of Illinois Press.

Sanford, L.T., & Donovan, M.E. (1984). *Women and self-esteem: Understanding and improving the way we think about ourselves.* New York: Penguin.

Sapiro, V. (1990). *Women in American society* (2nd ed.). Mountain View, CA: Mayfield.

Scharf, L. (1980). *To work and to wed: Female employment, feminism, and the great depression.* Westport, CT: Greenwood.

Scheyett, A. (1990). The oppression of caring: Women caregivers of relatives with mental illness. *Affilia, 5,* 32–48.

Scott, A.F., & Scott, A.M. (1975). *One half the people: The fight for woman suffrage.* Philadelphia, PA: Lippincott.

Smith, E.M.J. (1985). Ethnic minorities: Life stress, social support, and mental health issues. *Counseling Psychologist, 13,* 537–579.

Smith, B.E., & Chapman, J.R. (1987). Rape law reform legislation: Practitioners' perceptions of the effectiveness of specific provisions. *Response, 10,* 8.

Smith, S.A., & Tienda, M. (1988). The doubly disadvantaged: Women of color in the U.S. labor force. In A.H. Stromberg & S. Harkess (Eds.), *Women working: Theories and facts in perspective* (pp. 61–80). Mountain View, CA: Mayfield.

Special Issue on Women. (1976). *Social Work, 21,* entire issue.

Stanley, L., & Wise, S. (1993). *Breaking out again: Feminist ontology and epistemology.* New York: Routledge.

Steffensmeier, R. (1984). Suicide and the contemporary woman: Are male and female suicide rates converging? *Sex Roles, 10,* 613–631.

Stewart, D.E., & Cecutti, T. (1993). Physical abuse in pregnancy. *Canadian Medical Association Journal, 149,* 1257–1268.

Stock, W., Graubert, J., & Birns, B. (1982). Women and psychotherapy. *International Journal of Mental Health, 11,* 135–158.

Strom, S.H. (1975). Leadership and tactics in the American Woman Suffrage Movement: A new perspective from Massachusetts. *Journal of American History, 62,* 296–315.

Tangri, S., Burt, M.R., & Johnson, L.B. (1980). Sexual harassment at work: Three explanatory models. *Journal of Social Issues, 38*(4), 33–54.

Tavris, C.B. (1988). *Women and health psychology: Mental health issues.* Hillsdale, NJ: Lawrence Erlbaum Associates.

Thyer, B., & Biggerstaff, M.B. (1989). *Social work credentialing and legal regulation.* Springfield, IL: Charles C Thomas.

U.S. Department of Commerce, Bureau of the Census. (1980). *Current population reports* (#349). Washington, D.C.: U.S. Government Printing Office.

U.S. Department of Commerce, Bureau of the Census. (1987). *A statistical abstract of the United States.* Washington, D.C.: U.S. Government Printing Office.

U.S. Department of Commerce, Bureau of the Census. (1989). *A statistical abstract of the United States.* Washington, D.C.: U.S. Government Printing Office.

U.S. Department of Commerce, Bureau of the Census. (1993). *Current population reports* (Series P23-185). Washington, D.C.: U.S. Government Printing Office.

U.S. Department of Commerce, Bureau of the Census. (1994). *A statistical abstract of the United States.* Washington, D.C.: U.S. Government Printing Office.

U.S. Department of Education. (1994). *Digest of education statistics, 1994.* Washington, D.C.: U.S. Government Printing Office.

U.S. Department of Justice. (1987). *Uniform crime reports for the United States.* Washington, D.C.: U.S. Government Printing Office.

U.S. Department of Labor. (1989). *Employment and earnings* (January, 1989). Washington, D.C.: U.S. Government Printing Office.

U.S. Department of Labor. (1995). *Employment and earnings* (January, 1995). Washington, D.C.: U.S. Government Printing Office.

U.S. elections: Some gains for women. (1993). *WIN News, 19*(1), 68.

Vinton, L. (1992). Women's content in social work curricula: Separate but equal? *Affilia, 7,* 74–89.

Wagner, D. (1989). Fate of idealism in social work: Alternative experiences of professional careers. *Social Work, 34*(5), 389–395.

Walker, A. (1983). Care for elderly people: A conflict between women and the state. In J. Finch & D. Groves (Eds.), *A labour of love: Women, work and caring* (pp. 106–128). London: Routledge & Kegan Paul.

Weiner, L. (1985). *From working girl to working mother: The female labor force in the United States, 1920–1980.* Chapel Hill, NC: University of North Carolina Press.

Weiss, R.S. (1984). The impact of marital dissolution on income and consumption in single-parent households. *Journal of Marriage and the Family, 46,* 115–128.

Weitzman, L.J. (1985). *The divorce revolution: The unexpected social and economic consequences for women and children in America.* New York: Free Press.

Weitzman, L.J. (1988). Women and children last: The social and economic consequences of divorce law reforms. In S.M. Dornbusch & M.H. Strober (Eds.), *Feminism, children, and the new families* (pp. 212–248). New York: Guilford.

Wertheimer, B.M., & Nelson, A.H. (1989). "Union is power": Sketches from women's labor history. In J. Freeman (Ed.), *Women: A feminist perspective* (2nd ed., pp. 312–328). Mountain View, CA: Mayfield.

Witkin, S.L., & Gottschalk, S. (1988). Alternative criteria for theory evaluation. *Social Service Review, 62,* 211–224.

Women in the states: Governors, legislators, candidates. (1994). *Campaigns & Elections, 15*(10), 56.

Wool, H., & Pearlman, L.M. (1947). Recent occupational trends. *Monthly Labor Review, 65,* 139–147.

Chapter 6

SOCIAL WORK PRACTICE WITH THE AGED

Sophia F. Dziegielewski and Dianne Harrison

Introduction

In our society, aging or "old age" is typically accompanied by a unique set of circumstances with which an individual must cope in order to achieve and maintain a satisfactory existence. Most of these circumstances are viewed negatively; namely, declines in physical functioning, changes in physical appearance, loss of income, retirement and loss of partner and/or social supports. Because of some of these circumstances, old age has been defined not only chronologically (age 65) but also in terms of physical and social-psychological factors (Brieland, Costin & Atherton, 1980; Strawbridge, Camacho, Cohen & Kaplan, 1993; Segrin, 1994). This chapter reviews historical developments in the field of aging, current characteristics of this population, and issues relevant for social work practice.

HISTORICAL BACKGROUND

Aging—the "Problem" that Affects Everyone

Aging did not become a popular subject for study among professionals and scientists until the end of the 1930s (Shock, 1987). The eventual attention that elderly individuals attracted was related to three major events: (1) the implementation of the Social Security Act (Axinn & Levin, 1982); (2) the development of a scientific basis for study of the aged (Shock, 1987); and (3) population trends and shifts involving elderly individuals (Rhodes, 1988).

By the end of the 1930s, our country began to experience the aftermath of many major social changes. World War I had come to a close and many individuals had been thrust into poverty as a result of the Great Depression. With so many newly impoverished individuals, an increased

138

willingness by society to help certain disadvantaged groups had surfaced. Many individuals believed that the country had an obligation to help "old people" and "babies" (Frank, 1946). However, even stronger than the desire to help these disadvantaged groups was the work-ethic perspective, where every individual was thought to have the responsibility for being a productive part of society. It was at this time that social workers and the public began to insist that government take the necessary steps to ensure that these disadvantaged groups, and their inability to work, did not cause them to become burdens on society (Axinn & Levin, 1982).

The Social Security Act of 1935 was basically a response to the widespread unemployment crisis caused by the Great Depression which altered the existing income distribution system. As a result of legislation, elderly individuals were now provided with a government-assisted income, as they were considered unemployable (Axinn & Levin, 1982). This guaranteed income helped the elderly to compete in society on an economic basis and brought additional professional and societal attention to this population group.

A second reason for the increased attention given to the concept of the elderly in the late 1930s rests with the development of an improved scientific basis for the study of the aged. By 1942, a publication entitled *Problems of Aging* by E. Cowdry was introduced (cf. Shock, 1987). This book was a collection of contributions made by eminent scientists from many disciplines and represented the first compilation of the existing "scientific data on aging" (Shock, 1987, p. 34).

Following Cowdry's publication, the first edition of the *Journal of Gerontology* was printed in January 1946. This journal was the first in the field of gerontology, or the study of aging. It was designed "to provide a medium of communication and of interpretation in our efforts to gain a much surer knowledge of human growth and development" (Frank, 1946, p. 3). The journal was created as part of the newly formed Gerontological Society whose primary interest was to assist the elderly "against the present almost brutal neglect of the aged, by which many have been misused" (Frank, 1946, p. 3). The journal's founders supported the importance of expanding scientific endeavors to help the aging individual and the belief that human resources should not be wasted, and believed that science and technology could assist in preventing the loss of this valuable labor adage. Since the introduction of these two works to the field of gerontology, a large body of literature has grown which reflects the popularity of aging as an area of study. Professionals such as chemists, physicians, economists, dentists, psychologists, and social workers have all participated in the development of knowledge about the aging population.

The social work profession has a long-standing interest in the topic of aging as evidenced by proceedings from the 1947 National Conference of Social Work, the inclusion of the content on aging issues in the 1949 Social Work Yearbook, the Aspen Conference in 1958, and numerous other workshops, books and articles (Lowry, 1979). Much of this interest originated as the concept of aging became visible as a legitimate domain for scientific study. The problem of aging had been identified.

A third reason for the increased attention given to the concept of the elderly in the late 1930s rested with the population trends and shifts of this group. Interpretations of population statistics relevant to the late 1930s began to show increased numbers of elderly individuals (Axinn & Levin, 1982). The growth of this population caused much concern as they were not basically capable of contributing to the national economy in terms of work (Frank, 1946; Axinn & Levin, 1982). Although programs such as those supported by the Social Security Act continue, they may no longer be sufficient to assist this population group due to the sheer increase in the number of recipients. Given the new democratic administration in Washington, D.C., a sense of cautious optimism has developed, yet our lagging economy continues to limit the possibilities for new programs to address the needs of our elderly population (Morris, 1993).

CURRENT CHARACTERISTICS

Population Trends

Currently, the number of aged individuals continues to rise. Three reasons are suggested for this increase. The first deals simply with the large portion of the population that will be reaching old age. Prior to World War II, large numbers of immigrants came to America. Those who entered the country legally are reflected in the national statistics, yet those whose immigration was illegal are not (MacDonald, 1986). Many of these immigrants (legal or illegal) are now reaching retirement age. This trend will continue to increase, especially as infants born after World War II (often referred to as the "baby boomers," born from

1945–1965) continue to age (MacDonald, 1986; Rhodes, 1988). The baby boom generation is now estimated to constitute approximately 70 million Americans (Butler, 1994).

A second factor related to the growth in the number of aged individuals concerns the number of births in relation to the number of deaths. In recent years, there has been a trend toward less births and less deaths (Rhodes, 1988). It is further predicted that death rates will continue to decline, leaving more aged individuals in society, especially among the "old" old, or those over age 75.

The third and most obvious factor related to the growth of the elderly population rests with the strides that have been made by the scientific community in promoting and understanding the ingredients that lead to longer and healthier life spans (Belsky, 1988; Rhodes, 1988; Mosher-Ashley, 1994). We will review some of these strides in the remainder of this chapter.

Current Population Statistics

In 1950, there were 12.4 million individuals over the age of 65; by 1980, this group had more than doubled in size. Projections for the year 2000 approximate 35 million persons age 65 and over. By the year 2030 it is estimated that there will be 50 million aged persons in the United States, constituting about 20 percent of the entire population (Besdine, 1994; Rhodes, 1988). The proportion of the total population 75 and over is expected to increase disproportionately over the general population well into the twenty-first century. In conjunction with the increase in sheer numbers of elderly individuals, it is estimated that between 1992 and 2040 the non-white elderly population is expected to grow from 3.3 to 14.1 million (Lilienfield & Perl, 1994). Currently, the elderly constitute the fastest-growing age group in the United States.

Who Are the Aged?

As noted earlier, old age has been defined from physical, social-psychological and chronological perspectives. Use of the chronological age cutoff is the most common referent for defining who constitutes an aged person. This age definition began with the Social Security Act of 1935 and was based on the German precedent which established the age of 65 as the appropriate age for benefits to begin (Brieland et al., 1980). At the time the U.S. Social Security Act was initiated, age 65 marked the 95th percentile in the age distribution. By 1986, the percentile rating had dropped to 75 (Wolinsky & Arnold, 1988). In other words, the absolute number of individuals aged 65 and over has increased drastically over time.

Characteristics of the elderly have also changed over time, making this large group less homogeneous. One of the differences in group composition is based on sex. Increased life span and a decrease in the death rate among all individuals have presented particular problems for aged women. "Fifty years ago there was as many males as females at ages 65 and over; since then, there has been a constant reduction in the proportion of men and an increasing proportion of women in the elderly population" (Rhodes, 1988:9). Population estimates suggest that this trend will continue, and, in the year 2000, there will be 64 males per 100 females (Rhodes, 1988).

A second factor limiting the achievement of a homogenous elderly population rests with the diversity of the ages included in this group (Belsky, 1988). Some aged individuals are now living into their nineties. Elderly individuals in their eighties and nineties tend to have significantly more health problems, and it is difficult to combine descriptions of this group with aged individuals in their sixties and seventies. Distinctions have been made which divide these groups into young-old, medium-old, and old-old, simply because of the sheer numbers involved in this population (Rhodes, 1988). For purposes of simplicity, however, we shall use the terms "elderly" and "aged" to refer to all those individuals, including both men and women, 65 years of age or older. In summary, the aged population of all individuals 65 and older is growing in number and living longer. These two trends present issues that will be examined throughout this chapter.

Theories of Aging

Several theories have been described in the gerontological literature which attempt to explain and predict the various outcomes possible for aging individuals. We will discuss two major historical theories, disengagement and activity theories, and their application to the practice of social work.

Disengagement theory was introduced initially by Cumming and Henry (1961) and focused on the "normal" process of withdrawal from the social environment to which the aging person belonged. According to this theory, the aging person initiates withdrawal because of acknowledgement of one's own impending death and reduced physical energy and/or poor health. The process of disengagement is considered beneficial to both the individual and the society. Disengagement benefited the individual by helping to make the natural transition from adhering closely to societal norms to a focus on the self; disengagement facilitated society by physically separating the individual from mainstream life, thus fostering an adjustment period to his or her absence. Disengagement was viewed as an inevitable process that every aging individual must encounter. This theory suggested that if an individual resisted this natural process of "letting go," then problems in adjustment to the elderly years would develop (Cumming & Henry, 1961).

To date, most of the research on disengagement theory has been controversial and conflictive and it remains unclear whether disengagement has any direct relationship to the activity level the elderly individual will engage in after leaving mainstream society (Rhodes, 1988). Studies by Maddox (1964) and Sills (1980) supported the notion that the role elderly individuals assume after disengagement depends on the behavior patterns which they had established over their lifetime. Some individuals do not actively separate and continue to stay engaged by changing the focus of their prescribed activities; further, individuals who do not actively disengage do not always report increased difficulty in transition. Sills (1980) suggests that researchers interested in how disengagement affects the life of the elderly individual focus their attention on measuring how close the elderly individual views his or his own death. He hypothesized that if an individual perceived death to be close, he or she will initiate more of a desire to disengage in the sense that Cumming and Henry originally implied. More research is needed to determine whether or not disengagement is a natural part of the aging process.

A second major theory used to explain and predict the patterns of aging individuals is called activity theory. In activity theory it is assumed that elderly individuals have the same social and psychological needs as middle-aged individuals. Aging is a struggle to remain middle aged; in order for successful aging to be completed, the elderly individual needs to continue involvement similar to what was important in middle age (Lemon, Bengston & Peterson, 1972).

The concepts of activity theory were used prior to the 1961 introduction of disengagement theory; yet, activity theory was not formalized until 1972 with the work of Lemon, Bengston and Peterson. These authors were among the first to test activity theory in relation to reported life satisfaction. It was hypothesized that as activity increased, life satisfaction would also increase; and conversely, as role loss increased, life satisfaction would decrease. Although the Lemon et al. (1972) study did help to formalize the factors related to activity theory into testable hypotheses, it did little to support its general theses (Rhodes, 1988). Additional research is needed to establish a direct link between level of activity and life satisfaction (Hoyt, Kaiser, Peters & Babchuk, 1980).

Human life span developmental theory became popular in the 1970s as a broad-based theory which could take into account the positive aspects and challenges that individuals encounter as they mature in life. In this approach, the personality of an individual is assumed to remain consistent with the manner in which life tasks are developed and managed throughout one's lifetime (Rhodes, 1988). Probably the most comprehensive and widely used work in the area of human development is that of Erikson (1959). Erikson presented and described eight different stages of human development: basic trust vs. mistrust; autonomy vs. shame and doubt; initiative vs. guilt; industry vs. inferiority; identify vs. identity diffusion; intimacy vs. self-absorption; general activity vs. stagnation; and integrity vs. despair. Erikson (1959) believed that once an individual completed all these stages successfully, he/she would gain acceptance of one's self and responsibility for one's own life. In the last developmental stage termed "integrity vs. despair," an individual's life goals reach finalization, and time for reflection and contemplation becomes an important task. Ryff (1982), along with many other authors, expanded on Erikson's last developmental stage by including such tasks as: adjusting to the fact that the elderly person will no longer gain an identity through work; acceptance of the physical limitations brought about by the aging process; and learning to cope with the concept of the meaning of death and acceptance of one's own spirituality.

Rhodes (1988) states that more empirical research is needed to establish the actual utility of the developmental theories. Ryff (1982) argued that research must attempt to isolate the factors that result in accomplishment of the developmental stages and look at what factors actually allow elderly individuals to achieve optimal levels of performance. It is important to add another caution in the adherence to these theories, namely, the apparent middle-class and sexist biases which are present.

Historically, the concepts of disengagement and activity have been viewed as a normal and natural part of the aging process by many individuals in both the professional and lay communities. The development theories, on the other hand, became more popular in the 1970s.

While available research has not supported the validity of these theories as being comprehensive enough to explain all life changes experienced by the elderly (Rhodes, 1988), the influences of these theories to social work practice remain. Social workers need to be aware of these differing views of aging and how these views can affect the elderly individual. Whether these theories are valid or not, the fact that many professionals and lay persons believe them to be true may have an important influence on their expectations and behaviors. Non-critical adherence to these ideas may preclude the use of differing explanations for behaviors and innovative problem-solving techniques.

Unemployment In Relation to the Elderly

Today, the high rate of unemployment in the United States is causing social workers to look seriously at the social and economic problems that can result from being without a job (Rife & Belcher, 1994). This has helped to bring to the attention of the public the specific problems of certain groups of individuals such as older adults (Crown, 1991). Currently, the trend toward early retirement, in conjunction with the diminishing number of youths entering the labor market (as a result of lower birthrates), has attracted growing attention to the elderly as a potential labor source to help supplement this gap. Elderly individuals appear to be an underutilized labor pool that cannot be ignored (Mor-Barak & Tynan, 1993). In addition to this societal need, many elderly individuals can expect to live longer and healthier lives which may make the possibility of employment more desirable. The desire to remain a part of the work force also may be a factor, as supported by an archival study conducted by Mosher-Ashley (1994) on 298 mental health outpatient records. Mosher-Ashley (1994) found that elderly men between the ages of 60 and 98 expressed the loss of the "work role" as a major area of personal concern. Given the general turbulence of these economic times, Duke, Barton and Wolf-Klein (1994) remind us that many individuals, both young and old, may be affected. Therefore, supposedly retired elderly individuals may be called upon to assist their junior family members during periods of economic crisis. This may require the elderly to assume an active role in supporting the family unit and thus return to the work environment.

It is important to note that if an elderly individual decides to return to work, she/he is not guaranteed space in the work force. Even with some types of protective legislation, such as mandatory age-based retirement and re-entry criteria, age discrimination can and does take place (Sterns, Barrett, Czaja & Barr, 1994). Several authors argue that in order for elderly individuals to be able to assume work-role opportunities within the traditional work environment, modifications need to be made (Sterns, Barrett, Czaja & Barr, 1994; Mor-Barak & Turner, 1993).

Sterns et al. (1994) identify three critical situations that must be addressed in order for elderly individuals to be considered desirable and effective employees. First, they must be willing to update or maintain the current skills that will help them remain competitive throughout their careers. This remains a major consideration with the rapid techno-logical advances that are occurring today, as well as the computer and automation technologies that are used in most occupational settings. Learning and maintaining these types of skills can be a frightening prospect to the elderly individual. Therefore, the second area deals with the importance of utilizing human factor approaches which support the continued capability of older workers.

To facilitate the older worker, Mor-Barak and Tynan (1993) make the following suggestions: (1) programs are needed which adjust and accom-modate the needs of the older worker (e.g., work schedule modifications such as sharing between two or more workers, flex-time schedules and reduced workweeks); and (2) linkage programs designed to build worker skills, motivation and self-confidence, provided by either the employer (e.g., in-house programs) or the community (e.g., community-based programs). Programs such as the "job club" described by Rife and Belcher (1994) which utilized a specialized job assistance strategy pro-vide an excellent practice environment in which social work profes-sionals can assist older workers to become re-employed.

The third area presented by Sterns et al. (1994) is the issue of elder care or caregiving assistance that support and allow individuals to con-tinue working. Although several major companies have altered their benefit packages to include elder care provisions, many have not (Tennessee Eldercare Commission, 1994; Sterns et al., 1994; Mor-Barak & Tynan, 1993).

In a recent workshop sponsored by the Tennessee Eldercare Commis-sion (1994), the need for adult day care was continually voiced as a major concern of families who need to maintain employment outside the home. As the birthrate continues to decline and those reaching old age increases, elder care services will become a reality that cannot be avoided for family members to continue in the traditional work setting. Provision of this service can allow elderly individuals and their family members to continue in the work place. All employers are encouraged to embrace this need and consider adding it as a standard option in employee benefit packages.

RETIREMENT

History of Retirement

The aged population and the issue of retirement have been viewed very differently throughout the years, with differing views dependent upon changes in social, emotional, political and cultural climates. To appreciate how the view of retirement has changed, a brief history of the role of the aged in the labor force is presented.

Economic changes in the early twentieth century involved a shift from an agrarian and commercial economy to an urban industrial one (Axinn & Levin, 1982). In the agrarian society, each member of society had their role as part of a cohesive family unit. At this time, the problem of aging and retirement did not exist as we know it today. The family unit was held responsible for meeting all the needs of its individual members, including the needs of elderly family members. Industrialization changed this perspective, establishing different expectations, roles and methods. There was a decline in individual business or farm ownership, a trend which meant that many people had to obtain an income from outside sources (Atchley, 1976).

During the years 1890–1912, one family member often could not make enough money to support the family unit; work outside of the home by all family members, including women, children and the aged, became mandatory (Axinn & Levin, 1982). The inclusion of all these groups into the labor force, however, did not last long. The removal of family members from the work force was affected by two factors: (1) as industrialization increased productivity, fewer workers were needed in the production of output (an economic surplus had been created); and (2) a high new-immigrant rate in the early nineteenth century contributed to the availability of new workers to fill the job market (Morrison, 1982). Women, children and the elderly were no longer needed in the current labor market.

In the 1930s, millions of families became dependent on relief, and the

American people wanted the government to provide help to those in need. Since so many people were now unemployed who had never been before, unemployment became known as a social problem rather than a personal one. It was in this era that elderly individuals began to receive attention from the public. Morrison (1982) relates this increased attention to a growing elderly population and the possibility that this population growth might create competition for limited jobs with younger workers.

The Social Security Act of 1935 proved to be a major first step in government acknowledging responsibility toward assisting the elderly to acquire an income without actual participation in the labor market. The Social Security Act "set up a national system of old age insurance" which legitimized retirement at age 65" (Morrison, 1982:9). This pension act supported limited, although permanent, economic stabilizers for both elderly individuals and the enterprise system.

Over the years, social security has affected the aged in two ways: (1) retirement benefits moderate the reduction in income that workers must face when they retire, providing incentives for elderly individuals to choose leisure instead of work; and (2) social security may help to condition workers and employees that 65 is the normal retirement age (Morrison, 1982). In viewing the history of retirement, the conditions necessary for its inception had been achieved.

Current Perspectives on Retirement

In considering retirement as a role in the 1990s, social workers need to be aware of the following aspects of retirement and how these aspects can affect the aged individual. The definition and treatment of the aged individual is created and influenced by society. Most things that happen in society are complex reflections of what is, what has been, and the individual desires that motivate their introduction, intervention and discovery. The lives of the aged have not radically changed over the last fifty years; what has changed, however, is our view of the elderly and how this view has been acted on by society.

Over the short span of forty years, retirement has become an important concern for the American people; almost every day, articles and commentaries appear in publications throughout the country on the economic, social and psychological consequences of retirement. It is clear that this interest in retirement has been heightened primarily because of the rising cost of public and private retirement benefits and serious concern as to whether these costs can be afforded in the future (Morrison, 1985). As the "baby boomers" approach retirement age, there is the specific concern about the ability of the Social Security system to handle the anticipated growth in the number of retirees.

Social work intervention can assume a critical part in helping the aged individual complete a successful transition from the role of the worker to the new role of retiree. It is important, however, that the social worker clearly communicate to elderly clients his/her role in the delivery of services, as sometimes the provision of this type of service may be poorly understood (Scharlach, Mor-Barak & Birba, 1994). Counseling and assistance provided by the social worker can benefit in helping aged individuals plan for the role adjustments that will occur. In facing retirement, it is important to note that many aged individuals gain their status or identity through working (Mosher-Ashley, 1994). Many individuals enjoy the work they do and may not want to give it up, as they derive both internal and external rewards from it. Some elderly can afford to retire but choose not to because of the values placed on working for money in this society (Davidson & Kunze, 1979). Ekerdt (1986) suggested that the importance of the work ethic in our society should not be underestimated. He pointed out that it is important for the elderly reaching retirement to plan their leisure time as carefully as they planned their work time, and avoidance of this type of preparation may lead to decreased self-esteem. Social workers need to be sensitive to this issue and help elderly individuals find activities other than work that can help them adjust to this change.

In planning leisure time, the degree and type of activity that the individual can perform (and afford) must be considered. Social workers can assist elderly clients in creating a list of all positive options and discuss each of these options in a problem-solving, decision-making approach. Once the appropriate leisure activity has been chosen, individual contracts may be developed. The contracting of leisure-time activity can help give permission to engage in and to provide structure in approaching an otherwise ambiguous time period in the life of the elderly.

Another reason why elderly individuals may find the concept of retirement difficult stems from the decrease in financial assets that frequently occurs. Financial motives may deter an individual from entering retirement (Davidson & Kunze, 1979). Fear of not having enough income or being inundated with numerous medical bills and having difficulty securing health insurance may cause the elderly person to avoid facing retirement. Social workers need to be aware of the resources that will be available to the elderly individual and to help the individual in obtaining adequate financial counseling. Places of employment often will provide such counseling upon request. For securing information regarding health and life insurance, insurance brokers can be consulted. These individuals are generally able to discuss numerous policy options, as they are capable of underwriting policies for several different companies.

Social workers need to be aware when conducting retirement counseling that there is often resistance to change (Davidson & Kunze, 1979). Many individuals fear change and avoid what they cannot predict. They may have grown comfortable in their careers and achieved a sense of consistency with respect to job patterns being part of their lives. Elderly individuals need to be made aware of options that will be available to them in retirement, especially in regard to leisure activities.

Pre-retirement services offered to prospective retirees is an area of social work intervention that should probably be expanded. The rationale for such expansion rests with the facts that: (1) many individuals who are preparing to retire avoid or do not engage in this type of planning (Rhodes, 1988); and (2) in current social work practice, few pre-retirement services are generally offered (Montana, 1985). Most social work interventions in this area are generally after the fact and supportive in nature. Montana (1985) stated that pre-retirement counseling is necessary because it can help elderly individuals increase interpersonal acceptance while decreasing the anxiety of what retirement will bring. Social workers need to take a more active role in pre-retirement counseling by making aged individuals aware of its importance, as well as how to plan for the future and what to expect (e.g., what benefits are available, and so on). The attitude an elderly individual has toward retirement can be very important in determining the degree of life satisfaction that is obtained during retirement (Rhodes, 1988).

HEALTH AND AGING

Based on findings from a national interview survey, the National Council on Aging (1981) reported that health concerns were considered of primary importance by the elderly. The aged used hospital services, physician services and long-term care services more than any other age group (Rhodes, 1988), thus making health issues related to the elderly a significant concern in the United States today. In an archival study conducted on 298 clients treated by a mental health center, three types of issues predominated among elderly clients: (1) family conflicts, (2) poor physical health, and (3) feeling as if they were not in control of their lives (Mosher-Ashley, 1994).

Normal Versus Abnormal Aging

There are two general terms that are often used to describe elderly within the medical community. The first term, *aging,* is generally defined as the condition of growing old regardless of chronologic age; where the second, *senescence,* is generally restricted to term of old age characteristic of the later years within a life span (Peterson, 1994). The process of normal aging can be divided into two types: (1) intrinsic aging, which refers to the characteristics and processes that occur to all elderly of a given gender; and (2) extrinsic aging, the factors that influence aging in varying degrees which can affect individuals differently (e.g., life-style patterns and exposure to environmental influences). "Normal aging is therefore defined as the sum of intrinsic aging, extrinsic aging, and idiosyncratic or individual genetic factors in each individual" (Peterson, 1994, p. 46). One of the myths about aging is that "all older people are alike" and, therefore, predictable patterns of age-related behavior should occur. However, this has not been proven; if anything the opposite appears true "as people get older they are less alike" (Peterson, 1994, p. 46).

A term often used when describing the age-disease relationship is senility or senile. Generally, this term has limited professional use but is quite often used within the lay community (Peterson, 1994). Unfortunately, many of the aged in our society are stereotyped with the label "senile"; therefore, the elderly person may be labeled by peers, family and friends as "demented" or "insane." Some individuals believe that the normal aging process affects an elderly person's competency or ability to perform self-care. Research has not supported this notion; in fact, changes in memory and other intellectual capacities are relatively mild when there is no dementia illness present (Zarit, Orr & Zarit, 1985). Older but healthy individuals can retain and retrieve as much information as younger persons can, even if the process of retrieval is slower (Corvea, 1987). The skills that seem to remain the strongest as individuals age are verbal skills such as reading, writing, word usage and arithmetic (Corvea, 1987). It is important to remember when looking at normal versus abnormal aging that any changes related to normal aging are relatively mild in nature.

Intelligence Testing

"From childhood we have been taught to judge old people by a harsher mental standard, seeing evidence of confusion in even benign mistakes" (Belsky, 1988, p. 33). When an elderly person forgets something, we are more likely to stereotype the etiology as senility; we also tend to rely on standardized measurements of intelligence which generally do not allow for the inclusion of life experience. In our society, everyday survival is not based on making clear-cut choices between right and wrong solutions. In many situations, elderly individuals need to be able to make best choices, those which allow for the achievement of the maximum amount of life satisfaction possible. Unfortunately, intelligence tests generally do not do this (Belsky, 1988), and, for the aged person, who has been away from the academic setting for some time, relying strictly on the results of intelligence testing may lead to false conclusions. If intelligence testing or other cognitive measurement is the goal of the professional, it is suggested that a battery of tests be used which provide the researcher with the capacity to measure the more global skills needed for life success (Corvea, 1987), deemphasizing the importance of right and wrong answers.

The Myth of Dying of Old Age

How many times have you heard an individual describe the death of an aged loved one as stemming from old age? How many times have you heard professionals support this notion? How many times have you seen or heard of an elderly person seeking medical attention from a physician about a certain ache or pain, only to be told the pain is simply related to old age? To illustrate this point, suppose an elderly male visits a physician for pain in the elbow joint of his right arm. The physician offers the client no explanation for this pain, attributing its origin to old age. If this explanation is to be considered tenable, why doesn't the elderly client's other elbow hurt? After all, it is the same age.

Dying of old age is a myth, and it is important for all professionals to give elderly clients the respect they deserve by not encouraging this type of practice. No one has ever died of old age. There are many causes of illness in the elderly, including such serious conditions as heart disease, cancer and stroke (Rhodes, 1988), but death due to these and other causes should not be quickly and carelessly referred to as death related to **old age.** It is unfortunate that the diagnosis of many diseases of the respiratory system may go undetected because relevant symptoms characteristic of the disease may be related by both the client and the physician to the aging process itself (Anderson & Williams, 1989). Elderly individuals deserve the same professional treatment considerations as other age groups, and as social workers we have a role in educating and assisting elderly individuals in securing the health services they need in relation to their specific health concerns.

Chronic Conditions

Health issues considered important by aged individuals can be divided into two types: physical and mental health concerns. "Probably no factor is of more immediate concern to older persons than physical health" (Brody & Brody, 1987, p. 99). Many elderly fear the loss of individual unaided activity or perceived independence. The U.S. Special Committee on Aging (1982) reported that 45 percent of elderly individuals 65 and older experience some limitation of activity due to some type of chronic condition. This percentage is much higher than other age groups; for example, 23 percent of 45–64-year-olds reported some type of limitation of activity.

A chronic condition is generally defined as a disease that is of long duration, constituting a long drawn-out progression (*Taber's Cyclopedic Medical Dictionary,* 1977). An acute condition, on the other hand, generally has a rapid and severe onset that lasts for a short duration (*Taber's Cyclopedic Medical Dictionary,* 1977). Elderly individuals are most often affected by chronic as opposed to acute conditions. Acquiring a chronic condition is generally the elderly person's worst fear, because this type of condition often results in a loss of activity or unaided mobility (Rhodes, 1988).

Chronic conditions found in the elderly are either of a physical (biological/physiological) or mental health (psychological) nature. Although this distinction is made for simplicity's sake, it is important to note that physical and mental health conditions are often related and interdependent. For example, a physical (physiological) condition such as a stroke may develop into a mental health (psychological) condition known as dementia.

Physical Health Conditions

Of all the physical health conditions, heart disease is the leading cause of death among those 65 and older (Anderson & Williams, 1989), followed closely by cancer and stroke, respectively (Rhodes, 1988, p. 23). Although these conditions (excluding cancer) are generally considered acute, patients often gradually fall prey to chronic conditions such as paralysis and mental impairment resulting in some type of dementia (Crichton, 1987). Specifically, arthritis and hypertensive diseases are the most prominent chronic conditions among men and women 65 and older (Brody & Brody, 1987). Other major chronic conditions that result in the restriction of activity include rheumatism and hearing and vision impairments.

Vision impairment is a major physical health condition that often occurs in the elderly. As an individual ages, the lenses of the eyes become less elastic because of the accumulation of fibers. This decrease in elasticity leaves the retina and the optic nerve less sensitive, resulting in difficulty adjusting to different levels of light. It may take the elderly person longer for his or her eyes to adjust when entering from a dark to a lighted room. Glaucoma is a condition that occurs when the channels of aqueous material draining from the eye become blocked; as a result, increasing pressure causes the decay of the optic nerve (Belsky, 1988). Cataracts develop when the lens becomes scarred and an opacity results that does not allow light to enter.

When working with elderly clients who suffer from vision impairment, the following two suggestions should be considered. First, social workers should always encourage clients to receive regular checkups to aid in detecting conditions such as cataracts and glaucoma before permanent damage results. Second, it is important for social workers to consider how decreased vision can affect the counseling relationship. Safford (1988) has pointed out that individuals are often shocked and embarrassed by the changes in health they are experiencing, and these feelings of shock and embarrassment may lead to denial. An elderly individual may not want to admit that they cannot easily see to read or interpret what is happening around them, because admitting a vision deficit would mean admitting individual inadequacy. Counseling and interviewing should provide initial assessment to determine whether vision decrease is affecting the interview process. This can be done by simply asking the client if they are having any difficulties and explaining that vision decrease is often a normal part of aging. Questions such as, "When did you have your last vision checkup?" and "When did you purchase your last pair of eyeglasses?" can be asked while gathering information for completion of a routine health history. Family members and significant others who associate with the client on a daily basis can serve as important contributors in obtaining a client's health history.

The physical deficit of decreased hearing ability or hearing loss can occur at any age and not necessarily with age, although the probability does become more likely (Belsky, 1988). In our society, however, many professionals have the misconception that all hearing problems can be corrected by simply getting a hearing aid. Unfortunately, this is not always the case. If it is determined that a hearing loss is related to auditory nerve damage where sound is not carried to the brain, no correction can be made. In this case, a hearing aid is not an option. If, however, the bones of the ear are frozen, a blockage would occur. In this case, a hearing aid could provide relief. It is important to note that testing needs to be conducted by an audiologist before any determinations can be made.

Hearing loss presents a particular problem when working with the aged, because elderly individuals often deny having a hearing loss. A withdrawn individual who does not seem to respond to conversation may simply be suffering from a hearing loss or the individual may only be hearing part of what is said and hypothesizing what they could not hear. If the response is not appropriate, it may be interpreted as confusion. Denial, by the elderly individual, of the inability to hear what is being said may be particularly frustrating for family members. Family members may believe the aged relative is becoming confused and/or simply ignoring them, and confusion in the elderly tends to increase the stress felt by family members toward their aged relative (Smallegan, 1985).

When conducting the clinical interview with a suspected hearing-impaired client, the social worker should be aware that as an individual ages, higher frequency sounds become more difficult to hear and lower frequency sounds become more pronounced (Belsky, 1988). If a social worker tries to interview an aged client in a room that has a great deal of background noise, which is generally low frequency, the client may have a great deal of difficulty concentrating. This noise, while very distracting to the aged client, can go virtually unnoticed by the social worker completing the interview. When dealing with elderly hearing-impaired individuals, environmental manipulation becomes crucial for effective interviewing. Settings should be chosen which allow the maximum benefits to be obtained from the interview process by limiting all background noise and distractions.

Mental Health Conditions

Depression is considered a common mental health problem of the elderly, one that is frequently associated with physical symptoms and illness (Rhodes, 1988). However, there is little consensus among researchers regarding the prevalence of this condition and how to recognize this condition in the aged (Ban, 1987; Reynolds, Small, Stein & Teri, 1994). According to Belsky (1988), who interpreted the results of various community surveys, anywhere from five to fifty percent of the elderly population suffer from some level of depression; this is further classified into approximately 15–20 percent of the elderly who reside in the community (Reynolds et al., 1994). Depression is often treatable, and the existence of this condition in the elderly is unfortunate, as few elderly actually seek treatment for this or any other mental health condition (Maldonado, 1987; Belsky, 1988). It is believed that the condition of depression is related to the disproportionately high suicide rate found among the aged population (Ban, 1987; Perkins & Tice, 1994).

Common signs and symptoms of depression include feelings of sadness, loneliness, guilt, boredom, marked decrease or increase in appetite, lack or increase in sleep behavior, and a sense of worthlessness (American Psychiatric Association, 1994). When the etiology of depression is related to life circumstances, it is generally considered situational in nature. Situational depression presents a particular problem for the elderly because they generally endure many tragic life experiences including the loss of loved ones, jobs, status, independence and other personal disappointments. When dealing with situational depression, social work intervention and counseling can provide the elderly individual with the ability to achieve greater life satisfaction.

Social workers can assist elderly individuals suffering from situational depression by teaching them to control the frequency of their depressive thoughts. Relaxation techniques such as imagery and deep muscle relaxation can be utilized to help clients calm down during anxious times. Concrete problem solving and behavioral contracting can be implemented to help the elderly individual change problem behaviors. Whenever possible, family members should be included in treatment contracting to provide support and to assist in recording and observing behaviors that the elderly client is seeking to change.

Depression, however, is not always situational or reactive; it also can be related to biological causes (and sometimes labeled as endogenous depression). The etiology of depression is not always clear and may result from a combination of situational and internal factors. For example, many chronic medical conditions often found in the elderly are accompanied by depression. Some of these conditions include hypothyroidism, Addison's disease, idiopathic parkinsonism and congestive heart failure. It is also possible that symptoms of depression may be the by-products or side effects of medications being taken for another condition (Belsky, 1981). The American Psychiatric Association (1994) has warned that the diagnosis of depression in the elderly can be particularly problematic, as the symptoms of dementia in the early stages and the condition of depression are very similar. Symptoms such as loss of interest and pleasure in one's usual activities, disorientation and memory loss are common in both. Although many of the same signs and symptoms can exist in both cases, usually the individual suffering from early stages of dementia will not improve as a result of treatment.

In work with elderly clients who are believed to be suffering from depression, social workers should gather as detailed a medical and medication history as possible. Depressed elderly clients should always be referred for a medical exam to rule out any physical reasons for depressive symptoms. Although depression remains a problem that is often left unrecognized by professionals, when implemented, treatment for depression in the elderly can be as effective as that with other age groups (Reynolds et al., 1994).

Dementia. Within our culture, the type of mental disability known as dementia is acknowledged to be the most devastating and debilitating condition affecting the aged (Steur & Clark, 1982; Corvea, 1987). Approximately one million elderly individuals suffer from this chronic condition (Steur & Clark, 1982). Dementia can lead to death, and it remains the fourth leading cause of death for those aged 65 and older (Rosenwaike, Yaffe & Sagi, 1980). Specifically, in the case of mental impairment related directly to dementia, confusion, which is characteristic of this disease, generally precipitates admission to long-term care facilities (Dziegielewski, 1991; Smallegan, 1985); it is estimated that between 30 and 50 percent of all institutionalized elderly suffer from some type of dementia (Plum, 1979).

This disease is particularly problematic because it can affect an individual's functional independence, requiring that every need be met by others. The American Psychiatric Association (1994) described the essential feature of this condition as a loss of intellectual abilities of a sufficient nature to interfere with social or occupational functioning, thus limiting an individual's judgment, abstract thought, intelligence, and orientation.

Unfortunately, the term "dementia" has been used as a type of catch-all phrase when related to the elderly. In the professional community, there has not always been an attempt to diagnose or differentiate which type of dementia an individual is suffering. Possible reasons for this include: (1) the elderly person is sometimes viewed as hopeless, helpless and unworthy of careful evaluation and treatment (Eisdorfer & Cohen, 1978); (2) the general treatment approach for dementia is to treat symptoms as they appear since remedial treatments and a cure are not available (Corvea, 1987); (3) a definite diagnosis cannot be made until the person dies and a brain autopsy is performed (Kahn & Miller, 1978; Corvea, 1987); and (4) the term dementia, as linked to organic brain syndrome or organic mental disorders, can include many different types of organic mental disorders, and little attempt has been made to desig-nate these disorders by site of lesion or location of the most dramatic atrophy (Hussian, 1981). Conditions such as dementia of the Alzheimer's type (DAT) and vascular dementia, previously referred to as multi-infarct dementia (MID), are often linked together, although the etiology for both are different (American Psychiatric Association, 1994). DAT generally has a gradual deterioration for which there is no known cure. DAT has been linked to genetic, viral, and biochemical factors (Corvea, 1987), yet the cause remains unclear. Vascular dementia is generally characterized by small repeated strokes or infarcts in the brain. Frequently, these strokes or infarcts are so small that there are no overt symptoms at the time they occur. Occasionally, a major stroke may result, involving paralysis or other impairments (Zarit, Orr, & Zarit, 1985).

The differential diagnosis of dementia, although often neglected and avoided, is important. Professionals who seek early and improved diagno-sis of these elderly individuals can contribute to increased understanding and perhaps a cure, if one becomes available. In the case of DAT, in all likelihood, the destructive process and its accompanying clinical deterio-ration will proceed despite the professional's efforts (Wells, 1977). However, if the condition is vascular related, anti-hypertensive medication and anticoagulants can be administered early in the course of the disease, preventing the occurrence of additional small strokes and further mental deterioration (Roth, 1981).

Social workers need to be aware of the different forms of dementia and the signs and symptoms this progressive disease presents. We have the unique opportunity to educate and provide counseling and support for elderly individuals suffering from dementia and to provide support and education to their families and caregivers, thereby increasing support networks for all involved (Dziegielewski, 1990; Dziegielewski, 1991). In general, when assessing the problems an elderly individual is suffering, it is essential to remember: (1) it is important to help elderly individuals stay as active, independent, and psychologically stable as possible (Beck, Freedman & Warshaw, 1994); (2) keep assessment time and/or evaluations as brief as possible and establish changes in behavior that have occurred over time (Beck et al., 1994); and (3) never forget the importance of including the perceptions of family members or those in the immediate support system (Beck et al., 1994; Dziegielewski, 1990).

Medication Use and Misuse

The use and misuse of prescription medication can present particular problems for elderly individuals and is an area in which social work professionals need to keep informed. Medication prescribed to an elderly individual may react differently than if the same medication and dosage were given to a younger person. Elderly individuals often have slower metabolic rates, possibly related to decreased activity or physiological losses (Belsky, 1988). Medications taken to treat chronic conditions, such as arthritis, ulcers, heart conditions and hypertension, can cause depression when taken alone or with other medications (Safford, 1988). Commonly prescribed medications also can present side effects such as irritability, sexual dysfunction, memory lapses and/or a general feeling of tiredness (Harrison, 1986).

Elderly individuals often take numerous medications and are given multiple prescriptions. When taking more than one medication, the number of side effects and contraindications increases dramatically. Frequently, elderly individuals see more than one physician and each one may not be aware of what the other has prescribed. When taking multiple prescriptions, it is not uncommon for these individuals to simply forget and eat or drink prohibited foods that can lead to a toxic drug reaction. The problem of remembering what medications an individual is taking is further complicated by the number of medications being taken. Elderly individuals who take many medications daily are more likely to forget whether or not they took them (Rost & Roter, 1987; Wolfe, Hope and Public Citizen Health Research Group, 1993).

It is of utmost importance for social workers to be aware of the medications that the elderly client is taking. The side effects of these medications should be explored and examined in relation to whether or not they are affecting the social or interpersonal problems being presented by the individual. Before beginning any type of intervention, the social worker needs to explore whether the symptoms exhibited might be medication-related.

Overview of Physical and Mental Health Issues

The fear of activity loss, as well as the actual occurrence of such loss, are areas that should be addressed by social workers. Since many elderly individuals suffer from chronic conditions, the probability of the condition getting better is unlikely. We have a tendency in our society to deny that problems may be terminal. Family members, and some professionals, may tell aged individuals that the condition will get better, rather than helping the individual develop ways to cope with the existing condition.

It is important for social work practitioners to be knowledgeable of these chronic conditions, knowing the signs and symptoms and the expected progression of various diseases. Further, there is considerable evidence to support the importance of involvement and support of elderly individuals by family members in creating a general sense of well-being in the elderly individual (e.g., Rubinstein, Lubben, & Mintzer, 1994; Dziegielewski, 1990, 1991). Therefore, the role of the social worker remains essential in educating aged clients and family members to cope with and understand changes that will occur. A comprehensive assessment of the individual, taking into account health conditions and environmental factors, becomes critical.

UTILIZATION OF HEALTH CARE SERVICES

Societal Concerns Regarding Health

"In 1980, approximately 10.7 million persons over age 65 experienced some limitation. By the year 2000, this number will increase to 16.3 million and will reach 31.7 million by 2050" (Brody & Brody, 1987, p.

99). Of all the individuals who suffer from some type of health limitation, elderly individuals account for at least one third of the nation's health expenditures. They are more frequently hospitalized and have more costly hospital stays (Specht & Craig, 1982). The elderly make up 12 percent of the total population of the United States, but they actually account for 30 percent of the nation's annual health care costs (McCullough & Cody, 1993).

Hospital Care Utilization

In 1965, Title XVII (Medicare) was implemented to provide health insurance for the elderly, a high-risk group in terms of vulnerability to illness and poverty (Axinn & Levin, 1982). Medicare was one of the amendments to the Social Security Act of 1935. As an individual ages, the use of all health care services increases; however, a dramatic increase has been noted in the use of hospital services since 1965. Davis (1975) found that an increase in hospital admissions of the elderly did take place once the Medicare program was implemented. Rhodes (1988) linked the increase in hospital usage by the elderly to the implementation of the Medicare program.

With the implementation of the Medicare program, many elderly could afford health care that they could not afford previously; physicians and hospitals also benefited, as greater flexibility in providing needed health care services was secured. However, the concessions gained by health care recipients and providers became particularly problematic for the federal government because it was denied any leverage to control costs. As costs and services continued to escalate, the government acquired an independent interest to control costs (Starr, 1982). In 1983, Congress mandated a radical change in the payment structure for hospital care to rescue the Hospital Insurance Trust Fund from imminent bankruptcy (Lee, Forthofer & Taube, 1985). The original system, fee for service, required Medicare to pay whatever hospitals charged for a particular service. Many of the same services were costing different amounts, depending on who provided the services. The government wanted to achieve some regulation, and in an attempt to do so, the payment system based on diagnostic related groups (DRGs) was developed (Begly, 1985).

The DRG system was created to produce an equitable payment scale across all hospitals. In this system, elderly recipients were grouped together who had similar conditions and resources. These groups made up the hospital product called the case mix. Information was gathered and the short-term hospital cases were measured. These cases were classified into units called DRGs. Three classes of DRGs were designated: surgical, medical and psychiatric. Each diagnostic category was designated with a particular length of stay (e.g., gallbladder removal, 7 days).

This new system presented several problems for the elderly. First, since the DRG payment schedule was fixed, hospitals knew how much money they would receive for each individual. This provided little incentive for hospitals to treat individuals who might extend beyond the current average number of allowable days for a particular diagnosis. In this way, hospitals were given incentives to avoid or refuse to accept patients who might require an extended stay. Unfortunately, elderly individuals, who generally tend to have chronic or complicating conditions, can be highly affected by this practice. If a hospital accepts this type of patient and the hospital stay is longer than the allowable DRG days, the hospital might be motivated to discharge this patient as quickly as possible. This presents two problems for the elderly: (1) many of the ill elderly are of low income and have minimal supports in the community for extended care assistance (Blazyk & Canavan, 1985); and (2) many are being discharged to nursing homes in sicker condition than they were previously. Nursing home social workers have complained about the increase in serious illnesses which their new patients are suffering. Nursing staff are also stressed, as these new patients require much more care and observation. In many cases, increases in staff have not occurred to accommodate the additional needs of these new patients. At times, readmission, which is costly for the individual and the hospital, is required (Berkman & Abrams, 1987).

DRG limitations can cause particular problems for social workers as they generally handle the discharge and placement options for elderly individuals in both nursing home and hospital settings. Social workers must be aware of the community supports for discharges back into the community and the availability of any special treatments or services. Family members and care-givers need to be aware of the medical condition of the elderly, including signs, symptoms and how to deal with emergency situations. Education about the needed medical treatment can generally be handled by the physician or the home health care nurse. However, responsible social work practice requires initiating this process and ensuring that it has been completed.

Discharging elderly individuals who are sicker because of limited DRG days may place additional stress on the family and/or extended care staff. In discharges back into the community, family stress is often viewed as a major contributing factor to long-term care admission (Pratt, Wright & Schmall, 1987). Measures should be taken to allow families to communicate needs, problem solve, and have available support groups. Social workers provide an excellent entry point for supportive and educational services for both elderly individuals and caregivers. The admission of an elderly client who needs a great deal of individual care to a long-term care facility can create stress for the staff as well. Support groups and regular in-service training on how to treat these individuals becomes mandatory. If additional staff is needed to facilitate placement, recommendations for such support should be made.

Utilization of Mental Health Services

Elderly individuals suffer many life stresses including widowhood, social and occupational losses, and physical health problems which are often of a progressive nature. It would seem logical that they would also seek more mental health services than other population groups; however, this is not the case (Maldonado, 1987; Rhodes, 1988). Actually, elderly individuals use mental health services at less than half the rate of the general population (Maldonado, 1987). When living in the community, elderly psychiatric clients generally go to community mental health centers for checkups and medication. However, many elderly individuals will not use these available services if it requires leaving the home (Sherwood, Morris & Ruchlin, 1986). This refusal or absence of services is unfortunate; while many elderly are well adjusted mentally, the life stressors they experience could be addressed in a counseling relationship which provides the elderly client with a preventive and supportive atmosphere.

A second issue in regard to utilization of mental health services deals with the admission of many mentally impaired elderly to long-term care facilities. This trend has continued to increase as a result of deinstitutionalization; over the past 33 years, state mental hospitals have shrunk to one-third their former size (Talbot, 1988). In the last 30 years, many privately run long-term care facilities, including adult congregate living facilities (boarding homes), and intermediate and skilled level care nursing homes, have been opened. The number of nursing homes alone have tripled in the United States during this time period (Booth, 1985). These homes provide a discharge option for mentally impaired elderly clients that other population groups do not have. Most of the patients admitted to extended care facilities are over age 65. Several authors (Dobelstein & Johnson, 1985; Lusky, 1986; Diamond, 1986) have suggested that old-age homes are convenient but inappropriate placement options for the mentally impaired elderly, as old-age homes generally do not provide mental health services (Swan, 1987). Talbot (1988) argued that, according to the President's Commission on Mental Health, very few long-term care facilities provide psychosocial interventions, and medication is heavily emphasized as the sole method of treatment. Social workers need to question the practice of using the long-term care setting as a placement for the mentally impaired elderly. It is important to note that while each facility is different, it cannot be assumed that mental health services will be provided. Social workers need to be aware not only of what long-term facilities exist in an area but the services that these facilities can offer to the mentally impaired elderly client.

SEXUALITY AND AGING

Many men and women fear that aging will eventually prohibit them from having sexual intercourse and, in this society, old age is often related to sexlessness (Kelly & Rise, 1986). These current societal attitudes often cause the sexual needs of the elderly individual to be ignored by family, friends, peers, caregivers and society in general (Hodson & Skeen, 1994). These attitudes can extend from a variety of possible sources. The first source is related to the Victorian ethic of productivity and procreation as a means of establishing the worth of individuals. Since elderly people can no longer procreate, they often become members of the sexually oppressed in our society (Gochros, Gochros & Fischer, 1986).

A second source of bias rests with our own fears of growing old and the importance of separating from the elderly; this need and desire for separation may support the development of stereotypes of the elderly to create distance and distinct differences between the young and old. Another source of our attitudes toward the elderly simply rests with inadequate or misinformation regarding the effects aging actually has on the sexual functioning of elderly individuals. To examine sexuality among the aged, we must first expand the definition of sexuality from simply penile-vaginal intercourse and reproduction to include the broader notions of sensuality, intimacy, and sexual identity (Gochros et al., 1986). We should also recognize that in our society the concept of physical love being related to romantic love, to youth, beauty and passion, is an enduring one. Many individuals further believe that in order for sexual behavior to be truly satisfying, intercourse must involve an erect penis and a well-lubricated vagina and result in rapid orgasmic responses. Most experts do not support these notions (Leiblum & Pervin, 1980; Belsky, 1988; Rhodes, 1988), and many elderly individuals report satisfactory sexual experiences can and do exist (Hodson & Skeen, 1994; Kelly & Rice, 1986).

When dealing with sexuality issues among elderly clients, the first obstacle social workers must face involves dispelling the folk myths that permeate our society regarding the sexual habits of the elderly. The best way to dispel these myths is through education and instruction in the actual changes an elderly individual may experience in terms of sexuality. The belief that aging individuals are either physically unable or uninterested in having sexual intercourse is a myth. While there are several physical changes that do occur with aging, these changes alone do not have to interfere with satisfying sexual experiences.

In the aging male, there are several normal physical changes that generally occur. The first is that erections in elderly males occur less spontaneously and require more time and effort to develop. Males beyond age 50 may not be able to immediately obtain an erection without direct stimulation. Second, older males also tend to lose their erections more easily, may require continued stimulation for maintenance, and possibly only obtain a full erection moments prior to ejaculation (Belsky, 1988). Third, it becomes increasingly difficult as a man ages to be able to ejaculate more than one time during a particular encounter. Masters and Johnson (1966) found that most men past the age of sixty report having only one to two climaxes per week. However, since pressure (from partner or self) to ejaculate is often reduced (Kelly & Rice, 1986), it is possible that the aged male may be able to maintain the erection for a longer period of time without ejaculation (Belsky, 1988). This experience may be more pleasurable for both partners.

Many elderly males fear the common misconception that impotence or erectile failure is a significant problem for all elderly males. Actually, most cases of erectile failure in older males are compounded by medical conditions that prevent a man from having an erection full enough for intercourse to take place (Belsky, 1988). An erection is produced by increased blood flow to the penis and the engorgement of this organ with blood. The potential for erection can be disturbed by any upset in the delicate balance between the body and its systems (e.g. hormonal or neurological). Belsky (1988) estimated that among males over age sixty, 70 percent of the noted cases of erectile failure had an organic health-related etiology. Chronic conditions such as arteriosclerosis, high blood pressure and diabetes, which are commonly found in the elderly population, can also affect the blood flow to the penis. Prostate difficulties, which may require surgical intervention and result in erection difficulties, are relatively common at this age. The side effects of medications taken for treatment of chronic conditions can also factor into the increase of erectile dysfunctions in the elderly male. Most cases of male impotency in the elderly are due to physical, not psychological, causes. A physical checkup, and review of the medical and medication history, becomes imperative before any type of sexual counseling is initiated.

Females also encounter several physical changes as a function of aging. However, when compared to their male counterparts, females are sometimes referred to as the psychologically resilient sex (Belsky, 1988). Masters and Johnson (1966) found that older females are as capable of reaching orgasm as younger females. For females, certain physical changes that do exist include: (1) less production of lubricating fluid in the vagina; (2) the vaginal walls become thinner and less elastic; and (3) stimulation of the clitoris brings about a slower reaction time with decreased intensity of the climatic response.

Apart from noting the physical changes we have described, problems regarding sexuality among elderly individuals can be handled similarly to treatment techniques used for younger individuals. Many techniques exist to help with the problems of erectile failure, including the use of surgical implants and chemical or medication enhances. Elderly individuals face many important life circumstance events that can affect their general overall sense of well-being that should not be avoided. Intervention strategies for the elderly should include participation in sex education programs and activities such as support groups and workshops given by social workers to local and community-oriented, civic-minded audiences. Avoidance of ageist terminology in our institutions and in the media also should be encouraged (Kelly & Rice, 1987).

Social workers who generally work with the elderly in hospitals, homes or communities have a unique opportunity to help aged individuals understand and gain increased acceptance with their current level of sexual functioning. This can be accomplished by providing information to elderly individuals and family members regarding the changes that are specific to this age group. It is important for the elderly to realize that they are not alone and many of the feelings they are experiencing have been felt and openly expressed by others. Knowing that they are not alone may help to relieve feelings of guilt and frustration that otherwise might not be addressed and that, left unresolved, may lead to cessation of sexual activity.

Suicide Among the Elderly

Death from suicide constitutes the eighth leading cause of death in the United States and accounts for over 30,000 deaths each year. Elderly individuals tend to have a higher suicide rate than younger generations and elderly individuals account for 25 percent of all reported suicides (Lowry, 1979). "Among the general population, the suicide rate is 12.4 per 100,000 persons; the suicide rate for older people is higher than in the general population with a rate of 20 per 100,000 being recorded in 1990. Persons aged 65 and older compromise 12.5 percent of the population and account for 20.9 percent of the suicides annually" (Perkins & Tice, 1994, p. 438). Unfortunately, suicide rates among the elderly seem to be on the rise, particularly among elderly males, and some authors believe these rates are underreported (Perkins & Tice, 1994). Suggested reasons for this higher rate of suicide than that of the general population include: (1) that there may be a difference in coping skills and sex-role identification of elderly individuals (Canetto, 1992); (2) there appears to be a great deal of somatic preoccupation and dissatisfaction with functional status related to ill health and loss of functioning (Reynolds et al., 1994); and (3) these individuals have experienced a tremendous amount of life stressors (e.g., death of spouses, relatives, friends, changes in social status, employment status, etc.) in a relatively short period of time.

Suicide rates typically are considered indicative of the extent of mental health, satisfaction and well-being. Suicide in the elderly, however, is not always viewed in the same way as suicide involving a young person. For example, the rise in suicide rates among adolescents, generally attributed to such factors as inadequate coping abilities, has created much alarm and calls for solutions. At the same time, suicide is often accepted as an understandable option for elderly individuals (Kastenbaum & Coppedge, 1987). When an elderly person feels lost, trapped and alone, suicide as an option is not necessarily condemned by society (Kastenbaum & Coppedge, 1987). Kastenbaum and Coppedge (1987) have suggested that suicide is not only encouraged as an option but subtly implied, as evidenced by diminishing health care benefits and the rationing of "limited health care options" to the aged.

Widowhood presents a particular coping problem for the elderly, as the loss of a spouse may require the elderly survivor to assume duties that were previously not required (e.g., balancing a checkbook, driving, shopping for groceries). These new tasks, and the required transition, can create stress for the elderly. They may feel further isolated from married friends, and fear the loss of independence and possible dependence on family or friends.

Death and widowhood can represent particular problems for elderly women, as they generally outlive their male counterparts by approximately 15 years (Belsky, 1988). However, female widowhood may not be directly linked to attempted suicide, as suicide rates in elderly males are higher than elderly females (Specht & Craig, 1982). Wan (1985) has warned, however, that widowhood is likely to have negative effects on the survivor, including impairment of physical, psychological and social well-being. Suicide among the elderly is almost always considered a result of major life stresses and accumulated losses; therefore, widows and widowers maintain a high probability of committing suicide.

Social workers need to be aware of the probability of accumulated life losses an elderly client has or is enduring. Research indicates that the first year after the death of a spouse seems to be the hardest time of adjustment (Wan, 1985; Belsky, 1987). During this especially stressful period, social workers should be cognizant of a client's abilities and/or problems in coping with grief.

The role of the social worker in dealing with a potentially suicidal elderly client is essential. First, if a client, whether young or old, expresses ideation and a concrete plan, steps to ensure hospitalization must be conducted immediately. The person needs to be in a safe place. Unfortunately, many times the situational criteria are not so clear and the social worker is uncertain of the seriousness of the client's thoughts in regard to his/her actions. Regardless of whether the elderly client's behavior is action-focused or not, some type of counseling strategy needs to be employed. Perkins and Tice (1994) emphasize the use of a counseling strategy for older adults which focuses on the identification of client strengths. Here the elderly client joins with the social worker in elucidating pre-existing coping and survival skills. The elderly client begins to accept the role of survivor and this type of model, in conjunction with crisis services and bereavement counseling, can help the elderly client to regain control of his/her life.

Planning for Death

Much of the confusion in our society regarding death can be linked to the denial, secrecy and fear of death which we have created (Largue, 1985). Death is an inevitable part of life, yet many individuals in our society spend most of their time ignoring and avoiding this fact, at least until it affects them indirectly. It is usually at this time that an individual struggles with feelings of loss, separation, guilt, fear and anger. "No one rationally desires to be in a state of dying or have a terminal illness, most people do not enjoy being ill; persons, however, may want to die" (High, 1978, p. 89). Many individuals fear the unknown that death will bring and the loss of independence that often comes with a chronic illness. Family members fear making decisions about a loved one, especially in regard to continuing or discontinuing one's life. The elderly individual and the family member often turn to science and medicine for the answers. Physicians, as representatives of the scientific and healing community, are often sought out and expected to have the answers and make the decisions. However, physicians are taught from the day they enter medical school to preserve life, and many physicians are not prepared to deal with the psychosocial aspects of dying (Nolan, 1987). The training of a physician has prepared them "as rescuers from pain, and many times these physicians see themselves as arch rivals from death" (LaRue, 1985, p. 11). As physicians cannot always handle the full responsibility of dealing with the possibility of death, and because they are part of an interdisciplinary team which includes social workers, the social worker is often sought after to help the individual or the family cope with death.

Before a social worker can successfully help the family or the individual deal with death, there are several issues of concern to examine. The first is to become aware of one's own feelings toward death. Many social work practitioners, not unlike their medical counterparts, are uncomfortable with the subject of dying (LaRue, 1985). To assist in understanding the concept of death, it may help for the social worker to become acquainted with how death is viewed in other countries and by certain religions. By becoming aware of the alternate conceptions of death and the legitimation of the role of death, social workers may become somewhat desensitized to the perception of mysticism surrounding death in this country. Once the social worker feels more comfortable discussing death, these alternate concepts might be presented, when appropriate, to the elderly individual and family members.

The second concern in helping elderly individuals deal with death is to know the resources or services available in the community that might assist this population to prepare for death. One such service are hospice programs. Hospice, which is funded by Medicare, offers services to individuals who are suffering from a terminal illness and are expected to have six months or less to live (Crichton, 1987). This program does not focus on prolonging life beyond its natural end. Often, in these programs, the social worker serves as part of an interdisciplinary team designed to assist the individual and family members in preparation for natural death. A second service that may benefit many elderly clients is the implementation of a "living will." Most individuals are aware of the need for, and do complete, a "will" which declares who will receive their money, property and other worldly goods. However, the concept of a living will is less often contemplated and implemented (Patterson, Baker & Maeck, 1993). The living will is a document that allows an individual to state, in advance, preferences relating to the use of life-sustaining procedures, in the event of a terminal illness. In completing a living will, many individuals are given the chance to state when they want to avoid unwanted life-sustaining measures. This type of will can be especially helpful to family members who are frequently left with the burden of making this decision when their elderly relative is mentally incapacitated. Without such a will, family members may avoid making this type of decision, since they may feel that initiating such a procedure gives them too much control and responsibility over the disabled person. A living will is generally created by simply expressing one's wishes while in a state of sound mind and body, and having the document legally witnessed.

CONCLUSION

In general, growing old continues to be viewed negatively in our society by those who are not yet old, as well as by many health and mental health care professionals. The elderly themselves are also victimized by societal attitudes which devalue old age. Many individuals (young and old) will do almost anything to avoid or deny old age. Such prejudices are the result of both rational and irrational fears. Rational fears about declining health, income, loss of loved ones and social status can be exaggerated by negative stereotypes of the elderly, and the irrational fears of changes in physical appearance, loss of masculinity, femininity, and perceived mental incompetence also can be exaggerated. The elderly continue to be oppressed by myths and misinformation and by real obstacles imposed by various biological, psychological, social and economic factors.

Social workers, at a minimum, need to examine their own attitudes toward aging and the elderly. We should not contribute, directly or indirectly, to discrimination based on age, which results in ineffective and unethical practice. Practitioners need to recognize the aged as a valuable resource in our society and to provide services and advocacy which will assist the elderly to maximize their degree of life satisfaction and well-being.

REFERENCES

American Psychiatric Association. (1994). *Diagnostic and statistical manual of mental disorders* (4th ed.). Washington, D.C.: Author.

Anderson, F., & Williams, B. (1989). *Practical management of the elderly.* Boston: Blackwell.

Axinn, J., & Levin, H. (1982). *A history of the American response to need.* New York: Harper & Row.

Atchley, R. (1976). *The sociology of retirement.* New York: Halsted.

Ban, T.A. (1987). Pharmacological perspectives in therapy of depression in the elderly (pp. 127–131). In G.L. Maddox & E.W. Busse (Eds.), *Aging: The universal experience.* New York: Springer Hill.

Beck, J.C., Freedman, M.L., & Warshaw, G.A. (1994, February). Geriatric assessment: Focus on function. *Patient Care,* 10–32.

Begly, C. (1985). Are DRGs fair? *Journal of Health and Human Resources Administration, 8,* 80–89.

Belsky, J. (1988). *Here tomorrow: Making the most of life after fifty.* Baltimore, MD: Johns Hopkins Press.

Berkman, B., & Abrams, R. (1986). Factors related to hospital readmission of elderly cardiac patients. *Social Work, 31*(2), 99–103.

Besdine, R.W. (1994, February). Successful aging for all? *Patient Care,* 7–8.

Blazyk, S., & Canavan, M. (1985). Therapeutic aspects of discharge planning. *Social Work, 30,* 489–495.

Brieland, D., Costin, L.B., & Atherton, C.R. (1980). *Contemporary social work* (2nd ed.). New York: McGraw-Hill.

Brody, E., & Brody, S. (1987). Aged. In A. Minahan (Ed.), *Encyclopedia of social work* (pp. 106–126). Silver Spring, MD: NASW.

Butler, R.N. (1994). Baby boomers: Aging population at risk. *Geriatrics, 49*(2), 13–14.

Canetto, S.S. (1992). Gender and suicide in the elderly. *Suicide and Life Threatening Behavior, 22*, 80–97.

Corvea, M. (1987). Senile dementia of the Alzheimer's type and multi-infarct dementia: A clinical comparison. Florida State University, Fall, 1987.

Cowdry, E.V. (Ed.) (1942). *Problems of aging: Biological and medical aspects.* Baltimore, MD: Williams & Wilkins.

Crichton, J. (1987). *The age care source book: A resource guide for the aging and their families.* New York: Simon & Schuster.

Cumming, E., & Henry, W. (1961). *Growing old: The process of disengagement.* New York: Basic Books.

Davidson, W.R., & Kunze, K. (1979). Psychological, social and economic meanings of work in modern society: Their effects on the worker facing retirement. In W.C. Sze (Ed.), *Human life cycle* (pp. 690–717). New York: Jason Aronson.

Diamond, T. (1986). Social policy and every day life in the nursing home: A critical ethnography. *Social Science Medicine, 23*, 1287–1295.

Dobelstein, A., & Johnson, B. (1985). *Serving older adults: Policy, programs and professional activities.* Englewood Cliffs, NJ: Prentice-Hall.

Duke, W.M., Barton, L., & Wolf-Klein, G.P. (1994). The chief complaint: Patient caregiver and physician's perspectives. *Clinical Gerontologist, 14*(4), 3–11.

Dziegielewski, S.F. (1990). *The institutionalized dementia relative and the family member relationship.* Unpublished doctoral dissertation. Florida State University, Tallahassee.

Dziegielewski, S.F. (1991). Social group work with family members of elderly nursing home residents with dementia: A controlled evaluation. *Research on Social Work Practice, 1*, 358–370.

Ekerdt, D.J. (1986). The busy ethic, moral continuity between work and retirement. *Gerontology, 26*, 239–244.

Erikson, E. (1959). Identity and the life cycle. In *Papers by Erik H. Erikson.* New York: Universities Press.

Frank, L. (1946). Gerontology. *Journal of Gerontology, 1*, 1.

Gochros, H.L., Gochros, J.S., & Fischer, J. (Eds.). (1986). *Helping the sexually oppressed.* Englewood Cliffs, NJ: Prentice-Hall.

Harrison, D.F. (1988). The institutionalized mentally ill. In H.G. Gochros, J.S. Gochros, & J. Fischer (Eds.), *Helping the sexually oppressed* (pp. 191–209). Englewood Cliffs, NJ: Prentice-Hall.

High, D. (1978). Quality of life and care of the dying person. In M. Blaes & D. High (Eds.), *Medical treatment and the dying: Moral issues* (pp. 65–84). Salem, MA: G.K. Hall.

Hodson, D.S., & Skeen, P. (1994). Sexuality and aging: The hammerlock of myths. *Journal of Applied Gerontology, 13*, 219–234.

Hoyt, D.R., Kaiser, M.A., Peters, G.R., & Babchuk, N. (1980). Life satisfaction and activity theory: A multi-dimensional approach. *Journal of Gerontology, 35*, 935–981.

Hussian, R. (1981). *Geriatric psychology: A behavioral perspective.* New York: Van Nostrand Reinhold.

Kastenbaum, R., & Coppedge, R. (1977). Suicide in later life: A counter trend among the old-old. In G. Maddox & E. Bussee (Eds.), *Aging: The universal human experience.* New York: Springer.

Kelly, J.J., & Rice, S. (1986). The aged. In H.L. Gochros, J.S. Gochros & J. Fischer (Eds.), *Helping the sexually oppressed* (pp. 99–108). Englewood Cliffs, NJ: Prentice-Hall.

LaRue, G.A. (1985). *Euthanasia and religion.* Eugene, OR: The Hemlock Society.

Lee, E., Forthofor, R., & Taube, C. (1985). Does DRG mean disastrous results for psychiatric hospitals. *Journal of Health and Human Services Administration, 8,* 53–78.

Leiblum, S.R., & Pervin, I.A. (Eds.). (1980). *Principles and practice of sex therapy.* New York: Guilford.

Lemon, B.L., Bengston, V.L., & Peterson, J.A. (1972). An exploration of activity of aging: Activity types and life satisfaction among in-movers to a retirement community. *Journal of Gerontology, 27,* 511–583.

Lilienfeld, D.E., & Perl, D.P. (1994). Projected neurogenerative disease mortality among minorities in the United States. *Neuroepidemiology, 13,* 179–86.

Lowry, L. (1979). *Social work with the aging: The challenge and promise of later years.* New York: Harper & Row.

Lusky, R. (1986). Anticipating the needs of the U.S. elderly in the twenty-first century: Dilemmas in epidemiology, gerontology and public policy. *Social Science Medicine, 23,* 1217–1227.

Maddox, G. (1964). Disengagement theory: A critical evaluation. *The Gerontologist, 4,* 80–82.

Maldonado, D. (1987). Aged. In A. Minahan (Ed.), *Encyclopedia of social work* (pp. 95–106). Silver Spring, MD: NASW.

Masters, W.H., & Johnson, V.E. (1966). *Human sexual response.* Boston: Little, Brown.

McCullough, P.K., & Cody, S. (1993). Geriatric development. In Frederick S. Sierles (Ed.), *Behavioral science for medical students* (pp. 163–167). Baltimore, MD: Williams & Wilkins.

Montana, P. (1985). *Retirement programs: How to develop and implement them.* New York: Prentice-Hall.

Mor-Barak, M.E., & Tynan, M. (1993). Older workers and the work place: A new challenge for occupational social work. *Social Work, 38,* 45–55.

Morris, R. (1993). Do changing times mean changing agendas for the elderly? *Journal of Aging and Social Policy, 5*(3), 1–6.

Morrison, M. (1982). *Economics of aging: The future of retirement.* New York: Van Nostrand Reinhold.

Mosher-Ashley, P.M. (1994). Diagnoses assigned and issues brought up in therapy by older adults receiving outpatient treatment. *Clinical Gerontologist, 15*(2), 37–64.

National Council on Aging. (1981). *Aging in the 80s: America in transition.* Washington, D.C.: Author.

Nolan, K. (1987). In death's shadow: The meanings of withholding resuscitation. *Hastings Center Report, 17,* 9–14.

Paterson, S.L., Baker, M., & Maeck, J.P. (1993). Durable powers of attorney: Issues of gender and health care decision making. *Journal of Gerontological Social Work, 21,* 161–177.

Perkins, K., & Tice, C. (1994). Suicide and older adults: The strengths perspective in practice. *Journal of Applied Gerontology, 13,* 438–454.

Peterson, M. (1994). Physical aspects of aging: Is there such a thing as normal? *Geriatrics, 49*(2), 45–49.

Plum, F. (1979). Dementia: An approaching epidemic. *Nature, 279,* 373.

Pratt, C., Wright, S., & Schmall, V. (1987). Burden, coping and health status: A comparison of family caregivers to community dwelling institutionalized Alzheimer's patients. *Social Work, 10,* 99–112.

Reynolds, C.F., Small, G.W., Stein, E.M., & Teri, L. (1994, February). When depression strikes the elderly patient. *Patient Care,* 85–101.

Rhodes, C. (1988). *An introduction to gerontology: Aging in American society.* Springfield, IL: Charles C Thomas.

Rife, J.C., & Belcher, J.R. (1994). Assisting unemployed older workers to become reemployed: An experimental evaluation. *Research on Social Work Practice, 4,* 3–13.

Rosenwaike, I., Yaffe, N., & Sagi, P. (1980). The recent decline in mortality of extreme aged: An analysis of statistical data. *American Journal of Public Health, 70,* 1074–1080.

Rost, K., & Roter, D. (1987). Predictors of recall of medication regimens and recommendations. *The Gerontologist, 27,* 510–515.

Roth, M. (1981). The diagnosis of dementia in late and middle life. In J. Mortimer & L. Schuman (Eds.), *The epidemiology of dementia* (pp. 67–75). New York: Oxford University Press.

Rubinstein, R.L., Lubben, J.E., & Mintzer, J.E. (1994). Social isolation and social support: An applied perspective. *Journal of Applied Gerontology, 13,* 58–72.

Ryff, C.D. (1982). Self-perceived personality change in adult-hood and aging. *Journal of Personality and Social Psychology, 42,* 108–115.

Safford, F. (1988). Value of gerontology for occupational social work. *Social Work, 33,* 42–45.

Scharlach, A.E., Mor-Barak, M.E., & Birba, L. (1994). Evaluation of a corporate-sponsored health care program for retired employees. *Health and Social Work, 19,* 192–198.

Segrin, C. (1994). Social skills and psychosocial problems among the elderly. *Research on Aging, 16,* 301–321.

Sherwood, S., Morris, J., & Ruchlin, H. (1986). Alternate paths to long-term care, nursing home, geriatric day hospital, senior center and domiciliary care options. *American Journal of Public Health, 76,* 38–44.

Shock, N.W. (1987). The International Association of Gerontology: Its origins and development. In G.L. Maddox & E.W. Busse (Eds.), *Aging: The universal experience* (pp. 21–43). New York: Springer.

Sills, J.S. (1980). Disengagement reconsidered: Awareness of finitude. *The Gerontologist, 20,* 457–462.

Smallegan, M. (1985). There was nothing else to do: Needs for care before nursing home admission. *The Gerontologist, 25,* 364–369.

Specht, R., & Craig, G.T. (1982). *Human development: A social work perspective.* Englewood Cliffs, NJ: Prentice-Hall.

Starr, P. (1982). *The social transformation of American medicine.* New York: Basic Books.

Steuer, J., & Clark, E. (1982). Family support groups within a research project on dementia. *The Clinical Gerontologist, 1,* 87–95.

Sterns, H.L., Barrett, G.V., Czaja, S.J., & Barr, J.K. (1994). Issues in work and aging. *Journal of Applied Gerontology, 13,* 7–19.

Strawbridge, W.J., Camacho, T.C., Cohen, R.D., & Kaplan, G.A. (1993). Gender differences in factors associated with change in physical functioning in old age: A six year longitudinal study. *The Gerontologist, 33, 5,* 603–609.

Swan, F. (1987). The substitution for nursing home care for in-patient psychiatric care. *Community Mental Health Journal, 23,* 1.

Taber's cyclopedic medical dictionary. (1977). Philadelphia, PA: F.A. Davis.

Talbott, J. (1988). Taking Issue. *Hospital and Community Psychiatry, 39,* 115.

Tennessee Commission on Eldercare. (1993). *Workers in eldercare: Issues in practice* (pp. 1–25). Conference Proceedings, National Association of Social Workers Eldercare Conference, Nashville, TN.

U.S. Senate Special Committee on Aging. (1981). *Developments in aging: 1981* (vol. I). Washington, D.C.: U.S. Government Printing Office.

Wan, T. (1985). *Well-being for the elderly: Primary preventive services.* Lexington, MA: Lexington Books.

Wells, C. (1977). Dementia: Definition and description. In C. Well (Ed.), *Dementia.* Pittsburgh, PA: F.A. Davis.

Wolfe, S.M., Hope, R., & Public Citizen Health Research Group. (1993). *Worst pills, best pills II: The older adult's guide to avoiding drug induced death or illness.* Washington, D.C.: Public Citizens Health Research Group.

Wolinsky, F.D., & Arnold, C.L. (1988). A different perspective on health and health services utilization. In G.L. Maddox & M.P. Lawton (Eds.), *Annual review of gerontology and geriatrics* (vol. 8, pp. 77–94). New York: Springer.

Zarit, S., Orr, N., and Zarit, J. (1985). *The hidden victims of Alzheimer's disease: Families under stress.* New York: University Press.

Chapter 7

SOCIAL WORK PRACTICE WITH PERSONS WITH DEVELOPMENTAL DISABILITIES

NANCY P. KROPF AND KEVIN L. DEWEAVER

Introduction

The inclusion of a developmental disability (DD) chapter in a text on cultural diversity may be surprising to many readers. The assumption may exist that developmental, and other types of disabilities, are health or mental health issues and people with disabilities do not constitute a "cultural group." Even before the Civil Rights era, however, the argument was presented that people with disabilities need to be understood within the context of a minority group framework (Meyerson, 1948). This perspective suggests that people with disabilities experience problems in functioning more as a consequence of social and psychological barriers than as a result of their physical or mental status. Although the profession of social work has an historic mission to promote social justice, rarely are people with developmental disabilities considered a marginalized social group. In fact, frequently this segment of the population is not considered at all in professional preparation, practice, policy or research. This omission has prompted DeWeaver and Kropf (1992) to identify people with developmental disabilities as the "forgotten minority in social work education".

The content presented in this chapter will increase understanding and sensitivity to people with developmental disabilities as a way to promote effective practice, appropriate policy, and research with people who have developmental disabilities. The initial section will describe the population and present justification for perceiving them as a "minority group." Subsequent sections will take a life span perspective to address practice and policy, and present concerns for social work education and research in developmental disabilities. The final section will propose future trends and directions.

The Concept of "Diversity" Applied to People with Developmental Disabilities

As with other groups discussed in this text, people with DD are a heterogenous segment of our population. While several different diagnostic categories are included in the definition, the four major conditions are mental retardation, cerebral palsy, epilepsy, and autism. Other early onset, lifelong impairments are also considered "developmental disabilities" including blindness, deafness, spina bifida, orthopedic conditions, and learning disabilities. The Developmental Disabilities Assistance and Bill of Rights Act of 1990 defines *developmental disability* as a severe, chronic disability of a person five years or older which has these characteristics:

- is attributable to a mental or physical impairment, or combination
- is manifested before age 22 years
- is likely to continue indefinitely
- results from functional limitations in three or more of the following areas of major life activities: self-care, receptive/expressive language, learning, mobility, self-direction, capacity for independent living, economic self-sufficiency
- reflects the person's need for a combination and sequence of special interdisciplinary, or generic care or treatment, or other services which are of lifelong or extended duration and are individually planned and coordinated.

Although these criteria apply to children and young adults ages 5–22 years, infants and young children are also addressed in the act. Application can be made to youngsters less than five years of age, if these children have a substantial developmental delay, or a specific congenital or acquired condition with a high probability of a resulting developmental disability if services are not provided.

The term "developmental disability" is recent, originating in the late 1960s and initially defined in the Developmental Disabilities Services and Facilities Construction Act, 1970, P.L. 91-57 (DeWeaver, 1995). The earliest definitions mainly addressed cognitive impairment as displayed in subaverage intellectual functioning. Although mental retardation is still the predominate category, individuals with other forms of DD may have average or above average intelligence. Unfortunately, a developmental disability is still frequently misinterpreted to be cognitive impairment.

The general DD field can be very confusing due to the terminology and the ever-evolving changes in definitions and terms. Following the 1970 federal legislation, the concept of DD has been used by the federal government (P.L. 91-517) in its directives and various publications. DeWeaver and Kropf (1992) have stated that, "the definition of DD has become more generalized with the passage of new federal laws and currently is not used when discussing an individual's assessment" (p. 36). Regardless of whether the concept of DD or specific diagnostic conditions are referred to, the preferred terminology is "people first" language (e.g., person with mental retardation, not mentally retarded person).

The functional definition of DD makes estimating the prevalence difficult and complex. The common estimates for the four leading diagnoses are .3% for cerebral palsy, .4% for epilepsy, .032% for autism, and 3% for mental retardation (Malone & Kropf, in press). It is important to note that these estimates vary over the life course, as some types of DD are associated with higher infant mortality rates (e.g., Down's syndrome) or shorter life expectancies (e.g., cerebral palsy) (Thase, 1982; Turk & Machemer, 1993).

Thus far, intragroup variation among people with DD has been discussed. With all of the variability, how can people with DD be considered a minority group? This view is predominately based upon a sociopolitical paradigm, meaning that the "disabilities" are more a product of disabling environments, including physical, social and attitudinal, than of personal deficiencies (Hahn, 1988). The progress made by other groups discussed in this text, including people of color, the elderly, women, individuals who are gay/lesbian/bisexual/transgendered, has been based upon societal change promoted by social movements from individuals who share common membership in these groups. People with developmental and other disabilities are beginning to demand political resources and attention, as demonstrated by recent legislation. For example, the community of people with disabilities was instrumental in achieving the passage of the Americans with Disabilities Act (P.L. 101-336) which extends the civil rights protection similar to those provided to individuals based upon race, gender, national origin, and religion. People with disabilities, including developmental, are becoming more politically aware and can be considered a rising social movement (Scotch, 1988).

Concerns for Social Work Practice and Policy

Practices and policies in the area of DD need to reflect the philosophy that these clients experience problems that are primarily a result of barriers to full social participation. Unfortunately, previous practice and program approaches have emphasized individual pathology, limitations, and stresses instead of approaches which augment strengths and resources, and promote empowerment (McCallion & Toseland, 1994). Social work interventions and social policies need to refocus on the transactions and goodness-of-fit between the person with a disability and the physical, social and political environment. This type of person-environment approach also considers the life phase of the individual with a disability and his or her family. A life span perspective has been advocated as a way to increase understanding of people with disabilities in various phases from infancy to old age (Seltzer, Krauss, & Janicki, 1994). Practice and policies with people who have DD will be presented for childhood and adolescent years, adulthood, and late life.

Childhood and Adolescence

As defined in the Developmental Disabilities Assistance and Bill of Rights Act (1990), a child can be considered "developmentally disabled" until she or he reaches 22 years. Therefore, great variation exists in time of onset of a developmental disability and the associated risk factors. Risk factors can occur during prenatal (e.g., genetic conditions, maternal alcohol consumption during pregnancy), perinatal (e.g., trauma during birth) or postnatal (e.g., accident, severe illness) periods of development (McDonald-Wikler, 1987).

Primary prevention strategies can be provided by social workers to reduce risks both before and after a child's birth. Prevention objectives are currently part of 28 state DD councils and are included in the national health care objectives for the year 2000 (Crocker, 1992). Community projects have been enacted in many locales and serve as a way to educate the public to increase disability awareness, as well as target specific interventions in communities where particular problems are most acute. Adams and Hollowell (1992) provide a summary of various initiatives which include campaigns to increase awareness of fetal alcohol syndrome, projects to promote the proper use of infant seats in vehicles, initiatives to provide prenatal health care, and provision of skill development classes for parents at risk of physically abusing their children.

Social workers can be involved in these educational campaigns and provide linkages to particular resources which may be beneficial for parents such as prenatal health care programs, well-baby clinics and parenting classes.

Once a child is diagnosed with DD, social workers can assist with psychosocial issues, provide information about the condition and services, and serve as advocates and case managers to attain services. After a child is diagnosed, families can experience several psychosocial issues such as feeling anger, a sense of loss, and the need to reconstruct expectations about the child's development and needs. Reactions of loss or grief can recur through the child's development and are most acute at times when developmental mastery should have been achieved (e.g., beginning to walk, talk, enter school) (Gilson & Levitas, 1987; Wikler, 1981b, 1986). Practitioners should be available to families during times of recurring stress for consultation about the child's development, support in the family's continued adjustment to caregiving responsibilities, referral, and provision of support as needed.

For families raising a child with a DD, the school system is an important institution for support, education, and respite from caregiving demands. With the passage of P.L. 95-142 (1975), public education became mandatory for all children regardless of disability status. In 1986, P.L. 99-457 The Education of All Handicapped Children Amendments extended educational services to children of preschool ages. In addition, this law mandated that early intervention programs be established for children from birth to three years of age. Until these pieces of legislation were passed, children with disabilities were excluded from school systems and families were forced to purchase private schooling or have sons/daughters receive no educational services at all. Currently, educational placement may be in a segregated classroom with other children who have disabilities or an integrated setting with non-disabled peers depending on the structure of the school district and the student's level of functioning. Regardless of the type of setting, the school social worker has an important role in the interdisciplinary team to assist in coordinating educational goals and in working with the family to achieve consistency between the school and home environments.

In both the classroom and the home, one of most difficult problems is dealing with disruptive and self-injurious behaviors. In fact, problematic behaviors cause families a great deal of stress and may precipitate out-of-home placement requests for the child (Friedrich, Wilturner, & Cohen,

1985; Tausig, 1985). Parents and teachers who have children that are disruptive or self-injurious can learn effective methods for behavior management. Social workers can assist parents and teachers by constructing intervention plans to identify antecedents of problem behaviors, redirect to appropriate and engaging activities, refer for appropriate medical evaluations, use time-out strategies, and modify the environment (King, 1993; Pitonyak, 1992; Underwood & Thyer, 1990).

Social workers can be beneficial for siblings of children with disabilities. Children with a brother or sister who has a disability report both negative (e.g., jealousy or anger) and positive (e.g., acceptance or companionship) effects of these relationships (Wilson, Blacher, & Baker, 1989). Research on sibling relationships suggests that offspring are often expected to assume some caregiving responsibility for their sibling (Stoneman, Brody, Davis, Crapps 1989); in fact, parents may assume that non-disabled siblings will become the primary care providers for their brother or sister in later life. Brothers and sisters of children with disabilities often benefit from individual or group counseling with other siblings to address issues related to family and peer relationships, their perceptions about their own future, and to share feelings with peers who have similar family issues (Levy, 1995).

Adulthood

Two of the prominent roles of adulthood are family and vocational memberships. During adulthood, individuals are frequently involved in child care and/or elder care responsibilities. Vocational roles include being employed in the labor force and achieving a level of economic self-sufficiency. Family relationships and vocational opportunities for people in midlife who have DD will be discussed.

Although social and physical factors may preclude many adults with DD from having children, some adults do have responsibility for raising offspring. Intellectual disability of a parent, such as mental retardation, has been a concern due to questions about the child's welfare and the adequacy of parenting skills. Some studies suggest that children who are raised by parents with mental retardation evidence developmental delays and these parents experience difficulties in their caregiving role (Feldman, Case, Towns, & Betel, 1985; Keltner, 1994; Unger & Howes, 1988). Social workers can have a dramatic impact upon supporting parents with disabilities to ameliorate problems in parenting performance. Some of the interventions which can be helpful include assistance with accessing medical care and social resources; education about parenting skills and child development; and general case management to coordinate the multiple services which may be necessary to support parents in their roles.

In addition to being parents themselves, many adults with DD also provide support to their aging parents. While research about caregiving relationships has tended to identify the support provided by the parents, adults with DD are an overlooked source of support for their parents (Greenberg, Seltzer & Greeley, 1993). Sons and daughters with disabilities can provide emotional support (e.g., companionship), instrumental support (e.g., helping with household maintenance) and financial assistance (e.g., SSI payments, employment wages). Unfortunately, practitioners may subscribe to a paradigm of "caregiving burden" and neglect to evaluate the contributions that many adults with disabilities provide to their household. While older parents often face many demands and stresses in later life caregiving, they may also benefit from the support and assistance provided to them by adult sons and daughters with disabilities. The reciprocity in family relationships is important in the assessment and intervention process with older families.

In the vocational roles, adults with DD have historically suffered from discrimination in the workplace with the concomitant conditions of unemployment and low wage earnings. Recently, the Americans with Disabilities Act (P.L. 101-336) of 1990 extended civil rights protection to people with disabilities by guaranteeing equal opportunity in employment, public accommodation, transportation, and state and local government. This legislation attempts to eradicate barriers in the workplace to allow people with disabilities to be more involved in the labor force.

While the ADA has made legislative progress, some people with DD may require additional on-the-job training and support. In 1986, P.L. 99-506, The Rehabilitation Act Amendments, defined supported employment as competitive work in an integrated work environment for individuals with handicapping conditions that have traditionally made competitive work improbable. Part of these amendments asserted that as a result of the worker's disability status, ongoing support service was necessary to assist with maintenance of a job. Social work practice skills of all levels are required in these vocational interventions. Direct practice with the individual worker is necessary to assist with job training, ongoing support and problem solving, and monitoring placement progress. Work with coworkers is also imperative to assist with integration of the person with a disability into the job site. Additionally, advocacy and community organization with potential employers is also required to promote hiring and placement of workers who have disabilities.

Late Life

The "graying of the population" is a term that is commonly used to describe the current demographic shifts that are occurring nationally and internationally. Life spans for people with developmental disabilities parallel the general population which translates into more people who enter later years with a lifelong disability. For certain developmental disabilities, life span extensions have been dramatic. Only a generation ago, people with Down's syndrome were not expected to live past adolescence or young adulthood. Today, it is not unusual for individuals with this type of mental retardation to live into their fifties or sixties (Eyman, Call & White, 1991).

The physical changes of the aging process for people with DD may have an earlier onset than the general population. This factor has prompted "late life" to be defined earlier, most commonly at age 55 (Seltzer & Krauss, 1987). Some chronic physical problems are a result of the disability condition, such as increased swallowing difficulties in adults with cerebral palsy or early onset Alzheimer's disease in people who have Down's syndrome. However, other later life health problems are consequences of poor health practices and treatment across the life course. These factors include a lack of health professionals who practice with people who have DD, inadequate health care coverage, poor nutrition, and sedentary habits for many in this population.

Psychosocial issues of later adulthood are also areas where social workers can be helpful. Too often, people with DD are considered "eternal children" and believed to be immune to the issues facing the older population. However, people with DD do experience some of the usual issues of later life such as dealing with parental death and morbidity, and their own mortality (Deutsch, 1985; McDaniel, 1989; Yanok & Beifus, 1993). Life review, a common therapeutic technique with the older population in general, may be especially useful for older people with developmental disabilities and their families (Kropf & Greene, 1993). The life review process can help these older clients bring closure to some of the disappointments and frustrations of earlier life, as well as revisit positive aspects to promote a sense of competence and accomplishment.

On a policy level, the emphasis has been on inclusion of aging people and their supports in community programs and services. A number of efforts have attempted to "bridge the networks" of aging and DD service systems (cf. Ansello & Rose, 1989; Clements, 1994; LePore & Janicki, 1990; Wilhite, Keller & Nicholson, 1991). The political thrust toward inclusive service delivery has become part of the national agenda. The Older Americans Act of 1987 includes amendments that enable older persons with developmental disabilities to be served within the community services provided in the OAA. Other changes have also been mandated through OAA legislation including establishing cooperation between state divisions of aging and local mental retardation/developmental disabilities agencies, and providing additional support to home-based caregivers who are caring for older adults with DD (Janicki, 1994).

The issue of caregiving for older people with DD is an important one. One of the major issues facing older people with developmental disabilities and their families is the transition of care when primary care providers, usually older parents, can no longer function in their caregiving role. Many families cope with this emotionally laden process by neglecting to make any future plans (Kaufman, Adams & Campbell, 1991; Smith & Tobin, 1993). Unfortunately, this situation leaves many older adults with developmental disabilities in a very difficult predicament when a family crisis occurs, such as the death or illness of the primary caregiver. Practitioners can assist older adults and their families in transition planning and provide linkage and information about various options (Kelly & Kropf, 1995). As developmental service systems have changed to become more person-centered, additional options are available to older people with developmental disabilities, such as residing in their own home instead of automatic placement into some type of congregate living arrangement (O'Brien, 1994). Social workers need to be creative in resource development and service coordination since family needs and desires about future care are very individual.

Concerns for Social Work Education

Practice Background

Historically, the DD field and the profession of social work developed along parallel tracks (Horejsi, 1979) with few intersections, such as the children's movement, that began with the White House Conference in 1909 (DeWeaver, 1995). The field and profession converged significantly in the 1960s with the election of John F. Kennedy (whose sister is a person with mental retardation) as president in 1960. This convergence temporarily subsided in the 1970s with the emergence toward psychotherapy and privatization in the profession. In the late 1980s, however, another intersection occurred and continues into the 1990s. Concerning these events, DeWeaver (1994) has summarized that, "Similar to the decoupling in the 1970s, the reasons for the renewal of interest are unclear; however, we do know that a growing number of social workers were taking jobs in this area in the 1980s and that a significant number of these people had BSW degrees" (p. 1).

The convergence and renewed interest is reflected in one of the major publications of the National Association of Social Workers (NASW), entitled *The Encyclopedia of Social Work*. The two editions in the 1970s (i.e., 1971 and 1977) had no chapters on mental retardation or other types of disabilities. Their *Supplement* to the *Encyclopedia* that was published in 1983 did include a generic chapter on disabilities, which provided a terse overview of mental and physical disabilities. The 1987 edition of the *Encyclopedia* had a separate chapter on DD and another chapter on physical disabilities. The 1990 *Supplement* did not have a separate chapter on disabilities; however, it contained two chapters that were germane to this area. The first chapter was titled "Recent Trends in Case Management," and the second chapter was titled "Genetic Services." The 1995 *Encyclopedia of Social Work* has two chapters on DD for the first time in history. One chapter will focus on clinical issues and direct practice, while the other chapter will focus on definitions and policy issues. These publication events indicate a resurgence in interest in the field of DD by the social work profession.

Historical Events

While cultural diversity has been more central to social work education and has grown steadily over the decades, curricula in DD lagged behind practice and little development occurred before the 1950s. Materials about social work education and mental retardation proliferated in the 1960s. In 1961, for example, the proceedings of a conference that specifically addressed mental retardation and social work education was published (Katz, 1961). This conference was jointly sponsored by the Council on Social Work Education (CSWE) and the American Association on Mental Deficiency, which is a nonprofit organization devoted to advocacy for people with mental retardation. At this point in time, three classic books were published: (a) *Mental Retardation: A New Dimension in Social Work Education* (Hume, 1967); (b) *Field Instruction in Mental Retardation Settings Serving Children* (Lewis, 1967); and (c) *Source Book on Mental Retardation for Social Work* (Schreiber & Barnhard, 1967). Another major reference work, which was published by Schreiber (1970), was then used in schools of social work for over a decade. Another source of information was various articles that appeared in a variety of journals. Some of the major topics covered in the 1960s were the following: teaching of mental retardation content (Bertrand, 1967); using mental retardation content to enrich social work education (Dana, 1965); preparing social workers for practice in this field (Krishef & Levine, 1968); developing knowledge content and field work placements (Pisapia, 1964); and generating a call for further use of agencies that provide services to persons with retardation as viable field practica (Smith, 1964). DeWeaver and Kropf (1992) also noted that "many schools of social work connected content on mental retardation with maternal and child health programs and the university-affiliated programs of the era" (p. 37).

The proliferation of materials about social work education and mental retardation subsided in the 1970s. While the reasons for the waning interest are often associated with the profession (e.g., growing interest in psychotherapy), it appears that the graduate students of the late 1960s were not very interested in this population or field of practice. In his dissertation in which social work students were surveyed about mental retardation, Begab (1968) concluded that:

> Students with little or no direct contact or personal life experience with retarded persons demonstrate moderately unfavorable attitudes toward and limited knowledge of this group. . . . The retarded are ranked sixth among the client groups with respect to their preference as clients. Less than 4% of the students select them as their most preferred choice. (pp. 107–108)

The 1980s were characterized by a growing number of social workers entering this field (NASW, 1983), a "renaissance of interest" especially toward the end of the decade (DeWeaver, 1994), and the beginnings of additional curricula content in social work education. In a seminal study, Sterns and Jarrett (1976) reported that half (51%) of the graduate schools of social work had mental retardation as an area of interest; moreover, only seven (13%) schools reported having a course that dealt with mental retardation and only two schools stated that mental retardation was a major area of emphasis. In the early 1980s, Wikler (1981a) reported that "36% of the graduate schools provided at least one course on DD and another 15% offered a part of a course devoted to DD content" (p. 289). The increased interest at the graduate level continued throughout the 1980s especially near the end of the decade when more federal dollars became available. At the undergraduate level, the interest was more extensive in the 1980s. In a survey of BSW programs, DeWeaver (1981) found that 85.7% of the schools stated that DD was an area of interest, 22.6% had a course in this area, 26.2% devoted four weeks of another course on DD, and 92.9% had field practica in DD agencies. Although curriculum offerings in DD increased during this decade, from an overall standpoint it remained fairly modest and in some schools content was completely lacking.

Rationale for DD Content

Social work students will be encountering people with DD as services are provided in other fields of practice (e.g., medical social work, criminal justice, child welfare). One practice setting, school social work, grew tremendously after P.L. 94-142 was passed in 1975 which emphasized education and social services to the "handicapped." With the passage of P.L. 103-230 (DD Assistance and Bill of Rights Act Amendments of 1994), the broadest definition of DD, passed in 1990 (P.L. 101-496), was retained and over forty million people may meet the criteria sometime in their life in this country. While only a few social work students will specialize and seek careers in the DD field, the majority of students will practice in other areas and provide or administer services to people with disabilities who have other needs which require resources from their programs.

The nature of problems with people with DD and their families is best described as multiple needs (past terminology was *multiproblem* family). In an effort to alert consumers about services to people with DD, some urban communities have "published a directory of mental retardation services for its residents which included the following services: professional service committees and boards, information and referral, local Association for Retarded Citizens, medical clinics for diagnosis and referral, vocational training (both workshops and activity centers), vocational rehabilitation, family services (counseling, financial aid, advocacy), group homes, respite care, residential training center, special education (public and private), and recreation" (DeWeaver, 1983, p. 158). In contrast, rural communities may have only one or two of these needed services available to its residents.

Obviously with such multiple needs and services, a generalist (or advanced generalist) orientation is needed by most social work students who will become service providers to this population group—either as a primary provider or as an ancillary provider. This generalist concept has historical practice roots in social work in rural areas (Ginsberg, 1982) and historically educational roots in undergraduate social work education (Rasberry, 1977). A practice operationalization of the generalist concept is case management (DeWeaver & Johnson, 1983), which is sometimes called case coordination, service coordination, or service integration. Ironically, case management and the population of DD were near the bottom of preferences in a study of MSW incoming students (Rubin, Johnson & DeWeaver, 1986). It is important to note that in certain cases, very specific skills which may not be included in the normal generalist approach are needed to assist the client with DD. One example is when the client is a nonverbal institutional resident who is engaged in self-injurious behavior and needs a specific non-aversive behavioral technique (Underwood & Thyer, 1990).

In addition to the generalist orientation that future social workers will most likely apply in the DD field, students need to learn about the interdisciplinary approach to working with people with DD (Andrews & Wikler, 1981). Often social workers are part of a team effort that requires that "the client and the client's family participate in development of an individualized habilitation plan" (Horejsi, 1979, p. 42). All members of the interdisciplinary service team need to understand their particular duties and domain, as well as what other disciplines and professions are responsible for in the overall plan of service (cf. Thyer & Kropf, 1995).

Present Educational Efforts and Movements

Some suggestions of the past [e.g., using DD agencies as field agencies (Pisapia, 1964) and developing a DD course in schools of social work (Wikler, 1981a)] have been accomplished in many different programs. Often these accomplishments were the result of individual faculty members rather than a comprehensive and organized plan. The present strategy of the 1990s does not seek separate coverage as much as the past, and seeks for all students to gain knowledge about this population group and necessary services for them. The current approach of the 1990s is the curriculum infusion model, which has been presented in depth for persons with mental retardation in the human behavior and social environment course (DeWeaver & Kropf, 1992) and for older adults with DD across the foundation curriculum (Kropf, in press). In discussing persons with disabilities—the broadest conceptualization that combines mental and physical challenges—and curriculum for graduate schools of social work, Tomaszewski (1993) has posited that:

> Infusion of curriculum content enriches both the curriculum and the learning environment via efforts to sensitize students to the needs and strengths of persons with disabilities; by providing opportunities for students to acquire specialized skills with disability issues in a variety of settings; and, ensures that graduate schools of social work meet the needs of students with disabilities to ensure accessibility to and full participation in the learning environment. (p. 3)

It is suggested here that this infusion model be used in undergraduate social work education as well. It has been shown in one study that the undergraduate students were more open to working with the DD population and in accepting case management positions (Rubin & Johnson, 1984).

Regarding diversity and DD, there are two sources that should add to the infusion model. The first is a chapter by Beck (1994) that discusses people with disabilities as a specific population-at-risk while specifically addressing the diversity concept. In the policy course, DD and cultural diversity can be discussed as it is noted in the latest DD Amendments of 1994 (P.L. 103-230). Concepts such as discrimination, culturally competent services, and minority participation are explicitly discussed in the statutes of the law.

Social work's professional organizations have been more involved, active, and supportive of the DD field in the 1990s than the previous decade. In 1991, NASW convened a task force to develop curriculum materials specific to disabilities issues. A curriculum was published two years later that contains nine sections and "is designed to help faculty prepare students for professional interactions with persons with disabilities—whether the relationship is collegial, involves policy and/or research decisions, or is based on the provision of direct social work services" (Tomaszewski, 1993, p. 3). NASW cosponsored the first international conference on social work and disabilities, offered through the Young Adult Institute (YAI) in May 1994. NASW's Executive Director, Sheldon Goldstein, spoke at the opening of this initial conference and the second international conference took place in April 1995.

CSWE has also contributed to the rebirth in this area. Papers have been presented on disabilities during the last four annual program meetings (APM). Furthermore, CSWE has developed a Task Force on Persons with Disabilities, which is trying to organize a disability symposium at future APMs. Finally, the task force is producing a video as part of CSWE's diversity initiative which will serve as a resource for classroom learning and faculty development.

Beyond infusion, which is aimed at exposing all students to this population and service network, some other educational strategies are needed for other students and practicing social workers. Unfortunately, these offerings have only been partially conceptualized and implemented. Overall it has been suggested that more awareness of DD, more knowledgeable faculty (both full-time and part-time) to teach in this area, and more creativity in introducing DD to students are sorely needed (DeWeaver, 1994). These characteristics have been demonstrated at several schools. At the College of Staten Island, for example, the undergraduate social work program has an optional certificate program in DD, which is an idea that has been recommended since the last decade (DeWeaver, 1982). At the University of Wisconsin, there is an optional concentration for MSW students who wish to specialize in this area. Social work students can also become involved in multidisciplinary programs on campus, which provide courses, practicum sites, or research opportunities in DD. One example is the Interdisciplinary Leadership Program in Aging and Developmental Disabilities at the University of Georgia, which is jointly offered through the University Affiliated Program for Developmental Disabilities and the Gerontology Center (Kropf, Malone & Welke, 1993). Many other schools at the undergraduate and graduate levels offer a separate course on DD.

As we move toward the millennium, a variety of educational needs are still present. While models for continuing education of practicing social workers in this area exist (Monfils, 1984), very few schools are offering any courses or workshops on DD. In addition, the field work component in many schools needs to be expanded beyond institutions' doorsteps to include agencies that provide a variety of community services. Wikler (1979) has suggested that social work programs should develop closer relationships with University Affiliated Programs (UAP) and increase DD classes that are taught to social work students. Ironically, from discussions at several sessions at YAI's previously mentioned conference, the opposite appears to be occurring. Finally, there is a real need for a current text on social work and DD. The last text that was published concerned only mental retardation and is 14 years old (Dickerson,

1981). Published materials on cultural diversity and the profession, similar to what was done for special education (Harry, 1992), are also very much in need.

Concerns for Research

In the 1970s, Horejsi (1979) noted that there was a paucity of articles about mental retardation or DD in social work journals. Unlike other fields of practice (e.g., health, aging), DD does not have its own separate journal that is published under a social work auspice. When social workers do research and attempt to present it, one place that is willing to accept work in this area is the Social Work Division at the annual meeting of the American Association of Mental Retardation (AAMR). Unfortunately, there is no corresponding proceedings or social work sponsored outlet for publication of such research. Hence social workers who have presented at AAMR, such as Hanley and Parkinson (1994), have to look for venues of publication like AAMR's journal titled *Mental Retardation.* As previously mentioned, YAI seeks to publish a book or a reader of social work research in the future.

More outcome studies with empirical results (e.g., Levy, Murphy, Levy, Kramer, Rimmerman, & Botuck, 1993; Underwood & Thyer, 1990) are needed in the DD field, and social workers could contribute these studies especially with the addition of single-system research designs to social work curricula. Case management is one area where social workers could contribute to both practice (Rose, 1992) and empirical research (Rothman, 1991). Program evaluation is even more important now that states are closing all their ICF–MR institutions (e.g., Vermont) and seeking effective services totally from the community. Data will be needed to ascertain the best models of service. One example is the recent evaluation of a state program which provides cash subsidies to families who provide home-based care for children and adolescents with DD (Herman, 1994).

Social workers need to create and validate more measures of social work practice. To this date, few have been developed for the DD field. One noted exception is the Mental Retardation Practice Inventory (MRPI) which is an eight-item discomfort scale and an eight-item response probability scale (Fashimpar, 1989). Fashimpar (1989) stated that "A low response probability score combined with a low discomfort score indicates good practice skills, the motivation to apply them, confidence in the ability to apply them and assurance of the ethicality of one's professional behavior" (p. 58). Each scale measured three factors: advocacy, warmth, and normalcy. The MRPI had good reliability ratings and a fair amount of validity, but it was suggested that further work be done on both of these important aspects of an instrument.

Methodological originality is also needed by social work researchers in this area. In attempting to study older individuals with DD who are not part of a service system, for example, a way is needed to identify these people since no list is available. In cases similar to these, Rubin and Babbie (1993) have suggested the snowball sampling technique in which the researcher asks participants or their families if they know of other people who share similar characteristics or situations. It can be difficult to find the first few subjects; therefore, service providers or clients might initially be asked for leads in a particular research project. Another example is the recruitment of subjects to evaluate the SIBIS machine, which uses a slight "electrical stimulus" equal to a pinch, to eliminate self-injurious behavior. Researchers have found that clients in state residential institutions cannot be subjected to this type of aversive programming. However, researchers could use clients who reside in the community or possibly in some private institutions. Ethical ways around bureaucracy are part of the needed originality to test potentially important developments in practice.

Doctoral students in social work need to be encouraged to do their dissertation research in the DD field where appropriate. Lately, the number of dissertations by social work doctoral students has been increasing markedly, especially in the late 1980s. Some of these dissertations specifically address various aspects of cultural diversity such as black mothers' acceptance of their sons with DD (Morris, 1989), cultural differences among mothers of children with DD (Yee, 1993), programs for Chinese families (Chou, 1993), and older parents who care for their adult offspring at home (McCallion, 1993). Masters thesis research is also beginning to use the DD field for these projects.

Future Directions

This chapter has discussed the historic and current status of developmental disabilities in social work practice and policy, education, and research. Since content on DD is often omitted in the educational preparation of social workers, many students ignore this population when considering career goals, and numerous methodological and conceptual gaps exist in research with this client population. A great deal of effort and resources need to be introduced into the practice, policy and educational settings to ensure that people with DD receive the best interventions and most appropriate programs with qualified and trained practitioners. Future directions in DD and social work include attracting students and faculty to this field of practice, continuing to construct and evaluate practice models and programs in DD, and development of a comprehensive research agenda.

Promoting effective social work practice with people who have DD is built upon a solid foundation of practitioners and educators who have interest and expertise in this field of practice. Unfortunately, many students continue to ignore career possibilities with clients who have DD. In an analysis of factors which influence individuals to pursue careers in DD, Kobe and Hammer (1993) identified that prior exposure to people with DD was associated with higher degrees of career interest in this area. Generating greater interaction and personal involvement with people who have disabilities may increase individuals' desire to work with this population. The small, but committed, group in social work and DD needs to provide opportunities for colleagues and students to learn more and interact with this population. Hopefully, these endeavors will be supported by legislative changes such as the ADA that promote inclusive environments so greater numbers of people with DD will be in integrated educational, vocational, and social situations and have contact with non-disabled populations.

Cultural diversity within the population of people with DD also needs to be explored. Personal characteristics that impact practice modalities such as race/ethnicity, age or cohort group, gender, and sexual identity are relevant to people with DD just as with the general population. Unfortunately, many of these areas are unexplored for people who have developmental and other disabilities. For example, Edgerton and Gaston (1991) provide a case study of a gay man with retardation and his experiences upon deinstitutionalization from a state facility. Experiences of families who provide care to a child with DD have also been reported for families of different ethnic backgrounds (Heller, Markwardt, Rowitz & Farber, 1994; Mary, 1990). These are just a few examples of how issues of cultural diversity can be explored within the population who has DD.

In several areas of the profession, clarification and elaboration of a comprehensive agenda for social work in DD is needed. One such effort is a position paper by Hanley and Parkinson (1994) that outlines social work values in the DD field to provide greater awareness of the importance of social work roles in this field of practice. Future needs in this area include more organized multidisciplinary research in this area at the university level, additional exploration about ethical issues in DD, and stronger linkages to other fields of practice that will increasingly serve people with DD such as mental health, health care, and aging.

The future directions for social work research in developmental disabilities includes issues in both practice and educational realms. At the moment, there is no social work research agenda in DD. An agenda is needed to proceed in a logical manner toward identifying the present gaps and then proceed toward knowledge development through the use of a variety of research methods.

A four-part research agenda is offered to organize future research. The first part of the agenda is social work practice, which would be divided into three components: micro (direct), mezzo, and macro (indirect). The latter part is especially important, as research concerning policy practice (Figueira-McDonough, 1993) and social workers as administrators (DeWeaver, 1987) is in its infancy. The second part of the agenda is social work education, which traditionally has been about curricula models and schools' involvement. Additional information is needed regarding what information or skills practicing social workers, most of whom had no education in DD, need to practice more effectively.

A third area is research on the social workers who are presently in direct and indirect service positions in the DD field. Past research has indicated that although people of color are underrepresented among developmental disabilities professionals, those social workers active in it are fairly satisfied and plan to remain active in this field (DeWeaver, 1980). More research is needed regarding additional training, which leads to more effective practice in the DD field (Fashimpar, 1989).

The final part of the research agenda is involvement in interdisciplinary research, which could be part of a team effort similar to practice. Research on elderly people with DD and on the effect of ethnicity seem most appropriate topics for such efforts. Through University Affiliated Programs, there may even be federal grant money to support such joint research endeavors.

These areas for future practice, policy, education, and research seeks to organize the efforts of social work in the DD field. The reality is that people with developmental, and other disabilities, are experiencing longer life spans than previously and are living as members of families and communities instead of being institutionalized. The profession's mission of promoting social justice and eradicating barriers to full social participation would suggest that social work would be at the forefront of the DD field, yet this is certainly not the case. Hopefully efforts, such as this chapter, will prompt more members of our profession to become interested in this field of practice.

REFERENCES

Adams, M.J., & Hollowell, J.G. (1992). Community-based projects for the prevention of developmental disabilities. *Mental Retardation, 30,* 331–336.

Andrews, S., & Wikler, L. (1981). Developmental disabilities. *Health and Social Work, 6*(4), 62s–68s.

Ansello, E.F., & Rose, T. (Ed.). (1989). *Aging and lifelong disabilities: Partnership for the twenty-first century. The Wingspread Conference Report.* Baltimore, MD: The University of Maryland Center on Aging.

Beck, R.B. (1994). Diversity and populations-at-risk: People with disability. In F.G. Reamer (Ed.), *The foundations of social work knowledge.* New York: Columbia University Press.

Begab, M.J. (1968). *The effect of differences in curricula and experiences on social work student attitudes and knowledge about mental retardation.* Unpublished doctoral dissertation. The Catholic University of America, Washington, D.C.

Bertrand, P.T. (1967). Issues in social work education affecting the teaching of mental retardation content. *Occasional Paper of the School of Social Work, University of Wisconsin, 3,* 1–14.

Chou, Y.C. (1993). Developing and testing an intervention program for assisting Chinese families in Taiwan who have a member with developmental disabilities. *Dissertation Abstracts International, 53,* 3365A. (University Microfilm No. 92-33, 977.)

Clements, C. (1994). *The arts/fitness quality of life project: Creative ideas for working with older adults in group settings.* Baltimore, MD: Health Professions Press.

Crocker, A.C. (1992). Where is the prevention movement? *Mental Retardation, 30*(6), iii–iv.

Dana, B. (1965). Enriching social work education with mental retardation content. *Journal of Education for Social Work, 1*(2), 5–10.

DeWeaver, K.L. (1980). An empirical analysis of social workers in the field of mental retardation. *Dissertation Abstracts International, 41,* 1214A–1215A. (University Microfilm No. 80-20, 351.)

DeWeaver, K.L. (1981, May). *The role of the baccalaureate social worker in the practice field of developmental disabilities.* Paper presented at the 105th Annual Meeting of the American Association on Mental Deficiency, Detroit, MI.

DeWeaver, K.L. (1982). Producing social workers trained for practice with the developmentally disabled. *Arete, 7,* 59–62.

DeWeaver, K.L. (1983). Delivering rural services for developmentally disabled individuals and their families: Changing scenes. In R. Coward & W. Smith (Eds.), *Serving families in contemporary rural America: Issues and opportunities* (pp. 150–170). Lincoln, NE: University of Nebraska Press.

DeWeaver, K.L. (1987, September). *Social workers as administrators in the developmental disabilities field: Practice implications.* Paper presented at the annual conference of the National Association of Social Workers, New Orleans, LA.

DeWeaver, K.L. (1994, May). *Future directions for social work practice and education in developmental disabilities.* Paper presented at the first annual international conference on social work and disabilities, Young Adult Institute, New York.

DeWeaver, K.L. (1995). Developmental disabilities: Definitions and policies. In National Association of Social Workers (Ed.), *Encyclopedia of social work* (pp. 712–720). Washington, D.C.: Author.

DeWeaver, K.L., & Johnson, P.J. (1983). Case management in rural areas for the developmentally disabled. *Human Services in the Rural Environment, 8*(4), 23–31.

DeWeaver, K., & Kropf, N.P. (1992). Persons with mental retardation: A forgotten minority in education. *Journal of Social Work Education, 28,* 36–46.

Deutsch, H. (1985). Grief counseling with the mentally retarded client. *Psychiatric Aspects of Mental Retardation Reviews, 4,* 17–20.

Dickerson, M.U. (1981). *Social work practice with the mentally retarded.* New York: Free Press.

Edgerton, R.B., & Gaston, M.A. (Eds.). (1991). *"I've seen it all." Lives of older persons with mental retardation in the community.* Baltimore: Paul H. Brookes.

Eyman, R.K., Call, T.I., & White, J.F. (1991). Life expectancy of persons with Down's syndrome. *American Journal on Mental Retardation, 95,* 603–612.

Fashimpar, G.A. (1989). Mental retardation practice inventory. *Journal of Social Service Research, 12*(3/4), 49–69.

Feldman, M.A., Case, L., Towns, F., & Betel, J. (1985). Parent education project I: Development and nurturance of children of MR parents. *American Journal of Mental Deficiency, 90,* 253–258.

Figueira-McDonough, J. (1993). Policy practice: The neglected side of social work intervention. *Social Work, 38,* 179–188.

Friedrich, W.M., Wilturner, L.T., & Cohen, D.S. (1985). Coping resources and parenting mentally retarded children. *American Journal of Mental Deficiency, 90,* 130–138.

Gilson, S., & Levitas, A.S. (1987). Psychosocial crises in the lives of mentally retarded people. *Psychiatric Aspects of Mental Retardation Reviews, 8*(6), 27–31.

Ginsberg, L.H. (1982). Social work in rural communities, with an emphasis on mental health practice. In P.A. Keller & J.D. Murray (Eds.), *Handbook of rural community mental health.* New York: Human Sciences Press.

Greenberg, J.S., Seltzer, M.M., & Greenley, J.R. (1993). Aging parents of adults with disabilities: The gratifications and frustrations of later-life caregiving. *The Gerontologist, 33,* 542–550.

Hahn, H. (1988). The politics of physical differences: Disability and discrimination. *Journal of Social Issues, 44*, 39–47.

Hanley, B., & Parkinson, C.B. (1994). Position paper on social work values: Practice with individuals who have developmental disabilities. *Mental Retardation, 32*, 426–431.

Harry, B. (1992). *Cultural diversity, families, and the special education system.* New York: Teachers College Press.

Heller, R., Markwardt, R., Rowitz, L., & Farber, B. (1994). Adaptation of Hispanic families to a member with mental retardation. *American Journal on Mental Retardation, 99*, 289–300.

Herman, S.E. (1994). Cash subsidy program: Family satisfaction and need. *Mental Retardation, 32*, 416–421.

Horejsi, C.R. (1979). Developmental disabilities: Opportunities for social workers. *Social Work, 24*(1), 40–43.

Hume, M. (Ed.). (1967). *Mental retardation: A new dimension in social work education.* Louisville, KY: University of Louisville Press.

Janicki, M.P. (1994). Policies and supports for older persons with mental retardation. In M.M. Seltzer, J.W. Krauss, & M.P. Janicki (Eds.), *Life course perspectives on adulthood and old age* (pp. 143–165). Washington, D.C.: American Association on Mental Retardation.

Kaufman, A.V., Adams, J.P., & Campbell, V.A. (1991). Permanency planning by older parents who care for adult children with mental retardation. *Mental Retardation, 29*, 293–300.

Katz, A.H. (Ed.). (1961). *Mental retardation and social work education.* Detroit: Wayne State University Press.

Kelly, T.B., & Kropf, N.P. (1995). Stigmatized and perpetual parents: Older parents caring for adult children with lifelong disabilities. *Journal of Gerontological Social Work, 24*(1/2), 3–16.

Keltner, B. (1994). Home environments of mothers with mental retardation. *Mental Retardation, 32*, 123–127.

King, B.H. (1993). Self-injury by people with mental retardation: A compulsive behavior hypothesis. *American Journal on Mental Retardation, 98*, 93–112.

Kobe, F.H., & Hammer, D. (1993). Who is interested in careers in mental retardation and developmental disabilities? *Mental Retardation, 31*, 316–319.

Krishef, C., & Levine, D.L. (1968). Preparing the social worker for effective services to the retarded. *Mental Retardation, 6*(3), 3–7.

Kropf, N.P. (in press). *Infusing content on older people with developmental disabilities into the curriculum. Journal of Social Work Education.*

Kropf, N.P., & Greene, R.R. (1993). Life review with families who care for developmentally disabled members: A model. *Journal of Gerontological Social Work, 21*(1/2), 25–40.

Kropf, N.P., Malone, D.M., & Welke, D. (1993). Teaching about older people with mental retardation: An educational model. *Educational Gerontology, 7*, 635–650.

LePore, P., & Janicki, M.P. (1990). *The wit to win: How to integrate older persons with developmental disabilities into community aging programs.* New York: State Office for the Aging.

Levy, J.M. (1995). Social work. In B.A. Thyer & N.P. Kropf (Eds.), *Developmental disabilities: Handbook for interdisciplinary practice* (pp. 188–201). Cambridge, MA: Brookline Books.

Levy, J.M., Murphy, B.S., Levy, P.H., Kramer, M.E., Rimmerman, A., & Botuck, S. (1993). Monitoring process and employment outcomes over time: The YAI employment project. *Journal of Developmental and Physical Disabilities, 5,* 167–169.

Lewis, V.S. (Ed.). (1967). *Field instruction in mental retardation settings serving children.* Baltimore, MD: University of Maryland.

Malone, D.M. &, Kropf, N.P. (in press). Growing older. In P. McLaughlin & P. Wehmann (Eds.), *Mental retardation and developmental disabilities.* Austin, TX: Pro-Ed.

Mary, N.L. (1990). Reactions of black, Hispanic, and white mothers to having a child with handicaps. *Mental Retardation, 28,* 1–5.

McCallion, P. (1993). Social worker orientations to permanency planning with older parents caring at home for family members with developmental disabilities. *Dissertation Abstracts International, 54,* 1543A. (University Microfilm No. 93-24, 535.)

McCallion, P., & Toseland, R.W. (1994). Empowering families of adolescents and adults with developmental disabilities. *Families in Society, 74,* 579–589.

McDaniel, B.A. (1989). A group work experience with mentally retarded adults on the issues of death and dying. *Journal of Gerontological Social Work, 13,* 187–192.

McDonald-Wikler, L. (1987). Disabilities: Developmental. In A. Minahan et al. (Eds.), *Encyclopedia of social work* (18th ed.) (pp. 422–434). Silver Spring, MD: National Association of Social Workers.

Meyerson, L. (1948). Physical disability as a social psychological problem. *Journal of Social Issues, 4*(4), 107–109.

Monfils, M.J. (1984). A pressing need: Continuing social work education in mental retardation. *Journal of Continuing Social Work Education, 2*(4), 3–7.

Morris, J.K. (1989). Patterns of acceptance among black mothers of mentally handicapped sons (Doctoral dissertation, University of Chicago, 1989). *Dissertation Abstracts International, 51,* 22922.

National Association of Social Workers. (1983, November). Membership survey shows practice shifts. *NASW News,* p. 10.

O'Brien, J. (1994). Down stairs that are never your own: Supporting people with developmental disabilities in their own homes. *Mental Retardation, 32*(1), 1–6.

Pisapia, M.L. (1964). Mental retardation in the social work curriculum. *Mental Retardation, 2*(5), 294–298.

Pitonyak, D. (1992). Behavior management: Focus on self injury. In P.J. McAlughlin & P. Wehman (Eds.), *Developmental disabilities: Handbook of best practices* (pp. 206–227). Boston, MA: Andover.

Rasberry, B.H. (1977). Building rural content into undergraduate curriculum. In R.K. Green & S.A. Webster (Eds.), *Social work in rural areas: Preparation and practice* (pp. 137–147). Knoxville, TN: The University of Tennessee.

Rose, S.M. (Ed.). (1992). *Case management and social work practice.* White Plains, NY: Longman.

Rothman, J. (1991). A model of case management: Toward empirically based practice. *Social Work, 36,* 520–527.

Rubin, A., & Babbie, E. (1993). *Research methods in social work* (2nd ed.). Pacific Grove, CA: Brooks/Cole.

Rubin, A., & Johnson, P.J. (1984). Direct practice interests of entering MSW students. *Journal of Education for Social Work, 20*(2), 5–16.

Rubin, A., Johnson, P.J., & DeWeaver, K.L. (1986). Direct practice interests of MSW students: Changes from entry to graduation. *Journal of Social Work Education, 22*(2), 98–108.

Schreiber, M. (Ed.). (1970). *Social work and mental retardation.* New York: Day.

Schreiber, M., & Barnhard, S. (Eds.). (1967). *Source book on mental retardation for social work.* New York: Selected Academic Readings.

Scotch, R.K. (1988). Disability as the basis for a social movement: Advocacy and the politics of definition. *Journal of Social Issues, 44,* 159–172.

Seltzer, M.M., & Krauss, M.W. (1987). *Aging and mental retardation: Extending the continuum.* (Monograph No. 9). Washington, D.C.: American Association on Mental Retardation.

Seltzer, M.M., Krauss, M.W., & Janicki, M.P. (1994). *Life course perspectives on adulthood and old age.* Washington, D.C.: American Association on Mental Retardation.

Smith, G.C., & Tobin, S.S. (1993). Practice with older parents of developmentally disabled adults. *Clinical Gerontologist, 14*(1), 59–77.

Smith, W.E. (1964). Services to the retarded as social work education. *Children, 11*(5), 189–192.

Sterns, C.R., & Jarrett, H.H. (1976). Mental retardation content in the curricula of graduate schools of social work. *Mental Retardation, 14*(3), 17–19.

Stoneman, Z., Brody, G.H., Davis, C.H., & Crapps, J.M. (1989). Role relations between children who are mentally retarded and their older siblings: Observations in three in-home contexts. *Research in Developmental Disabilities, 10,* 61–76.

Tausig, M. (1985). Factors in decision-making about placement for developmentally disabled individuals. *American Journal of Mental Deficiency, 89,* 352–361.

Thase, M.E. (1982). Longevity and mortality in Down's syndrome. *Journal of Mental Deficiency Research, 26,* 177–192.

Thyer, B.A., & Kropf, N.P. (Eds.) (1995). *Developmental disabilities: Handbook for interdisciplinary practice.* Cambridge, MA: Brookline Books.

Tomaszewski, E.P. (1993). *Disabilities awareness curriculum for graduate schools of social work.* Washington, D.C.: National Association of Social Workers.

Turk, M.A., & Machemer, R.H. (1993). Cerebral palsy in adults who are older. In R.H. Machemer & J.C. Overeynder (Eds.), *Understanding aging and developmental disabilities: An in-service curriculum* (pp. 111–129). Rochester, NY: University of Rochester.

Underwood, L., & Thyer, B.A. (1990). Social work practice with the mentally retarded: Reducing self-injurious behaviors using non-aversive methods. *Arete, 15*(1), 14–23.

Unger, O., & Howes, C. (1988). Mother child interactions and symbolic play between toddlers and their adolescent or mentally retarded mothers. *Occupational Therapy Journal of Research, 8,* 237–240.

Wikler, L. (1979). Has the UAF seed money germinated? Consider schools of social work curricula. *American Association of University Affiliated Programs Newsletter,* Washington, D.C.

Wikler, L. (1981a). Social work education and developmental disabilities. In J.A. Browne, B. Kirlin, & S. Watt (Eds.), *Rehabilitation services and the social work role: Challenge for change* (pp. 285–295). Baltimore: Williams & Wilkins.

Wikler, L. (1981b). Chronic stresses of families of mentally retarded children. *Family Relations, 30,* 281–288.

Wikler, L. (1986). Periodic stress of families of older mentally retarded children. *American Journal of Mental Deficiency, 90,* 703–706.

Wilhite, B., Keller, M.J., & Nicholson, L. (1990). Integrating older persons with developmental disabilities into community recreation: Theory to practice. *Activities, Adaptation & Aging, 15*(1/2), 111–130.

Wilson, J., Blacher, J., & Baker, B.L. (1989). Siblings of children with severe handicaps. *Mental Retardation, 27,* 167–173.

Yanok, J., & Beifus, J.A. (1993). Communicating about loss and mourning: Death education for individuals with mental retardation. *Mental Retardation, 3,* 144–147.

Yee, S. (1993). Cultural differences in psychological adaptation of mothers of children with developmental disabilities. *Dissertation Abstracts International, 54,* 4261A. (University Microfilm No. 94-10, 170)

Chapter 8

SOCIAL WORK PRACTICE WITH PERSONS WITH ADULT ONSET DISABILITIES

DONALD R. LESLIE AND LAURA L. MYERS

Introduction

One of the most complex, challenging, and potentially fruitful areas of practice is that of work with individuals who have experienced an adult-onset disability. These individuals, their families, their environments, indeed society as a whole, are faced with a wide range of possible needs. Not only do these needs require serious social work consideration, but also the interactions among these areas of need can be significant for all concerned.

As indicated, social work practice in the area of adult-onset disabilities is very complex. In attempting to view practice in this area in conjunction with issues of cultural diversity, the complexity is expanded rather than simplified. For example, this book has reviewed issues of cultural diversity and their implications for social work practice with respect to a number of identifiable populations. Each of these populations contains within it individuals who have adult-onset disabilities. The cultural implications for disabled members within these populations are not simply added to but often multiplied through the interaction of disability and other cultural diversity issues. The causes of adult-onset disabilities may be directly or indirectly linked to racial, ethnic, or gender determinants, or may be linked to behavioral determinants which are in turn linked to life-style or cultural factors. In addition, the meaning of or sense of responsibility for the needs of individuals with adult-onset disabilities may be based on other forms of cultural diversity. Since the incidence of adult-onset disability cuts across all areas of cultural diversity, the possible interactions between elements of diversity related to adult-onset disability and other culturally diverse areas are not only possible but probable.

As if this interactional component of cultural diversity were not enough, the picture is further complicated by the wide variety of possible adult-onset disabilities. This variety encompasses disabilities which may make the individual highly visible or which remain entirely hidden, thus posing no issues of visibility for the individual (Asch, 1984). As well, the range of functional disturbance is also great. Adult-onset disabilities may leave individuals faced with imminent death, or dealing with rehabilitative features lasting for the rest of their lifetime. On the other hand, the adult-onset disability may involve changes in functional ability which are merely irritating or frustrating to the individual but pose no significant life problems.

The variety of possible adult-onset disabilities is far too lengthy a list to document in this chapter. It is not simply this lengthy list of disabilities or the vast numbers involved (36,000,000 in the USA) which creates complexity for this area of social work practice, but also that the level of severity or functional impact of each disability may vary widely for individuals with that same disability (Asch, 1984; Tuttle, 1984). The myriad of functional implications for individuals are contributed to by both the type and severity of disability along with the prevailing and particular cultural attitudes toward this disability which in turn are interpreted through and mediated by the individual's own personal sense of responsibility.

In addition, the range of helping professionals, treatment or rehabilitation procedures, and service organizations vary widely. Within the area of restorative, curative, supportive, and assistive treatments and technological devices, there exists an immense diversity of services and products. A major repercussion of this complexity is the serious detraction from the ability of each individual with adult-onset disability to take responsibility for his/her own situation.

As social workers reviewing the potentially overwhelming challenge of dealing with these complexities of diversity, it is tempting to throw up our hands and allow the specialized professionals dealing in each disability area to set the helping agenda. However, if there was ever a clear helping situation requiring the particular skills and abilities of trained social workers, this is it. The responsibility for social work as a profession is to both attempt to understand the nature of these complexities and search for commonalities among individuals, families, and helping services involved in this area. Even more importantly, social work practitioners need to look for these commonalities while basing their assessment on the needs and situation of each individual client, a task well suited to this profession.

This chapter will attempt to explore some issues of commonality in dealing with this field of practice. In order to do so efficiently, the particular situations of individuals with adult-onset hearing and vision impairments will be presented for the sake of illustration. However, it must be remembered that the issues presented and the concerns underlying effective social work involvement in the area of adult-onset disabilities apply to a very wide range of practice situations appropriate to this field of endeavor.

Adult-Onset Hearing Loss

Why has this vast population been scarcely noted by psychologists and social scientists, who study so many other groups? Why are there so few organizations that represent and serve their interests? Why do we know so little about feelings and conduct of these people; their personal, social, and occupational problems; and the different ways, good, poor, and tragic, by which they and their families adjust to their condition? (Orlans, 1985, p. 179)

The needs of persons with hearing impairments differ significantly depending on the age of onset of the hearing loss. Hearing impairment occurring prelingually interferes with the acquisition of language and speech, thus having a profound impact on the education and communication skills of the deaf or hearing-impaired person. Because of significant problems with the English language, many prelingually hearing-impaired people have formed a Deaf Community, centered on their use of sign language as a means of communication (Thomas, 1984). The literature in this area is fairly extensive, concentrating on the education, vocational rehabilitation, and psychology of the deaf.

People who are post-lingually hearing impaired form a much more heterogeneous group, including young children and adolescents who may or may not learn sign language and join the Deaf Community, adults participating in the work force or raising children, and older adults who suffer hearing loss late in life. The literature on adult-onset hearing loss is very scant, even though there are approximately three times as many people experiencing significant hearing loss after reaching 21 years of age as before this age (Ries, 1985). Vernon and Andrews (1990) point out that in the United States, "professionals have essentially ignored these people" (p. 260). Glass and Elliott (1993) agree, stating,

"The unique characteristics of persons who lose hearing as adults often are recognized only incidentally, even by specialized professionals trained to provide rehabilitation services for deaf and hard-of-hearing persons" (p. 403). Meadow-Orlans (1985) adds, "It is surprising how often scholars have confused those individuals who became deaf before they acquired speech, and who may or may not use sign language, with the much larger population of deafened adults, whose experience and problems differ radically" (p. 35).

The problems of this population are certainly different from those experienced by children who are hearing impaired before learning to speak. A psychiatrist summarizes the difference in the following way: "Those suffering from a profound prelingual deafness suffer a sensory deficit; those deafened in adult life suffer a sensory deprivation. The problems of the one are developmental, of the other traumatic. They cannot be equated" (Denmark, 1969, p. 965). Jack Ashley (1985), in his personal account, describes the difference like this, "The born deaf are denied the advantages gained by the deafened before their hearing loss, yet they are spared the desolating sense of loss" (p. 61).

Problems caused by adult-onset hearing loss may include a traumatic psychological adjustment, as well as profound effects on one's career, marriage, and social life (Vernon & Andrews, 1990). The problems suffered by individuals in this group vary greatly as do the individuals themselves. The problems, however, can be extreme:

> Fear of failure, fear of ridicule, fear of people, fear of new situations, chance encounters, sudden noises, imagined sounds; fear of being slighted, avoided, made conspicuous; these are but a handful of fears that haunt the waking and even the sleeping hours of the sufferer from progressive deafness. Small wonder that, at best, he tends to live in an atmosphere of despondency and suspicion. Small wonder that, at worst, he may not particularly want to live at all. (Hunt, 1944, pp. 230–231)

This part of the chapter focuses on those people who suffer hearing loss post-vocationally, or after entering the work force. The age this refers to differs within the literature but is usually between 18 and 25 years of age. First the prevalence of the impairment will be analyzed, then the various etiologies will be considered, the attitudes toward the hearing impaired discussed, and finally the problems of adjusting to a hearing loss and issues regarding social work services to adult-onset hearing-impaired clients will be examined.

Prevalence of the Problem

The most recent census of deaf persons, conducted by New York University in 1971, reported more than 13 million people with a significant hearing loss, making it one of the most prevalent chronic physical impairments in the United States (Schein & Delk, 1974). Of these, 6.5 million experience a significant bilateral impairment (affecting both ears), with 2 million being profoundly deaf. Gentile (1971) reports that of those suffering a bilateral impairment, over 75 percent became impaired after turning 21 years of age. The Health Interview Survey in 1981 reports over 18 million people with hearing impairments (Ries, 1985). In the same year, Leske claimed hearing loss to be the most common source of disability in the United States.

Minority Groups

Hearing loss is considerably less prevalent among African American children than among white children (Schein & Delk, 1974). This is probably due to the infrequency of certain medical problems among black and brown-skinned people that have shown to cause deafness (Vernon, 1969). Hairston and Smith (1983) estimate that approximately two million African Americans have a hearing impairment serious enough to require medical or educational services, with about 22,000 being profoundly deaf. They also note that the education of African Americans who are deaf has historically been inferior to that of other hearing-impaired persons. In addition, black individuals who are deaf have lower average incomes, have a higher rate of unemployment, come from lower socioeconomic brackets, and receive less adequate medical care than white people who are deaf.

Research studies looking at Hispanic, Native American, and Asian American hearing-impaired persons reveal underachievement in school, greater difficulty obtaining medical, educational, and rehabilitative services, higher incidence of multiple handicaps, and misdiagnoses due to professional insensitivity to cultural differences (Christiansen, 1987; Delgado, 1984; Maestas y Moores & Moores, 1984). Deaf females are slightly less prevalent than deaf males, but females show higher unemployment rates, lower personal incomes, and a lower educational achievement than do deaf males (Barnartt, 1987; MacLeod-Gallinger, 1985; Schein & Delk, 1974).

Etiologies of Hearing Loss

The etiologies of hearing impairment among children are reported by Vernon and Andrews (1990) as follows: Heredity (26%); Prematurity (17.4%); Rubella (9.5%); Meningitis (8.7%); Rh factor complications (3.7%); Other causes (9.6%); Unknown causes (30.4%). (There is some overlap in categories.) Other etiologies are present when looking at adult-onset hearing loss. Some drugs, including aspirin and antibiotics, when used incorrectly, may have side effects that result in hearing loss (Vernon & Andrews, 1990). Exposure to noise can result in hearing loss (Alberti, Morgan & LeBlanc, 1974; Cantrell, 1974; Fishbein, 1971; Kryter, 1973; O'Neill, 1973). The prevalence of significant hearing loss due to noise exposure increases with the length of exposure. Therefore, the risk of older people being hearing impaired because of noise is several times higher than for younger people (Hetu & Getty, 1993). Certain illnesses, such as syphilis, Meniere's disease, cancer, measles, hyperthyroidism, cerebral palsy, and multiple sclerosis, can also cause adult-onset hearing loss (Vernon & Andrews, 1990).

Byl (1975) estimates that fifteen thousand people in the United States each year experience a sudden profound (and usually permanent) deafness. The etiologies are varied, including poor circulation, lightning, underwater diving, head injury, hormones, and viral disease (Byl, 1975; Pang, 1974; Podoshin & Fradis, 1975; Schiff & Brown, 1973; Simmons, 1973; Wright & Silk, 1974).

Etiologies among Older Adults

Ries (1982) reports that severe hearing loss can be found in approximately 16.5 percent of persons over 64 years of age, causing him to reach the conclusion that hearing loss competes with loss of teeth as the most prevalent impairment in the United States. Corso (1977) suggests that hearing loss among older adults is probably caused by a number of variables, some inherent in the physiology of auditory aging. Changes in the cochlea have been found in older hearing-impaired persons, but it is not understood why these changes occur at different rates in different people. Glass (1985) suggests, "Hearing loss in old age may not be "normal"; it may result in part from unnoticed, lifelong insults, some of which may be preventable" (p. 171).

Adjusting to Adult-Onset Hearing Loss

Psychological Adjustment

Vernon and Andrews (1990) suggest that for the individual who suffers a hearing loss during adulthood, psychological adjustment is often traumatic. The experience of one lipreading teacher illustrates the dramatic effects hearing loss can have on a person's life:

> Threats of suicide, rage, depression, isolation, self-hate, shame, and suspicion are part of her daily contacts with her pupils as they go through the period of intense emotional struggle due to sudden loss of hearing or sudden realization that the handicap is permanent or progressive. (Levine, cited in Thomas, 1984, p. 31)

Levine goes on to describe the psychological problems sometimes faced by those experiencing a hearing loss:

> Where the individual is accustomed to being an integral part of a close relationship, as in the family, on the job, and in the community, to be suddenly left alone is tantamount to ostracism. It is not surprising, therefore, to find many such persons engulfed in torments of despair, panic, rage, and a feeling of worthlessness. (p. 65)

Professionals often do little to help during this adjustment period since "only a minutia of psychologists, psychiatrists, and social workers have any concept of how an individual can effectively cope with hearing loss" (Vernon & Andrews, 1990, p. 260). The individual's ability to adjust is affected by the age of onset of the hearing loss, the severity of the hearing loss, the rapidity of the loss, and the amount of residual hearing (Meadow-Orlans, 1985). Glass (1985) adds that adjustment is not a short-lived phase: "There is no respite; the newly deafened must continually cope; silence and adaptation never cease" (p. 168).

Many efforts have been made to determine if the hearing-impaired population experience certain mental health problems proportionately more often than do hearing people. The overall higher prevalence of attention deficit disorders, including hyperactivity, has been clearly established and is probably linked to the brain damage caused by some of the etiologies of hearing loss (Levine & Wagner, 1974; Vernon, 1969). Most anxiety disorders do not seem to be overrepresented among the hearing-impaired population; however, post-traumatic stress disorder may be a little more common as a consequence of sudden late-onset deafness. Despite very prevalent stereotypes of the hearing-impaired population, recent research suggests that paranoid disorders and affective disorders are not diagnosed disproportionately more often among hearing-impaired clients (Vernon & Andrews, 1990).

Social Adjustment

During the period when hearing is diminishing, individuals may deny having a hearing problem; they may begin to dominate the conversation rather than having to understand others; they may become a master of the neutral response, responding with "Hmms," smiles and nods; they may become suspicious of others because of misunderstandings; and they may find hobbies or interests in which the communication required is minimal (Vernon & Andrews, 1990). When such efforts no longer work satisfactorily, some hearing-impaired individuals withdraw from social contact, resulting in isolation and loneliness (Thomas, 1984). Nett (1960) suggests that hearing-impaired people feel alienated and excluded from the larger society, "forgotten" rather than "discriminated against" (p. 117). This personal statement illustrates the profound effect hearing loss can have on one's psychological and social well-being:

> Though endowed with a passionate and lively temperament, and even fond of the distractions offered by society, I was soon obliged to seclude myself and live in solitude. If at times I decided just to ignore my infirmity, alas, how cruelly was I then driven back by the intensified sad experience of my poor hearing. . . . For there can be no relaxation in human society, no refined conversations, no mutual confidences. I must live quite alone and may creep into society only as often as sheer necessity demands. I must live like an outcast. If I appear in company, I am overcome by a burning anxiety, a fear that I am running the risk of letting people notice my condition. . . . Such experiences have almost made me despair, and I was on the point of putting an end to my life—the only thing that held me back was my art. (cited in Thomas, 1984, p. 28)

This quote was made by Beethoven in 1802 while experiencing a progressive hearing loss. It was 16 years before he became totally deaf.

Adjustment in the Work Place

Individuals may cope with hearing loss in the work place through "concealment of hearing difficulties, avoidance of demanding situations, and social withdrawal, especially at times of breaks, lunches, and meetings" (Hetu & Getty, 1993, p. 398). In concealing their impairment, they attempt to compensate for their hearing loss without the use of appropriate accommodations. By avoiding demanding situations, Getty and

Hetu (1991) found that hearing-impaired workers often restrict their own career advancement.

For the hearing-impaired person working in an environment where sound is an important source of primary information, Glass and Elliott (1993) point out that "the loss of hearing, whether progressive or sudden, introduces major hazards into their work environment" (p. 403). Despite the many obvious difficulties, Glass and Elliott discovered that 65 to 70 percent of people who had become deaf while in the work force "had continued successfully in their jobs and were promoted or did not change occupations subsequent to acknowledgment of problems with their hearing" (p. 412). They feel this is an important finding to convey to clients since initial reactions to hearing loss usually include feelings of frustration, anger, depression, isolation, and a sense of hopelessness (e.g., Elliott & Glass, 1991; Luey, 1980; Rousey, 1971).

Adjustment of Older Adults

Hearing loss accentuates the social isolation, dependency, and loss of status for the older adult (Beattie, 1981). The older adult may inappropriately be deemed "senile" because of the presence of a hearing impairment (Maurer & Rupp, 1979, p. 97). Meadow-Orlans (1985) points out the dual trauma experienced by elderly men (and women) who have retired from working and are concurrently experiencing a hearing loss. Criswell (1979) maintains that such elderly deafened people may "find themselves virtually prisoners in solitary confinement" (p. 36).

Ironically, older adults deafened in childhood often have a strong support system established in the Deaf Community and do not suffer from the isolation and dependency of those older adults deafened late in life. Glass (1985) points out the two very distinct populations of older hearing-impaired persons: "the deaf who are growing old and the old who are growing deaf" (p. 167). The emotional, social and behavioral effects of the hearing impairment on these two groups are very different, therefore their needs are also quite different.

Communication Issues in Social Work Practice

Levine (1981) suggests that in providing social services, the "main operational tool is communication—linguistic, conceptual, and behavioral. When communication ceases to function effectively, . . . practice suffers a crippling handicap" (p. 222). Shiels (1986) warns, "Where there is not good communication, behavioral observations will lack insight, interviewing will be difficult and likely quite artificial, and obtaining all-important client reactions to various activities will be hard to do" (p. 101). In order to communicate with the hearing-impaired client, the social worker must master the communication forms used by the hearing-impaired population and determine what modes of communication are preferred by a particular client.

Lipreading

Lipreading or speechreading is a skill that requires the hearing-impaired person watch for clues from the lips, tongue, and facial expressions. Vernon and Andrews (1990) warn evaluators that even the best lipreaders only get about 25 percent of what is said, mainly because only 33 percent of the English speech sounds are visible. They add that deaf children usually get only about 5 percent of what is said through reading lips. Levine (1981) and Elliott and Lee (1987) offer some guidelines that allow the lipreader to get as much as possible of what is being said (see Table 1).

Hearing Aids

It should not be assumed that a client who wears a hearing aid can hear everything that is said. Vernon and Andrews (1990) point out that hearing aids do not restore a normal level of hearing for the ear the way that glasses can give normal vision to the eyes. Kaplan (1985) explains that there are two types of hearing problems: one of loudness and one of clarity. Amplification with a hearing aid can only be effective with the first type. In the second type, language is distorted. Amplification does not eliminate the distortion. The vast majority of people with hearing loss experience both types of hearing impairment. This limitation of hearing aids should be clearly understood by the social worker and the client.

Meadow-Orlans (1985) points out that many older adults have trouble operating a hearing aid because of arthritic fingers, decreased coordination, and slower responses. Another problem with hearing-aid use is that some younger adults associate it with the stigma of growing old and therefore refuse to use them (Hetu & Getty, 1993). Some suggestions for interviewing the client who wears a hearing aid are included in Table 1.

Table 1
SUGGESTIONS WHEN INTERVIEWING
THE HEARING–IMPAIRED CLIENT

When client uses lipreading/speechreading:

1. Sit facing the client no more than four feet apart.
2. Sit so that light is behind the client rather than the interviewer.
3. Use your natural speaking voice and expression.
4. Do not distort mouth movements by grimacing, shouting, mouthing words without voice, or slowing down the delivery of speech.
5. Do not smoke, chew, rest with cheek or chin in hand, bend head down, turn face away, or move about while talking.
6. Stop for a break if the client appears to be fatigued.
7. Attend immediately to puzzled expressions.
8. Rephrase the concept or reword the language into simpler and/or more visible forms when the client does not understand—never simply repeat the same words.
9. When necessary, clarify ideas by discussing them with the client.
10. Keep pads and pencils nearby to clarify especially difficult concepts.
11. Obtain the client's attention before beginning to speak.*
12. Expect a decrease in understanding each time the topic is changed, and if necessary clarify statements until the new context is established.*

When the Client Uses a Hearing Aid

1. The interview room should be kept quiet, with special precautions against loud noises, such as a ringing telephone or an intercom buzzer.
2. Since many of these clients also rely heavily on reading lips, follow all the suggestions presented above for interviewing clients who read lips.
3. The interviewer's voice should be maintained at a level agreed upon by the interviewer and the client.
4. Keep a supply of hearing-aid batteries on hand.

Source: Information paraphrased from Levine (1981, pp. 329–331).
*Information from Elliott and Lee (1987).

Other Assistive Devices

Other devices are often used by the hearing-impaired client to assist in communication. These devices may be designed to aid communication in large groups, enhance personal listening in large areas, such as auditoriums and outdoors, enhance telephone, television and radio listening, or for signaling the telephone, doorbell, alarm clock, smoke alarm, or other warnings through the use of blinking lights, extremely loud sounds, or vibration (Kaplan, 1985).

Speaking

It is sometimes difficult to understand the speech of a hearing-impaired person. Levine (1981) offers the following suggestions to enhance the communication process: (a) allow the client to talk uninterrupted for a period of time to give the interviewer's ear a chance to get used to the particular speech patterns of the client; (b) the interviewer may have to depend to some extent on his/her lipreading skills to enhance understanding; (c) written or manual communication may also be used to help clarify certain words; (d) the interviewer should always ask for clarification when words are not understood; and (e) the interviewer should never correct the client's speech (pp. 331–332).

Written Communication

Writing may be the preferred communication mode of a hearing-impaired person who has a strong command of English. Writing materials and a comfortable setting should be made available. This can be an effective means of communication, but the social worker must be willing to take the necessary time to give and receive the desired communications (Elliott & Lee, 1987).

Sign Language

While the majority of people who become hearing impaired during adulthood do not learn sign language, some do choose this form of communication. One of the significant aspects of the deaf culture in the United States is the cultural language of the Deaf Community, American Sign Language (ASL). This language has its own grammar and syntax and cannot be directly translated into English. Many hearing people who use sign language use Signed English, which uses the same manual signs as ASL but uses the syntax and word order of English. Many deaf people are willing to use Signed English when communicating with a hearing person. Others have a strong pride in ASL and prefer not to use Signed English (Elliott & Lee, 1987). When it is necessary to use an interpreter with a client who uses sign language, Levine (1981) and Halgin and McEntee (1986) make several suggestions (see Table 2).

Body Language

It is important to be aware of the significance of body language when assisting a hearing-impaired client. Wright (1956) reminds the social worker:

Table 2
SUGGESTIONS WHEN USING AN INTERPRETER
WITH THE HEARING–IMPAIRED CLIENT

1. The interviewer should maintain the focus of interest on the client and not on the interpreter.
2. The client should be seated nearer to the interviewer than to the interpreter.
3. The interviewer should speak directly to the client and not to the interpreter.
4. The interpreter should begin interpreting after the other parties have finished speaking/signing.
5. When the interpreter is signing to the client, the interviewer should pay attention to the client's facial expressions and behavior.
6. The interviewer should keep the client's attention as much as possible.
7. The interviewer and interpreter should be aware of their own expressions and what they communicate to the client.
8. There should be no side conversation between the interviewer and the interpreter.
9. The interviewer should maintain friendly control over the process to encourage the building of rapport between the interviewer and the client rather than between the client and the interpreter.
10. The decision regarding the use and choice of an interpreter should be made with the client's assistance.*

Source: Information paraphrased from Levine (1981, pp. 334–335).
*Information from Halgin and McEntee (1986).

The deaf and the hard of hearing are very observant. (They have to be.) The way you stand or sit, the way you shrug your shoulders (perhaps in impatience), the way you walk from your desk to the door tell a great deal to the keen observer. Your manner, your poise, your smile, the expression in your eyes and on your face, the way you use your hands, all tell a story of indifference or understanding. (p. 19)

Future Directions

To become deaf as an adult is to be cut off in the midst of one's dreams and plans for the future, whatever they may be. Life comes to a halt. (Anderson, cited in Meadow-Orlans, 1985, p. 37)

The population of adults who suffer hearing loss seem to have been overlooked by the social services profession. Glass and Elliott (1993) report that few people who are deafened as adults receive vocational rehabilitation assistance compared to clients with early onset hearing impairments. Many of these clients are not even aware of the services available to them.

Orlans (1985) asks, "Why has this vast population been scarcely noted by psychologists and social scientists" (p. 179)? He suggests that this lack of attention is due, in part, to the heterogeneity of the population. Nevertheless, this is a population that, because of the difficulties of adjusting to this impairment, could benefit from social work services. Hopefully, in the future, social workers will take the lead in providing services and educating the public on the issues of importance to this diverse population. By looking at the cultural diversity issues of the population with visual impairments, an attempt will be made to reinforce, broaden and explore other aspects of this leadership role.

Population With Visual Impairment

Who are the disabled and what is the appropriate terminology to be used when referring to them? Let us explore the issues involved in answering these questions rather than the answers themselves. In doing so, we can use the example of issues involved in determining who is visually impaired and what labels or terms are appropriate for use in describing them generally.

Traditionally individuals without sight have been referred to as blind and have been considered to comprise this disability group. However, it has never been that simple when seen in terms of who needs assistance or should be eligible to receive services designed for this group of disabled individuals. A lay conception of blindness assumes that it means without sight or alternately having no light perception. While this may have been adequate as a descriptive category for those not involved with individuals with vision impairments, it has never been sufficient for those who are including the individuals themselves. Little difference exists between individuals who can perceive shapes and shadows, and those totally without sight. Having acknowledged this simple difference, it opens the door to the issue of where along a continuum from totally without sight to "20/20" vision does a limitation in vision become a disability?

For this purpose, the expertise of medical and paramedical practitioners was brought to bear in order to provide guidance in achieving some resolution. Medical practitioners involved with issues of sight have long expressed functional sight in terms of acuity of vision or completeness of field of vision (Kirchner & Peterson, 1981; National Society to Prevent Blindness, 1980). Most political jurisdictions have used these medically derived measures of functional vision to set definitions of eligibilities for consideration as disabled. For example, a fairly widely accepted definition of blindness based on visual acuity indicates that individuals whose vision, after the use of corrective measures (glasses etc.), remains at 20/200 or less are to be considered blind (Giarratana-Oehler, 1976; Stoddard & Shanks, 1983; Tuttle, 1984). That is to say an individual who sees at 20 feet what an individual with "20/20" vision would see at 200 feet would be termed blind. Thus the definition based on expert knowledge includes individuals with some residual sight and those who are totally without sight leading to the expanded label of "legally blind."

The obvious difficulty of an arbitrary definition of visual disability can be illustrated by thinking of the implications of the above terminology "legally blind." Does this not inspire thoughts of the "sight police"? Let's imagine these publicly funded control agents patrolling our communities looking for individuals whose visual acuity is slightly better than 20/200 but who illegally persist in pretending to be suffering some form of disability; imagine the shame of being picked up on such a charge. Ridiculous? Perhaps, but such arbitrary definitions still control the provision of many services to this population. Such definitions based on expert knowledge and observation are not only arbitrary but remove the individual from an ability to officially know and be involved in his own assessment of disability. Such arbitrary definitions become further complicated when differences in vision efficiency or functional usage are taken into account (Barraga, 1980).

Some theorists in social work would recommend a more functionally and interventionally based definition for this disability. From the social work perspective, what is of crucial importance is the impact of the vision limitation upon the individual as he interacts with the systems around him in the performance of everyday life skills. In this instance, social work values and consumer wishes seem to be headed in the same direction. The National Federation for the Blind, a major consumer organization in the United States, recommends the following definition for the disability arising from impairments to vision.

> One is blind to the extent that he must devise alternative techniques to do differently those things which he would do with sight if he had normal vision. An individual may properly be said to be blind or a blind person when he has to devise so many alternate techniques, that is if he is to function efficiently, that his pattern of daily living is substantially altered. (Vaughan, 1993, p. 102)

As can be readily seen, the definition not only removes the arbitrary nature of the fixed cutoff point but also removes the necessity for expert knowledge in assessing disability and directly involves the individual in this process.

With reference to terminology, this chapter has already alluded to a number of labels to describe individuals with a visual impairment. From this point forward, an attempt will be made to use consistently the terminology "person(s) with a visual impairment." This appears to be a term which has been accepted by the social work profession and by many persons with a visual impairment. It is felt that using the terminology, "person(s) with a visual impairment," emphasizes the person first and the disabling condition second. However, it would be inappropriate to proceed without identifying that this remains a controversial issue for those who are involved in this area (Stoddard & Shanks, 1983; Vaughan, 1993).

The National Federation of the Blind, speaking on behalf of consumers, strongly recommends the terminology "blind person." Spokepersons for this organization argue that this issue is not one of terminology but rather of changing the perspective and attitudes of society at large. Others argue that the term "blind" is too out of date and holds for many the idea of individuals who are totally without sight.

Clearly, persons with a visual impairment, helping professionals working with them, and society in general, have not arrived at a universal agreement upon appropriate terminology. However, the persons with the visual impairment and those working with them would be in general agreement with the National Federation's view that the perception of what it means to have a visual impairment must change (Vaughan, 1993). There is a need to see persons with a visual impairment as full participants in society, meeting their highest potential through the exercise of their individual skills and abilities (Meyerson, 1988; Phillips, 1985).

Images and Stereotypes

The cultural diversity issues in the disability field are most significant in the area of myth and stereotype. While these myths and stereotypes vary widely depending upon the nature of the disability, there are some commonalities which can be illustrated by looking at those applicable to individuals with visual impairments. The applicable myths and stereotypes are both positive and negative in nature, although all tend to inappropriately distort reality with any given individual (Lowenfeld, 1981; Lukoff, 1972; Resnick, 1981; Roberts, 1973).

Individuals who are visually impaired, particularly those who are totally without sight, have generally been attributed with compensating increased sensation from the other senses and with special talents such as increased musical ability (Kessler, 1976; Lukoff, 1972; Scott, 1969; Tuttle, 1984; Winkler, 1972). While it is true that some individuals develop an ability to utilize other senses to a greater degree, there is no empirical evidence to support the idea of augmented sensory acuity. Nonetheless, this mythology continues to permeate public perception and finds its way into the helping areas.

In the area of human sexuality, individuals with a visual impairment are seen with a dual mythology. On the one hand, they are attributed with having special tactile abilities and sensitivities as lovers, while on the other hand, professionally accepted ideologies link visual impairment with sexual perversion and punishment for sin (Cholden, 1958; Tuttle, 1984). Despite the fact that psychological theories with regard to the link to sexuality and sin were developed and espoused, they relate more clearly to the realm of imagination than reality (Winkler, 1972). While most individuals with a visual impairment find these mythologies humorous and learn to laugh at questions about their piano-playing abilities, they do nonetheless present distortions of the image of persons with a visual impairment and contribute to both stereotyping and stigmatization.

Probably the most significant area of stereotyping affecting persons with visual impairment revolves around the understanding of the individual's deficits. People with visual impairments are generally seen as living in worlds of isolation and darkness, struggling mightily against heavy odds, but nonetheless dependent and pitiable (Bogdan, Bilken, Shapiro, & Spelkoman, 1982; Meyerson, 1988; Resnick, 1981; Tuttle, 1984; Vaughan, 1993). This view has had the positive impact of defining persons with a visual impairment as being deserving of individual help and charity as well as appropriate for the efforts of societal assistance. The downside of course is that these individuals are not appropriately viewed in terms of strengths and abilities and there is no general acceptance of the idea that they should be.

It is quite recent that individuals with a disability have come to be seen as a minority group which has suffered oppression and discrimination (Barker, Wright, & Gonick, 1946). Persons with visual impairments might well be described as the "harmless minority" since they are not seen as being inferior in any personal characteristic or identity but rather as being inferior for very sound and logical reasons. This was clearly illustrated by the example of an applicant to graduate studies at Stanford University, who was visually impaired and who was turned down by the admissions committee in order to protect the student from experiencing frustration and failure in an area in which they assumed him to be unsuited. The assumption was that he would be unable to skim written material and would not be able to keep up in assigned readings. Since no test of these abilities exist for other students, this is a clear example of discrimination but also a clear example of patronage where those in power felt they were undertaking a very benevolent act by exercising such discrimination (Vaughan, 1993). For individuals with a visual impairment and most other persons with disabilities, this benevolent patronage acts as clearly oppressive prejudice. The fact that this prejudice may be well meaning in no way diminishes its impact. The process of assessing an individual based on one identifiable characteristic is no less discrimination than are universal assumptions made on the basis of skin color, ethnicity or gender. In working with persons with disabilities, the impact of this form of supposed logical prejudice must be taken into account and guarded against.

Implications for Practice

The above issues of prejudice, discrimination, patronization, and complexity all have serious implications for social work practice. Since practitioners are people as well, they must recognize the possibility of and guard against their holding similar forms of prejudice and stereotypical ideation. This becomes a particularly challenging task when working with individuals with adult-onset disabilities since it is easy to imagine ourselves in the same situation. In this case, our ability to empathize through imagining the impact of loss of function, particularly that of sight, gives rise to an inadvertent assumption that we understand the impact of the loss.

This tendency to overidentify with understanding the client's loss can have the effect of focusing practitioner attention upon the area of deficit. The practitioner's tendency to focus upon the functional deficits are further reinforced by the various complexities surrounding adult-onset disabilities. The social, physical, political, rehabilitative, and technological issues that abound around and within each area of disability conspire to maintain this focus upon deficits. The need to have some knowledge with regard to all of these complex issues inadvertently can focus the practitioner's efforts upon understanding the disability at the expense of understanding the individual. Since by definition many of these areas involve expert knowledge and specialized understanding, it is a short step from the knowledge of the implications of the individual's disability to assuming the knowledge of what is best for the individual. Although these two areas of knowledge are worlds apart, well-meaning and intelligent practitioners cross the line on an all-too-frequent basis. The truly important area of knowledge for practitioners in providing assistance is that of understanding the individual within the context of his situation (Maas, 1984; Neukrug, 1994; O'Neil, 1984; Robertson & Brown, 1992; Schmolling, Youkeles, & Burger, 1993; Tuttle, 1984). This means developing the ability to take into account the disability along with its various complexities without falling into the trap of losing sight of the individual within the area of disability.

Notwithstanding the above admonishments, in order for the practitioner to be helpful, there must exist an understanding of the commonalities among individuals who have experienced an adult-onset visual impairment (Turner, 1983). It is determining these commonalities that allow the professional practitioner to become skilled in the process of differential diagnosis and, subsequently, in the ability to provide quick and appropriate assistance to individuals in need. In the case of persons with an adult-onset visual impairment, many of these commonalities relate to loss or the reaction to and grieving of this loss (Monbeck, 1973; Schulz, 1980; Tuttle, 1984).

The adult onset of visual impairment has been seen to involve reactions of denial, depression, and dependence when viewed from a psychodynamic framework. These theories or frameworks for understanding the individual's adjustment to visual impairment utilize the constructs of phases or stages, seeing reactions progress from shock to acceptance. They are usually dynamic in nature, allowing for individual differences, but all assume individual reactions and psychological adaptation (Dover, 1959; Fitzgerald, 1970; Hicks, 1979; Kubler-Ross, 1969; Riffenburgh, 1967; Schulz, 1980; Tuttle, 1984). When seen from a systems approach, similar stages are seen to occur but are looked at in terms of crisis points in a process of transition (Brammer, 1991; Hopson & Adams, 1976; Robertson, 1992; Schlossberg, 1984).

In using conceptualization of these methods of ego defense or progression through the stages of acceptance and transition, it must be remembered that these commonalities provide a diagnostic road map; they do not specify exact routes or the only way of proceeding. The applicability of such constructs must be mediated by an understanding of the individual's characteristics or personality. A unique pattern or personality structure for persons with adult-onset visual impairment does not exist but rather varies markedly from individual to individual (Foulke, 1972; Kertley, 1975; Schulz, 1980; Tuttle, 1984). Social work practitioners are well positioned to see these defense mechanisms or stages of reaction to loss as being a dynamic process rather than things that must or even should occur. The theoretical conceptualization of loss may assist the practitioner in his assessment of an individual. Ultimately, that assessment must be based on the individual's perception of and reactions to the adult-onset disability.

Just as the assessment process and attribution of characteristics of the individual can become focused upon the existence of the disability, so can treatment modalities become overly focused. The evolvement of and training in behavioral approaches to assisting individuals in developing functional skills and abilities often require careful attention of both the practitioner and the client (Kessler, 1976; Tuttle, 1984; Vaughan, 1993). This degree of focus can lead the practitioner to ignore signs and signals which indicate that the individual with an adult-onset disability is wrestling with issues unrelated to the disabling condition or at best tangentially related to it. Brown points out the case of an individual client who was encouraged by the rehabilitation counselor to continue to develop coping skills in order to return to work as a means of increasing his quality of life. However, the counselor was completely missing the individual's request to deal with the impact of the loss of his wife and child who had separated from him after the onset of the disability (Brown, 1992). While behavioral techniques or technological adaptations may be extremely important and useful, the practitioner must take responsibility for ensuring that their acquisition is under the control of the person with a visual impairment in order to maximize their utility (Brown, 1992; Thyer & Stocks, 1986).

Similarly, there has been a tendency to focus upon the individual with the disability, thus ignoring a whole range of family systems theory. The identification of an adult-onset disability as an incident of loss and a transition in the individual's life is equally true for family members. In fact, all of those persons who are involved with the individual through significant relationships are affected. Probably the most important of these are those which take the form of familial relationships (Coopersmith, 1984; Kew, 1975; Schmolling, Youkeles, & Burger, 1993; Shapiro, 1983; Zastrow, 1993). The practitioner must be prepared to assess and intervene in family situations in order to assist with their reactions. This assistance must not only be viewed as a means of helping the individual with the adult-onset disability but must be seen as necessary and appropriate for the other individuals who are involved in their own right. Whether or not directions taken by family members in handling their reactions to the adult-onset disability and the individual are seen as positive or in the best interest of that individual, they must nevertheless be seen as having needs themselves. To make the focus of all assessment and intervention, the individual with the adult-onset disability not only ignores the legitimate needs of his significant others but also falls into that pitfall of patronizing the individual, albeit with the best of intentions.

Concerns for Policy and Service Delivery

The need to address common needs while respecting individual differences of persons with visual impairments makes both policy development and service delivery very challenging. Organizations designed to provide services to the visually impaired constituency have long been criticized for what most consumers see as a patronizing attitude and the tendency to see all persons with visual impairments in the same way (Robertson & Brown, 1992; Scott, 1969; Tuttle, 1984; Vaughan, 1993). The low focus of such organizations upon physical, psychological, and technological accommodation to the functional loss in sight results in criticism that such organizations in fact create an identity for persons with visual impairments (Scott, 1969).

Many of these organizations benefit from the charitable appeal provided by this client constituency but in the process set up an expectation that persons with a visual impairment must be seen as different from the overall population and of necessity must be segregated in order to receive appropriate services. This segregation or alienation of persons with visual impairments from the mainstream of society plays into the deficit view or stereotype cited above. These organizations, through their specialization and limited focus, tend to make it more difficult for a person with a visual impairment to compete in a sighted society and to be judged on the basis of strength and ability as opposed to one set of notable deficits.

The situation for policymakers is very challenging. It is essential for a caring society to promote social policies which assist in providing equal opportunities for all of its citizens. In the case of individuals with visual impairments, this focus needs to be on providing adaptation and assistance which leads toward accommodating the person with the visual impairment in terms of equal accessibility to all elements of social life. These elements of social life include leisure activities, recreation, employment, travel, etc. Policies or assistance programs designed to facilitate access in any of these areas must be sensitive to a wide range of possible needs existing within the constituent population. Assistance programs must allow individuals to choose from a range of possible accommodative services in order to respect the varying levels of skills, abilities, needs, and motivations to exist within the constituency. Similarly, policymakers must explore issues of funding structures such as the attaching of funds to the individual as recommended by the 1989 Brassard Committee Report (Brown, 1992).

Finally, the programs need to address real needs and provide meaningful assistance. Persons with visual impairments have long experienced the tokenism of a well-meaning but ignorant society. For example, the instillation of audible traffic signals frequently occurs at intersections adjacent to organizations providing services to persons with visual impairment. This is clearly a situation of tokenism since society has no intention of making all traffic lights audible and, therefore, the assistance which audible cues provide is meaningless to persons with visual impairments as they can be accessed at only one or two locations in any city. This ignores the realities of individual's actual lives and the abilities of even persons who are totally without sight to be able to function using other types of cues (Vaughan, 1993). One cynically might assume that these traffic signals are located near organizations serving the visually impaired to remind the sighted world of their existence and encourage the flow of charitable dollars. They certainly serve no useful purpose for the client constituency.

Token programs are not only useless attempts to accommodate but also do significant damage in terms of public perceptions. Once again, they focus attention on issues of deficit while ignoring areas of adaptive skill and ability. It is important that social policies on accommodations be available on a universal basis and be designed to enhance accessibility and opportunity on the basis of individual choice and assessment. It is clear that no one service or system of services can accommodate all persons with visual impairments. Identity, personal characteristics, motivations, and needs of persons with visual impairments do not lend themselves to a one-size-fits-all approach.

Concerns for Social Work Educators

Social work education is well positioned to provide society with professional graduates who can make a significant impact in accommodating the cultural diversity issues appropriate to persons who have visual impairments. Social work educators need to continue to emphasize the core values of professional practice as part of the educational process. This is particularly true in terms of the values of client self-determination and general respect for all individuals.

These core social work values are essential to any sensitive and meaningful approach to working with persons with disabilities. As has been pointed out throughout this chapter, there is no one-size-fits-all approach to working with persons with visual impairments, hearing impairments, or with any other adult-onset disability. While it is important that social work educators make students aware of the commonalities which exist among individuals with adult-onset disabilities, it is important that this be done in the context of individualized assessment. Social work educators can encourage their students to pay more than lip service to the conceptualization of problems as situations that must be understood through the meaning and functions which they possess for the individual. The expert's attempts to understand and assist based on specialized knowledge of the disability area is to be viewed as additive to the process rather than deterministic.

Finally, social work educators can ensure that individuals with disabilities are considered as a vulnerable or marginalized minority in need of consideration in all aspects of social work practice. The teaching of social policy, social work practice methodologies, and family and general systems theories could address the implications of cultural diversity from the standpoint of a multiplicity of minority groups. One of the major minority groups which needs to be included in this constellation of minorities and minority issues should be that of persons with physical disabilities.

Concerns for Research

An amazingly large body of research exists in the area of adult-onset disabilities. However, the bulk of this research takes the form of medical or quasi-medical-based research and research on technological adaptations. While this research is extremely important and must continue, there needs to be some effort put into balancing its impact.

At the present time, much of the research conducted upon individuals with visual impairments has been based on or influenced by this prevailing body of research knowledge. Research designed to look at rehabilitation process and effectiveness has been mechanistic or behavioristic in nature (Meyerson, 1988). While there is nothing implicitly wrong with this type of research, it has created a problem in that so little effort has been placed on understanding the nature of disabilities from the point of view of those individuals with the disability (Brown, Bayer, & MacFarlane, 1989; McHugh, Loeske & Frieze, 1986; Shontz, 1977).

Not to place more emphasis on the perspective of the person with the visual impairment leads to a depersonalization of both the treatment services and the approach to the individuals themselves. For example, Brown cites a study where a good deal of information was collected about the rehabilitation process and the views of the client towards this process. However, the subjects with physical disabilities were not seen as being important enough as individuals to be described demographically (Brown, 1992). While this can be written off as poor research, it illustrates the lack of attention paid to the overall identity of persons with visual impairments. This seems out of step with the holistic approach of social work and its adaption in many other professions. In fact, when it comes to persons with disabilities, we have not progressed far from the days when doctors treated "the broken leg in bed three."

Future Trends

Medical advances hold out many promises for hoped-for restoration procedures. While these are of great importance for individuals with particular conditions where breakthroughs may provide restorative services, they do not hold much promise for most people with disabilities. Most people look forward to a combination of advances in technology and enhanced accessibility within society as areas of hope for the future.

Legislation such as The Americans With Disabilities Act and employment equity programs combined with access to available technology encourage real hope and excitement among persons with adult-onset disabilities. For example, the impact of increased technology in the form of reading machines, braille transcription equipment, and mobility aids for persons with visual impairments, in and of themselves, have limited impact. However, when they are viewed as adaptive tools to allow the person with a visual impairment to exercise his/her skills and abilities through increased accessibility to a sighted world, the potential is noteworthy.

A cautionary note must be inserted at this point. The advancement of technology in our society creates as many areas of difficulty as it resolves. The advent of banking machines, computer screen ordering, and information systems, etc., places additional demands on the adaptive abilities of individuals with visual impairments, while Star Trek's portrayal of Jody's magic sight visor remains clearly in the realm of science fiction. The dominant sighted culture may see these adaptations as boons to persons with visual impairments, but it is crucial that the evaluation of adaptive equipment be based on its practical usability for the individual involved (Goode, 1988; Halpern, Close, & Nelson, 1986). There are numerous examples of technological advances hailed by the sighted community which ultimately proved to be next to useless as adaptive measures. Also, there is a tendency for the general population to overestimate the functional usefulness of adaptive equipment. The expectation that the development of reading machines and computer-assisted programs have or will make persons with visual impairments equal in a sighted society is purely erroneous. It is changing society's attitudes, provision of equal opportunities, and the making available of accommodative equipment and services which will accomplish this task. The most important advances in overcoming the negative implications of adult-onset disabilities will come from these efforts.

Whether social work practice focuses upon specific needs of individuals relative to their adult-onset disability or upon the broader cultural and societal aspects of work with this client group, it can play a major leadership role. The very complexity of cultural diversity issues applicable to individuals with adult-onset disabilities makes a person-in-situation approach essential for work in this area. The ability to both view and reinforce the individual as the primary actor in this world of complexity holds out promise for social work practitioners to intervene both sensitively and successfully with individuals and the systems effecting them.

REFERENCES

Alberti, P.W., Morgan, P.O., & LeBlanc, J.C. (1974). Occupational hearing loss—An otologist's view of a long-term study. *The Laryngoscope, 84,* 1822–1834.

Asch, A. (1984). The experience of disability: A challenge for psychology. *American Psychologist, 39,* 551–552.

Ashley, J. (1985). A personal account. In H. Orlans (Ed.), *Adjustment to adult hearing loss* (pp. 59–70). San Diego, CA: College-Hill Press.

Barker, R.G., Wright, B.A., & Gonick, M.R. (1946). *Adjustment to physical handicap and illness: A survey of the social psychology of physique and disability.* New York: Social Science Research Council.

Barnartt, S.N. (1987). Deaf population: Women. In J.V. VanCleve (Ed.), *Gallaudet encyclopedia of deaf people and deafness* (pp. 267–270). New York: McGraw-Hill.

Barraga, N. (1980). *Program to develop efficiency in visual functioning.* Louisville, KY: American Printing House.

Beattie, J.A. (1981). *Social aspects of acquired hearing loss in adults.* A report on the research project funded by the Department of Health and Social Security and carried out in the Postgraduate School of Applied Social Studies, University of Bradford (England), 1978–1981: Summary of Contents and Findings.

Bogdan, R., Bilken, D., Shapiro, A., & Spelkoman, D. (1982). The disabled: Media's monster. In M. Nagler (Ed.), *Perspectives on disability* (pp. 138–142). Hamilton, Ontario: Health Markets Research.

Brammer, L. (1991). *How to cope with life transitions: The challenge of personal change.* Washington, D.C.: Hemisphere.

Brown, R.I. (1992). Some challenges to counselling in the field of disabilities. In S.E. Robertson & R.I. Brown (Eds.), *Rehabilitation counselling* (pp. 133–175). San Diego: Chapman & Hall.

Brown, R.I., Bayer, M.B., & MacFarlane, C. (1989). *Rehabilitation programmes: Perform-ance and quality of life of adults with developmental handicaps.* Toronto, Ontario: Lugus.

Byl, F. (1975). Thirty-two cases of sudden profound hearing loss occurring in 1973: Incidence and prognostic findings. *Transactions of American Academy of Ophthalmol-ogy and Otolaryngology, 80,* 298–305.

Cantrell, R.W. (1974). Prolonged exposure to intermittent noise: Audiometric, biochemical, motor, psychological and sleep effects. *The Laryngoscope, 84*(Suppl. I), 3–55.

Cholden, M.D. (1958). *A psychiatrist works with blindness.* New York: American Foundation for the Blind.

Christiansen, J.B. (1987). Deaf population: Minorities. In J.V. VanCleve (Ed.), *Gallaudet encyclopedia of deaf people and deafness* (pp. 270–276). New York: McGraw-Hill.

Coopersmith, E.I. (1984). *Family therapy with families with handicapped children.* Rockville, MD: Aspen.

Corso, J.F. (1977). Auditory perception and communication. In J.E. Birren & K.W. Schaie (Eds.), *Handbook of the psychology of aging* (pp. 535–553). New York: Van Nostrand Reinhold.

Criswell, E.C. (1979). Deaf Action Center's senior citizen program. *Journal of Rehabilitation of the Deaf, 12,* 36–40.

Delgado, G.L. (1984). Hearing-impaired children from non-native language homes. In G.L. Delgado (Ed.), *The Hispanic deaf: Issues and challenges for bilingual special education* (pp. 28–37). Washington, D.C.: Gallaudet College Press.

Denmark, J.C. (1969). Management of severe deafness in adults: The psychiatrist's contribution. *Proceedings of the Royal Society of Medicine, 62,* 965–967.

Dover, F. (1959). Readjusting to the onset of blindness. *Social Casework, 40,* 334–338.

Elliott, H.H., & Glass, L.E. (1991). Psychological aspects of hearing loss in adulthood. *Proceedings of the XIth World Congress of the World Federation of the Deaf* (pp. 237–242). Tokyo: Secretariat of the World Federation of the Deaf.

Elliott, H., & Lee, M. (1987). The process: An overview. In H. Elliott, L. Glass, & J.W. Evans (Eds.), *Mental health assessment of deaf clients: A practical manual* (pp. 23–34). Boston, MA: College Hill Press.

Fishbein, M. (1971). Quiet please. *Medical World News, 12,* 76.

Fitzgerald, R.G. (1970). An exploratory study of adults with recent loss of sight. *Archives of General psychiatry, 22,* 370–379.

Foulke, E. (1972). The personality of the blind: A nonvalid concept. *New Outlook, 66*(2), 33–37.

Gentile, A. (1971). *Persons with impaired hearing, United States, 1971* (Series 10, No. 134). National Center for Health Statistics. Washington, D.C.: U.S. Government Printing Office.

Getty, L., & Hetu, R. (1991). The development of a rehabilitation program for people affected by occupational hearing loss—II: Results from group intervention with 48 workers and their spouses. *Audiology, 30,* 317–329.

Giarratana-Oehler, J. (1976). Personal and professional reactions to blindness from diabetic retinopathy. *New Outlook, 70,* 233–239.

Glass, L.E. (1985). Psychosocial aspects of hearing loss in adulthood. In H. Orlans (Ed.), *Adjustment to adult hearing loss* (pp. 167–178). San Diego, CA: College-Hill Press.

Glass, L.E., & Elliott, H. (1993). Work place success for persons with adult-onset hearing impairment. *The Volta Review, 95,* 403–415.

Goode, D.A. (1988). *Discussing quality of life: The process and findings of the work group on quality of life for persons with disabilities.* Valhalla, NY: Mental Retardation Institute, Westchester County Medical Center.

Hairston, E., & Smith, L. (1983). *Black and deaf in America: Are we that different?* Silver Spring, MD: T.J. Publishers.

Halgin, R.P., & McEntee, D.J. (1986). Psychotherapy with hearing-impaired clients. *Professional Psychology: Research and Practice, 17,* 466–472.

Halpern, A.S., Close, D.W., & Nelson, D.J. (1986). *On my own. The impact of semi-*

independent living programmes of adults with mental retardation. Baltimore, MD: Paul
H. Brookes.

Hetu, R., & Getty, L. (1993). Overcoming difficulties experienced in the work place
by employees with occupational hearing loss. *The Volta Review, 95,* 391–402.

Hicks, S. (1979). Psycho-social and rehabilitation aspects of acquired visual handicap.
New Beacon, 63, 169–174.

Hopson, B., & Adams, J. (1976). Towards an understanding of transition: Defining
some boundaries of transition dynamics. In J. Adams, J. Hayes, & B. Hopson
(Eds.), *Transitions: Understanding and managing personal change.* London: Martin
Robertson.

Hunt, W.M. (1944). Progressive deafness. *Laryngoscope, 54,* 229–234.

Kaplan, H. (1985). Benefits and limitations of amplification and speechreading for the
elderly. In H. Orlans (Ed.), *Adjustment to adult hearing loss* (pp. 85–98). San Diego,
CA: College-Hill Press.

Kertley, D.D. (1975). *The psychology of blindness.* Chicago: Nelson-Hall.

Kessler, F.A. (1976). *The unseen minority: A social history of blindness in the United States.*
New York: David McKay.

Kew, S. (1975). *Handicap and family crisis.* London: Pitman.

Kirchner, C., & Peterson, R. (1981). Statistical brief number fifteen. *Journal of Visual
Impairment and Blindness, 74,* 267–270.

Kryter, K.D. (1973). Impairment to hearing from exposure to noise. *Journal of the
Acoustical Society of America, 53,* 1211–1234.

Kubler-Ross, E. (1969). *On death and dying.* New York: Macmillan.

Leske, M. (1981). Prevalence estimates of communicative disorders in the U.S. *ASHA,
23,* 229–237.

Levine, E.S. (1981). *The ecology of early deafness: Guides to fashioning environments and
psychological assessments.* New York: Columbia University Press.

Levine, E.S., & Wagner, E.E. (1974). Personality patterns of deaf persons: An interpretation based on research with the Hand Test. *Perceptual and Motor Skills Monograph*
(Suppl. 4-V39).

Lowenfeld, B. (1981). *Bertold Lowenfeld on blindness and blind people.* Selected papers.
New York: American Foundation for the Blind.

Lukoff, I.F. (1972). Attitudes toward the blind. In I.F. Lukoff & O. Cohen (Eds.),
Attitudes toward blind persons (pp. 1–13). New York: American Foundation for the
Blind.

Luey, H.S. (1980). Between worlds: The problems of deafened adults. *Social Work and
Health Care, 5,* 253–265.

Maas, H.S. (1984). *People and contexts.* Englewood Cliffs, NJ: Prentice-Hall.

MacLeod-Gallinger, J. (1985). *Secondary school graduate follow-up program for the deaf*
(Sixth Annual Report). Rochester Institute of Technology, National Technical
Institute for the Deaf, Division of Career Opportunities.

Maestas y Moores, J., & Moores, D. (1984). The status of Hispanics in special
education. In G.L. Delgado (Ed.), *The Hispanic deaf: Issues and challenges for
bilingual special education* (pp. 14–27). Washington, D.C.: Gallaudet College Press.

Maurer, J.F., & Rupp, R.R. (1979). *Hearing and aging: Tactics for intervention.* New York: Grune and Stratton.

McHugh, M.C., Loeske, R.D., & Frieze, I.H. (1986). Issues to consider in conducting nonsexist psychological research: A guide for researchers. *American Psychologist, 41,* 878–890.

Meadow-Orlans, K.P. (1985). Social and psychological effects of hearing loss in adulthood: A literature review. In H. Orlans (Ed.), *Adjustment to adult hearing loss* (pp. 35–57). San Diego, CA: College-Hill Press.

Meyerson, L. (1988). The social psychology of physical disability: 1948 and 1988. *Journal of Social Issues, 44*(1), 173–188.

Monbeck, M.E. (1973). *The meaning of blindness.* Bloomington, IN: University Press.

National Society to Prevent Blindness. (1980). *Vision problems in the U.S.* New York: National Society to Prevent Blindness.

Nett, E.M. (1960). *The relationships between audiological measures and handicap.* A project of the University of Pittsburgh School of Medicine and the Office of Vocational Rehabilitation, U.S. Dept. of Health, Education, and Welfare.

Neukrug, E. (1994). *Theory, practice, and trends in human services.* Belmont, CA: Wadsworth.

O'Neill, J.J. (1973). Hearing conservation. *Rehabilitation Record, 14,* 508.

O'Neil, M.J. (1984). *The general method of social work practice.* Englewood Cliffs, NJ: Prentice-Hall.

Orlans, H. (1985). Reflections on adult hearing loss. In H. Orlans (Ed.), *Adjustment to adult hearing loss* (pp. 179–194). San Diego, CA: College-Hill Press, Inc.

Pang, L.Q. (1974). Sudden sensorineural hearing loss following diving and treatment by compression: A report of two cases. *Transactions of the American Academy of Ophthalmology and Otolaryngology, 78,* 436–443.

Phillips, M.J. (1985). "Try harder": The experience of disability and the dilemma of normalization. *The Social Science Journal, 22*(4), 45–57.

Podoshin, L., & Fradis, M. (1975). Hearing loss after head injury. *Archives of Otolaryngology, 101,* 15–18.

Resnick, R. (1981). *The relationship between self concept, independence and the life styles of congenitally blind persons in terms of integration.* Doctoral dissertation, University of San Francisco.

Ries, P.W. (1982). *Hearing ability of persons by sociodemographic and health characteristics: United States* (Series 10, No. 140). National Center for Health Statistics. Washington, D.C.: U.S. Government Printing Office.

Ries, P.W. (1985). The demography of hearing loss. In H. Orlans (Ed.), *Adjustment to adult hearing loss* (pp. 3–21). San Diego, CA: College-Hill Press.

Riffenburgh, R. (1967). The psychology of blindness. *Geriatrics, 22,* 127–133.

Roberts, A. (1973). *Psychological rehabilitation of the blind.* Springfield, IL: Charles C Thomas.

Robertson, S.E. (1992). Counselling adults with physical disabilities: A transitions perspective. In S.E. Robertson & R.I. Brown (Eds.), *Rehabilitation counselling* (pp. 133–175). San Diego: Chapman & Hall.

Robertson, S.E., & Brown, R.I. (Eds.). (1992). *Rehabilitation counselling: Approaches in the field of disability*. San Diego: Chapman & Hall.

Rousey, C.L. (1971). Psychological reaction to hearing loss. *Journal of Hearing and Speech Disorders, 36,* 382–389.

Schein, J.D., & Delk, M.T. (1974). *The deaf population in the United States*. Silver Spring, MD: National Association of the Deaf.

Schiff, M., & Brown, M. (1973). Hormones and sudden deafness. *The Laryngoscope, 84,* 1959–1981.

Schlossberg, N.K. (1984). *Counseling adults in transition*. New York: Springer.

Schmolling, P., Jr., Youkeles, M., & Burger, R. (1993). *Human services in contemporary America*. Belmont, CA: Wadsworth.

Schulz, P. (1980). *How does it feel to be blind?* Vanives, CA: Views.

Scott, R.A. (1969). *The making of a blind man*. New York: Russell Sage Foundation.

Shapiro, J. (1983). Family reactions and coping strategies in response to the physically ill or handicapped child: A review. *Social Science Medicine, 17,* 913–931.

Shiels, J.W. (1986). Vocational assessment. In L.G. Stewart (Ed.), *Clinical rehabilitation assessment and hearing impairment: A guide to quality assurance* (pp. 95–110). Silver Spring, MD: National Association of the Deaf.

Shontz, F.C. (1977). Six principles relating disability and psychological adjustment. *Rehabilitation Psychology, 24,* 207–210.

Simmons, F.B. (1973). Sudden idiopathic sensorineural hearing loss: Some observations. *The Laryngoscope, 83,* 1221–1227.

Stoddard, E.R., & Shanks, S.L. (1983). Social types and differential rehabilitation within "the blind" role: A sociological view of the visually compromised. *California Sociologist, Summer,* 105–124.

Thomas, A.J. (1984). *Acquired hearing loss: Psychological and psychosocial implications*. London: Academic Press.

Thyer, B.A., & Stocks, J.T. (1986). Exposure therapy in the treatment of a phobic blind person. *Journal of Visual Impairment and Blindness, 80,* 1001–1003.

Turner, F.J. (Ed.). (1983). *Differential diagnosis and treatment in social work*. New York: Macmillan.

Tuttle, D.W. (1984). *Self-esteem and adjusting with blindness: The process of responding to life's demands*. Springfield, IL: Charles C Thomas.

Vaughan, C.E. (1993). *The struggle of blind people for self-determination: The dependency rehabilitation conflict, empowerment in the blindness community*. Springfield, IL: Charles C Thomas.

Vernon, M. (1969). *Multiply handicapped deaf children: Medical, educational and psychological considerations*. Reston, VA: The Council for Exceptional Children.

Vernon, M., & Andrews, J.F. (1990). *Psychology of deafness: Understanding deaf and hard-of-hearing people*. New York: Addison-Wesley Publishing Co., Inc.

Winkler, D.M. (1972). The blind: Psychological and emotional needs. *The Social Worker, 40,* 262–269.

Wright, B.C. (1956). *Orientation training for vocational rehabilitation counselors: A syllabus on special problems of the deaf and the hard of hearing for orientation institutes*. Washington, D.C.: American Hearing Society.

Wright, J.W., & Silk, K.L. (1974). Acoustic and vestibular defects in lightning survivors. *The Laryngoscope, 84,* 1378–1387.

Zastrow, C. (Ed.). (1993). *Introduction to social work and social welfare.* Pacific Grove, CA: Brooks/Cole.

Chapter 9

SOCIAL WORK PRACTICE WITH GAY MEN, LESBIAN WOMEN, AND BISEXUAL INDIVIDUALS

SOPHIA F. DZIEGIELEWSKI AND DIANNE F. HARRISON

Introduction

Sexual orientation as described by Hyde (1990) is defined as "whom we are sexually attracted to and also have the potential for loving" (p. 418). In Western society, any sexual preference other than hetero-sexuality, attraction toward someone of the opposite sex, is typically frowned upon as a socially unacceptable sexual orientation. The belief that all people are heterosexual is common and this myth is often reinforced by the media, laws, advertising, sex education and by health and mental health professionals.

Toward a Definition of Non-Heterosexuals

In American society, heterosexual behavior is considered to be the norm against which all other sexual orientations are compared. Bisexuality, having sexual preferences toward both sexes, and *homosexuality,* having sexual preferences toward members of the same sex, are considered by many Americans to be unacceptable forms of affectional attraction (Davis & Smith, 1984). The term homosexual is derived from the Greek root meaning same and can be applied to both males and females. Homosexuals, particularly males, are often referred to as gays. Female homosexuals are generally referred to as *lesbians.*

This word was originally derived by the Greek poet Sappho who lived on the island of Lesbos. Although Sappho was married and had a child she often wrote love poetry about other women, and her lesbian feelings were the focus of her life. In the black communities of the Diaspora women also have termed the erotic fasination they have found with other women. *Mati* (or matisma) is the Sranan Tongo word for women who have sexual relationships with other women. These women also have sexual relationships with men, during the same time period

(Wekker, 1993). Many times these women have children; and, culturally they are believed to be more consistent with Afrocentric heritage than their female counterparts termed *black lesbians* (whose only sexual partners are other women) (Wekker, 1993).

The terms *gay males* and *lesbians* are the preferred way to address male and female homosexuals. Gay activists prefer these terms because they believe that the term homosexual emphasizes the sexual aspects of the life-style, and homosexuality has often been used as a derogatory label negatively ingrained into society.

Defining what constitutes a gay male or a lesbian is somewhat more difficult to do. There are many stereotypical and derogatory terms used to define gay males and lesbians, and some individuals believe that non-heterosexuals are readily definable by their mannerisms or dress. For example, gay males are often thought to be effeminate and *limp wristed,* and lesbians are believed to be masculine and of the *butch* type. In reality, however, non-heterosexuals as well as heterosexuals, do not exhibit clear lines of behavior. Similar to heterosexual relationships there also appears to be a complex intersection of race, gender and sexuality (Kader, 1993). The stereotypical definition of gay males as effeminate and lesbians as masculine simply does not hold true. It is impossible to define homosexual or heterosexual behavior based on dress or sex role characteristics. Each individual exhibits different degrees of these traits, and if all individuals were placed on a continuum of feminine to masculine there would be little correlation between where heterosexuals and non-heterosexuals were placed.

There have also been attempts to define homosexuality and heterosexuality by merely identifying an individual's sexual preference. Research evidence, however, does not support this (Kelly, 1990). The problem with adopting such a simple definition is that sexual activity may not be limited only to those individuals to whom the non-heterosexual is attracted, and varying degrees of sexual attraction and preference can be exhibited (Kelly, 1990).

According to Kinsey, Pomeroy, Martin and Gebbhard (1953), there are no binary distinctions that can be made between what is a *homosexual* or a *heterosexual.* Rather, most sexual behavior exists on a continuum between exclusive homosexual experiences and exclusive heterosexual experiences. Berger (1983) believed that "homosexual identity is [was] the result of a system of interacting influences that included life experiences, cultural and religious values, social reaction, self-attribution, and association with others" (p. 135). Simply stated, the psychosocial factors (e.g., self-acceptance, peer association, sexual encounters, identity confusion, social reaction and self-labeling) that surround an individual are important in the search for a definition.

In summary, strict definitions of homosexuality, bisexuality and heterosexuality are difficult to make. To further complicate this definition Billy, Tanfer, Grady and Klepinger (1993) found in a recent study of United States males between the ages of 20–39 that sexual behavior varied tremendously based on the reported frequency of sexual acts preferred and performed (vaginal, anal and oral) and this was further influenced by the social and demographic characteristics of the subject. Definitions based solely on current behavior do not take into account situational factors or an individual's inner interests, needs or fantasies (Kelly, 1990). As a result, general distinctions can be made based on the current attractions or activities which predominate: homosexual (same sex), heterosexual (opposite sex) and bisexual (both sexes).

Prevalence of Non-Heterosexual Behaviors

Although heterosexuality is considered the norm, the incidence of homosexuality has occurred across all times and cultures and involves about 5 percent of the total population (Hyde, 1990). Some researchers (Fay, Turner, Klassen & Gagnon, 1989; Nichols, 1989; Kinsey, Pomeroy & Martin, 1948) believe this figure is higher, representing up to 10 percent of all men and a slightly lower percentage for women. Most researchers agree that the incidence of homosexuality is higher among males than females (Hyde, 1990; Kelly, 1990). It is believed that a bisexual orientation, also known as ambisexual, characterizes approximately 20 percent of the population (Nichols, 1989). Bisexuality (at least one sexual experience with a male and one sexual experience with a female) is more common than exclusive homosexuality (no experiences with the opposite sex) (Hyde, 1990). Given the incidence estimates of non-heterosexual contacts, regardless of how a society views non-heterosexual behavior, it is found universally and it is practiced by some individuals in all societies at all times.

Homosexuality: Cross-Cultural Perspectives

In Western societies (including the United States) fears or negative attitudes toward homosexuality, also known as *homophobia,* are prominent; however, this is not the case in other societies. For example, in Melanesia, an area of the southwest Pacific, homosexual behavior is a necessary part of the entrance into male adulthood. In Melanesia it is believed that if a carefully selected older male gives semen to a younger male, either orally or anally, it will strengthen the younger male (Herdt, 1984). These older male partners were usually selected by the father of the younger male. It is believed that this period of homosexual intercourse served to increase the preparedness of the young male for upcoming heterosexual relationships.

Anthropological research also exists in regard to a tribe of Peruvian natives which allegedly engage in homosexual activity openly, and where the women and children of the tribe maintain separate quarters (Kelly, 1990). Documented accounts of same-sex behavior are common among Buddhists and Moslems, especially among Buddhist monks and priests (Gramick, 1983). During the eighteenth and nineteenth century in Egypt, homosexuality among men in many instances was accepted as a normal part of the patriarchal system (Hatem, 1986). It was believed that male homosexual relationships not only supported and cemented the ties between men but also perpetuated the patriarchal way of life. Heterosexual rivalry was viewed as counterproductive to the forming of necessary political alliances. This, however, was not the case for lesbians. Lesbianism was viewed as a threat to patriarchal authority. Lesbian relationships were denounced, as women were viewed as important insomuch as they could satisfy the needs of males.

In ancient Greece, sculptures of nude young males clearly fostered interest and attraction in the male body. Weitz (1977) believed that this art was not used to attract and appeal to women. Women in ancient greece had no status or power, and, in this patriarchal society, their role was to satisfy and birth sons, not to be entertained. This interest in the young male physique was strongly related to the ideal of humanity. The wealthy in ancient Greece often utilized the private services of young male servants and the ethos involved in these relationships remains questionable (Weitz, 1977).

Homosexuality: For the Rich

Throughout history some societies have accepted and documented homosexuality, but only for the rich. For example, in ancient Chinese literature homosexuality was viewed as acceptable for royalty (Ruan & Tsai, 1987). Several prominent Chinese leaders openly wrote about their attraction and affection for younger males, and during the Ching Dynasty a temple was established that provided young monks whose sole purpose was to entertain. These monks only served royalty, as the fees charged were high. Although, for the most part, homosexuality was accepted for the rich, this was not the case for the entire population. In the literature, this type of behavior met with covert societal opposition, and, oftentimes, the later literary writings attacked the practice by punishing the characters that engaged in such behaviors (Ruan & Tsai, 1987).

During the feudal period in Japan, male homosexual love was considered more "manly" than heterosexual love (Gramick, 1983). Interested men frequented teahouses which employed male geishas. The sole purpose of these young males was to satisfy the request of the benefactor. These facilities were quite common until the end of World War II. The use and number of these facilities decreased with the influence of Western culture and the occupation invasion of American forces into the country.

Homosexuality Among Native Americans

Although non-heterosexual activity is generally frowned upon in the United States, documented cases of accepted non-heterosexual activity exists. For example, among the North American Indians, the practice of *berdache*, in which an individual adopted one or more behaviors, occupations, or social roles of the other sex, was accepted. Much of this literature has been gathered and published as a history project of the Gay American Indians (GAI) in San Francisco (Roscoe, 1987). The objective of this publication of source material was to help researchers and educators become aware of the historical and cultural aspects of gay Native Americans. In many tribes berdache status was part of traditional religious and/or ceremonial life. Male berdaches were sometimes reported to be medicine men, and female berdaches were sometimes linked with prophecy telling.

Oppression and Homosexuality

Gay males and lesbians have often been the targets of overt and covert prejudice and discrimination. The film *Pink Triangles* (Cambridge Documentary Films, 1982) depicts that in Medieval and early modern history *gay men and lesbians* were declared heretics and burned at the stake. The word *faggot,* which means a bundle of kindling, became another term for gay males because they were used as human stakes in the burning of witches.

In Nazi Germany a tremendous injustice to many minority groups including women, Jews and homosexuals took place. The degree of covert intense prejudice directed toward these groups will never be matched. In the Nazi camps, all minority prisoners were labeled with patches which corresponded to their crime (e.g., Jews wore a yellow star, Jehovah's Witnesses wore a purple triangle, and gay men wore a pink triangle). Tens of thousands of gay men were imprisoned and executed simply because of their homosexual orientation (Cambridge Documentary Films, 1982). These men were senselessly killed as they were used in *dress rehearsals* for the mass executions of the Jews. Himmler, Chief of the Gestapo, hated women, and because he equated gay males with women, he believed these males had no value or purpose in society. In Nazi Germany, gay males were viewed as detriments to the supremacy of the German race and, therefore, they had to be eliminated.

The situation was somewhat different for lesbians. In Nazi Germany, the primary purpose for Aryan women was defined as the reproduction of male Aryan children. If a woman was non-Aryan or she did not fulfill her childbearing role, she was viewed as having very little purpose. If a lesbian admitted her same-sex orientation, she was considered deviant and persecuted as such. Lesbians did not wear the pink triangle, as their existence was not recognized by the state.

Non-Heterosexuals: Where Do They Fit?

After having reviewed the existence of non-heterosexual preferences in Melanesia, Peru, Egypt, Greece, China, Japan, and America, it is apparent that non-heterosexual behavior has existed in all societies throughout history. Sometimes, it has been accepted and encouraged, and at other times it has been condemned or punished. Homosexual subcultures seem to appear in all societies, although documented cases appear more commonly among royalty or the wealthy.

A society's climate, race, affluence, typical family structure or state of development seem to have little effect on whether homosexual orientations emerge; however, the rules and sanctions in the society have affected the degree of visibility and openness of homosexual behavior. If homosexual behaviors were approved and praised, the incidence would increase in societies where homosexuality was condemned, such behavior would decrease. It is also possible that homosexual behaviors that were once accepted can become unacceptable over time.

Today, incidences of *gay bashing,* where young gang members physically attack gay men or lesbians for the simple reason that they are homosexual, appear to be on the rise (Wertimer, 1988). While some segments of our society have shown increased tolerance of or support toward homosexuals, this continues to be a slow, painful process. However, it is important to note that tolerance does not always mean acceptance. Many individuals in our society continue to prefer to just ignore the influence that these forms of alternate relationships can have on a gay, lesbian or bisexual individual's life. For example, Reimoneng (1993) stated that many of the admirers of the work of Countee Cullen, a hailed poet laureate of the Harlem Renaissance, prefer to ignore the influence of his openly admitted homosexuality. Further, in a study conducted at a midwestern state university with 177 respondents, most reported increased alienation from the greater society when they held more positive attitudes about homosexual life-styles than negative ones (Wells & Daly, 1992). Research also supports that homosexuality finds even less tolerance in the minority black community than it does in the majority white community (Ernst, Francis, Nevels & Lemek, 1991). Unfortunately, with attitudes and beliefs such as this, many individuals still continue to deny or denounce the awareness and support of the individual who subscribes to an alternative life-style.

In protest of how they are viewed and treated in society, many gay men and lesbians continue to wear the *pink triangle* in an attempt to show the discrimination to which they have been subjected, to demonstrate gay/lesbian pride, and to make society aware that injustices will not be tolerated any longer.

Oppression and discrimination against non-heterosexual individuals has occurred throughout history—and continue to occur. Although such oppression may not be as extreme as in Medieval times and Nazi

Germany, the subtle and sometimes not so subtle means of discrimination remain. The myths, misdefinitions and stereotypes that surround non-heterosexual orientations continue to abound.

Myths and Stereotypes

There are many myths and stereotypes about gay men and lesbians which continue to create prejudice and discrimination toward these individuals. Some of the most common and the most destructive include the following:

(1) *All gay men are effeminate and all lesbians are masculine or "butch."* This stereotype represents a confusion between sexual identity, or an individual's sex role or gender behaviors (masculine, feminine, or androgynous), and sexual orientation, which refers to the preferred sex of the sexual partner. Apart from a small number of cases, it is impossible to determine a person's sexual orientation from their appearance, mannerisms, interest, or job (Hyde, 1990).

(2) *Homosexual couples play heterosexual roles in their relationships, sexual or otherwise.* This stereotype refers to the belief that one of the partners always assumes the dominant or male role in the relationship, while the other partner assumes the passive or female role. On the contrary, research has not supported that such role playing is typical (Peplau, 1981). Any such role playing which does exist is probably due to the lack of relationship models which are available to gay and lesbian couples; the only available model is a heterosexual one. As such, it appears that this type of role playing may be more common among older couples than younger couples (Hyde, 1990). These types of generational differences also appear in heterosexual couples.

(3) *Most male homosexuals are child molesters, and gay men and lesbians are constantly trying to recruit others into their life-style, especially children.* Again, research has not supported either of these myths. In fact, most child molesters (80%) are heterosexuals and are usually male heterosexuals molesting young girls (Kelly, 1990). Adolescents who are initiated into homosexual activity are most often persuaded by another teenager, not by an adult (Sorensen, 1973).

(4) *Homosexuals dislike members of the opposite sex, and all a lesbian really needs is a "good man who can show her a good time."* Contrary to this stereotype, most gay males are not woman-haters and most lesbians are not man-haters. Exclusive homosexuality is a relatively rare phenomena;

many predominately gay males and lesbians engage in heterosexual activity from time to time (Kelly, 1990).

(5) *All gay men have AIDS.* While disproportionately higher numbers of gay men are represented among those persons with AIDS, currently the fastest-growing group with HIV are heterosexuals (HIV/AIDS Report, 1993). AIDS is a devastating illness that has currently reached pandemic proportions. In the United States alone it is estimated that 1.5 million individuals suffer from AIDS and those at the greatest risk of exposure are: (1) sexually active individuals which includes homosexuals, bisexuals and heterosexuals; (2) substance abusers, both men and women who may have used interveneous drugs; and (3) persons who have received blood or blood products in the early 1980s, including hemophiliacs and surgery patients (Treatment Team Handbook, 1991). Based on race, only 12% of the nation's population is black, yet current statistics show that 28% of the people with AIDS are black (Jemmott, 1993); this leaves black males disapportionately affected by AIDS (Icard, Schilling, el-Bassel & Young, 1992). Taking this into account, research is being conducted to elucidate the probable reason(s) for the disproportionate number of minority gay males infected with the disease (blacks and Hispanics) when compared to their white counterparts. Differences in sociodemographic status, history of sexually transmitted diseases, or sexual and drug-use behaviors appear to be factors that contribute to this division (Easterbrook, Chmiel, Hoover, & Saah, 1993). To date, the reported cases of AIDS among lesbians remain rare, with only two documented cases of female-to-female transmission (Monzon & Capellan, 1987).

(6) *Homosexuals choose this life-style and orientation and they could change if they wanted to.* At this point in time, no single factor has emerged from the research as to what causes a homosexual orientation or any other sexual orientation. It appears that sexual orientation seems to be determined prior to adolescence, and it is likely that there is a biological explanation for sexual preference, although evidence for the biological explanation has not yet been collected (Hyde, 1990). No support has been found for explanations of homosexuality which emphasize parental relationships (e.g., absent father or domineering mother), early unpleasant heterosexual experiences, or a child's seduction by a same-sex adult (Hyde, 1990; Kelly, 1990). While the development of sexual orientation is a complex issue, it is apparent that homosexuals do not "choose" their sexual preferences any more than heterosexuals do. Perhaps the only element of choice is whether or not to "act" on these preferences.

Therapists who claim to have "cured" homosexuals have probably simply taught such individuals not to act on their same-sex attractions.

Homosexuality and Religion

Often, religion has been a block for many non-heterosexual individuals. In the Old Testament of the Bible several texts have been quoted as condemnations of homosexuality. The texts that are usually referred to are: Leviticus 18:12, Genesis 9, Corinthians 6:9 and Timothy 1:10. Some individuals believe that these texts were actually intended to condemn sex outside of marriage, male prostitution and marrying or loving someone from a different race or country, not homosexuality per se (Cambridge Films, 1982). There are also passages in the Bible that support slavery and the inferiority of women; therefore, the individual subjective interpretation of the Bible cannot be underestimated. Basically, when dealing with the interpretation of biblical views it is important to note that these interpretations vary widely, with advocates on both sides seeking to find justification for their religious views (Berger, 1987). There are several Christian and Jewish organizations (e.g., Dignity Integrity Universal Fellowship) established specifically for gays, lesbians and bisexuals which are supported by either the major denominations (e.g., Catholic, Jewish, Episcopal and Methodist) or nondenominational sects (e.g., Metropolitan Community Churches, Unity).

Homosexuality and the Medical Model

Previously, it was believed that homosexuality was a sin. In the twentieth century this idea was replaced with the medical model and the notion that homosexuality was an illness or sickness that needed to be treated (Hyde, 1990). The medical community literature addressed and labeled this as a disease, and during this pathology became the central role of treatment. For years the inclusion of homosexuality in the American Psychiatric Association's *Diagnostic and Statistical Manual* was used to support treatment of homosexuality as a disease and that homosexuality was a mental illness (Berger, 1987). In the 1970s, however, this concept of homosexuality as a disease or a congenital condition (existing at birth) was challenged. Therefore, on December 15, 1973, a landmark treatment event occurred when the American Psychiatric Association's board of trustees voted to remove it as a psychiatric disorder. The rationale for excluding homosexuality as a mental illness was that the definition of a mental disorder had not been met; no evidence of social impairment or emotional distress was found. Since many gay men and lesbians were found to have lived happy, well-balanced lives, the concept of homosexuality was changed from the concept of disease to a way of life. Professionals were no longer to address this issue as pathologic unless problems were evidenced in the sexual orientation an individual had chosen.

Homosexuality and Legal Implications

Various laws have also complicated the development of homosexual liberation. Although homosexuality and bisexuality are not directly outlawed per se, some of the behaviors and processes held in common, such as sexual behaviors other than heterosexual intercourse, including anal or oral sex, are illegal in many states. These laws, known as sodomy laws, also apply to heterosexual couples; however, in regard to heterosexuals, these laws are less likely to be enforced. Numerous cases of acts of sodomy involving two consenting male adults have been brought to court; however, the same acts involving a heterosexual couple are rarely prosecuted. Although these acts remain illegal, the differential way the violations are enforced and the sentences granted remains open to interpretation and controversy (Kelly, 1990).

Changes in the laws have occurred over the years, and, as of 1990, 26 states and the District of Columbia had decriminalized consensual homosexual activity (Kelly, 1990). In some states, women are still at risk of prosecution if they are identified as being in a lesbian relationship. "With the exception of Wisconsin, most government systems and private sector organizations continue to reserve the right to deny lesbians equal rights in education, employment, lending, housing, and medical settings" (Woodman, 1987, p. 809). The military and many government positions have clearly established policies against non-heterosexual activity. If a service person admits or is found to be engaging in non-heterosexual activity, he or she will be released from military service. If the admitting person is a government employee in the civilian sector, although they would not be released, he or she could be denied a security clearance.

Gay men and lesbians should carefully weight the medical, religious and legal realities before deciding to come out.

Homosexuality and Coming Out in America

At the start of the 1960s homosexuality was referred to as primarily a private affair (Berger, 1986), supported by the universal belief that homosexuality was a disease or a sin. In a Harris poll conducted from 1965 to 1969, the majority of Americans indicated that homosexuals were considered harmful to American life (Kelly, 1990). A fear, dislike, hatred or prejudice of gay men and lesbians, known as *homophobia*, became widespread (Martin & Lyon, 1984). Americans found that their homophobic attitudes surfaced in the following irrational fears: (1) a fear of homosexual tendencies in oneself; (2) the fear that heterosexuals would be converted to the homosexual life-style; and (3) fear that if homosexuality was accepted, procreation, and therefore the human race, would be altered, if not extinct (Gramick, 1983).

In general, the climate of the 1960s was turbulent. This decade was marked by numerous political movements, reflecting support for non-establishment themes. The *"sexual liberation movement"* became a popular cause. This intensified social/political interest helped many disadvantaged groups to receive support and attention that previously had never been received. As part of the nation's desire for sexual political liberation, gay liberation became visible.

Of critical importance to the gay liberation movement was an incident that occurred in Greenwich Village, New York. In June, 1969, the Stone Wall Inn, a bar frequented by gays, was invaded by police. The gay consumers of the club became angered by what they believed was unprovoked harassment. The consumers fought police for several nights, refusing to have the bar closed (Newton, 1976). This incident, generally referred to as Stonewall, has been noted as the beginning of the awakening of gays into personal and sexual liberation (Kelly, 1990; Nichols, 1989).

After this rebellion, homosexual individuals began to openly express their non-heterosexual preference or "closet existence" and the term "coming out" was coined. Substantial differences existed between how gay men and lesbians reacted to their coming out of the 1960s. For lesbians, it was more of a political battle and the patriarchal approaches to sexual activity were frowned upon, in many cases leading to sexual avoidance (Nichols, 1989). For gay men, on the other hand, sexual freedom was often linked to frequent casual sex. In support of this mind-set, bathhouses and sex clubs became popular. Here, males could meet with other men for the specific purpose of having anonymous sexual relations (Hyde, 1990). Unfortunately, these facilities led to the rapid spread of venereal diseases, hepatitis and enteric disorders. It is also believed that the sexual *coming out* during the 1970s contributed to the rapid spread of the HIV virus among the gay community, although it took years for scientists to make this connection to the disease and how it was being spread.

> Once the HIV virus and how it was being communicated was identified a noticeable change in the gay community occurred. This type of frequent casual sex took a downward swing. However, recently a 250 member gay and bisexual sample of African American males in the San Francisco Bay area yielded some alarming information. Approximately 50 percent of the males reported having unprotected sexual relations, and this was considerably higher than what was reported by white males in San Francisco between 1988 and 1989. (Peterson, Coates, Catania, & Middleton, 1992)

Discrimination Differences Between Gay Males and Lesbians

Throughout history there appears to have been greater discrimination against gay males than lesbians (Cambridge Films, 1982; Nichols, 1989). There may be several reasons for this. First, in early socialization and throughout life, effeminate behavior in males is viewed negatively. The girl who has masculine traits is labeled a *tomboy* and expected to grow out of it. The boy, on the other hand, who shows effeminate behavior is feared and severely ridiculed by his peers and family. It is unclear how this basic difference in socialization can and might affect the non-heterosexual in later life.

The second reason for greater discrimination against gay males may be due to the power issues in society and the status of women in general. In Nazi Germany and in other foreign countries lesbians were not persecuted because they were viewed as non-people (Cambridge Films, 1982; Hatem, 1987). The loss of a male in American society (to a homosexual life-style) may be viewed as more of a wasted human resource than the lesbian female due to the perceived greater importance of men in our society. However, as the roles for females continue to diversify and women gain more economic power, this world view may be shaken.

A third possible reason for the apparent greater discrimination of gay males as opposed to lesbians is more complex. It deals with the number of frequency of sexual relationships and the actual sexual acts associated with gay men and lesbians. As stated earlier, some lesbians have often been turned off to sex, as it is viewed as a patriarchal restraint (Woodman, 1987); sex to them is more of a political stance with conservative sexual practices being highlighted; and lesbians typically change their partners less frequently than gay males. Recent research has suggested that gay males tend to have more sexual partners than both lesbians and heterosexuals, and in the male gay community non-monogamous relationships are more accepted (Berger, 1987). The days of the tearoom and bathhouse trade, although now almost nonexistent, have left lasting impressions. The *high-tech* practices of the 1970s, which involved elements of masochism and sadomasochism, are not easily forgotten, and it becomes almost too simple to blame and target the dreaded disease of AIDS as the problem of gay males alone.

Practice Issues

There are several practice issues that gay males, lesbians and bisexuals have in common. Before discussing these issues, it should be pointed out that most of the problems confronting these individuals are no different than those experienced by heterosexuals. Further, simply because a person has a non-heterosexual orientation does not necessarily mean that the difficulties for which they are seeking help are related to sexual orientation. Nonjudgmental assessments can assist in targeting the exact nature of the client's concerns. Some clients may prefer to be helped by competent gay or lesbian professionals, if available; for other clients, the services of competent and *straight* professionals is satisfactory.

One practice concern that may be unique to gay male and lesbian clients is the personal and social acceptance involved in admitting to oneself and/or others that a sexual attraction toward the same sex exists. This can be a very confusing and upsetting time. Although this identity confusion often occurs in adolescence or early adulthood, it can occur at any age (Berger, 1986). Acknowledging this type of preference is in contrast to many accepted beliefs and, therefore, open to alienation from family and friends. Anti-homosexual messages denouncing this type of behavior almost always come from parents, peers and the community. At times, these messages can affect an individual's self-concept and self-esteem, and the choice to accept this stigmatized role can be a difficult one.

Just as homophobia may be manifested in those who surround the non-heterosexual, it can also be internalized by the individual. In internalized homophobia, gay males or lesbians can begin to hate or resent themselves, feeling inferior to their heterosexual friends. They may become frightened of what they feel and become unsure of how they can fit. These feelings can cause confusion and may result in their denying, hiding or justifying their non-heterosexual preferences (Nichols, 1989). Berger (1983) suggested that for therapy to be effective with these individuals a task-centered approach should be employed. In this approach, the individual must accomplish certain tasks such as learning how to manage information about self and deriving support from peers. The acquisition of these tasks can help the individual gain self-acceptance. Berger (1983) warned, however, that in discovering and accepting the self, many individuals pass through a militant phase characterized by a need to assert their homosexuality. This phase is considered a normal part of the adjustment process and should not be viewed as a pathological state. When the announcement to and the acceptance by significant others become an issue, questions to be considered are: (1) how much information about self-identity and sexual preferences should be released? and (2) how should this information be conveyed to the individual's parents, family, friends, heterosexual peers and employers?

A second practice issue concerns family structure and patterns. Although many gay men and lesbians establish and maintain satisfying long-term relationships (McWhirter & Mattison, 1984; Hyde, 1990), the factors that keep heterosexual couples together do not always apply to non-heterosexual couples. For example, non-heterosexual couples generally differ from heterosexual couples in that their relationships tend to be non-monogamous (Nichols, 1989; Kelly, 1990). Non-heterosexual couples may change partners more often than their heterosexual counterparts, and in the homosexual culture, this behavior is usually viewed as acceptable. A second difference is financially based. Non-heterosexual couples, especially gay males and lesbians, tend to be financially independent. The incentive to stay together for purely financial reasons generally does not apply. A third difference is that maintaining a relationship for the children's sake may also not apply. In non-heterosexual couples, especially gay men and lesbians, often there are fewer children living in the home. Therefore, relationships are not cemented together for the sake of the children. Often, it is easier to let go of a relationship than to address the family and societal prejudices that this type of an *unconventional* relationship will attract. Therefore, non-heterosexual couples may be more likely to leave their mates without the same attachments found in heterosexual couples. This makes couple counseling or group couples counseling, with a focus on increasing communication skills, a critical issue.

A third practice issue deals with the sexual practice on non-heterosexual couples. These practices may be more varied than their heterosexual counterparts. It is important to note that individuals who participate in the behavior of crossdressing, referred to as transvestites, are not necessarily homosexual or bisexual (Brown, 1990). In non-heterosexual couples there is a tendency toward less vaginal penetration and more oral, anal and *uncommon* sexual practices (Nichols, 1989). Non-heterosexual couples, whether they engage in uncommon practice such as *watersports, sadistic masochistic practices,* or *fist fucking* (either vaginally or anally), generally are aware of them and how they are used (Nichols, 1989; Kelly, 1990). Gay males or lesbian couples may be aware of more sexual variations than the therapist treating them. Practitioners must examine their own feelings in regard to these practices and educate themselves regarding the various forms of sexual expression prominent in the non-heterosexual repertoire. The role of the therapist is to aid these couples in choosing and deciding what practices are best for them, in a well-informed, nonjudgmental, supportive atmosphere. Readers are referred to Nichols (1989) for a more detailed discussion of sex therapy with gay males, lesbians and bisexuals.

A fourth practice issue concerns the common method of socialization for non-heterosexual couples and the fact that many non-heterosexual couples (especially gay males) use *gay bars* as a social outlet (Israelstam & Lambert, 1986; Nichols, 1989; Kelly, 1990; DiNitto & McNeece, 1990). These bars serve a variety of needs that might be met for heterosexual couples through church affiliation, community centers and country clubs (Schwartz, 1980). Although many gays have formed their own churches and community groups (Hyde, 1990), the gay bar is still the primary unit of socialization (DiNitto & McNeece, 1990). Therefore, leisure time in the life-styles of many gays is linked to a drinking milieu. This environment is not a healthy one for developing long or satisfying relationships (DiNitto & McNeece, 1990). Although the research is limited on substance abuse in gay males and lesbians, Israelstam and Lambert (1986) believe that this is an area that needs valid attention and research.

This makes the role of the social workers twofold: (1) to initiate and support further research into the area of alcohol consumption and how this information relates to the substance treatment offered to this population; and (2) to become aware and make referrals to alternate means of homosexual socialization. Some alternate methods include: Alcoholics Anonymous (AA) groups (some of which are specifically offered to gay individuals) and groups and organizations (social and religious) dedicated to supporting the gay movement. Many of these activities and services available to the gay community are advertized in publications designed for gay men and lesbians and in local newspapers.

Gay Males and AIDS

Acquired immune deficiency syndrome (AIDS) has become a tremendous issue in the gay community. When society first acknowledged the disease it was termed gay-related immune deficiency (GRID), because it was believed that only homosexuals could get it (Stulberg & Smith, 1988). Sexually active gay males and bisexual males still constitute the largest group of individuals at risk for AIDS, constituting 66 percent of all reported cases (Centers for Disease Control, 1987). Society's attempt to make AIDS a problem belonging solely to homosexuals has helped to increase the level of homophobia in general and increase the anxiety, fear and doubt experienced by gay males themselves. The internalization of homophobic feelings in regard to the disease has become more prominent (Kreiger, 1988). Just as society has blamed the homosexual, the homosexual may blame himself or herself. In the past, frequent impersonal sexual contacts allowed gay males to avoid exploring their feelings. With fewer, more consistent relationships, the intimacy between partners becomes very important, and this new role can be anxiety-producing. The role of the therapist becomes crucial in supportive counseling and educating gay males about the disease, its transmission and safe-sex practices.

The treatment effectiveness of using a counseling-education approach to help prevent AIDS transmission was measured by a team of AIDS researchers in Sidney, Australia (AIDS Conference Bulletin, 1990). This team took one hundred asymptomatic homosexual males and tracked them from 1983 thru 1990. Muhall (AIDS Conference Bulletin, 1990) stated that he and his research associates believed that their intervention may have stopped the spread of AIDS into the research group. According to the researchers, a highly significant decrease in the number of sexual partners among group members was reported. A decline in the frequency of unsafe sex practices with increased use of condoms was also evidenced. The researchers concluded that the counseling and education of homosexual men had reduced sexual practices that were thought to be unsafe.

Both Puckett and Bye (1987) and the AIDS researchers in Australia agree that education is a powerful tool in changing sex-related behaviors. To further support of this contention, Flowers, Miller and Booraem (1994) also reported positive responses by 771 gay and bisexual men to single-session STOP AIDS discussion groups. This study found that there was a significant increase in reported attitudes about personal effiacy in controlling the spread of the HIV virus and intended safer sex practices after just one single-session intervention.

Haney (1988) believed that psychological support at the time of diagnosis was extremely important in *"preventing reactions of fear and anger from being transformed into self-destruction"* (p. 251). The barren and bleak prognosis of the disease outcome can complicate disease adjustment and the following reactions may occur: suicidal ideation or intent, denial of the disease, anger, hostility, frustration and depression. Each of these feelings and emotions must be treated as a normal part of the acceptance process, and dysfunctional degrees of these feelings must be treated on an individual basis.

Haney (1988) suggested that we change the mind-set of the professional community in dealing with the patient from preparing him for death, to preparing him for life. This can be accomplished in part by decreasing negative talk. For example, instead of saying, *"there is nothing we can do"* and *"you have so many months to live,"* focus on the possibilities of living. Concrete problem-solving skills become essential with a focus on what can and cannot be done. Kreiger (1988) suggested that the following stepwise approach be used to help those who need help coping with, understanding and handling the sexual transmission of AIDS: (1) dispense accurate information about the condition and transmission of AIDS; (2) assess the individual's fear of prior exposure; (3) help the individual learn to protect self and others; (4) assess support systems and encourage the building of support networks; and (5) address the related issues and fears as they apply.

In summary, it is important to stress that those afflicted with AIDS had a life before diagnosis and they will continue to live after it. The goal of the practitioner becomes to work with the client to improve the quality of their life in the here and now. Social workers who work with gay males and lesbians need to be aware of the psychosocial consequences this disease can have on the gay community. Social workers also need to promote and support groups, policies and programs which combat AIDS-related discrimination against the gay community (Stulberg & Smith, 1988).

Bisexuals

As stated earlier, a bisexual or an *ambisexual* person is an individual whose sexual orientation is toward both men and women. A slang term often used to address this group is AC/DC (alternating current-direct current). The proponents of bisexuality often view themselves as entrepreneurs of sexuality and are open to the widest variety of sexual experiences possible. In a recent data bank survey of 65,389 men who had admitted to having sex with other men since 1977, 26% reported that they were bisexual. More black (41%) and Hispanic men (31%) than white men (21%) reported bisexual behavior (Chu, Peterman, Doll, Buehler, & Curran, 1992). However, the exact number of all who participate at least once in some type of bisexual activity is unknown.

There is no easy definition in regard to how often and with which sex bisexual individuals prefer to spend their time. Some bisexuals prefer heterosexual experiences over homosexual ones half of the time and are referred to as "fifty-fifty" bisexuals (Hyde, 1990), and others only tolerate or accept same-sex or opposite-sex behavior but do not choose it. Others briefly choose this type of sexual intimacy while later moving on to a strictly heterosexual or homosexual relationship. There have been documented cases where the same-sex orientation did not become desirable until age 40 or 50 (Hyde, 1990).

Doll (1990) warned, however, that if education is used in treatment of bisexuals it must consist of more than just education regarding sexual identity. Some experts view bisexuality as a *natural* state of being. The bisexual, however, does not really fit in the homosexual or the heterosexual orientation. Although bisexuals may often seek comfort in either group (Nichols, 1989), they may not feel as they truly belong in either one. Further, they may be seen as *fence sitters* by both gays and straights and face discrimination and negative attitudes from both groups. Taking into account the diversity in the type, stage and frequency of bisexual behaviors, it becomes important to approach the individual in the context of what the individual appears to need. The following questions should be considered: (1) Is his or her bisexual preference causing any marital or family problems? If they are involved in a heterosexual monogamous relationship the probability of this being problematic is high. (2) Are they experiencing sexual identity problems, not knowing quite where they fit? (3) Are they frightened and/or confused by the same-sex orientation they are experiencing? and (4) Are they able to talk over their feelings with their primary significant other? If not, do they have any other type of support network available to them?

Individual counseling which focuses on problem identification and concrete problem solving should be considered. The search for the availability of self-help groups, support groups or other community or religious resources should be obtained, and the importance of workshops, books, magazines and other educative resource materials should be recommended.

Summary of Practice Issues

Social workers need to address the following issues when working with gay males, lesbians or bisexual individuals. The practitioner needs to be knowledgeable about and nonjudgmental toward these individuals (Keyy, 1990; Hyde, 1990; Falco, 1991). As products of society, most of us have been socialized into the stereotypical and prejudicial behaviors we must now identify and work to eliminate. Identifying how we are affected by our traditional beliefs and values (what we believe to be right and wrong) is not an easy task. Homophobic behavior needs to be viewed in the same context as any other prejudice against a particular minority group (e.g., women, blacks, etc.). The social worker must first educate himself or herself on the subject. This can be done through reading the professional literature and attending workshops, in-services and seminars which cover non-heterosexual behaviors in general and homophobic reactions in particular. Generally, in education the materials that need to be reviewed include: myths and realities, life-style issues, sexual practices, parenting, religious concerns, health issues, and specific counseling in regard to communicative diseases. For the treatment of AIDS victims in particular, Grossman and Silverstein (1993) suggest a support group format for the professional health care worker. Here, workers can be helped to relieve their own stress and burnout when dealing with their own emotional reactions and/or frustrations.

The social worker should also be involved in educating others, including other mental health professionals. Martin and Lyon (1984) have documented how some male therapists have been noted to subscribe to the myth that all a lesbian really needed was a good heterosexual experience with a man. Others may use homosexually based jokes and stories for entertainment. That type of behavior needs to be discouraged; humor at the expense of others is neither funny nor professionally responsible.

Some gays, lesbians and bisexual individuals may be reluctant to share their life-style preference with the helping professional. For example, research has shown that lesbians are less likely than primarily heterosexual women to disclose their sexual orientation (Cochran & Mays, 1988). This makes it essential that the client feel comfortable with the therapist. As noted earlier, some homosexual individuals may prefer to see a homosexual therapist rather than a heterosexual one. This is because homosexual individuals do not have to explain much of what they are experiencing or feeling, as they believe the other person more readily understands. When this happens it is important to refer the client, if possible, to get the treatment he or she is requesting.

The social worker must also become familiar with resources in the gay male and lesbian communities. For example, a client once came into the office and stated he was ready to *come out;* however, he could no longer attend his regular church and he did not want his only social contacts to be provided by the local *gay bar.* By knowing what churches would accept the gay male and the number and contact person for a local gay men's support group, the client expressed great relief. As social workers, we need to know what resources are available, as this enables the social worker to perform the roles of educator counselor, advocate and broker, which are all part of our social work domain.

As social workers in practice with gay males and lesbians we must not adhere to the *sickness* or *mental illness* theory that we have subscribed to for years. According to Gonsiorek (1982), researchers in the 1960s and 1970s overwhelmingly suggested that homosexuality is not related to psychopathology or psychological adjustment. As stated earlier, this does not mean, however, that gay males and lesbians do not have problems, only that their problems many times are similar to problems experienced by heterosexuals. There are also unique problems of these individuals that makes knowledge of these alternate life-styles of paramount importance for social workers. Sexual identity problems can include: the fears and repercussions of coming out (Gramick, 1983); the denial and suppression of homosexual erotic fantasies (Storms, 1980); and changing roles in midstream from a heterosexual family system to a homosexual one. Proctor and Groze (1994) further reminded the practitioner that many gay, lesbian and bisexual adolescents and young adults have attributed feelings of suicide to related issues of sexual gender. These are only a few examples of the unique problems that can originate in this group.

It is important not to pity or try to change sexual orientation. The sexual orientation chosen belongs to the individual as both his or her own right and responsibility. Your role is not to help individuals merely adjust to their problems. Your role as the therapist is to help the client identify the problem, establish a plan of action to address it, and provide support and guidance as they work through this process.

At all times, social work practitioners need to subscribe to the highest of ethical and moral standards. These must include the right of client self-determination and respect and support for whatever sexual preference(s) a client has chosen (Wyers, 1987). Being a gay male, a lesbian, or a bisexual, in a homophobic society where they are often stigmatized and ostracized simply for the company they choose to keep, is a difficult burden for even the strongest of individuals. What better goal for social workers than to support this unnecessarily stigmatized group.

Conclusion

There is much variability in gay male, lesbian and bisexual experiences, and these experiences are affected by the sex of the individual (male vs. female), class occupation, personality, geographic location (small town versus large city) and other factors. Some individuals choose to be open about their sexual preferences and others do not. Of those who do not, many maintain conventional relationships and live outwardly as heterosexuals. Our society tends to behave in a *heterosexist* manner, i.e., assuming everyone is heterosexual and that only images and models of a heterosexual life-style are permissible. Same-sex relationships do not conform to this model, and for individuals who are uncomfortable with their own sexuality or with differences from the status quo, homosexuality and bisexuality can be very threatening. As social workers, we must work toward a society which is more accepting of all human differences.

REFERENCES

Berger, R. (1983). What is a homosexual: A definitional model. *Social Work, 28,* 132–134.

Berger, R. (1986). Gay men. In H. Gochros, J. Gochros, & J. Fischer (Eds.), *Helping the sexually oppressed* (pp. 162–180). Englewood Cliffs, NJ: Prentice-Hall.

Berger, R. (1987). "Homosexuality: Gay men." In A. Minahan (Ed.), *Encyclopedia of social work* (pp. 795–805). Silver Spring, MD: National Association of Social Workers.

Billy, J.O., Tanfer, K., Grady, W.R., & Klepinger, D.H. (1993). The sexual behavior of men in the United States. *Family Planning Perspective, 25,* 52–60.

Brown, G. (1990). The transvestite husband. *Medical Aspects of Human Sexuality, 35,* 39–40.

Cambridge Documentary Films. (1982). *Pink Triangles* [Film]. Cambridge, MA: Author.

Chu, S.Y., Peterman, T.A., Doll, L.S., Buehler, J.W., & Curran, J.W. (1992). AIDS in bisexual men in the United States: Epidemiology and transmission to women. *American Journal of Public Health, 82*(2), 284–287.

Cochran, S.D., & Mays, V.M. (1988). Disclosure of sexual preference to physicians by black lesbian and bisexual women. *Western Journal of Medicine, 149*(5), 616–619.

Davis, J.S., & Smith, T. (1984). *General social surveys, 1972–1974: Cumulative data.* New Haven: Yale University/Roper Center.

Doll, L. (1990). Discrepancies found between sexual identity behavior. *AIDS CONFERENCE BULLETIN, 1*(3), 12–16.

DiNitto, D.M., & McNeece, C.A. (1990). *Social work: Issues and opportunities in a challenging profession.* Englewood Cliffs, NJ: Prentice-Hall.

Easterbrook, P.J., Chmiel, J.S., Hoover, D.R., & Saah, A.J. (1993). Racial and ethnic differences in human immunodeficiency virus type 1 (HIV 1) seroprevalence among homosexual and bisexual men. *American Journal of Epidemiology, 138,* 415–29.

Ernst, F.A., Francis, R.A., Nevels, H., and Lemeh, C.A. (1991). Condemnation of homosexuality in the black community: A gender specific phenomenon? *Archives of Sexual Behavior, 20,* 579–581.

Falco, K.L. (1991). *Psychotherapy with lesbian clients.* New York: Brunner-Mazel Publishers.

Fay, R., Turner, C., Klassen, A., & Gagnon, J. (1989). Prevalence and pattern of same-gender sexual contact among men. *Science, 243,* 338–348.

Flowers, J.V., Miller, T.E., Smith, N., & Booraem, C.D. (1994). The repeatability of a single-session group to promote safe sex behavior in a male at risk population. *Research on Social Work Practice, 4,* 240–247.

Gonsiorek, J.C. (1982). Results of psychological testing on homosexual populations. In W. Paul, J.D. Weinrich, J.C. Gonsiorek, & M.E. Hotvedt (Eds.), *Homosexuality: Social, psychological and biological issues.* Beverly Hills, CA: Sage.

Gramick, J. (1983). Homophobia: A new challenge. *Social Work, 28,* 137–141.

Grossman, A.H., & Silverstein, C. (1993). Facilitating support groups for professionals working with people with AIDS. *Social Work, 38,* 144–151.

HIV/AIDS Task Force Report. (1993). Racial minorities at increased risk: An Arkansas HIV/AIDS report. *Journal of the Arkansas Medical Society, 89,* 390–393.

Haney, P. (1988). Providing empowerment to the person with AIDS. *Social Work, 33,* 251–253.

Hatem, M. (1986). The politics of sexuality and gender in segregated patriarichal systems: The case of eighteenth and nineteenth century Egypt. *Feminist Studies, 12,* 2.

Herdt, G.H. (Ed.). (1984). *Ritualized homosexuality in Melanesia.* Berkeley, CA: University of California Press.

Hyde, J. (1990). *Understanding human sexuality.* New York: McGraw-Hill.

Icard, L.D., Schilling, R.F., el-Bassel, N., & Young, D. (1992). Preventing AIDS among black gay men and black gay heterosexual male interveneous drug users. *Social Work, 37,* 440–445.

Israelstam, S., & Lambert, S. (1986). Homosexuality and alcohol: Observations and research after the psychoanalytic era. *International Journal of Addictions, 21,* 509–537.

Jemmott, L.S. (1993). AIDS risk among black adolescents: Implications for nursing interventions. *Journal of Pediatric Health Care, 7,* 3–11.

Kader, C. (1993). The very house of difference: Zami, Audre Lorde's lesbian-centered text. *Journal of Homosexuality, 26,* 181–94.

Kelly, G. (1990). *Sexuality today: The human perspective.* Guilford, NY: Duskin.

Kinsey, A.C., Pomeroy, W.B., & Martin, C.E. (1948). *Sexual behavior in the human male.* Philadelphia, PA: Saunders.

Kinsey, A.C., Pomeroy, W.B., Martin, C.E., & Gebhard, P.H. (1953). *Sexual behavior in the human female.* Philadelphia, PA: Saunders.

Kreiger, I. (1988). An approach to coping with anxiety about AIDS. *Social Work, 33,* 263–264.

McWhirter, D.P., & Mattison, A.M. (1984). *The male couple: How relationships develop.* Englewood Cliffs, NJ: Prentice-Hall.

Martin, D., & Lyon, P. (1984). Lesbian women and mental health policy. In L.E. Walker (Ed.), *Women and mental health policy.* Beverly Hills, CA: Sage.

Monzon, O.T., & Capellan, J.M. (1987). Female to female transmission of HIV. *The Lancet, 6,* 23–28.

Muhall, L. (1990). Australian counseling program may have halted the spread of AIDS in a select group. *AIDS Conference Bulletin, 1*(4).

Nichols, M. (1989). Sex therapy with lesbians, gay men, and bisexuals. In S. Leiblum and R. Rosen (Eds.), *Principles and practices of sex therapy* (pp. 269–296). New York: Guilford Press.

Peplau, L.A. (1981, March). What homosexuals want in a relationship. *Psychology Today, 15*(3), 28–38.

Peterson, J.L., Coates, T.J., Catania, J.A., & Middleton, L. (1992). High risk sexual behavior and condom use among gays and bisexual African-American men. *American Journal of Public Health, 82*(11), 1490–1494.

Proctor, C.D., & Groze, V.K. (1994). Risk factors for suicide among gay, lesbian and bisexual youths. *Social Work, 39,* 504–513.

Puckett, S.B., & Bye, L.L. (1987). *The stop AIDS project: An interpersonal AIDS prevention program.* San Francisco, CA: The Stop AIDS Project.

Reimoneng, A. (1993). Countee Cullen's Uranian soul windows. *Journal of Homosexuality, 26,* 143–165.

Roscoe, W. (1987). Bibliography of berdache and alternate gender roles among North American Indians. *Journal of Homosexuality, 14*(3/4), 81–171.

Ruan, F., & Tsai, Y. (1987). Male homosexuality in traditional Chinese literature. *Journal of Homosexuality, 14*(3/4), 21–34.

Schwartz, L.R. (1980). *Alcoholism among lesbian/gay men: A critical problem in critical proportions.* Phoenix, AZ: Do It Now Foundation.

Sorensen, R.C. (1973). *Adolescent sexuality in contemporary America.* New York: World.

Storms, M.D. (1980). Theories of sexual orientation. *Journal of Personality and Social Psychology, 38,* 783–791.

Stulberg, I., & Smith, M. (1988). Psychosocial impact of the AIDS epidemic on the lives of gay men. *Social Work, 3,* 277–281.

Treatment Team Handbook. (1991). *Management of HIV Infection Handbook, Update.* New York: World Health Communications.

Weitz, S. (1977). *Sex roles: Biological, psychological, and social sex role foundations.* New York: Oxford University Press.

Wekker, G. (1993). Mati-ism and black lesbianism: Two ideal expressions of female homosexuality in black communities of the Diasora. *Journal of Homosexuality, 24,* 145–58.

Wells, J.W., & Daly, A. (1992). University students felt alienation in their attitudes toward African Americans, women and homosexuals. *Psychological Reports, 70,* 632–636.

Wertimer, D.M. (1988, January). Victims of violence: A rising tide of anti-gay sentiment. *USA Today Magazine,* pp. 52–54.

Woodman, N.J. (1987). Homosexuality: Lesbian women. In A. Minahan (Ed.), *Encyclopedia of social work* (pp. 805–812). Silver Spring, MD: National Association of Social Workers.

Wyers, N. (1987). Homosexuality in the family. *Social Work, 32,* 143–148.

Chapter 10

SOCIAL WORK PRACTICE WITH NATIVE AMERICANS

MARY BLOUNT

The vast majority of social workers providing services and counseling to minority clients are non-minority practitioners. Most find themselves poorly equipped by virtue of training to adequately serve culturally diverse populations. This has been a source of continuing difficulty for the profession and for the minority communities that must rely on services and treatment offered by Western-trained human services professionals. A multicultural training strategy should have three foci: (1) for agencies to develop and deliver culturally relevant services; (2) for colleges and universities to develop and implement multicultural curricula; and (3) for social work education and human service agencies to attract and retain a more representative number of minority students and professional staff.

The multicultural perspective is now an accreditation requirement for schools of social work across the United States as a result of the Council on Social Work Education's (CSWE) continuing pursuit for educational excellence. This educational content is expected to enhance social work skills with culturally diverse clients, but the clinician will not be expected to learn all the subtle within-group differences of any given culture group. In-depth awareness of multicultural training requirements as prescribed by the CSWE will enable positive improvement in at least six service delivery areas to minority clients: (1) improved accuracy in assessment diagnosis and treatment planning; (2) enhanced skills in developing culturally relevant resources and treatment interventions; (3) increased utilization of available services; (4) a reduction in premature service dropouts; and (5) measurable increases in the number of positive outcomes.

This chapter will focus specifically on the American Indian and Alaskan Native cultural groups. The terms Native American, American

Indian, and Indian are used interchangeably throughout the chapter since there is disagreement within this population as to a preference for either term. There are seven sections in the chapter covering: (1) cultural values and history, (2) characteristics of American Indians, (3) education, (4) social problems, (5) therapeutic variables, (6) research issues, and (7) future implications for social work practice.

Cultural Values and History

Values

A common theme in social work and related literature for the past decade has been to recommend that human service professionals be informed about American Indian values and history in order to work effectively with this culture group (Katz, 1981; LaFromboise, 1988; McDonald et al., 1993; Thomason, 1991). Historical events and native values strongly influence the Indian concept of self, and social workers who fail to take these factors into consideration run the risk of inaccurate assessment (Hull, 1982; Katz, 1981). Understanding the social milieu in which the client lives and functions not only facilitates practitioner assessment but aids in distinguishing between psychopathology and culture-bound beliefs or behaviors (Neligh, 1990; McDonald et al., 1993).

A review of the human services literature for the past ten years yielded eighteen regularly cited American Indian and Anglo American value differences. Recitation of these contrasting values over the years has tended to stereotype American Indians as a homogeneous culture and Anglo Americans as overly aggressive. However, it is important to consider these contrasts as guidelines. Within every culture group there are many variables affecting individual belief systems. For example, the degree of assimilation into the dominant culture, history, experiences, environmental variables, religious beliefs, education, the passing of time, and even child-rearing practices influence which values are strongly held or loosely regarded.

The American Indian and Anglo American value differences below are those cited most often in the literature. Some of these will be discussed in detail later in the text.

Selected American Indian and
Anglo American Value Differences

Traditional Indian	*Anglo American*
Pragmatic	Theoretical
Harmony with nature	Dominance over nature
Indirect criticism	Direct criticism
Extended family	Nuclear family
Cultural pluralist	Assimilationist
Limited eye-to-eye contact	Direct eye contact
Non-intrusive	Aggressive
Oral tradition	Written history
Gentle handshake	Firm handshake
Respect for age	Respect for youth
Religion way of life	Religion segment of life
Work for current need	Work ethic
Giving/sharing	Saving
Spiritual/mystical	Scientific
Listening/observing	Verbal skill
Permissive child rearing	Punitive child rearing
Free use of property	Ownership
Group emphasis	Individualism

Sources: Lurie, 1971; Red Horse, 1978; Katz, 1981; Hull, 1982; LaFromboise, 1988; Sue & Sue, 1990; Wasinger, 1993.

American Indian values and history are intertwined with Anglo culture dominance. Katz points out that this knowledge will enable clinicians to "begin almost immediately to open the issue of Indian-White relationships so the patient knows the therapist is mindful of the hostilities that are bound to have developed in that interface" (1981, p. 455). The history of interaction between Indians and Whites is too long and complex to cover here. However, it is best characterized as a political tug-of-war spanning several centuries, with Indians attempting to hold on to traditional life-styles against the pull of federal laws and policies aimed first to eradicate and later to assimilate the American Indian. Federal Indian policy and American Indian history are woven together in a unique political-legal relationship that at times is shaky. Those interested in legal details should read Title 25, U.S. Code of Federal Regulations, Cohen's (1982) *Handbook of Federal Indian Law*, or Pevar's (1992) book, *The Rights of Indian Tribes* (with excellent commentary).

Characteristics of American Indians

Demographics

Who is an Indian and what constitutes indianness is one of the longest-running unsolved debates in U.S. history. One consistent error made over the years has been to view American Indians as a heterogeneous population. Prior to implementation of the 1830 Indian Removal Act, the Office of Indian Affairs used the general term "Indian" for all the various tribes, and enumerated an eastern population of 105,064 and an aggregate census of 313,130 both east and west of the Mississippi. More than one hundred years later in 1950 the government was making preparations for the Indian Relocation Program, and three distinct census counts were produced to ensure an accurate total.

First, the Census Bureau discarded the term "Indian" for "American Indian" and enumerated 343,410 individuals (Lee, 1988). The Bureau of Indian Affairs (BIA) produced a second count of 402,286 "Federal Indians" using tribal rolls and personal knowledge. A third estimate of 571,784 resulted from a private census taken by University of Chicago anthropologist, Sol Tax, who defined an Indian as anyone living within an Indian community and identifying themselves as Indian. These disparate findings are a small indicator that enumerating Indians depends on many factors, not the least of which is who is reporting and how Indian is defined.

Prior to 1960, the determination of race was the responsibility of the census enumerator and misclassifications of White, Black, or Hispanic rather than American Indian were common (Snipp, 1989). Although self-report is far from a perfect solution, it furthered two long-range goals of the Census Bureau, including: (1) increased community participation in the census and (2) reduction of population under-counts. Self-report became effective with the 1960 census, and the Indian population counts increased 47% over 1950 estimates. Snipp (1989) correctly acknowledges the correlation between increased population counts and increased Indian birthrates. However, the influence of self-report should not be ruled out.

Successive census reports from 1960 through 1990 affirm sustained growth of the American Indian population. One explanation for this has been steady increases in Indian fertility rates: Several authors report statistics that show American Indian births have increased over American Indian deaths (Passel & Berman, 1984; Young, 1988; Snipp, 1989). Young (1988) notes that American Indian fertility research shows the

American Indian birthrate was twice that needed to replace the current generation of Native Americans. He also found that fertility rates among American Indian women living in urban areas were 80% higher than other women living in the same area and 210% higher by comparison with rural areas (Young, 1988). Indian Health Service (IHS) data for 1987–1989 confirms that reservation birthrates were 1.8 times greater than the U.S. All Races Rate. However, reservation mortality rates during this time were 25% higher than the national average and have been so since 1960 (IHS Regional Trends, 1993).

Another factor is the increase in ethnic pride since the Civil Rights Movement of the 1960s which resulted in a greater willingness to be identified as Indian (Deloria, 1985; Hughes, 1992). A third determinant has been the Census Bureau strategy to reduce under-counts in the Indian population. This strategy included hiring Native American census takers and the inclusion of two questions on primary race and ancestry. *Primary race* was defined as those respondents who reported American Indian without mixture and *ancestry* as having at least one parent with American Indian ancestry (E. Pasiano, personal communication, July 7, 1994). The primary race question yielded an aggregate of 4,864,263 individuals which includes all South American Indians, Mexican and other Hispanic Indians, Canadian and French Canadian Indians, Eskimos, Aleuts, Native Hawaiians, Guam and American Samoan Islanders, and American Indians. Primary race American Indians account for 1,878,285 of this general category (Frost, 1991).

The ancestry question produced a count of 3,833,957 mixed heritage American Indians which raised concerns within the federal Indian community. The fear is that more Indians means a smaller share of the federal financial pie. To avoid political controversy, the Census Bureau now includes a disclaimer on all American Indian census data stating that designation as American Indian on the census does not represent certification of Indian heritage, degree of Indian blood, or eligibility for federal status.

Population Centers

There are 314 federal Indian reservations and trust lands spread across a 352-county, 33-state area (excluding Alaska) (IHS Trends Report, 1994). Reservation boundaries are established by treaty, statute, and executive or court order and are recognized by the federal government as territory in which American Indian tribes have legal jurisdiction (U.S. Census Report, 1990). This area is known as "Indian Country" and is administratively subdivided into the following units: Aberdeen, Tucson, Navajo, Billings, Albuquerque, Phoenix, Bemidji, Oklahoma, Portland, Nashville, Alaska, and California. In 1990, only 22% (437,431) of the American Indian population were living on reservations and trust lands. The Navajo tribe is the largest of the federal tribes with a membership of more than 200,000. However, only 87,590 individuals live on the reservation. States with the largest Indian populations include: California with 265,069, Oklahoma with 257,796, Arizona with 214,430 and New Mexico with 137,625 (Census Report by County and State, 1992). Reservation states have several distinct federal tribes, and all states boast multi-national and culturally diverse American Indian populations.

Statistical area map data from the 1990 census show American Indians are concentrated in the same metropolitan areas to which they were relocated in the 1950s. For example, the Southern California metroplex comprising Los Angeles/Long Beach, San Diego, San Bernardino and Riverside Counties account for about forty percent of the state's 285,069 Indian population. In Texas, the majority of Native Americans are concentrated in the Dallas-Fort Worth and Houston metro areas, while Missouri's Indian population continue to live in St. Louis City and St. Louis County. Lastly, more than half of the 24,175 Indians in the state of Illinois were located in Cook County in the city of Chicago. Recent data show the Indian populations in each of these areas has remained consistent from 1980 to 1990 with regular incremental growth (Census Report by State and County 1980–1990, 1990).

The Federal Relationship

American Indians and Alaska Natives are unique among minority groups, in that the Congress of the United States has established criteria by which to determine if Indian tribes are entitled to federal recognition (Pevar, 1992; Trimble & Fleming, 1989). Rules for federal recognition appear in Volume 43, No. 172, codified as Part 83 of Title 25 of the *Code of Federal Regulations.* As stated above, the BIA is responsible for 542 federally recognized tribes with an estimated 1.8 million membership. Indian descendants who are not members of federally recognized tribes may be issued a Certificate of Degree of Indian Blood by the BIA with documentation of at least one-quarter degree of Indian ancestry. One-quarter heritage is the minimum requirement for entitlement to some education and social welfare programs.

Federal "recognition" or federal "acknowledgment" are interchangeable terms used to describe a relationship between governments. Federal recognition conveys sovereign nation status and rights to self-determination to Indian tribes. Prior to 1978, tribal groups were recognized by treaties, executive orders, special acts of Congress, or the courts through the judicial process. The Federal Acknowledgment Project was formally adopted in 1978 as part 83 of Title 25, Code of Federal Regulations. Many petitioners fail the stringently applied criteria. Amendments to the regulations enacted in 1994 promise to improve the petition process.

Federally recognized tribes are eligible for more than five hundred service programs including education assistance, health and welfare services, housing, legal aid, gaming, tax-exempt sales, and legal protections not available to non-recognized tribal groups or individual Indian descendants (Pevar, 1992). The government publication, *Federal Programs of Assistance to American Indians* (Jones, 1990), gives a complete description of all assistance programs available to federally recognized tribes from each governmental agency.

Indian arts and crafts protection was legislated in 1991 with the intention of protecting Indian artisans from federal tribes from sales of inexpensive look-alike imports. Under this law only federal Indian artisans may mark, advertise, and sell products as American Indian made. Threats of heavy fines and loss of business licenses for noncompliance has resulted in strict observance by those who buy and sell Indian arts and crafts. Thus, what was once a free market for all Indian artisans has become restricted to those with federal status and BIA numbers. Non-federal groups and American Indian descendants who once made their living selling handicrafts have suffered severe economic hardship. Although Native American by blood, these artisans may not sell or mark their wares as American Indian made.

Of all the federal entitlement programs, the Indian Health Service is among the most highly valued. Members of federally recognized tribes entitled to these benefits are referred to as "the eligible population" (IHS Trends Report, 1994). An important subset of the eligible population is the "eligible user population" that consists of 1.15 million individuals who take advantage of Indian health benefits (IHS Trends Report, 1993). IHS defines eligible users as those who live on or near a reservation and have used health care services within the past three years (IHS

Trends Report, 1993). IHS reports based on the health profile of the eligible user population are the most comprehensive source for Indian health status on the reservation. A major flaw in this information is that findings are often generalized out of context as representative of all American Indians in the U.S.

Social workers should use caution in relying upon Indian Health Services statistical reports unless the population of concern is represented in these statistical reports. Some limitations of IHS data include: (1) health services are provided only to federally eligible individuals living on or near reservations and reservation dwellers account for only 22% of the total Indian population; (2) statistical data are not tribal specific; (3) the majority of IHS eligibles live in medically underserved areas and are poorer and have more complex health problems than the general population (Jepson, 1994); and (4) the IHS is consistently underfunded and unable to meet all identified medical needs of the eligible population (Smith, 1987; Cunningham, 1993; Jepson, 1994). Eligibility determination is also problematic, and even the IHS stipulates that not all individuals who receive medical services may be eligible users (IHS Regional Differences Report, 1994). Finally, IHS data reports are passive in the sense that only those who receive health services are reported. However, there may be many reservation Indians with serious health problems who do not seek medical care for one reason or another. Taking the IHS data or any other American Indian findings at face value without considering the data source and the methodology involved leads to misinterpretation and a "one size fits all" stereotype (McDonald, 1994).

Unacknowledged Indian Groups

Title 25, part 83 of the Federal Code specifies that Indian groups who fail to be recognized under the regulations are not non-Indian; they just do not meet the federal criteria required for determining that they exist as an Indian tribe. Unacknowledged groups vary greatly. Some have maintained tribal customs, language, and various forms of government. Many are incorporated under the laws of their states of residence, and at last report at least thirty-two have even been formally recognized as tribes by their state governments (U.S. Census Bureau Report, 1990). A few Indian groups were so isolated that they went virtually unnoticed and thus have difficulty proving their existence. Others have chosen to keep to themselves and avoid any interaction with the U.S. government, and some tribal groups would like to become recognized but lack the financial resources necessary to complete the process (Greenbaum, 1991). Federal grants are available from the federal agency Administration for Native Americans (ANA). The ANA assists petitioners with competitively based grants that help tribes pay the costs of preparing petitions for recognition. However, not all tribes have members with technical writing skills necessary to prepare a polished grant, and substantially more requests for financial aid are declined than are granted.

As of 1988, the BIA estimated that there were approximately 240 non-federally recognized tribal groups. Of these, 180 were actively petitioning for recognition (BIA Testimony at Oversight Hearing on Federal Acknowledgment, 1988). The last tribe to be federally recognized was the Jenna Choctaw. Remaining non-federalized groups vary in size from thousands to a very few. The largest of these is the Lumbee Tribe of North Carolina with a population of 2,863. The Hassanamisco of Massachusetts is the smallest tribe with a single member. Both tribes are also recognized by their individual states (U.S. Census Report CPH–L-73, 1990).

Unrecognized tribes are equally as culturally heterogeneous as their federal counterpart. But, the social work literature is silent on this class difference. Consequently, there are no social work studies that can shed light on social problems resulting from this two-class system. For example, when Indians meet as strangers, the information exchange begins by first asking the tribal affiliation, then blood degree, and lastly federal status if not evident in the tribal affiliation. Responses to this line of questioning influence the nature of interaction or prescribed social distance since federal tribes view non-federal status as a stigma. Failure of the clinician to understand this class difference can frustrate the success of therapeutic groups with mixed members. It can also thwart well-meaning referrals to link individuals to perceived cultural supports. In sum, mismatched confederations can frustrate the best of social work treatment or case management plans.

Terminated Tribes

Terminated tribes are in the same category as non-federal Indians since they have no relationship with the federal government and receive no benefits. As noted above, in 1953 more than 100 American Indian tribes were terminated, ordered to disband their governments, and distribute land and other real property among the membership (Pevar, 1992). Relocation programs implemented simultaneously with termination policy resulted in resettlement of many thousands of reservation Indians in large metropolitan areas throughout the U.S. Nearly four thousand Indians were relocated to Chicago and Los Angeles in 1954, and by 1956 another 245,000 had been sent to Dallas, St. Louis, and Oklahoma City. Since that time, approximately seventy terminated tribes have been restored through congressional action. The Catawba tribe of North Carolina was the last terminated tribe to be restored, and other cases are pending (Federal Register, 1993).

Tribal Diversity

Federal tribal populations range in number from 100 to more than 100,000 individuals and non-federal tribes numbering from a few members to as many as 35,000. Within these tribes there are over 200 different dialects and languages spoken (Lurie, 1971; Young, 1988). In the state of Washington alone there are at least 12 distinct American Indian tribal languages (Bobo, 1987). The 1990 census shows that Native Americans constitute .08% of the national population. Only 437,431, or 24% of the federal Indian population, reside on reservations and federal trust lands. With the majority of American Indians now living in urban areas without Indian Health Service, non-Indian social workers are much more likely to encounter an Indian client who will offer a unique challenge to practitioner skills.

Medicine (1988) calls attention to cross-tribal diversity suggesting that degrees of tribalism, tribal sovereignty, cultural and linguistic traditions, land bases, and treaty obligations place each tribe in a distinctive category. Added to these traditional differences are the contemporary factors of cross-tribal and interracial marriages, social disintegration, within-group culture conflict, identity issues, and survival in urban settings, to name a few. A rule of thumb for non-Indian social work clinicians and practitioners is to always view Native Americans as a broadly diverse cultural group. Never assume that tribal traditions impact individual clients in the same way. Determining the degree of influence that a specific tribal culture may have or still has on the client is a critical part of the initial assessment process.

While an exhaustive study of the various tribal cultures might be ideal, it is not a practical approach. Competent non-Indian practitioner/clinicians should focus more on gathering culturally specific information from the client. Cultural questions sensitively asked about tribal affiliation, clan membership, tribal-specific values held, degree of ancestry, federal status, and position or role within the tribal structure should produce responses that help determine the degree to which the client has taken on dominant culture values and practices (McDonald et al., 1994).

American Indians often see themselves as an extension of the tribe with their sense of self, security, and belonging centered in this affiliation (Sue & Sue, 1990). This force is strong while on the reservation or in near proximity, but as economic demands force more Indians into urban settings, tribal ties may become weakened. This is especially true when transportation costs are too expensive to permit frequent visits back home (Red Horse, 1978). It is critical to understand that the tribe versus the individual is not necessarily an important factor in treating all Indian clients. For example, urban and rural landless Indian people have no reservation land base. They live only with an abstract notion of tribal affiliation and gain their strength through group gatherings and powwows. This tribal connection was also lost to many Indian children who were removed from their families and tribes prior to the Indian Child Welfare Act of 1978. As adult survivors of assimilation policies, these individuals often seek reconnection with a tribal identity and an Indian self, but they need culturally sensitive guidance to regenerate their cultural roots. Bachman's (1992) interviews with adult Indian adoptees and boarding school students reveal painful memories of family disruption. One man reported running away many times from his adopted family; never feeling he belonged anywhere:

> The social worker took me and my brother to a hotel room where we stayed overnight. I remember my brother just crying all night. I was nine and he was just six. I mean we didn't even know why we were taken from our parents. They just did it. (p. 39)

In another example, an older Indian man gave details of family separation during boarding school days. "I was just holding on to my mother's dress and screaming. My mother was crying too. They literally dragged me away and put me on a bus with other crying kids" (Bachman, 1992, p. 39). In this latter case, at least the children remained together at the Indian school and kept their cultural identity, but they were deprived of the rich cultural traditions of their tribal identity.

Pan Indian Movement

Experiences of adoptees and other displaced Indian individuals have combined with factors such as intertribal and intracultural marriages and urban life-styles to form the diversity which is at the heart of the pan-Indian movement. Pan-Indianism places the importance of Indian identity over that of a tribal identity (Snipp, 1989), creating a subculture where "not-so-traditional Indians" may participate. A major factor contributing to the development of the pan-Indian subculture has been the Indian intermarriage.

In 1980, census data showed 48.3% of Indian women were married to White men, 48% of Indian men were married to White women, 2% of Indian men are married to Black women and 1% of Indian women are married to Black men (Snipp, 1989). Moreover, Indians who marry other Indians frequently select mates from tribes other than their own. It is common to encounter Indian individuals who append hyphenated nationalities to their surname: e.g., Rachel Harjo, Cherokee-Creek; Luther Wolf, Cheyenne-Sioux; Bear Smith, Kiowa-Shawnee; and other such combinations. According to a recent federal projection, by the year 2060 the American Indian population will be less than 10% full blood and this rate will decline to less than 5% by 2080 (American Indian Health OTA Report, 1986). Intermarriage deepens the cultural maze, posing challenges for the non-Indian social worker.

Traditionalists

Some tribes hold strongly to ancient tribal traditions retaining their religious rituals and ceremonial rites. Especially important among traditionalists are the puberty rites that admit adolescents into the clan or society and link them with adult mentors. Traditional tribes also observe ancient forms of government, the priesthood and healing practices, and take their customs seriously. Failure of members to conform according to group custom is cause for social disgrace within the community.

Strictly observed traditions help preserve individual integrity and perpetuate the cultural community. On the other hand, strongly held traditions can become a double-edged sword for tribal members. Especially at high risk are children and youth of traditional tribes who must attend public schools, spending the majority of their day in an environment that challenges values and traditional teachings of the tribal culture.

Berlin (1987) and Buchanan (1992) point out that traditionally reared Indian children are at great risk for attempted suicide when they must live in two worlds with conflicting values. Consider, for example, the Indian value of non-intrusiveness cited earlier. Among traditionalists this value constrains one individual from striving to be better than another. Thus, if Indian youth from traditional tribes are singled out for academic or athletic superiority, they loose face within their own community and risk being ostracized (Berlin, 1987). Whether a traditionally reared Indian child survives culture clash depends in large part on the stability and support of his or her immediate and extended family system.

American Indian Families

Although the American Indian family structure varies from tribe to tribe due to intermarriage and migration patterns, it remains the cornerstone of American Indian society (Red Horse, 1978). Family and culture are inseparable from individual mental health because the sense of "self" is derived from an historic culture transmitted through family socialization. The unifying factor for American Indian family life has been reliance on the extended family where uncles, aunts, grandparents and cousins of varying degrees all play a vital role (Red Horse, 1978). Closeness, collective problem solving, equal responsibility for young children, sharing of resources and of labor are all a way of life evolving out of the clan system in which the family was the core and the clan the extension. Much of the traditional strength of the extended family life-style has been worn away over time by many complex factors, not the least of which is inconsistent federal policy. The resulting family disintegration, abbreviated life spans, and the magnitude of mental health problems may already exceed the healing strength of the extended family or spiritual belief system of the tribal community.

Religion and Spirituality

Religious practices have changed among families and within the tribal communities over time. Both Christian faith and traditional spiritual practices are observed in the Native American population. There are Indian churches associated with almost every Protestant denomination with American Indian pastors and parishioners. Likewise, traditionalists continue to celebrate according to ancient customs of the particular tribe. For example, some Muscogee Creek Indian tribal groups observe traditional rites four times each year. These are called Busks and are named: Berry, Little Green Corn, Green Corn and Harvest. Each Busk has a special purpose and prescribed set of ritual activities with appropriate medicine bundles. The celebrations are conducted on a tribal square ground and are customarily not open to public participation or view. Among traditionalists these spiritual celebrations are considered a special opportunity for extended family unity, interaction, and renewal. On the other hand, value conflict between traditionalists and Christians is often an abrasive issue that affects immediate and extended family and tribal community relations as well.

Native American Church and Peyoteeism

The Native American Church and peyoteeism fits somewhere between traditionalism and Christianity as a spiritual/religious preference. Spindler and Spindler (1977) describe peyoteeism as one of the most widely shared Indian religions in North America involving individuals from many American Indian tribes. Use of peyote in a religious ceremony is pre-Columbian in origin, but contemporary rituals and ideology are products of recent history (Slotkin, 1956). Establishment of the Native American Church has been viewed as a direct response to the defeat, deprivation, and confinement which Indians experienced nearly everywhere after the first half of the nineteenth century (Spindler & Spindler, 1977). Ceremonies combine both traditional and Christian elements with many of the traditional elements traceable to Plains Indian culture (Spindler & Spindler, 1977). There are no instructions in the peyote way, and individuals are allowed to find their own path to salvation, revelation, knowledge, or cleansing from sins through visions and dreams (Slotkin, 1956). On the other hand, all members are helped by group efforts that include prayers, singing, drumming, shakers, and dance-like movements in a circular direction. Worshipers pray aloud and give testimonials at prescribed periods during the ceremony, often breaking into tears. This is an emotional time, at once both an individual experience yet a time of community support and joint healing efforts.

American Indians and Professional Social Work Groups

The National Indian Social Workers Association (NISWA) is the oldest professional organization of American Indian social workers in the United States. It was founded in the early 1970s under the guiding influence of Jere Brennen and a few of other dedicated American Indian social workers. Past-president Evelyn Lance Blanchard has character-ized the NISWA as a struggling organization (E.L. Blanchard, personal communication, April 24, 1990). This is in part related to the relatively few numbers of Native American social workers and to their widespread geographic dispersion. The association attempts to hold at least one national conference per year where Indian social workers from the U.S. and Canada gather to discuss and plan strategies related to current issues of concern to the Native Indian population. The organizational newslet-ter is entitled *The Association* and it is published four times each year in February, May, August, and November.

The National Association of Social Workers (NASW) supports several minority special-interest groups under the direction of the National Committee on Racial and Ethnic Diversity. The American Indian repre-sentative to this committee serves a three-year term of office and helps keep Indian issues in the forefront of national social work concern. American Indian social workers have fewer members in the NASW than any other minority group (Ghelman & Schervish, 1994). Past-repre-sentative C. Manygoats (personal communication, November 16, 1994) states that the small number of Indian social workers within the NASW and the diversity and overall magnitude of Indian problems makes it difficult to generate and keep interest focused on Indian issues.

INDIAN EDUCATION

Early Indian Schools

As early as 1803, the federal government established a fund for the "civilization" of the American Indian people. The task was given to several missionary societies who found little success in their endeavors to Christianize Indian adults on native reserves. In 1818, the Congress introduced a bill to establish a permanent fund for the education of American Indian children, and in 1825 the Choctaw Academy was the first national Indian boarding school to be established with federal funds. Founder and teacher, Colonel Richard M. Johnson, was a member of the United States Congress and hero (at least to non-Native Americans!) of the Indian wars under Andrew Jackson. Johnson gained political status by killing Tecumseh, a renowned Indian leader and prophet.

The academy was located at Great Crossings, Kentucky on a farm owned by Colonel Johnson. Indian children were mandated to attend by inserting educational requirements in Indian treaties subsequent to 1825 (Kappler, 1904; Macmillan, 1950). The all-male student body ranged in age from 6 to 22 years. Two to three hundred boys were in attendance at the school at any given time, bringing considerable income to Senator Johnson and free labor for his farm (Foreman, 1928). Johnson continued the school after he became vice-president of the United States in 1837, and the issue of conflict of interest was never raised.

Early Indian school policies were strict. The students' hair was cut and no native dress or speaking of an Indian language were allowed. Indian names were dropped and students renamed for contemporary white leaders of the time such as Benjamin Franklin, G. Washington, Andrew Jackson, Henry Clay, Thomas Jefferson, and Richard M. Johnson. Visitations with families were not permitted for the term of the school which lasted more than ten years (Foreman, 1932). As Blanchard (1988) points out, the boarding schools became a primary placement resource for Indian children whom the federal and state agencies determined were in need of protection. In the case of the early schools, protecting the child meant removing him or her from uncivilized and heathen influences of the tribe and family.

Indian boarding schools were a mandatory way of life for Indian families and children that lasted well into the 1950s. During the child-removal policy period, many Indian couples lost confidence in their own ability to parent and looked to the federal government as a preferable surrogate parent (Goodluck & Eckstein, 1978). Many children displaced by such policies experienced adjustment difficulties as adults as shown in Bachman's (1992) study of 30 American Indian inmates serving sentences for homicide. Findings showed family disruption and Indian identity crisis to be consistent variables across subjects as a factor in violent behavior.

BIA Sponsored Schools

Today, the bureau operates fifty-seven day schools, forty on-reservation boarding schools, six off-reservation boarding schools and nine dormitories that facilitate Indian student attendance in public schools. Off-reservation boarding schools serve three groups of students: (1) those living in isolated areas; (2) those with family or home problems; and (3) those with learning disabilities and behavior problems. The federal schools are also used for adult education programs, and the BIA reports that more than 18,500 students are enrolled in the bureau's adult education programs and 90% of all school-age Indian children attend public schools.

Student Financial Assistance

The popular notion that all Indian students receive educational aid from the government is a myth. Eligibility requirements for student financial aid vary widely depending upon the funding source. Federal funds are always limited and not all Indian students who are able to successfully complete college receive funds. Indian Education Reports show for school year 1993–1994 that there were 325 eligible applications submitted for the Indian Fellowship Program and only 114 fellowships awarded. Funding limitations account in part for the small number of American Indians with college degrees.

The Indian Fellowship Program has been sponsored by the U.S. Department of Education (DOE) since 1974. In twenty years of operation the program has assisted only 2,000 Indian students. These students have been helped to get degrees in areas of study selected by the department. Areas selected for undergraduate study include: business administration, engineering, natural resources or related fields. Graduate degrees are also funded in the above areas in addition to education, law, medicine, clinical psychology, or related fields. Social work is an eligible field in the undergraduate and masters level and may be considered on an individual basis for a doctoral program. Limited interest in doctoral social work degrees perhaps relates to a perceived greater need in the IHS for Indian professionals with doctoral degrees in psychology. A problem with this restriction is the limitation it places on the availability of American Indians qualified to teach BSW and MSW students.

Indian Fellowship applicants must document membership in a state or federally recognized Indian tribe or band including terminated tribes. Applicants may be Indian descendants with a parent or grandparent who was a member in any of the above tribal categories. In addition, members of organized (non-federal) Indian groups that have received early education grants under the Indian Education Act of 1988 may also apply. However, the number of awards granted to non-federal groups has been negligible. Indian Fellowship awards have a payback provision.

Renewed Federal Interest in Indian Education

With the enactment of P.L. 100-297 in 1988, the government showed renewed interest in improving Indian education across the board. Provisions of the law included a White House Conference on Indian Education that began in the fall of 1991 and concluded in 1992 with a final report of seventeen goals to be implemented by the year 2000. Three consistent themes emerged from pre-conference meetings with Indian representatives in thirty states. These themes included: (1) a desire for local control of education and local determination of educational needs; (2) a demand for inclusion of appropriate cultural values, language, beliefs, accurate histories, and other culturally sensitive expressions at every educational level; and (3) provision of funding adequate to ensure high quality and standards in every school and classroom (Whitehouse Conference Report, 1992).

Stress and the School Environment

The primary purpose of schools is to educate, but it is also a place where students learn to conform to peer pressure. In 1989, reservation students completing the University of Minnesota study of adolescent Indian youth indicated strong pressures to drink, use drugs, sniff substances such as glue, paint, liquid paper, etc., destroy property, fight, and steal things (Blum et al., 1992). This survey also found a strong relationship between adolescents at academic risk and those with multiple physical, social, and psychological risk indicators. Students who reported poor health were at least three times more likely than White children of the same age group to have a history of substance abuse and attempted suicide.

According to a recent federal study, Indian adolescents with histories of poor physical and mental health, substance abuse, peer pressure and family stresses leads are at higher risk of early school dropout than non-Indian youth with similar problems (OTA Report, 1990). Meta-analysis of studies on Indian and non-Indian schoolchildren demonstrate that Indian children compete at or above the achievement level of non-Indian children until about the sixth grade when the "crossover effect" sets in among Indian children (Neligh, 1990). When achievement falters, degeneration is rapid and the stage is set for school drop out among very young Indian children (Neligh, 1990). Lack of Native American teachers, attitudes of non-Indian teachers and a curriculum insensitive to Indian culture combine to create stress and little incentive for Indian children and adolescents to remain in school (Tippeconnic, 1988).

SOCIAL PROBLEMS

Poverty

The true picture of Indian poverty is unknown since the majority of statistical and descriptive information is derived from the federal reservation population and U.S. Census demographics from areas on or near the reservations. Extreme poverty and high unemployment are common problems for Native Americans living on or near reservations and trust land areas, but little is known about urban and rural landless Indians. Three of the five poorest counties in the United States include Indian reservations, and 32% of Indians residing in reservation states are below the poverty level. This is 2.4 times greater than the U.S. all races rate (IHS Trends, 1993). Aberdeen, Navajo, Billings, Albuquerque, and Phoenix are the poorest IHS areas with poverty percentages ranging from a high of 49.6% to a low of 41.8%. Poverty is often linked to greater need for mental health and other health care services which in many instances are not available (Jepson, 1994; Neligh, 1990).

Poverty and extended periods of unemployment or underemployment have resulted in substandard housing, malnutrition, inadequate health care, and a shortened life expectancy as well as less formal education. The 1990 census shows only 65% of Native Americans age 25 years and older residing in reservation states are high school graduates; only 8.9% have a college education. LaFromboise (1988) reported this problem several years ago noting that almost one-third of all Native Americans are classified as illiterate and only one in five have a high school education. American Indian students enter a school system with a background and value set significantly different from those which the system seeks to develop. The value clash causes a negative self-image for the student and this combines with other life stresses that lead to academic failures and a cycle of poverty. Bachman (1992) cites poverty as an influential link in a cycle of events that ultimately leads to high rates of death and violence on Indian reservations.

Alcohol Abuse

The extent of alcohol abuse in American Indian communities is a long-standing problem. Alcoholism is second only to tuberculosis in the top ten causes of death. Alcohol abuse has long been described as the foremost medical and social problem among Native Americans (Weibel-Orlando, 1986–1987). Since the mid 1960s there has been a great surge of federal and state level interest in studying alcohol use and abuse among the American Indians. The majority of studies have focused on alcohol use and abuse and how it might be related to drinking patterns in various tribal rituals. The Indian "drinking party" studied by Weibel-Orlando (1986–87) is cited by some as the reason for high rates of alcoholism in the Native American population.

Other studies have demonstrated that the problem is much more complex. Neligh (1990) attributes alcoholism more to pervasive depression, which often has its onset in early childhood. About twenty-five percent of Indian children suffer from serious emotional disorders. Since more than half of the Indian population is in the childhood and adolescent age range, Neligh (1990) suggests a strong possibility exists that tens of thousands of Indian children are in urgent need of mental health services yet less than 10% of IHS mental health contacts are designated for children. Alcohol abuse is not limited to isolated geographic areas nor is there a uniform problem among the various tribes.

Use and abuse of alcohol varies with virtually every tribe. Two tribes in Oklahoma, the Creek and the Cherokee, have relatively low rates of alcohol-related deaths and arrest, while the Cheyenne-Arapaho area in western Oklahoma accounts for 20 percent of the arrests for public drunkenness (Weibel-Orlando, 1986–87). The Weibel-Orlando (1986–87) study also shows that across the board, in all tribes and in all locations, women drink considerably less than men and more infrequently in urban settings. The "drinking party" has become a regular recreational activity for many Sioux men and women. This party is a social event in which participants rapidly consume inexpensive, low-quality alcoholic beverages. Drinking usually ends when the alcohol is gone or when the participants have reached a state of unconsciousness. Few negative sanctions are placed on intoxicated behaviors, and aggressive behavior is usually overlooked. When the member has "sobered up," he or she is permitted to return to the group without sanctions or criticism (Weibel-Orlando, 1986-87).

Research among Native American youth in grades 7 through 12 has shown that 78 percent of the students had tried alcohol, and 61% of these respondents also reported using alcohol within the last two months (Young, 1988). The Minnesota Adolescent Indian Health Survey of 1989 was conducted among seventh through twelfth grade students within the IHS service areas and recorded similar findings. Several researchers have found that alcohol and other substance abuse are so pervasive within some Indian communities that children under the age of six have been found using alcohol or sniffing some form of inhalant (Young, 1988; LaFromboise, 1988).

The occurrence of fetal alcohol syndrome (FAS) varies among tribes but occurs on average once in 633 live births and can run as high as one in every 100 births (May & Hymbaugh, 1983). By comparison, Niccols (1994) cites research showing FAS affects one to three infants per 1000 live births in the general population. FAS results in high rates of mental retardation, physical deformity, and attention deficit and hyperactivity disorder among Indian children. Young's (1988) research shows that 75 percent of all Native American deaths can be traced to alcohol in some form. Research reports show that five of ten leading causes of death among Indian individuals in the IHS service areas result from alcohol-related accidents, cirrhosis of the liver, alcohol dependency, suicide and homicide (Young, 1988; IHS Regional Report, 1994).

Some authors argue that alcohol use is a coping strategy used to offset the loss of culture, stresses of assimilation, and abandonment of tribal traditions (Weibel, 1982; Neligh, 1990). Mail, McKay and Katz (1989) extend this to include a causal relationship between alcohol abuse and stress and alcohol as a stressor. Another popular theory is that American Indians metabolize alcohol at a different rate than whites; however, studies undertaken to test this hypothesis have revealed almost identical metabolic rates between the two groups (Young, 1988). Alcoholism is one of the most widely studied of American Indian social problems, and every researcher has some part of the answer as to causation since stress can result from most any source.

A common recommendation for corrective action is to implement programs that reduce stress in those Indian communities with high incidence of alcohol abuse (Beauvais & Laboueff, 1985; Mail et al., 1989). Well-meaning recommendations are usually more difficult than simplistic recommendations presume. For example, in response to the alcohol problem in Indian country, the IHS adopted the Alcohol Program in 1974. After ten years of service and few positive results, the IHS added a substance abuse treatment component in 1986 but failed to adequately staff either program with properly trained professionals. Alcohol and drug abuse remain dominant problems that appear to be increasing.

Drug Abuse

Drug abuse has recently become a core problem in Indian country. Drugs and other substance abuse is often seen as a correlate with the abuse of alcohol, especially in the case of Native American youth (Schinke et al., 1985, 1987a, 1987b, 1988; Gilchrist et al., 1987). The Minnesota Adolescent Indian Health Survey found that the most prevalent use of substances other than alcohol included marijuana, peyote, and inhalants. Those students who reported using marijuana included 31.2% in the younger grades and 50.1% in the upper grade levels. Peyote use was reported by 22% of Indian students and inhalant users accounted for 20.8%. The Minnesota study fails to specify whether the use of peyote among any of the respondents was connected with religious practices common in the Native American Church.

Voluntary use of inhalants for mind-altering purposes is twice as high for Native American youths as it is for white youth (LaFromboise, 1988). Substances such as gasoline, glue, spray paint, lighter fluid, nail polish remover, marker pens, and typewriter correction fluid are among the first drugs abused by Native American youth and their use most often preceded the first time being drunk (Wingert & Field, 1985). Easy access and inexpensive costs of inhalants partially account for the high rate of use among Indian youth; effects dissipate rather quickly and the user is able to experience many "highs" at a relatively low cost. Young's (1988) research shows that the average age of first non-alcohol drug use is

11.5 years and the average age of first time being intoxicated by liquor was 12.3 years (Young, 1988).

The use of "crack" cocaine is prevalent in Indian communities and prices are low enough to make this highly addictive drug affordable to children and youth. Crack is a highly addictive drug, but the more dangerous phencyclidine (PCP), also known as "angel dust," "dust," or "hog," is a growing problem (Neligh, 1990). Reports also cite problems with underground prescription sales on the reservations, with illicit sales and exchanges so widespread as to be considered a commonplace economic activity. Unfortunately, what appears to be an enormous drug abuse problem on the nation's reservations remains essentially unaddressed (ATO Report, 1990).

Even if the badly needed funds were available to finance the necessary programs and services, IHS physicians and others in the health care system lack the exposure and specialized skills required for the acute treatment and detoxification of drug-abusing patients (Neligh, 1990). Clearly, prevention of substance abuse among Indian children and adolescents is a more cost-effective alternative than belated treatment of its effects. However, culturally sensitive prevention strategies and hiring of professional American Indian staff lag behind current need.

Suicide

Suicide within the American Indian population might well be considered the ultimate sign of community pathology. In attempting to understand the reasons for suicide among Native Americans, one must consider the history, experiences, and the stress levels generated by contact with the dominant society, and the group and individual's attempts to adapt to the stress (May, 1974). Prior to removal of Indians to federal reservations suicide among American Indians was virtually unknown.

Contemporary IHS statistics show suicide in Indian country is 21.3/100,000 compared to the U.S. All Races Rate of 11.5/100,000 (IHS Trends, 1994). Areas with the highest prevalence are: Alaska at 34.6, Billings at 27.8, and Aberdeen at 26.9 per 100,000 population. These data also reveal that American Indian men between the ages of 15 and 34 years account for over 60% of suicide deaths per 100,000 population, as opposed to 25% per 100,000 among white men of the same age cohort. On the other hand, suicide rates among Indian females is very low in comparison to Indian males and on average is somewhat lower than suicide rates among white females (IHS Trends, 1994). Alaska's higher suicide rate appears related to acculturation stress that includes the shift to a cash economy, migrations from villages to towns, where too few jobs are available (Hippler, 1970). Traditional values and marriage preferences are also changing. Hippler (1970) noted in his study that a growing preference for "things" that can be bought has influenced the preference of eligible Native Alaskan females for American servicemen with money as more desirable mates than Native Alaskan men. As a result, Native Alaskan males suffer from feelings of inadequacy and poor self-esteem that are exacerbated by low frustration tolerance (Hippler, 1970).

Across cultures and nationalities factors such as age and sex appear relatively consistent, with the highest percentage of suicides among males 15–24 years and with female suicides in the same age group well below those of males (Hollinger, Offer, Barter, & Bell, 1994). Beginning with Durkheim's observations in 1897, the connection between age and suicide has been thoroughly researched and correlations documented. Researchers conducting postmortem research on American Indian adolescents have found several factors that lead to suicide. Some of these include: parent, friend or other relative attempted suicide, severe within-family conflict usually involving a stepparent, long-term foster care that was abusive, serious alcohol problems in the family in addition to long-term unemployment, living alone without parental care or care from another, personal abuse of drugs and/or alcohol, and family and tribal instability (Berlin, 1987).

Durkheim's theory of altruistic suicide has applicability to American Indians during the hunting and gathering period when collective survival outweighed individual importance. When circumstances required action to maintain tribal balance, the elderly, invalid, and/or any member whose life or care became a burden to the tribe would go away on their own to await death in service to the tribe as a whole (Davenport & Davenport, 1987). Durkheim's theory of anomic suicide also has relevance to the contemporary Native American population. This form of suicide results when cultural or community change requires adaptations of such major proportions that many members of the community are unable to accommodate to the demands. Given the tragic history of forced assimilation, it is likely that some American Indians have experienced psychological agitation and depression of a magnitude capable of making them take their own life. However, this theory fails to explain statistically significant differences by sex, age group, and tribal nationality.

Developmental psychologists working with the IHS have speculated on suicide causality in light of Erickson's model which focuses on the adolescent tasks of identity versus identity diffusion. For example, Neligh (1990) suggests that the lack of viable adult identities for Indian adolescents from tribes experiencing extreme cultural stress may well be a factor contributing to unusually high-risk behaviors during this developmental phase. Bachman (1992) speculates that negative self-images are due to school racism, abuse and neglect at home, or other environmental factors that increase the frequency of depression and other symptoms of mental health problems that contribute to suicide.

Suicide research has identified several mental health factors that help identify youth at highest risk for self-destruction. Some of these factors are: psychiatric disorders, affective disorders such as bipolar disorder or major depression, personality disorders, and a family history of psychiatric disorder (Hollinger et al., 1994). IHS mental health professionals cite major depression, bipolar disorder, and schizophrenia as significant mental health problems among American Indian youth, and these factors are commonly documented in the majority of Indian suicides and homicides (Neligh, 1990).

Indian youth living on reservations have been shown at high risk for suicide. Unfortunately, there are too few trained professionals in Indian country to provide the treatment that would reduce the probability of self-destructive behavior. For example, more than 397,000 children and adolescents live in the IHS service areas, but there are only 17 IHS mental health providers trained to treat them (Inouye, 1993). This is due in large part to budget constraints that result in hiring freezes and staff turnover within the IHS (Neligh, 1990). Young (1993) hypothesizes there may be a correlation between "the relative shortage of medical resources among IHS districts and the high suicide and homicide rates" (p. 103) and suggests further research is urgently needed.

Persons working extensively with Indian violence report that most all assaults, homicides and suicides involve persons who had been drinking just prior to the event. In-depth investigations of these cases often show that a history of mental health problems preceded the bout of alcohol or drugs that lead to the violent act (Neligh, 1990). Isolation of many factors involved in incidences of suicide within the American Indian culture has promoted better understanding. But, unraveling precipitating causes after the fact has made substantive progress toward prevention slow and tedious.

An alarming discovery since 1990 is the increasing rate of suicide among younger children ages 10 to 14 years and in the incidence of cluster or contagion suicides (ATO Report, 1990). Cluster suicides are defined as when at least three or more suicides occur in a series within a short time and space. Very little is known about the causes of cluster suicides among Indian youth. IHS clinical records show that a higher percentage of male than female youth are involved in cluster suicide which is opposite to general findings of most studies (ATO Report, 1990). The IHS has urged community social support for tribal children, adolescents, youth or adults seen as high risk for self-destruction. However, it is not clear to what extent the cultural value of non-interference might mitigate against discouraging such behavior. In general, Indian country mortality patterns between suicide and homicides are similar to general population findings, suggesting that these problems may be epidemiologically related (Hollinger et al., 1994). More research is necessary, especially that which integrates the exploration of psychological commonalities with epidemiological and clinical viewpoints.

Homicide

Homicide in Indian country is 80 percent greater than the national average. The Tucson area is most problematic, with age-adjusted homicides three-and-one-half times greater than the national rate of 10.2 per 100,000 population (IHS Regional Report, 1994). The IHS Regional Report for 1994 also shows that homicides occur most frequently among American Indian males starting at age 15. However, unlike suicides which decline after age 25, the high-risk period for homicide extends to age 45. Indian females are less frequently homicide victims, but those who are fall within the same age cohort as Indian males.

Another disturbing finding within American Indian mortality rates is the high percentage of infant homicides under one year of age. Indian male infant homicide per 100,000 population is 19.9 versus 9.0 for Indian females. These mortality figures compare to 7.6 for males and 8.7 for females in all other races (IHS Trends, 1993). The fact that Indian infant homicides exceed the U.S. All Races Rates is particularly troublesome, since the U.S. ranks fourth among 21 world nations in infant homicide (Christoffel, 1990; Hollinger, Offer, Barter, & Bell, 1994).

Infant mortality rates in Indian Country exceed the U.S. national average by 30 percent, with the majority of infant deaths per 1000 live births occurring in Aberdeen (17.5), Billings (16.1), and Alaska (IHS Regional Report, 1994).

Violent deaths involving suicide and homicides have been shown to be associated with such factors as poverty, minority status, high unemployment, extreme social pressures, substance abuse, prevalence of guns in the community, and poor physical and mental health (Holinger et al., 1994). These factors are so commonplace on Indian reservations that most every family or individual is impacted in some way. It is rare to find any Indian who has not personally experienced the loss of a relative or other person well known to them. Living with constant deprivation and loss explains in part the widespread depression found among Native Americans. Finding ways to mitigate against depression especially among Indian youth requires a special sensitivity to identity issues which are magnified for this culture and age group. It also requires a commitment from the federal government to improve the overall mental health services in all IHS service areas. As Senator Inouye (1993) has said, "This nation must stand by its commitment to Indian tribes by committing resources to solving these problems" (p. 8).

Social Disintegration

American Indian families living on the reservation have become especially vulnerable to problems of social disintegration and acculturation. For example, Hopi families who enter into traditionally disapproved marriages across tribes, mesas, and even clans have been labeled "deviant" by their community. Uncommonly high rates of suicide have been found among the children of these extra-tribal unions (OTA, Report, 1990). Interculture and intraculture tribal value clashes are often complicated by alcoholism, poverty, unemployment, and physical and mental illness. All of these factors compromise individual and family functioning. Clinicians working with Indian families report that major episodes of depression, personality disorders and psychotic states are found in family members with high levels of violence and other problems such as alcohol and drug abuse (Neligh, 1990). The effects of family disruption are especially evident among Indian adolescents who report biological parents not living together, one or both parents dead, poor health of close family member, and similar factors that lead to single-parent households or

children living without either parent (Blum et al., 1992). Other consequences of family disruption may be seen in high rates of child abuse and
neglect, and in mental and physical health problems that the IHS is not
equipped to handle (OTA Report, 1990). Family breakdown as an
indirect indicator of community well-being has some clinical professionals worried that mental health problems among most all age groups
are more serious than generally known (Neligh, 1990).

American Indians living on the reservations seem to have elements of
both self and other-directed violent subcultures coexisting within their
cultural environment. Living in a constant state of economic deprivation
blocks opportunities and reduces political power. This condition gener-
ates a state of frustration, anxiety and depression that are easily capable
of contributing to the development of such a violent subculture. Those
living under these circumstances learn to tolerate both inward and
outward forms of aggression, and ultimately the sanctity of all life (one's
own and others') becomes devalued (Bachman, 1992).

More than a decade ago, authors noted the prevalence of anxiety and
depression among Native Americans was four to six times higher than
that of non-Indian communities (Rhodes et al., 1980). Today, the IHS
professionals say that use of mental health services is far below the
projected needs of the American Indian community (ATO Report,
1990). While an increasing number of Native American university students are beginning to seek mental health services during their schooling
(especially if a Native American counselor is available), the fact remains
that most American Indians are not fully utilizing available mental
health services. LaFromboise (1988) suggests that many Native Americans view mental illness as an outcome of human weakness. Such a view
is not unique to the American Indian culture, but it is a strongly held
belief that influences whether or not mental health services should be
sought. Neligh (1990) supports this position, noting that "Indian people
still avoid using the IHS mental health service system because they
believe that if a person were tough enough they could pull themselves
out of problems of behavior, feeling, and thinking" (p. 101).

La Fromboise (1988) makes a counterargument, stating that more
Indian people would use mental health care if it were not for bureaucratic ineptitude. She points out that Indians are blocked from seeking
mental health services because they are not always made aware of the
variety of all the entitlement programs available to them. In addition,
bureaucratic red tape often frustrates access to mental health counseling

when these services are sought out. Other factors complicating delivery of IHS mental health programs and services include: too few Indian counselors, frequent reorganizations within the IHS, and inadequate funding.

Inadequate funding for Indian health services is a perennial problem and source of argument between tribal leaders and the Congress. For example, in 1994, American Indian leaders complained that the IHS budget of $1.9 billion represented just $1,500 per capita which is less than half the amount of Medicaid dollars spent on other Americans (Jepsen, 1994). Limitations in the medical program budget have forced some IHS eligibles to seek health care outside the IHS system even though the majority have no private insurance (Cunningham, 1993). Those without enough money to buy private insurance, yet have too many personal resources to qualify for state aid, simply do not get the health care they need. Senator Inouoye (1993) acknowledged that federal promises for culturally sensitive mental health services have not kept pace with needs.

THERAPEUTIC VARIABLES

Client/Therapist Issues

The Native American population requires other than conventional therapeutic practices for several reasons. Factors such as confusion, skepticism, and lack of cultural awareness by therapists regarding Native American customs and traditions result in barriers to service between the Indian client and the non-Indian therapist. Fear and mistrust on the part of the American Indian client combine with insensitivity and lack of understanding by therapists to result in underutilization of available mental health services (LaFromboise & Bigfoot, 1989).

Misunderstanding American Indian clients, their cultural values, and behavioral nuances can be frustrating to counselors who are inexperienced in working with this minority group. For example, some clinicians might find Indian clients excessively passive during treatment sessions. However, with increased experience, this passivity might be viewed as the result of the client's lack of familiarity with clinical surroundings or in just not knowing what is expected of them. One remedy might be for the counselor to take time to discuss office protocol or other conventions in a way that allays fears and eliminates client confusion prior to beginning therapy. On the other hand, passivity in some clients may result from difficulties in describing presenting problems in an individualistic way. Those clients with close tribal connections sometimes perceive their problems as inexorably tied to or affecting the entire community. In such cases, therapist patience and flexibility are key determinants in helping the client open up to persons external to the Indian community.

Another Native American cultural behavior that bothers some non-Indian therapists is lack of eye-to-eye contact. In the Anglo culture, great value is placed on the individual who can "look you in the eye." However, lack of eye contact is relatively common across tribes, although it can have various meanings depending upon the particular tribal culture. For example, some Native Americans consider direct eye contact a sign of aggression or intrusiveness and to avoid it is an act of respect. On the other hand, looking away in some tribal cultures serves to restrict one from asking for help from others (Hull, 1982). Finally, eye-to-eye contact between males and females in some tribes is viewed as a sexually aggressive gesture, and infractions can result in serious trouble (Attneave, 1982, 1985). While the meaning or purpose of averting the eyes varies among tribal groups, the behavior is one of the most prevalent and noticeable differences between Anglo and Indian cultures. Therapists working with American Indian clients should not apply Western value standards in evaluating the meaning of limited eye contact.

A sign of goodwill in many cultures is the handshake. Anglos expect to find a hearty grasp when engaging in the custom, but this is not the case among Native Americans. Among Indians, the handshake is accomplished as a gentle touch of the other person to show friendly respect and acceptance (Attneave, 1982). Touching one another during conversations is a nonverbal expression of friendship and closeness within some tribes. This behavior is usually reserved to close friends and family members. Observation of American Indians in group interaction discloses relatively quickly which group members are comfortable with the custom and which are more reserved. Social workers and therapists should feel comfortable in offering to shake hands but should not view a gentle response as a sign of weakness or lack of enthusiasm. It is just a universal custom observed in a culturally different way.

A reasonably good understanding of the Indian client requires patience and flexibility, because the Indian client is sometimes slow in deciding to open up to a non-Indian therapist. It is not uncommon for an Indian client to observe the therapist for several visits before deciding whether to commit to a trusting relationship. For this reason, it is usually best to adopt a facultative style rather than that of a directive therapist (Noftz, 1988; Neligh, 1990). Gaining respect of the American Indian client is an important first step because this respect assumes that a trust relationship has been established. Once confidence is established, treatment may proceed and the client or client group will be more likely to disclose personal issues. Thus, keeping the discussion at a general level for several meetings offers the client more opportunity to reveal material that might be crucial to the diagnostic assessment.

Therapeutic Approaches

Despite contemporary evidence of extended family disintegration, American Indians still maintain a strong sense of responsibility to family, kinship group, and tribe (Noftz, 1988). Collective treatment of psychologically troubled clients in extended family groups has been shown to promote individual healing as well as that of the whole group involved in the treatment (LaFromboise, 1988). Family network therapy is not a common practice in Indian communities because clinicians have found difficulty in getting participation of all relevant family members or couples involved in the treatment process (Attneave, 1982). Nevertheless, the strong socializing influence within some extended families suggests that family network therapy can be effective when sensitively applied (Attneave, 1982; Red Horse, 1980).

Currently, there are five programs utilizing the family network model in the IHS service areas. However, none have been evaluated for their effectiveness (OTA Report, 1990). Non-Indian practitioners who are interested in implementing family network therapy might wish to contact the IHS Mental Health Administration in Albuquerque for consultation on the specific area programs that appear most successful.

Use of traditional healers remains a strong preference among some American Indians (LaFromboise, 1988). Many of the well-known Indian healers are quite old in their seventies and eighties (Neligh, 1990). Some have passed on their healing skills to younger apprentices in the tribe, ensuring the traditions will survive. In other Indian communities, medicine traditions have not been handed down and the knowledge and practice will end with the passing of the traditional healer. Recognizing the value of traditional medicine to Indian people, the IHS attempted to incorporate traditional medicine techniques and beliefs into the health care system, only to find traditional healers did not wish to be associated with "Anglo Medicine" (Neligh, 1990).

Another problem with incorporating traditional medicine practices in the public hospitals is that Native healers belong to particular medicine societies. They practice according to ancient beliefs that are tribally specific, presented in the tribal language, and with medicine bundles preserved and revered only by the tribal group to which the healer belongs. Unlike the non-Indian practitioner with translatable skills, traditional healers are not generalists. They are effective only at home and among those constituents who believe in the power of traditional healing.

The traditional healer is highly revered in many tribes, playing a variety of roles such as doctor, counselor, teacher, priest and historian. This important person is known by different titles which roughly translates in English to "medicine maker." Traditional healers possess a great deal of experience and training in various healing arts and are held in high esteem within the tribe among traditionalists (Attneave, 1982). On the other hand, some tribal members who follow the Christian religion consider these medicine makers and their practices as satanic, pagan, and cult oriented. This schism results in no small amount of dissension within tribes that have traditional and Christian constituents. Nevertheless, traditional healing practices remain a strong and vital part of spiritual life and religious ceremony in many of the tribes (Weibell-Orlando, 1987).

Group psychotherapy has become more prevalent in the IHS service areas primarily due to lack of trained professional staff. Because of the preference of most Indian people for conjoint activities in such things as the sweat lodge, the council, and various societies, group work has been one of the more successful of treatment options (Neligh, 1990). Single-issue groups such as veterans, panic disorder, diabetes, adult survivors of sex abuse, Alcoholics Anonymous, etc., have proven most effective when the therapist uses a facilitative style to maximize group participation drawing on cultural traditions. One highly successful group in Montana relies heavily on testimonials from group members and stresses members working together to support those having hard times even outside the therapeutic meeting (Neligh, 1990). The testimonial approach is related to "soft teaching" accomplished through storytelling.

Most American Indian tribes share some form of moralistic storytelling custom whereby the tribal people learn not only the tribal traditions but the expectations for social behavior within the community. Storytelling is a nonintrusive technique that assumes no individual pathology. This custom implies respect for the individual's capacity to understand the morality issue raised and to draw parallels from it for their own situation. In areas of substantial Indian populations, it is not difficult to locate a local storyteller who is willing to consult with the therapist and share some of the local stories and their importance to Indian people. Use of such collateral resources can substantially improve the therapist's understanding of local Indian culture. Tribal stories and character roles vary among tribes and make story content nontransferable. Thus, when learning local customs and traditions, the social worker should not expect this knowledge to be effective with Indian clients from any other tribal group. For example, the rabbit, the coyote, and raven are all forms of "the trickster," depending on the tribal belief system, but the role model does not translate between Indian nationalities who use the particular animal totem.

In social work practice with American Indians, programs that attempt to place personal adjustment or recovery first are usually seen as less successful than those which consider other factors first (Rogan, 1984). Success in counseling programs for American Indians may be attributed first to taking the client's cultural and racial identity into account at the outset (Sue & Sue, 1990). This aids in facilitating easy access to the social network and support system already established in the Indian community and family and serves to reinforce confidence in the clinician (Trimble & Hayes, 1984) and rounds out a successful intervention. To summarize, there are three strategies to effective social work with the American Indian culture: (1) observe and abide by local convention, (2) be open-minded and respectful of differences, and (3) provide the services that are promised.

Prevention

Tertiary prevention is accomplished through the IHS or tribally run clinics and hospitals. These facilities provide mental health and other medical interventions that reduce the incidences of death, morbidity, and other consequences of illnesses and disease. *Secondary prevention* involves public service education, and there are many such education and training programs that instruct the American Indian population about the dangers of alcoholism, drugs, unprotected sex, failure to immunize children, and more. This level also stresses early diagnosis, screening, and regular treatment follow-up. Social workers involved in secondary prevention should recognize that advertising and education strategies are not always transferable among tribes. Special attention must be given to local culture and language if this form of prevention is to be successful.

Primary prevention consists of programs where social workers and other professionals try to identify special at-risk groups. Unfortunately, there has been very little primary or secondary prevention research with outcome measures disclosing the most successful therapeutic approaches in dealing with the Native American population. Schinke et al. (1985, 1987) was reasonably successful working with Indian youth groups using cognitive behavioral strategies for reducing peer pressure in connection with substance abuse. By teaching alternative coping methods, values integration and communication skills, Schinke et al. (1987) found that clients were able to successfully reject peer pressure without damaging group cohesion. These cognitive-behavioral strategies also improved communication skills between the client and peers and between the client and their immediate and extended families.

The social work literature offers few examples of well-documented and empirically sound instances of culturally defined research (cf. Lopez & Hernandez, 1986). At best, the literature generally indicates that there are some cultural differences dealing with people of the Native American population and other ethnic groups, but few treatment guidelines are proposed. More empirical research in cultural diversity among Indian people and other culture groups should provide knowledge that offers improved diagnostic reliability and validity (Lopes & Hernandez, 1986). Another research imperative is the need for non-biased personality assessment instruments. Until this is accomplished, neither clinicians or psychometrists are able to make accurate findings with predictive value. Existing protocols, even those labeled as culture free, are useless in determining current functioning of the culturally different (Lopez & Hernandez, 1986).

RESEARCH ISSUES

The cultural diversity within the Native American population makes practice and related research a difficult but not an impossible undertaking. Because of this diversity, the majority of social work studies with Native

Americans have tended to be descriptive in nature and focused more on epidemiology and demography than on developing and evaluating effective cultural intervention programs. This problem is due in part to the finding that the majority of Native Americans demonstrate a strong preference for treatment by Native American social workers and therapists (Haviland et al., 1983; Litterell & Litterell, 1982; Cook & Helms, 1988). In spite of this known preference, there remains a severe shortage of professionally trained Native American clinicians. Several studies have shown that it is difficult and possibly inappropriate to attempt to treat this population with conventional, Western-oriented methods of treatment such as uncovering psychotherapies, counseling or casework (Neville, 1960; Tyler & Thompson, 1965).

There are very few empirical studies on specific social work treatment methods with Native Americans and an even greater paucity of those with positive outcomes. As previously mentioned, the Bicultural Competence Skills Approach was utilized as a measure of preventing substance abuse among Native American adolescents (Schinke et al., 1988). In this study, Schinke and his colleagues found that several factors contributed to the abuse of substances by Native Americans. One factor is the spiritual values some tribes place on substance use (cf. Spindler & Spindler, 1977). Another factor is the acculturation process which is seen as stressful to adolescents, and substance use is viewed as a coping response to stress (May, 1988). Based on these assumptions, Schinke et al. (1989) proceeded by attempting to enable Native American adolescents to blend their own values and roles with those of the culture in which they presently are surrounded (see also Bobo et al., 1985).

Operationally, it was theorized that preventative intervention includes knowledge and practice of both sets of cultural values and skills. Activities were presented to a group of volunteer Native American adolescents who were roughly comparable to one another in terms of demographic background and all were living on reservations at the time of the study. After randomly dividing the teenagers into a control group and treatment group, they were provided with instructions in communication skills, coping skills, discrimination skills, as well as information dissemination and social network building procedures to help them receive social work services.

By administering two outcome measures, a written scale and a self-report questionnaire before and after treatment, Schinke and his colleagues were able to demonstrate a positive improvement. The group which received skills intervention demonstrated a modest difference in pretest to posttest to follow-up measurements. Studies such as this show it is possible for social workers to conduct well-planned outcome studies with appropriately designed instruments that demonstrate the effectiveness of social work interventions with Native Americans. Continued success in this area requires additional research and development of valid and reliable, bias-free assessment instruments. Lastly, efforts must be made to augment funding for delivery of culturally relevant social welfare services to Native Americans and for measuring outcome effectiveness.

FUTURE DIRECTIONS

The future of social work with Native Americans should center on four major domains: social work education, social work practice, empirical clinical research, and community action research. Some degree of attention has been given toward training social workers in effectively working with minorities (e.g. Brown, 1978; Garland & Escobar, 1986; Schinke et al., 1987b), but few of these authors have specifically addressed the Native American population and its rich diversity. This lacunae in the field of professional social work education should be remedied through adjustments to the curriculum content at all degree levels of social work education, through in-service training, and continuing education programs. A further proactive strategy would be for institutions and organizations such as schools of social work and the Council on Social Work Education to develop rigorous affirmative action programs aimed at recruiting Native American students into BSW, MSW, and Ph.D. programs via scholarships and grants. Such outreach efforts will ultimately build a larger pool of bicultural social workers from which private and public social work agencies may select employees.

Additional support and encouragement should be devoted to promoting empirical clinical research in social work services provided to Native Americans. The previously cited studies by Schinke and his associates are a good example of the kind of practice-related inquiries which help improve the social work knowledge base. Empirical research such as this is necessary to determine valid and effective methods for reducing many of the problems previously discussed.

The major proportion of social work's involvement with Native American programs has been focused on the provision of services to Native American children and youth (Hogan & Siu, 1988). Some of the core programs that have involved social work expertise include foster care, adoptions, health care, housing, educational programs and nutritional improvement and AFDC. According to the IHS there is a need for increased attention to the needs of the mentally ill and chronically mentally ill, the elderly, domestic violence, and special groups such as Indian veterans. As for the latter group, Silver (1985) points out that effective Native American psychological healing practices with Indian war veterans must take into account the whole person including religious, spiritual, psychological, physical, and systemic functioning. Special-issue groups, such as Indian veterans, have already been widely accepted on the reservations and hold promise also for all American Indian veterans regardless of federal status or place of residence. Neligh (1990) contends that culturally sensitive psychiatric social workers have proven especially valuable in providing both group and individual mental health services on reservations and trust lands. However, with the majority of American Indians now living in urban areas where IHS provides only limited medical or mental health care, social workers in most every area of practice are more likely to encounter an Indian client or family needing assistance.

Social service needs of Native Americans both on and off the reservation are many and complex and there are too few Native social workers available to adequately meet these needs. Therefore, the challenge to all social work professionals, from practitioner to administrative system level, is to find ways to fill this service gap. The best medicine begins with adequate cultural sensitivity training and a desire to make a measurable difference in the lives of American Indians.

REFERENCES

Attneave, C. (1982). Practical counseling with American Indian and Alaska Native clients. In P.B. Pedersen (Ed.), *Handbook of cross-cultural counseling and therapy* (pp. 135–140). Westport, CT: Greenwood.

Attneave, C. (1985). American Indians and Alaskan Native Families. In M. McGoldrick, J.K. Pearce, & J. Giordano (Eds.), *Ethnicity and family therapy* (pp. 55–83). New York: Guilford.

Bachman, R. (1992). *Death and violence on the reservation.* New York: Auburn House.

Beauvais, F., & Laboueff, S. (1985). Drug and alcohol abuse intervention in American Indian communities. *International Journal of Addictions, 20,* 139–171.

Berlin, I.N. (1987). Suicide among American Indian Adolescents: An overview. *Suicide and Life-Threatening Behavior, 17,* 218–232.

Blanchard, E. (1988). American Indians and Alaskan Natives. In A. Minahan (Ed.), *Encyclopedia of social work.* Silver Spring, MD: National Association of Social Workers.

Blum, R., Harmon, B., Harris, L., Bergeisen, L., & Resnick, M. (1992). American Indian Alaska Native Youth Health. *Journal of the American Medical Association, 267,* 1637–1643.

Bobo, J.K. (1987). Preventing drug abuse among American Indian adolescents. In I.D. Gilchrist & S.P. Schinke (Eds.), *Preventing social and health problems through life skills training.* Seattle, WA: University of Washington.

Bobo, J.K., Snow, W.H., Gilchrist, L.D., & Schinke, S.P. (1985). Assessment of refusal skills in minority youth. *Psychological Reports, 57,* 1187–1191.

Brown, E.F. (1978). Native American Indians in modern society: Implications for social policy and services. In D.G. Norton et al. (Eds.), *The dual perspective: Inclusion of ethnic minority content in the social work curriculum* (pp. 68–80). New York, NY: Council on Social Work Education.

Cook, D.T., & Helms, J. (1988). Visible racial/ethnic groups supervise satisfaction with cross-cultural supervision as predicted by relationship characteristics. *Journal of Counseling Psychology, 35,* 268–273.

Congress of the United States, Office of Technology Assessment. (1990). *Indian adolescent mental health.* Washington, D.C.: U.S. Government Printing Office.

Crestoffel, K.K. (1990). Violent death and injury in U.S. children and adolescents. *Journal of Diseases of Children, 144,* 697–706.

Cunningham, P.J. (1993). Access to care in the Indian Health Services. *Health Affairs, 12,* 224–233.

Davenport, J., & Davenport, J. (1987). Native American suicide: A Durkheimian analysis. *Social Casework, 68,* 533–539.

Deloria, V., Jr. (Ed.). (1985). *American Indian policy in the twentieth century.* Norman, OK: University of Oklahoma Press.

Foreman, G.T. (1928). The Choctaw Academy. *Chronicles of Oklahoma, 6*(4), 452–480.

Foreman, C.T. (1932). The Choctaw Academy. *Chronicles of Oklahoma, 10*(1), 77–115.

Frost, D. (1991). American Indians in the 1990s. *American Demographics, 3*(12), 26–34.

Garland, D.R., & Escobar, D. (1986). Education for cross-cultural practice. *Journal of Social Work Education, 24,* 229–241.

Ghelman, M., & Schervish, P.H. (1993). *Who we are: The social work labor force as reflected in NASW membership.* Washington, D.C.: National Association of Social Workers.

Gilchrist, L.D., Schinke, S.P., Trimble, J.E., & Cvtkovich, G.T. (1987). Skills enhancement to prevent substance abuse among American Indian adolescents. *International Journal of the Addictions, 22,* 869–879.

Goodluck, C., & Eckstein, F. (1978). American Indian adoption program: An ethnic approach to child welfare. *White Cloud Journal, 1,* 3–7.

Greenbaum, S. (1991). What's in a label? Identity problems of Southern Indian tribes. *Journal of Ethnic Studies, 19,* 107–119.

Haviland, M., Horswill, R., O'Connell, J., & Dynneson, B. (1983). Native American college students' preference for counselor race and sex and likelihood of their use of counseling centers. *Journal of Counseling Psychology, 30,* 267–270.

Hippler, A.E. (1970). *From village to town: An intermediate step in the acculturation of Alaska Eskimos.* Training Center for Community Affairs: University of Minnesota.

Hogan, P., & Sui, S. (1988). Minority children and the child welfare system: A historical perspective. *Social Work, 33,* 493–498.

Hollinger, P., Offer, D., Barter, J., & Bell, C. (1994). *Suicide and homicide among adolescents.* New York: Guilford.

Hughes, G.F. (1992). A categorized work force. *Bureaucrat, 20*(4), 23–26.

Hull, G. (1982). Child welfare services to Native Americans. *Social Casework, 62,* 340–347.

Inouye, D.K. (1993). Our future is in jeopardy: The mental health of Native American adolescents. *Journal of Health Care for the Poor and Underserved, 4,* 1–8.

Jepsen, B. (1994). Indians seek supplemental funding. *Modern Health Care, 24*(26), 78.

Jones, R. S. (1990). *Federal programs of assistance to American Indians.* Washington, DC: U.S. Government Printing Office.

Kappler, C.L. (Ed.). (1904). *Indian affairs: Laws and treaties* (Vol. II). Washington, D.C.: U.S. Government Printing Office.

Katz, P. (1981). Psychotherapy with native adolescents. *Canadian Journal of Psychiatry, 20,* 455–459.

LaFrombosie, T. (1988). American Indian mental health policy. *American Psychologist, 43,* 388–395.

LaFromboise, T., & Bigfoot, D.S. (1989). Cultural and cognitive considerations in the prevention of American Indian adolescent suicide. *Journal of Adolescence, 11,* 139–153.

Lee, A. (1988, April). *The census and definitions and semantics of race.* Paper presented at the Annual Meeting of the Population Association of America, New Orleans, LA.

Littrell, J., & Littrell, M.A. (1982). American Indian and Caucasian students' preference for counselors: Effects of counselor dress and sex. *Journal of Counseling Psychology, 29,* 48–57.

Lopez, S., & Hernandez, P. (1986). How culture is considered in evaluations of psychopathology. *The Journal of Nervous and Mental Disease, 176,* 598–606.

Lurie, N.O. (1971). The contemporary American Indian scene. In E.B. Leacock & N.O. Lurie (Eds.), *North American Indians in historical perspective.* New York: Random House.

Mail, P.D., McKay, R.B., & Katz, M. (1989). Learning from American Indian patients. *Patient Education and Counseling, 13,* 91–102.

May, P.A., & Hymbaugh, K.J. (1983). *Epidemiology of fetal alcohol syndrome among the Ogala Sioux of the Pine Ridge Reservation.* Washington, D.C.: DHEW Publication No. HSM 72.

May, P.A. (1988). The health status of Indian children. *American Indian and Alaska Native Mental Health Research, 1*(1), 222–283.

McDonald, J.D., Morton, R., & Stewart, C. (1994). Clinical concerns with American Indian patients. In L. Van de Creek, S. Knapp, & T.L. Jackson (Eds.), *Innovations in clinical practice: A source book, 12,* 437–454.

McMillan, E. (1950). The first national Indian school: The Choctaw Academy. *Chronicles of Oklahoma, 28*(1), 52–80.

Medicine, B. (1988). Native American women: A call for research. *Anthropology and Education, 19,* 86–92.

Neligh, G. (1990). Mental health programs for American Indians: Their logic, structure and functions. *American Indian and Alaska Native Mental Health Research, The Journal of the National Center Monograph Series, 3*(3).

Nevill, R.J. (1960). Casework in an igloo: Adaptation of basic casework principles in work with Eskimos. *The Social Worker, 28,* 5–19.

Niccols, G.A. (1994). Fetal alcohol syndrome: Implications for psychologists. *Clinical Psychology, 14*(2), 91–111.

Noftz, M. (1988). Alcohol abuse and culturally marginal American Indians. *Social Casework, 69,* 67–73.

Passel, J., & Berman, P. (1984). Quality of 1980 census data for American Indians. *Social Biology, 33,* 163–183.

Pevar, S. (1992). *The rights of Indians and Indian tribes* (2nd ed.). Carbondale, IL: Southern Illinois University Press.

Red Horse, J.G. (1978). Family behavior of urban American Indians. *Social Casework, 59,* 67–72.

Rhodes, E.R., Marshall, M., Attneave, D., Echohawk, M., Bjork, J., & Beiser, M. (1980). Mental health problems of American Indians seen in outpatient facilities of the Indian Health Service, 1975. *Public Health Reports, 96,* 329–335.

Rogan, A. (1986, Fall). Recovery from alcoholism: Issues for Black and Native American alcoholics. *Alcohol Health and Research World,* 42–44.

Schinke, S., Botvin, G., Trimble, G., Orlandi, M., Gilchrist, L., & Locklear, B. (1988). Preventing substance abuse among American Indian adolescents: A bicultural competence approach. *Journal of Counseling Psychology, 35,* 87–90.

Schinke, S., Schilling, R., Gilchrist, L., Barth, T., Walter, R.H.E., & Cvtkovich, G.T. (1987a). Preventing substance abuse among American Indian youth: Research issues and strategies. *Journal of Social Service Research, 9*(4), 53–67.

Schinke, S., Schilling, R., Gilchrist, L., Barth, R., Bobo, J., Trimble, H., & Cvtkovich, G. (1985). Preventing substance abuse with Native American youth. *Social Casework, 66,* 213–217.

Schinke, S., Schilling, R., Palleja, J., & Zayas, L. (1978b). Prevention research among ethnic-racial minority group adolescents. *The Behavior Therapist, 10,* 151–155.

Silver, S.M. (1985, August). *Lessons from child of water.* Paper presented at the Annual Convention of the American Psychological Association, Los Angeles, CA.

Slotkin, S. (1956). *The peyote religion: A study in Indian-White relations.* New York: The Free Press.

Smith, E. (1987). Health care for Native Americans: Who will pay? *Health Affairs, 6*(1), 123–128.

Snipp, C. (1989). *American Indians: The first of this land.* New York: Russell Sage.

Spindler, G., & Spindler, L. (Eds.). (1977). *Native North American cultures.* New York: Holt, Rinehart and Winston.
Wiley & Son.

Sue, D.W., & Sue, D. (1990). *Counseling the culturally different* (2nd ed.). New York: Wiley & Son.

Thomason, T. (1991). Counseling Native Americans: An introduction for non-Native American counselors. *Journal of Counseling & Development, 3,* 321–327.

Tippeconnic, J.W. (1988). A survey: Attitudes toward the education of American Indians. *Journal of American Indian Education, 28*(1), 34–36.

Trimble, J.E. (1984). Drug abuse prevention research needs among American Indians and Alaska Natives. *White Cloud Journal, 3,* 23–24.

Trimble, J.E., & Fleming, C.M. (1989). Providing counseling services to Native American Indians: Client counselor and community characteristics. In P.B. Pedersen, J.G. Draguns, W.J. Lonner, & J.E. Trimble (Eds.), *Counseling across cultures* (pp. 177–204). Honolulu, HI: University of Hawaii.

Trimble, J., & Hayes, S. (1984). Mental health intervention in the psychosocial contexts of American Indian communities. In W. O'Connor & B. Lobin (Eds.), *Ecological models: Applications to clinical and community mental health.* New York: Wiley & Sons.

Tyler, I.M., & Thompson, S.D. (1965, April). Cultural factors in casework treatment of a Navajo mental patient. *Social Casework,* 215–220.

U.S. Congress, Office of Technology Assessment. (1990). *Indian adolescent mental health.* Washington, D.C.: U.S. Government Printing Office.

U.S. Department of Commerce, Bureau of the Census. (1989). *Tribal liaison handbook.* Washington, D.C.: U.S. Government Printing Office.

U.S. Department of Commerce, Bureau of the Census. (1992). *American Indian Census by State and County 1980–1990.* Washington, D.C.: U.S. Government Printing Office.

U.S. Department of Commerce, Bureau of the Census. (1990). *Census Report CPH-L-73.* Washington, D.C.: U.S. Government Printing Office.

U.S. Department of Health and Human Services, Indian Health Service Office of Planning, Evaluation and Research. (1993). *Trends in Indian health.* Washington, D.C.: U.S. Government Printing Office.

U.S. Department of Health and Human Services, Indian Health Service Office of Planning, Evaluation and Research. (1994). *Trends in Indian health.* Washington, D.C.: U.S. Government Printing Office.

U.S. Department of Health and Human Services, Indian Health Service Office of Planning, Evaluation and Research. (1994). *Regional differences in Indian health.* Washington, D.C.: U.S. Government Printing Office.

U.S. Senate Select Committee on Indian Affairs. (1988). *Oversight Hearing on Federal Acknowledgment Process* (One hundredth Congress, second session). Washington, D.C.: U.S. Government Printing Office.

U.S. Department of the Interior, Bureau of Indian Affairs. (1988). *Acknowledgment Information Bulletin.* Washington, D.C.: Author.

Wasinger, L. (1993). The value system of the Native American counseling client: An exploration. *American Indian Culture and Research Journal, 17*(4), 91–98.

Weibel, J.C. (1982). American Indians, urbanization, alcohol: A developing urban Indian drinking ethos. *Alcohol Monograph, 4,* 331–355.

Weibell-Orlando, J. (1986–87). Drinking patterns of urban and rural American Indians. *Alcohol Health and Research World, 13,* 54–55.

Wingert, J., & Field, M. (1985). Characteristics of Native American users of inhalants. *International Journal of the Addictions, 20,* 1575–1582.

Young, T. (1988). Substance use and abuse among Native Americans. *Clinical Psychology Review, 8,* 125–138.

Young, T. (1993). Suicide and homicide among Native Americans: The medical resources hypothesis. *American Indian Culture and Research Journal, 17*(4), 99–105.

Chapter 11

CULTURAL DIVERSITY AND SOCIAL WORK PRACTICE: FUTURE DIRECTIONS

CHERYL DAVENPORT DOZIER AND LARRY NACKERUD

Introduction

There is and will continue to be a dramatic increase in cultural and ethnic diversity in American society (Ronnau, 1994; Manoleas, 1994). Social workers of the mid-nineties and beyond will intervene with increasing numbers of culturally diverse clients with unique racial, ethnic, and cultural backgrounds (Baruth & Manning, 1991). According to the 1990 census, one of every four Americans is a person of color (Black, Hispanic, Asian and Pacific Islander, American Indian, Eskimo, and Aleut Americans), and in the year 2000, one of every three Americans and half of all school-age children will be persons of color (Henderson, 1994). What will this mean to those social work practitioners employed in culturally diverse communities? What will this mean to social work education, practice, policy and research? In addition, the rise in reported acts of racism and hate crimes in American society and on college campuses cries out for responses from institutions of higher education (Ronnau, 1994). Are schools of social work preparing students to address these serious issues?

This chapter will address some of the major issues that social work practitioners and educators face regarding cultural diversity and social work education, social work practice, social work policy, and social work research.

Future Directions for Culturally Diverse Practice

Social work practice is almost always cross-cultural, in the sense that very few clients are the same race, ethnicity, age, gender, religion, and sexual orientation as their social worker. Therefore, social work practitioners must be able to bridge these cultural and diversity gaps (Thornton & Garrett, 1995).

The Council of Social Work Education's (CSWE) accreditation standards clearly identify the need for practice content to include approaches and skills for practice with clients from differing social, cultural, racial, religious, spiritual, and class background (CSWE, 1994). To accomplish this goal, it is imperative that social work educators adopt a cultural competence approach to social work practice and training (Manoleas, 1994).

Defining the "appropriate terminology" is a difficult task because social work educators and practitioners have not agreed on a set of terms when discussing cultural diversity. Several of these terms and definitions will be discussed and challenged in the section on social work education. However, in social work practice, practitioners are attempting to become culturally competent, culturally sensitive, ethnically sensitive, multicultural and culturally appropriate. In social work practice as in social work education, one must first define and agree upon the definitions and relevance of culture, race, ethnicity, diversity, social class, oppression, and multiculturalism.

Ethnic-Sensitive and Culturally Competent Practice

Ethnic-sensitive practice is defined in the nineteenth edition of the *Encyclopedia of Social Work* as "being based on the view that practice must be attuned to the values and dispositions related to clients' ethnic group membership and social class position" (Schlesinger & Devore, 1995a, p. 903). "Ethnic-sensitive social work practice builds on: (1) the components of a professional perspective conceptualized as the layers of understanding; (2) a series of assumptions; and (3) prevailing practice principles, skills, and strategies" (Schlesinger & Devore, 1995a, p. 904). The approach involves the adaptation of prevailing social work principles and skills to take account of ethnic realities and includes social workers' need to be aware of, and to redress, the oppression experienced by members of minority groups (Schlesinger & Devore, 1995a).

Ethnic-sensitive practice requires the support and cooperation of social work educators, field practicum agencies, and students. It integrates the needs of racial and ethnic individuals, families, groups, and communities. It also provides a broad-based process of assessment, goal formulation, intervention, and evaluation of these diverse individuals, families, groups, and communities (Haynes & Singh, 1992). Such practice could also be expanded to include other vulnerable populations such as women, the handicapped or disabled, gays and lesbians, the elderly or veterans (Haynes & Singh, 1992).

Social work practice includes working with male and female clients whose sexual orientation cannot be assumed to be heterosexual and who are more racially and ethnically diverse than at any other time in the history of social work (Marshack, Hendricks, & Gladstein, 1994). Social work practitioners also have to be prepared to address the needs of clients with physical disabilities, diverse religious and spiritual orientations, and who may be very poor and disenfranchised (Marshack, Ortiz, Hendricks, & Gladstein, 1994). Social work practice in the twenty-first century will include working with a much larger and older elderly population, some with good financial resources and some with very limited resources.

Cross-cultural encounters between workers and clients involve issues of race, culture, social class, minority status, and ethnicity (Green, 1982). Each of these terms must be clearly defined by the practitioner or agency and explored as to its significance in the treatment process. Effective programs and treatment interventions demand that those providing the services understand and be sensitive to the values, culture and special needs of all groups served, especially ethnic and racial groups (Jacobs & Bowles, 1988). There has also been an ongoing debate about the clinical relevance of issues such as ethnicity, social class, minority group membership, therapist-patient match, and culturally relevant treatment (Chau, 1991; Brisbane & Womble, 1991; Boyd-Franklin, 1989). These issues must be addressed by social work practitioners as they attempt to provide culturally competent treatment.

In providing culturally competent practice, social work practitioners must learn about clients both as individuals and as members of a cultural or ethnic community. They must investigate the relevance of culture to the clients' lives and then build on this knowledge and incorporate it into the helping process (Thornton & Garrett, 1995). Social workers must pay attention to culture as a factor in clinical assessments. This process includes problem identification, diagnosis, and the intervention plan. Orlandi (1992) defines cultural competence as a set of academic and interpersonal skills that allow individuals to increase their understanding and appreciation of cultural differences and similarities within, among, and between groups. A cross-cultural practice model and a cultural competence continuum are aides to developing ethnic sensitivity in a social work practitioner (Kilpatrick, 1995).

Pinderhughes (1989) identified several questions that practitioners should ask to ensure that their own cultural lens is not the basis of assessment. These questions address issues of transition (migration and immigration), culturally interpreted explanations of phenomena and behaviors, environmental deficits, cultural conflicts in identity and values, and client's cultural strengths.

The use of the dual perspective in social work practice is another means of focusing on client's cultural diversity. The dual perspective forces social workers to recognize diverse groups and to understand that disparities between these groups' beliefs and behavior and those of the wider society can often be explained by historical and cultural experiences such as discrimination, racism, or social and economic structural dislocation, rather than by personal psychopathology (Norton, 1993).

Research has suggested that the impact of racism and race on a client's life must be assessed and addressed at the initial phase of treatment (Robinson, 1989). It is important for clients to know that racist acts, perceived or factual, are treatment issues (Brisbane & Womble, 1991). A need for increased knowledge and sensitivity about the interrelationships between the concepts of race, culture, ethnicity, class, and gender will enhance and broaden educators' and practitioners' frames of reference and help them reformulate their assessment and treatment of African American clients (Logan, 1990) and other ethnically diverse clients.

Social work practitioners need to be prepared to address racial issues as they emerge in multiracial treatment groups. Race is such an emotionally charged area of practice that group leaders may fail to identify and deal with racial issues. To achieve effective outcomes in multiracial treatment groups, social workers must confront racial issues that are inherent in these groups (Davis, Galinsky & Schopler, 1995).

It is also important for social work practitioners to understand that skin color is an issue for various cultures that have an African heritage and it must be explored in treatment (Harvey, 1995). All Black people and persons of color are aware at a very early age that their skin color makes them different from mainstream White Americans. Their skin color (especially their Blackness) sets them apart from other White immigrant groups who were not brought here as slaves and whose assimilation experience into mainstream culture was much different (Boyd-Franklin,

1989). Social work practitioners need to raise the issue of skin color because it can be perceived as a positive dynamic or a negative factor in their client's lives (Harvey, 1995). This issue is pervasive, also occurring to some extent among Black clients, professionals, and staff (Hall, 1992).

Social work practitioners must examine the political and economic impact of oppression on client systems by evaluating the impact of oppression in relation to policy, practice, program development and implementation, and resource allocation in both public and voluntary agencies. "Cultural oppression is the imposition of the dominant group's culture on oppressed or powerless groups, wherein the culture of the oppressed is considered marginal, illegitimate, or nonexistent" (Schiele, 1993, p. 20). Although all groups of color have experienced some form of cultural oppression, they have not experienced cultural oppression monolithically (Schiele, 1993).

Empowerment and Strengths Perspective Models

Social work practitioners must shift from pathology-focused practice to an empowerment-based practice (Saleeby, 1992) when working with oppressed groups. Several scholars (Solomon, 1976; Boyd-Franklin, 1989; Pinderhughes, 1989; Lee, 1994) have presented the process of empowerment as an approach that social workers can engage clients to reduce the powerlessness that has been created by negative valuations based on membership in a specific ethnic, racial, or other oppressed group.

Empowerment practice "seeks to create community with clients in order to challenge with them the contradictions faced as vulnerable, hurt, or oppressed persons in the midst of an affluent and powerful society" (Lee, 1994, p. 13). Social work practitioners must develop effective strategies and interventions to confront the client's individual pain by taking social forces into account (Lee, 1994).

Empowering African American families means revisiting a multigenerational history of victimization by poverty and racism. African Americans, for a variety of historical reasons, have not been well acculturated into American society (Williams & Wright, 1992). This has resulted in the maintenance of a distinctive culture that possesses elements of the dominant culture, other subcultures as reflected in language, family structures, religion, and relationships with other systems (Billingsley, 1990; Boyd-Franklin, 1989). Empowering African American families means assessing these families within the context of their own unique experiences.

Social work practitioners require knowledge and understanding of traditional values and beliefs held by African Americans and other diverse cultural groups. The assessment of African American circumstances in social work practice should emphasize the identification of coping skills and capacities for developing them to enhance individual, family, and community functioning (Daley, Jennings, Beckett, & Leashore, 1995).

Many authors have stressed the importance of focusing on clients' strengths as a treatment strategy, especially when working with racially and ethnically diverse clients (Pinderhughes, 1989; Solomon, 1976; Brisbane & Womble, 1992). Social work practitioners need to emphasize, celebrate, and nurture families' strengths, capacities, pride, and knowledge in the therapeutic process instead of doting on problems and failures (Weick & Saleebey, 1995). Many therapeutic models used in social work agencies with clients focus on the recognition of clients' strengths and coping skills as a key to achieving successful treatment outcomes.

Women and Gender Content

Social work practitioners need to better integrate the diverse issues of women and gender into their practice. There is new and emerging knowledge about how women's experiences relate to the contextual dimensions of practice. Therefore, traditional therapeutic models that are taught in schools of social work and intervention approaches at practicum agencies may not incorporate this new knowledge into practice (Carter et al., 1994).

Practice models that focus on families, groups and social justice must incorporate the relevance of gender and recognize the roles of power and conflict in relation to gender issues. An important consideration of social work practice is how different practice strategies relate to the empowerment of group and family members (Carter et al., 1994). In addition, these authors emphasize that social workers must be cognizant of the impact that diverse gender issues have on all interactions with clients. Consciousness-raising has served to focus attention more on the oppressiveness of patriarchy, thus precipitating changes in both genders (Kilpatrick, 1995).

Social work practitioners must address the gender terminology and go beyond calling all women "minorities" regardless of the obvious diversity among them, particularly their experiences with racism, sexism and sexual oppression in this society. The term *women of color* has been adopted by many African American, Latina, Asian, and Native American women in the United States as a way of unifying the commonalities, especially in contrast to the experiences of European American women. The use of this term, however, does not minimize the differences between and within these racial and ethnic groups. These authors believe that feminist methods provide one useful framework for ensuring that attention be given to both sexism and racism when organizing with women of color (Gutierrez & Lewis, 1994).

Macro Practice Issues

On a macro practice level, human service organizations need to assess their organization's cultural competence and ethnic sensitivity as it relates to their employee and client relations. There continues to be a lack of cultural diversity among the staffing patterns at many social service agencies, especially in the management level. Many social service agencies with a clientele of predominantly racial and ethnic groups of color have administrative staff and often a clinical staff that is predominantly white. Recent studies indicate that clinical services in child welfare are predominantly delivered by White workers, while the predominant recipients of these services are ethnic and racial groups of color (Siegel, 1994). This must be addressed by social work agencies at an organizational level.

The staffing of social work agencies should be reflective of the diversity of the client groups. This involves a conscious effort by management to first recognize the value of a diverse staff and to insure its implementation at all levels. Simply having a bilingual staff is not always the solution to having an effective clinical team that can relate to clients who speak a foreign language and have a unique culture. Spanish, for example, may be one of the only obvious similarities between Puerto Rican clients and Mexican clients. If the clientele is predominantly Mexican Americans, then having a bilingual and bicultural social worker would better meet the needs of the clients versus a worker who speaks Spanish.

Cultural diversity training has been provided in many organizations, usually as half- or full-day in-service trainings by consultants, with the purpose of addressing the racial, ethnic, gender and cultural issues that are inherent in these agencies. These one-day sessions have been viewed by some managers as igniting the racist, sexist, homophobic, and other bias attitudes among the workers. In these situations, often the trainer gets blamed for the reactions and for not doing the healing. There is a need for managers to recognize that conflict which may exist in their organizations may need a major overhaul, not a one-time awakening to the conflicts. One-shot training sessions are usually not effective when dealing with cultural diversity at the organization level. At a minimum, cultural awareness involves an ongoing discussion among workers of the various ways to design services so that they better match the diversity and experiences of the clients (Green, 1982). Management often does not recognize that it's multicultural conflicts are affecting interpersonal relations and work productivity.

Human service agencies and other organizations must prepare for the dramatic shift in the makeup of the work force in the twenty-first century. Building a pluralistic work place is one alternative to addressing the diverse racial, ethnic, gender, and cultural issues in the new work force. The new work force will have workers who are older, and the new arrivals will be largely people of color, women, and new immigrants (legal and illegal) (Nixon & Spearman, 1991). These authors describe pluralistic management as "leadership that aggressively pursues the creation of a workplace in which the values, interests, and contributions of diverse cultural groups are an integral part of the organization's mission, culture, policies, and procedures and in which these groups share power at every level" (Nixon & Spearman, 1991, p. 156).

Some principles of pluralistic management that need to be embraced by social work macro practitioners include: changing the organizational rules to accommodate cultural differences in style, perspectives, and world views; incorporating issues of diversity in organizations-wide policies and practices versus being restricted to EEO policies and practices; empowering employees through career development, team building, mentoring, and participatory leadership; and working to overcome barriers that hinder successful and authentic relationships among peers and subordinates who are culturally different from the mainstream stereotype (Nixon & Spearman, 1991).

As social work practitioners prepare for the future, they must be cognizant of the true meaning of incorporating diversity values and principles into their thinking and practice. It must not be an afterthought when issues of difference affect the therapeutic or organizational environment. It must be a conscious and primary goal to first consider the issues of diversity. Clients must not be blamed or expected to raise the issues of how differences and similarities may be affecting their lives. Social work practitioners must first raise the questions and continue to address the issues with their clients.

It is important for social work practitioners and social work administrators to assess the reasons why clients who are culturally diverse or from vulnerable populations may not return or continue treatment. Often the lack of addressing the diversity issues, or not seeing agency personnel and clinicians who resemble the client's background, may have a great impact on client follow-through and treatment outcomes. Clients may not voluntarily share these reasons for not continuing in treatment, but it should be investigated. Seeking help is taboo in many cultures and becomes more difficult when persons do not feel comfortable with the agency policies, staffing and structure.

As we move into the twenty-first century, social work practitioners must be aware of and understand the ongoing debates in the field regarding diversity and culture. Their role as practitioners must be one of incorporating the social work values, knowledge, and skills and continuing to gain knowledge of diverse ethnic, cultural, and vulnerable groups.

CULTURAL DIVERSITY AND SOCIAL WORK RESEARCH

Until the present it has been appropriate that the interplay between cultural diversity and social work research focus on such minimal goals as (1) a need for increased awareness, (2) knowledge acquisition regarding culturally diverse variants, and (3) facilitation of the use of non-biased, non-sexist language (Eichler, 1988). However, in a spirit of continued improvement, social work researchers need to move beyond these minimalist goals. Continued improvement in social work research will take place when social work researchers infuse cultural diversity issues and concerns into the more complex aspects of research. Gold and Bogo (1992) identify question formulation, research design, instrumentation, data analysis, and interpretation leading to reported findings as examples of these more complex aspects. Another important aspect would be empirical investigations regarding the extent to which ethnic, gender, and racial factors on the part of both clients and practitioners are related to service outcomes. Just as such factors may not be safely ignored, it should not be assumed that they exert a consistent monolithic impact.

Shifting perceptions and redundancy in presentations of cultural diversity material related to social work research are witness to this need for continued improvement. For instance, consider the change in perception of such a seminal work as Margrit Eichler's (1988) *Nonsexist Research Methods.* Once considered a radical presentation, the book is now considered to contain merely a standard reference text on gender-sensitive research. Redundancy of cultural diversity material presented in social work research textbooks also speaks to the need for continued improvement by social work researchers. For example, the following paragraph is a condensation of Eichler's material on sexism in research repeated almost word for word in many social work research methods.

> Gender and cultural bias and insensitivity can hinder the methodological quality of a study and therefore the validity of its findings. Much has been written about these problems in recent years, and some have suggested that when researchers conduct studies in a sexist manner or in a culturally insensitive manner, they are not committing just methodological errors, but are also going awry ethically. (e.g., Rubin & Babbie, 1993, p. 76; Williams, Tutty, & Grinell, 1995, p. 42)

The fourth edition of the *Publication Manual of the American Psychological Association* (APA) (1994) also includes an explicit expression of the cultural diversity standards by which all writing in social work research reports is to be judged. An entire section of guidelines (e.g., appropriate level of specificity, sensitivity to labels, acknowledgment of participation, gender, sexual orientation, racial and ethnic identity, disabilities, and age), specific to the goal of reducing bias in language contained in research reports, is provided to the reader. Social work researchers are summarily exhorted in the APA manual that "long-standing cultural practice can exert a powerful influence over even the most conscientious author. Just as you have learned to check what you write for spelling, grammar, and wordiness, practice reading over your work for bias" (American Psychological Association, 1994, p. 47).

Empirical Research/Outcome Studies

Reid (1994) states that since its beginnings in the 1960s, the empirical practice movement in social work has addressed three major goals: (1) advancement of the use of research methods in practice as a means of facilitating assessment, guiding intervention planning, and evaluating cases; (2) promotion and use of interventions whose effectiveness has been demonstrated through empirical research; and (3) knowledge building through studies carried out by practitioner-researchers. Continued improvement of social work research will be operationalized by blending cultural diversity issues and concerns directly into these three empirical foundation goals.

For example, practice-based empirical research focused on cultural diversity issues and concerns will augment the claim of social work professionals that they are effective in dealing with clients who are members of culturally diverse groups. Schlesinger and DeVore (1995) stress that social work research related to cultural diversity has been too narrowly focused on capturing how aware an individual social worker may be of his or her own biases and how knowledgeable he or she may be of culturally diverse values. Social work research has failed to focus on assessments of specific skill development, enhancement, and performance as related to a social worker's cultural competency (LaFromboise & Rowe, 1983; Ponterotto, Rieger, Barrett, & Sparks, 1994). This is particularly true when the claim is made that a social work practitioner has demonstrated an ability to work with persons from a number of culturally diverse groups (Ponterotto et al., 1994).

The completion of outcome studies with a focus on cultural diversity issues and concerns will help address global research questions about what it means for a social worker to be culturally competent. What skills are necessary for social work professionals to achieve effectiveness in working with members of culturally diverse groups? Schinke, Gilbert, Trimble, Orlandi, Gilchrist, and Lochlear (1988) emphasize the need for research focused on theory-based, culturally sound, and sensitive interventions. More specific research questions, such as whether culturally diverse clients more readily achieve their desired goals when working with social workers assessed to be highly culturally competent, could also be addressed. As well, social service programs that reportedly work well with members of culturally diverse populations must document that success via outcome studies (Thornton & Garrett, 1995). Some progress is being made along these lines. For example, Thyer (1994) describes some applications of social learning theory as one approach to social work practice which does possess a considerable body of empirical research evidence supporting the effectiveness of these approaches.

Empirically based outcome studies could help answer some important questions regarding cultural diversity, cultural competency, and social work education. What are the measurable effects upon social work students of the inclusion over the last decade of cultural diversity coursework and a cultural diversity emphasis throughout the curricula of accredited social work programs from culturally diverse groups? Which teaching methods are most effective in achieving enhanced cultural competency in social work students? Is there an empirical foundation for the informal standard in social work education of cultural diversity courses being taught by persons of color and/or women? Most importantly, do "culturally sensitive" social workers achieve more effective outcomes with diverse client groups? The answer to these simple questions is usually assumed to be yes, but it is clear that documenting such contentions are crucial to justify the whole initiative called "culturally diverse" training.

Research curricula in graduate and undergraduate social work programs must also increasingly emphasize how awareness of cultural diversity issues and concerns can complement the acquisition of research skills by social work students (Marlow, 1993). For example, students can easily be required to include consideration of culturally diverse variants (e.g., race, gender, ethnicity, sexual orientation) as covariants or independent variables in their research efforts.

Social Work Assessment Methods

Relative to the total amount of social work literature on cultural diversity issues and concerns, little attention has been directed toward developing psychometrically sound and conceptually anchored instrumentation for evaluating culturally competent social work practice. Data-collection instruments designed to measure the cultural competence of social work practitioners and social work students need to be developed. As well, social work researchers need to have at their disposal an objective guide by which to assess the respective strengths and weaknesses of different instruments (Ponterotto et al., 1994). While it may be valuable to borrow instrumentation from other academic areas (e.g., psychology, anthropology, sociology), continued improvement in social work research will not be achieved if the burden of developing and validating such instruments continues to fall outside of social work. The new journal *Research on Social Work Practice* (produced by Sage Publications, Inc.) is one social work periodical which regularly publishes examples of new developments in culturally diverse assessment methods (e.g., Julia, 1993), and similar examples are frequently found in other disciplinary outlets.

While ethnic and cultural differences have been studied via the application of various psychometric instruments (e.g., Minnesota Multiphasic Personality Inventory, MMPI) for decades, the results have been generally inconclusive and major questions remain. For example, are interpretations based on any specific instrumentation equally valid when used with members of various culturally diverse groups? Are the interpretations based on instrument-derived data as accurate for members of all culturally diverse groups? The fact is that the majority of standardized tests have been normed only on subjects belonging to the dominant White culture (Gold & Bogo, 1992). Timbrook and Graham (1994) caution social work researchers to consider that any instrument may tend to overpathologize or underpathologize members of culturally diverse groups.

Of course, the whole notion of "norms" can be problematic. Even if it is clearly shown that, for example, Cuban Americans meeting the *DSM–IV* criteria for major depression score above a given value on a standardized depression inventory, and a given Cuban American client does indeed score above that value, that *does not* mean that the client meets the criteria for major depression. To claim so represents the philosophical error called "affirming the consequent." Here are two examples of both correct and incorrect syllogistic reasoning involved:

Correct Reasoning

Major Premise: All Cuban American meeting the criteria for major depression score above "X".

Minor Premise: Mr. Garcia, a Cuban American, meets the criteria for major depression.

Conclusion: Mr. Garcia would score above "X".

Incorrect Reasoning

Major Premise: All Cuban Americans meeting the criteria for major depression score above "X".

Minor Premise: Mr. Garcia scores above "X".

Conclusion: Mr. Garcia meets the criteria for major depression.

The latter example is similar to reasoning that since all birds have two legs and that since John Wodarski has two legs, John Wodarski is a bird! It may well be safer, logically and empirically, to use standardized rapid assessment instruments with clients in an "ipsative" manner, rather than to rely on so-called normative data which may not really be representative of your particular client. Ipsative use involves repeatedly administering the instrument with a given client periodically during treatment, and looking for changes in scores, *comparing the client's present scores with his/her own past scores* to help determine any changes, rather than comparing his/her scores to some normative values accompanying the published instrument.

Combining Quantitative and Qualitative Methods

If a truly adequate methodology for the assessment of the cultural competence of social work practitioners is to be achieved, strong consideration needs to be given to the use of mixed (qualitative and quantitative) methods (cf. Fraser, 1994). For example, prolonged engagement, a central feature of the interpretive inquiry paradigm (Lincoln & Guba, 1985), is congruent with the idea that social work researchers, prior even to question formulation and final decisions about research design, spend some time immersed in the culture of the people with whom the research will be conducted. Thornton and Garrett (1995) suggest that social work researchers consider incorporation of ethnographic methods as a means of capturing a rich description of a culture from the insider's point of view. The use of ethnographic studies as a partial substitute for the heavy reliance in social work research on survey research may lead to more culturally relevant questions, participant-friendly research design, and less culturally biased interpretations (Logan, Freeman, & McRoy, 1990).

Qualitative and quantitative methods can be used in a complementary fashion in the pursuit of standards for assessment of culturally competent practice. For instance, the use of qualitative research methods, such as case studies and life histories of social workers considered to be highly culturally competent, may enrich the process of studying cultural diversity and social work practice from a purely quantitative perspective. Semi-structured or unstructured interviews aimed at assessing the kinds of qualities culturally diverse clients look for or see in culturally competent social workers are additional qualitative methods to be considered (Ponterotto et al., 1994).

The views of members of culturally diverse groups, which previously may have had limited access to the traditional scientific paradigm, may benefit from the increased use of feminist research methods. Feminist research methods may serve as a more sensitive approach by which social work researchers can meld cultural diversity issues and concerns into their work. Central to the feminist approach is the concept of allowing the research participants to be fully involved in the research process, including the question and design elements (Marlow, 1993).

Conceptualization of Risk

Ginsberg (1994) hypothesizes that the conceptualization of what is a social problem and determination of which social problems are most appropriately addressed by social work practitioners, researchers, and educators has become more complex through the years. In effect, concern has turned from looking not just at the problems themselves but also increasingly to a focus on those who have the problems (Meenaghan & Kilty, 1994). This shift in focus has promulgated the use of populations-at-risk as a conceptual foundation for not only social work practice and education but also for social work research. Care, however, must be taken in using this concept of at-risk populations in social work research, especially when using this designation with members of culturally diverse groups. For research purposes, members of culturally diverse groups are typically distinguished on the basis of demographic characteristics, when, in fact, they may have little in common besides a racial, age, gender, or sexual orientation category that is devalued in society (Meenaghan & Kilty, 1994).

Indeed, by identifying risk factors and characteristic variables which are associated with specific social problems or poor outcomes in life, social work researchers have informed social work practice. On the other hand, it is important to remember that data analysis, interpretation, and reporting may be based on variables with very weak associations. When we know that a characteristic is statistically related to a particular social problem or need, we can use that knowledge to predict future occurrences of the conditions about which we are concerned. For example, we may find a correlation between gender and alcohol abuse, such that men are more likely than women to display alcohol problems. If a relationship between two variables is discovered, we can use information about one of those variables to predict the other variable. In contrast, if there is no association or a weak association, using one variable (e.g., race, ethnicity, age, gender, or sexual orientation) as a predictor of the other yields nothing more than a haphazard forecast. The statistical research-related concepts of correlation and regression, then, are a means by which we can estimate the occurrence of specific conditions under particular circumstances, but not just in any case, in any context, or for members of any culturally diverse group (Meenaghan & Kilty, 1994).

Serious ethical and value problems are associated with the use of the concept of population-at-risk and social work research focused on a culturally diverse group (Schlesinger & DeVore, 1995b). In general, identification of such populations will be overly inclusive and more potential cases will be identified than will actually occur. In many cases, most people who are members of a population-at-risk will never develop the condition. For example, the vast majority of African Americans do not become drug users or alcoholics, just as they do not live out their lives in poverty. The point is not to reject as improper all social work research efforts that try to determine what characteristics are associated most strongly with particular problems or conditions, but rather to emphasize that we are dealing with group-level phenomena, from which we can distinguish greater or lesser odds of having problems by identifying relevant social categories. Rarely will we be able to state categorically that nearly every member of a certain culturally diverse group will have a certain problem, whereas the majority of another group would not (Meenaghan & Kilty, 1995).

CULTURAL DIVERSITY, SOCIAL WORK, AND SOCIAL POLICY

Within the ensuing years the polarities created by the desire for and the demands of cultural diversity in American society will be most strongly evident in the social policy arena. This will be true for the country as a whole, for the specific context of higher education, and most certainly for social work practice and education. Extensive dialogues and heated debates about the merits of such diversity-driven and diversity-driving social policies as affirmative action and U.S. immigration policy have begun and will surely continue.

The major question is will there be continued support for the development and implementation of social policies which have tended to promote and enhance cultural diversity in the United States. An accompanying question is how powerful will be the backlash against social policies, such as affirmative action and U.S. immigration policy, which have resulted in a diversification of cultures throughout American society?

Foundation of Social Work Involvement in Social Policy

Social work practitioners and social work educators with an eye to the future first need to become better informed of the issues linked with specific social policies of merit, such as affirmative action policies in employment and education, and of the interplay of cultural diversity issues within distinct social policy arenas (Kingdon, 1984), such as the policy arena of U.S. immigration. Secondly, there is a need for social work practitioners and social work educators to articulate a position on social policies which resonates the cultural diversity and social policy mandates of the social work practice and education communities. Finally, social work practitioners and educators need to take steps to assume proactive roles in local, state, or national policy circles (Jansson, 1993).

The foundation for the involvement of social work professionals in the arena of social policy emanates from a number of sources. A core element of the definition of social work adopted by the National Association of Social Workers (NASW) in 1973 was the recognized need for social work practitioners and educators to work to *create societal conditions favorable to the goals* of helping individuals, groups, or communities to enhance or restore their capacity for social functioning (Hepworth & Larsen, 1993, p. 3). It is the emphasis accorded by social work educators to the body of knowledge concerned with social policy which most sharply differentiates social work curricula from the curricula of all other disciplines (Hepworth & Larsen, 1993).

The study and knowledge of social policy by social work professionals is considered, however, not to be enough. Social work practitioners and social work educators are obligated to do something about social policy. The 1990 statement of the NASW *Code of Ethics* includes the following elements under the heading of the *Social Worker's Ethical Responsibility to Society* (Hepworth & Larsen, 1993, p. 3).

• The social worker should act to prevent and eliminate discrimination against any person or group on the basis of race, color, sex, sexual orientation, age, religion, national origin, marital status, political belief, mental or physical handicap, or any other preference or personal characteristic, condition, or status.

• The social worker should promote conditions that encourage respect for the diversity of cultures which constitute American society.

• The social worker should advocate changes in policy and legislation to improve social conditions and to promote social justice (Ginsberg, 1994).

The practice skills necessary for social work professionals to effectively enter into the arena of social policy have been thoroughly delineated by a burgeoning group of social work educators focused on policy practice. Notable among these efforts are those of Bruce Jansson (1994) who proposes that policy practice be considered as all efforts to influence the development, enactment, implementation, or assessment of social policies (p. 8).

Social work education programs are mandated to provide students with the skills to promote social change and to implement a wide range of interventions that advance the achievement of individual and collective social and economic justice (Fisher, Haynes, Latting, & Buffum, 1994). To be in full accordance with the mission and ethics of the profession, social worker practitioners and social work educators have a responsibility to participate in the development and utilization of social policies that enhance social justice (Hepworth & Larsen, 1993).

Cultural Diversity and U.S. Immigration Policy

Immigration policy has always been a force for change in the United States (Meissner, 1992) and a context within which cultural diversity concerns have been consistently dialogued and debated. Throughout the nineteenth and early twentieth centuries the vast majority of the immigrants coming into the United States were from European countries (Ramakrishnan & Balgopal, 1995). From 1924 to 1965, immigration to the United States was primarily based on a national origins system, which, in accordance with the Immigration Act of 1924, limited the yearly quota for each sending country to 3 percent of the individuals born in that country who were residing in the United States as enumerated in the 1890 census. Because most of the White population in 1890 was of northern and western European ancestry, countries in those regions were favored. The system restricted the immigration of people from Asia and the Pacific and from eastern and southern Europe and totally excluded immigrants from Africa (Drachman, 1995). Although the quota system was modified in 1929 to accept immigrants more readily from eastern and southern Europe, the racial and ethnic foundation in the national origins concept continued to drive immigration policy until 1965 (Briggs, 1984).

The Immigration and Nationality Act of 1965 created a major policy shift by doing away with the national origins quota system (Drachman, 1995). For the first time the United States was truly open to the whole world for the potential reception of immigrants. The fact that most of the recent immigrants to the United States are from Latin America and Asia (Ramakrishnan & Balgopal, 1995) is a clear indicator of the cultural diversification of the country which has resulted from this shift in immigration policy (Reimers, 1992).

The 1990 census showed that the racial and ethnic composition of the American population changed more dramatically in the past decade than at any time in the twentieth century, with nearly one in every four Americans identifying themselves as African American, Hispanic, Asian, Pacific Islander, or American Indian. Statistics reflect the fact that in recent years more than four out of five legal immigrants to the United States have been of non-European ancestry (Gould, 1995). Between 1960 and 1990, 15 million people, representing a mosaic of diverse cultures, were allowed to enter the United States via the immigration process (Ramakrishnan & Balgopal, 1995).

The percentage of foreign-born persons in the overall population is dramatic and presently occurring at rates not seen since the turn of the century. According to the 1970 census, 9,619,302 foreign-born persons were residing in the United States. By 1980, 14,079,906 foreign-born persons were living in the United States, and by 1990, the number of foreign-born people residing in the United States was 19,767,316 (Drachman, 1995). The newcomer population increased 46 percent between 1979 and 1980 and 40.4 percent between 1980 and 1990 (Drachman, 1995, p. 188). While past changes in U.S. immigration policy have driven cultural diversity in this country, present demands to restrict immigration (legal and illegal) may be viewed as an attempt to restrict cultural diversity.

While Americans tend to favor a description of the country as a "nation of immigrants," all has not been rosey in that element of our history. In reality, the movement of people from other countries into the United States has been characterized by varying degrees of acceptance and rejection (Reimers, 1992). Just as immigration policy and the result-ant diversification of cultures represented in the United States has pres-ently become a lightning rod for America's fears of social chaos and national decline, so was this the case at the turn of the century (Unz, 1994). Consider that the Germans, the Swedes, and others of the "old immigration" all came in for discrimination by the early English settlers but eventually became accepted because they were considered as a superior race of tall, blond, blue-eyed "Nordics" or Aryans. However, the people of eastern and southern Europe who began immigrating in the 1880s were not so lucky. The Italians, Slavs, and Jews were depicted as uncivilized, unruly, and dangerous and were even subjected to lynchings, shootings, and killings. Nevertheless, for these and other groups, cultural acceptance was a bit more easy because of their perceived European ancestry and white skin. The physically or culturally distinct groups, such as persons from Africa, Asia, Mexico, and the culturally indigenous American Indians, have all encountered nearly insurmountable barriers to cultural acceptance in the United States (Ramakrishnan & Balgopal, 1995).

If social work practitioners and social work educators are to publicly support the profession's commitment to racial, ethnic, and cultural diversity (Gould, 1995), they must be aware that American society has been receptive to culturally diverse immigrants but usually only if those people are willing to abandon their cultural distinctiveness. The desired ideal for social work professionals seems to be a social policy context where culturally diverse immigrants can continue in their expression of cultural traditions and the maintenance of a group identity, all the while being able to fully, and without prejudice or discrimination, participate in American civic life (Ramakrishnan & Balgopal, 1995).

Cultural Diversity and Affirmative Action Policies

"Affirmative action" began when the Kennedy administration ordered companies doing business with the federal government to root out discrimination in their ranks. Now the phrase refers to a wide range of policies undertaken by colleges, corporations, and government agencies to help members of protected groups, particularly women and persons of color (Fineman, 1995). Affirmative action refers to those social policies designed and implemented to (1) offset the impact of past experiences of discrimination, (2) eliminate racial, gender, and other bases of discrimination in education and employment (Ramakrishnan & Balgopal, 1995), and (3) create a social environment whereby equity of opportunity would exist for all people. What began, however, as a single corrective social policy has developed into a cohort of social policies.

Social policies have often been formulated with the purpose of serving as a socially corrective measure. Targeted populations which are identified as disadvantaged often receive social policies aimed at correcting instances of perceived social injustice or inequality. Much of the civil rights legislation, War on Poverty programming formulated in the 1960s, and social policies collectively referred to as affirmative action exemplify this line of reasoning and process of policy formulation. The problem is that although most Americans claim a kinship to such value ideals as social justice, equality, and opportunity for all, there exists as many opinions about what they really mean and recommended routes to their attainment as there are persons in this country. A negative offshoot of this is that often when corrective social policies are formulated, there can be an accompanying occurrence of stigmatization or social disapproval for members of the targeted population (Spicker, 1984).

If in fact Americans were a society bonded by a unified commitment to the goals of social justice, equality, opportunity, and diversity, the task of corrective social policy formulation would be a simple one. Social work policy advocates could first assess the discrepancy between the present situation and the perceived ideal, diagnose the causes of the discrepancy, and propose remedies. Then social work practitioners and social work educators could press policymakers for decisive movement to the formulation of social policies which would result in the eradication of any instance of social disadvantage (Shotland & Mark, 1985). Stigmatization of members in a targeted population which receives the corrective benefits of a social policy would simply not occur. However, it is easy to see how even this brief scenario differs from the current reality.

The current dialogue and debate about affirmative action includes a question about the ability of these social policies to function as a method of correction for past instances of social injustice, inequality, or lack of opportunity. An additional and important element of the current dialogue and debate is whether corrective social policies like affirmative action can be targeted for specific populations, such as persons of color and women, and the increased policy impact not be offset by the increased stigmatization of individual members of that population or the group as a whole. As well, members of disadvantaged populations often themselves fear being in receipt of the benefits of a corrective social policy. They recognize the possibility of negative repercussions such as stigmatization and backlash sentiment developing in members of more advantaged segments of the population. The fear is that if these negative repercussions are strong enough, their circumstance will be actually worsened by the perception that they are now in receipt of positive discriminating policies (Miller, 1973). For example, while Jesse Jackson speaks eloquently of the positive impacts of affirmative action and the dire need for their continuance, noted African American author, Shelby Steel, argues that affirmative action programs create a kind of implied inferiority among African Americans and other persons of color who are made to feel that they have acquired their positions, in either an educational or employment setting, not because of their knowledge and competence but because of preferential treatment (Ramakrishnan & Balgopal, 1995).

Will the elimination of affirmative action policies result in a fair, level playing field for all? Will eliminating affirmative action put Americans on the path to a color-blind, gender-neutral existence where achievement is honored and favoritism defunct? If, in fact, affirmative action policies have diversified the educational and employment environments of the United States (and there is no doubt they have particularly done so for women), it seems paramount to require that critics of affirmative action explain how abolishing these policies can lead to a meritocracy as long as other forms of favoritism continue (e.g., legacy admissions to prestigious universities) (Cose, 1995). Critics of affirmative action tend to overlook the fact that there has always been affirmative action in the United States for White men (Ramakrishnan & Balgopal, 1995).

While social work practitioners and social work educators cannot answer the affirmative action question for everyone else, they can help frame the issues to be addressed during the dialogue and debate process. Social work professionals should press for inclusion of the question of what will happen if affirmative action policies are eliminated or seriously modified. For instance, will there be a stepping up of enforcement of anti-discrimination laws if affirmative action policies are eliminated (Cose, 1995)?

Too often, social work practitioners and social work educators have acknowledged an awareness of the ethical responsibility to be active in the development, implementation, and modification of social policies while failing to articulate a position or take action in regards to a particular social policy, such as affirmative action, or within a distinct social policy arena, such as U.S. immigration policy. Social work practitioners and social work educators need to be informed, articulate a position, and get involved in the interplay of issues between cultural diversity and social policies. This is true irrespective of the social worker's political ideology. There is plenty of room for everyone in the policy dialogues and debates that are sure to take place over the ensuing years, particularly in regards to diversity-driven and diversity-driving social policies like affirmative action and U.S. immigration policy.

Social work practitioners and social work educators need to take a proactive stand in advocating for social policies that champion the needs of all racial, ethnic, and cultural groups in their efforts to preserve and practice their heritage. The social work profession needs to ensure that social policies go beyond just rhetoric (Ramakrishnan & Balgopal, 1995).

FUTURE DIRECTIONS FOR CULTURALLY DIVERSE SOCIAL WORK EDUCATION

The Council on Social Work Education's (CSWE) Curriculum Policy Statement (1994) (CPS) mandates the general educational requirements for all accredited schools of social work. Undergraduate and master's level programs have been required to include content on women, ethnic, and racial minorities for the past twenty years. The 1992 CPS strengthens the imperative to oppose oppression and expanded the curriculum requirements to include content on sexual orientation, persons with disabilities, and other at-risk populations (Van Soest, 1995).

The 1994 CPS section, (M 3.0) "Premises underlying social work education," states:

> The purpose of social work education is to prepare competent and effective social work professionals who are committed to practice that includes services to the poor and oppressed, and who work to alleviate poverty, oppression, and discrimination. (M 3.1, p. 134)

It further states that one of the purposes of the master's level social work education is to "prepare graduates to practice with diverse populations" (CSWE, CPS, p. 136). Under the section "Social work values and ethics," it states that "social workers demonstrate respect for and acceptance of the unique characteristics of diverse populations" (M 6.5.5. p. 139). It is clear that the Council of Social Work Education's intention is that social work education will effectively address throughout the curriculum issues of diversity, promotion of social and economic justice, and populations-at-risk.

As interest concerning ethnicity and culture has increased, social work educators and analysts have struggled to find appropriate language to describe and discuss these issues (Schlesinger & Devore, 1995a). "Minorities" is a term that is being used in social work and the larger society to encompass a diverse number of groups of people and vulnerable populations. There are a number of scholars who challenge this terminology and question whether it should include all oppressed groups as well as vulnerable populations. The term minority has been extended over the years to include people affected by racism, poverty, or discrimination. Women, gays, lesbians, the elderly, and the disabled have also been referred to as minorities. The term *"minority"* has no scientific criteria and is defined differently by government agencies and by each group (Greene, 1994).

Racial groups that have traditionally been referred to as "racial minorities" in this country clearly represent a majority in the world. Designating people of color as minorities obscures the fact that the world is made up largely of people of color and this will soon be a reality in the United States as well. This is a political and social issue that most social work practitioners don't like to discuss and most clients are afraid to raise.

The term "ethnic group" to refer to members of minority groups or people of color has also been challenged (Schlesinger & Devore, 1995a). The term cultural identity is preferred to ethnic minority identity or racial identity when used to describe the cultural identity of people of color, because this term does not relegate African Americans and other groups of color to a marginal "minority" status which is offensive to some (Schiele, 1993).

It is strongly recommended that the term "people of color" be utilized instead of minorities in social work education and training. When possible, it is always better to refer to persons by the specific group that they identify themselves. It is also important to recognize that there are persons of every group who may have difficulty with new terminology and some may find this terminology insulting. There has never been or ever will be a general term that makes all persons feel comfortable.

Cultural diversity must include an exploration of the "isms" (e.g., racism, sexism, classism, ageism, and heterosexism) in our society and their relationship to oppression. Institutional racism and poverty are the key components that cause a great deal of the distress that social workers are addressing in practice today. Cultural diversity must address institutional racism, sexism, and classism that are the root of many problems clients face. Social workers in practice deal with profoundly vulnerable populations, overwhelmed by oppressive lives, and by circumstances and events that they are powerless to control (Gitterman, 1991).

Keys (1994) raises several questions regarding the teaching of multi-cultural content to social work educators. "In which courses should multicultural content be taught, in specific multicultural courses, or infused throughout the curriculum" (p. 1)? He further questions whether social work educators know how to teach multicultural content and whether faculty development should include content to facilitate teaching. His final question relates to the monitoring and evaluation of the teaching of multicultural content in schools of social work. These are critical questions that social work educators and administrators need to address, related to the fundamental ones such as "Does training in cultural diversity result in more accurate and functional social work assessments?" and "Does training in cultural diversity result in more effective treatment outcomes?" (Keys, 1994)

There are several other questions that also need to be raised regarding the culturally diverse curricula in schools of social work. Who (race and ethnicity) are the faculty teaching this curricula? Is the faculty culturally diverse, or has this role been relegated to the "minority faculty?" What are the topics that faculty are comfortable teaching? What are the topics that get little attention? How does the faculty respond to questions of racism and sexism at the university or department level? What is the comfort level of White faculty as they teach about racism and oppression to predominantly Black students versus with White students? What is the comfort level of Black faculty as they teach the content to White students versus Black students? Which faculty can best respond to students' racist, sexist, or homophobic attitudes? Are these issues addressed? Should social work students be required to learn a foreign language (e.g. Spanish or an Asian language) to confront the issues of diversity among the clients of the future?

Social work educators must examine the diversity curriculum for gaps, inadequacy and covert hostility. One must recognize the pervasiveness of oppression in society and encourage examination of the residues of racism, sexism, and homophobia on both individual and organizational levels. In addition, social work educators must examine the power dynamics operating in faculty-faculty, faculty-student, worker-client relationships (Van Soest, 1995).

Singleton (1994) reported the findings of an exploratory study on the comfort level of social work faculty when teaching content specific to oppression. She defined comfort work as those steps taken by an instructor to achieve a tolerable level of personal ease in response to experiences of discomfort to the presentation of oppression content. An interesting finding was that racial oppression emerged as a prominent definition, with few references to women's issues and class oppression but virtually no discussion of homophobia, discrimination against the handicapped, the aged, anti-Semitism, or other expressions of oppression. Social work instructors in this study either avoided or minimized oppression terminology, rejected all content on oppression, or included oppression content. Their decisions were influenced by student feedback or the attitudes of their colleagues (Singleton, 1994).

It is incumbent upon social work educators to provide students with the skills needed to interact with individuals from backgrounds different from their own, to show students how they can become, in a sense, anthropologists who learn about the culture of each client they meet (Thornton & Garrett, 1995). It is important that the learning process begin with the student's awareness of their own cultural background and exposure of the pervasive influence of race, gender, ethnicity, and power on the social worker's own identity (Van Soest, 1994).

All components of social work education should prepare students for the realities of multicultural and multiracial societies. The goal is to prepare social work students to work with immigrants, refugees, and other ethnic and racial groups. The major strengths is that it provided opportunities for students to incorporate knowledge and skills relevant to social work practice through experiential learning (Christensen, 1992).

It is clear that social work education should provide innovative means for students to gain experience in working with clients of other cultures and backgrounds. Having students use ethnographic research techniques with classmates and other interviewees in courses on social work practice and human behavior in the social environment helps students gain the knowledge, values, and skills needed for practice with diverse groups. These authors' recommendation is to also extend ethnographic research into fieldwork courses with a requirement that students conduct ethnographic interviews and observation with clients (Thornton & Garrett, 1995). Of course, the effectiveness of this instructional approach requires empirical documentation as to effectiveness in its own right.

Teaching diversity in field instruction is as important as teaching it in the classroom (Keys, 1994). It is also important to confront issues of differences and similarities between field instructors and the student. Multicultural content needs to be introduced to field instructors in the field instruction seminars. This helps to facilitate their recognition of their own biases, fears, racism, and homophobia. As field instructors become more aware of the impact of differences and similarities on the teaching relationship, they are able to model a practice approach for students to use when working with diverse groups (Marshack, Hendricks, & Gladstein, 1994).

Women and Gender Issues

There have been inroads made in the inclusion of content on women and sexual orientation into the curricula. The difficulty has been more with the application of this knowledge in the classroom, field instruction, supervision and agency-based practice (Marshack, Hendricks, & Gladstein, 1994). Many scholars (e.g., Carter et al., 1994) address the issue that the integration of women's issues in social work curricula has not been seriously attempted. These authors believe that changing social conditions that influence women and even social work practice have had little impact on the way social work students are educated. Much of this lack of influence can be attributed to the fact that attention to women's issues in academia has often been handled through special women's classes or the addition of special sections in regular courses. They propose a revised social work curriculum approach based on historico-structural perspective reinforced by social work values and ecological and critical perspectives. Theories, research, and practice models must address gender as a central variable (Carter et al., 1994).

De Lange (1995) discusses the difference in men's and women's communication skills used in interviewing and social work practice. Students should be made aware of the biases and assumptions that characterize acculturation into a gendered use of language. Specific content on possible gender-based differences in communication should be integrated into discussions on communicating with clients and staff. Social work educators need to present material in class on the nature of possible gender differences in communication and the impact of such differences in practice (De Lange, 1995). Using a cross-cultural perspective may help discourage stereotyping and finger pointing, and free the communication style of women from devaluation by both sexes.

Multicultural training of employees is in demand in both the public and private sector. There is a need for social workers to receive training in order to be multicultural trainers. Many social workers are doing this with little guidance from the field of social work. This should be a major thrust in continuing education programs at schools of social work. Social work practitioners and social work educators should be the leaders in the field of multicultural training in the twenty-first century.

Social workers have competing visions of community, diverse perspectives on educational quality, and opposing views on social change that are rooted in the tradition of the profession. The development and implementation of educational policies related to diversity require an open dialogue about how to resolve conflicts between competing perspectives (Van Soest, 1994).
01

CONCLUSION

Cultural diversity is a crucial issue for the social work profession. From the view of both social practitioners and social work educators, the profession has repeatedly emphasized the principle that all social workers must be prepared to understand and appreciate racial, cultural, and social diversity (Gould, 1995). Achievement of this principle requires the ongoing commitment of social work practitioners and social work educators to cultural diversity. This book is another step in this ongoing process.

REFERENCES

American Psychological Association. (1994). *Publication Manual* (4th ed.). Washington, D.C.: Author.

Baruth, L.G., & Manning, M. (1991). *Multicultural counseling and psychotherapy: A life span perspective.* New York: Macmillan Publishing.

Billingsley, A. (1990). Understanding African-American family diversity. In J. Dewart (Ed.), *The state of Black America* (pp. 85–108). New York: National Urban League, Inc.

Boyd-Franklin, N. (1989). *Black families in therapy.* New York: The Guilford Press.

Briggs, V. (1984). *Immigration policy and the American labor force.* Baltimore, MD: Johns Hopkins University Press.

Brisbane, F.L., & Womble, M. (1991). *Working with African Americans: The professional's handbook.* Chicago, IL: HRDI.

Carter, C., Coudrouglou, A., Figueira-McDonough, J., Lie, G.Y., MacEachron, A., Netting, F.E., Nichols-Casebolt, A., Nichols, A.W., & Risley-Curtiss, C. (1994). Integrating women's issues in the social work curriculum: A proposal. *Journal Of Social Work Education, 30,* 200–216.

Chau, K.L. (1991). Social work with ethnic minorities: Practice issues and potentials. *Journal of Multicultural Social Work, 1*(1), 23–39.

Chau, K.L. (1992). Educating for effective group work practice in multicultural environments of the 1990s. *Journal of Multicultural Social Work, 1*(4), 1–15. social policy (pp. 59–74). Washington, D.C.: NASW Press.

Christensen, C.P. (1992). Training for cross-cultural social work with immigrants, refugees and minorities: A course model. *Journal of Multicultural Social Work, 2*(1), 79–97.

Cose, E. (1995, April 3). The myth of meritocracy, opinion: Why do racial preferences get us so steamed? *Newsweek,* 34.

Council on Social Work Education. (1991). Commission on accreditation. *Handbook of accreditation standards and procedures.* Alexandria, VA: Author.

Council on Social Work Education. (1994). *Handbook of accreditation standards and procedures* (4th ed.). Alexandria, VA: Author.

Daley, A., Jennings, J., Beckett, J.O., & Leashore, B. (1995). Effective coping strategies of African Americans. *Social Work, 40,* 240–247.

Davis, L.E., Galinsky, M.J., & Schopler, J.H. (1995). RAP: A framework for leadership of multiracial groups. *Social Work, 40,* 155–165.

De Lange, J. (1995). Gender and communication in social work education: A cross-cultural perspective. *Journal of Social Work Education, 31,* 75–81.

Drachman, D. (1995). Immigration statuses and their influence on service provision, access, and use. *Social Work, 40,* 188–197.

Eichler, M. (1987). *Nonsexist research methods: A practical guide.* Boston, MA: Allen and Unwin.

Fineman, H. (1995, April 3). Affirmative action, race and rage: When preferences work—and don't. *Newsweek,* 22–25.

Fisher, R., Haynes, K. S., Latting, J. K., & Buffum, W. (1994). Empowerment based curriculum design: Building a program in political social work. In L. Gutierrez & P. Nurius (Eds.). *Education and research in empowerment practice.* Seattle, WA: University of Washington Press.

Fraser, M. (1994). Scholarship and research in social work: Emerging challenges. *Journal of Social Work Education, 30,* 252–266.

Ginsberg, L. (1994). *Understanding social problems, policies, and programs.* Columbia, SC: University of South Carolina Press.

Gitterman, A. (Ed.). (1991). *Handbook of social work practice with vulnerable populations.* New York: Columbia University Press.

Gold, N., & Bogo, M. (1992). Social work research in a multicultural society: Challenges and approaches. *Journal of Multicultural Social Work, 2*(4), 7–22.

Gould, K. (1995). The misconstruing of multiculturalism: The Stanford debate and social work. *Social Work, 40,* 198–205.

Green, J.W. (1982). *Cultural awareness in the human services.* Englewood Cliffs, NJ: Prentice-Hall.

Greene, R.R. (1994). *Human behavior theory: A diversity framework.* New York: Aldine De Gruyter.

Gutierrez, L.M., & Lewis, E.A. (1994). Community organizing with women of color: A feminist approach. *Journal of Community Practice, 1*(2), 23–44.

Hall, R.E. (1992). Bias among African-Americans regarding skin color—Implications for social work practice. *Research on Social Work Practice, 2,* 479–486.

Harvey, A. (1995). The issue of skin color in psychotherapy with African-Americans. *Families in Society, 76,* 3–10.

Haynes, A., & Singh, R. (1992). Ethnic sensitive social work practice: An integrated, ecological, and psychodynamic approach. *Journal of Multicultural Social Work, 2*(2), 43–52.

Henderson, G. (1994). *Social work interventions: Helping people of color.* Westport, CT: Bergin & Garvey.

Hepworth, D.H., & Larsen, J. (1993). *Direct social work practice: Theory and skills* (4th ed.). Pacific Grove, CA: Brooks/Cole.

Jacobs, C., & Bowles, D. (Eds.). (1988). *Ethnicity and race: Critical concepts in social work.* Silver Spring, MD: NASW Press.

Jansson, B.S. (1994). *Social policy: From theory to policy practice* (2nd ed.). Pacific Grove, CA: Brooks/Cole.

Julia, M. (1993). Developing an instrument to measure the Spanish-speaking clients' perception of social work intervention in prenatal cases. *Research on Social Work Practice, 3,* 329–342.

Keys, P.R. (1994). Introduction. *Journal of Multicultural Social Work, 3*(1), 1–3.

Kilpatrick, A.C. (1995). Contexts of helping: Commonalities and diversities. In A.C. Kilpatrick & T.P. Holland (Eds.), *Working with families: An integrative model by level of functioning.* Boston, MA: Allyn and Bacon.

Kingdon, J. (1984). *Agendas, alternatives and public policies.* Boston: Little, Brown.

LaFromboise, T., & Rowe, W. (1983). Skills training for bicultural competence: Rationale and application. *Journal of Counseling Psychology, 30,* 589–595.

Lee, J. (1994). *The empowerment approach to social work practice.* New York: Columbia University Press.

Lincoln, Y., & Guba, E. (1985). *Naturalistic inquiry.* Beverly Hills, CA: Sage.

Logan, S. (1990). Black families: Race, ethnicity, culture, social class and gender issues. In S. Logan, E.M. Freeman & R.G. McRoy (Eds.), *Social work practice with Black families: A culturally specific perspective* (pp. 18–37). New York: Longman.

Manoleas, P. (1994). An outcome approach to assessing the cultural competence of MSW students. *Journal of Multicultural Social Work, 3*(1), 43–57.

Marlow, C. (1993). *Research Methods: For generalist social work.* Pacific Grove, CA: Brooks/Cole Publishing.

Marshack, E., Hendricks, O., & Gladstein, M. (1994). The commonality of difference: Teaching about diversity in field instruction. *Journal of Multicultural Social Work, 3*(1), 77–89.

Meenaghan, T.M., & Kilty, K.M. (1994). *Policy analysis and research technology: Political and ethical considerations.* Chicago: Lyceum Books.

Meissner, D. (1992). Managing migrations: International migration and emigration policy. *Foreign Policy, 86,* 66–83.

Miller, S. (1973). The case for positive discrimination. *Social Policy, 4*(3), 65–71.

Nixon, R., & Spearman, M. (1991). Building a pluralistic workplace. In R. Edwards & J. Yankey (Eds.), *Skills for effective human service management* (pp. 155–170). Silver Springs, MD: NASW Press.

Norton, D. (1993). Diversity, early socialization, and temporal development: The dual perspective revisited. *Social Work, 38,* 82–90.

Orlandi, M.A. (1992). Defining cultural competence: An organizing framework. In M.A. Orlandi (Ed.), *Cultural competence for evaluators: A guide for alcohol and other drug abuse prevention practitioners working with ethnic/racial communities* (pp. 293–299). Rockville, MD: U.S. Department of Health and Human Services.

Pinderhughes, E. (1989). *Understanding race, ethnicity and power.* New York: Free Press.

Pinderhughes, E. (1995). Empowering diverse populations: Family practice in the twenty-first century. *Families in Society, 76,* 131–140.

Ponterotto, J., Rieger, B.P., Barrett, A., & Sparks, R. (1994). Assessing multicultural counseling competence: A review of instrumentation. *Journal of Counseling and Development, 72,* 316–322.

Ramakrishnan, K.R., & Balgopal, P.R. (1995). Role of social institutions in a multicultural society. *Journal of Sociology and Social Welfare, 22*(1), 11–28.

Reid, W.J. (1994). The empirical practice movement. *Social Service Review, 68,* 165–184.

Reimers, D.M. (1992). *Still the golden door: The third world comes to America.* New York: Columbia University Press.

Robinson, J.B. (1989). Clinical treatment of Black families: Issues and strategies. *Social Work, 34,* 323–329.

Ronnau, J.P. (1994). Teaching cultural competence: Practical ideas for social work educators. *Journal of Multicultural Social Work, 3*(1), 29–42.

Rubin, A., & Babbie, E. (1993). *Research methods for social work* (2nd ed.). Pacific Grove, CA: Brooks/Cole Publishing.

Saleeby, D. (1992). *The strengths perspective in social work practice.* New York: Longman.

Schiele, J.H. (1993). Cultural oppression, African Americans, and social work practice. *Black Caucus, 2,* 20–34.

Schinke, S.P., Gilbert, B.J., Trimble, J.E., Orlandi, M.A., Gilchrist, L.D., & Lochlear, V.S. (1988). Preventing substance abuse among American Indian adolescents: A bicultural competence skills approach. *Journal of Counseling Psychology, 35,* 87–90.

Schlesinger, E.G., and Devore, W. (1995a). Ethnic-sensitive practice. In R.L. Edwards (Ed.), *Encyclopedia of Social Work* (19th ed.) (pp. 902–908). Washington, D.C.: NASW Press.

Schlesinger, E.G., & DeVore, W. (1995b). Ethnic-sensitive social work practice: The state of the art. *Journal of Sociology and Social Welfare, 22,* 29–58.

Shotland, R., & Mark, M. (Eds.). (1985). *Social science and social policy.* Beverly Hills, CA: Sage.

Siegel, L. (1994). Cultural differences and their impact on practice in child welfare. *Journal of Multicultural Social Work, 3*(3), 87–96.

Singleton, S.M. (1994). Faculty personal comfort and the teaching of content on racial oppression. *Journal of Multicultural Social Work, 3*(1), 5–16.

Solomon, B. (1976). *Black empowerment: Social work in oppressed communities.* New York: Columbia University Press.

Spicker, P. (1984). *Stigma and social welfare.* New York: St. Martins Press.

Thornton, S., & Garrett, K.J. (1995). Ethnography as a bridge to multicultural practice. *Journal of Social Work Education, 31,* 67–74.

Thyer, B.A. (1994). Social learning theory: Empirical applications to culturally diverse practice. In R.R. Greene (Ed.), *Human behavior theory: A diversity framework* (pp. 133–146). New York: Aldine-deGruyter.

Timbrook, R.E., & Graham, J.R. (1994). Ethnic differences on the MMPI-2? *Psychological Assessment, 6,* 212–217.

Unz, R.K. (1994). Immigration or the welfare state: Which is our real enemy? *Policy Review,* 33–38.

Van Soest, D. (1995). Multiculturalism and social work education: The non-debate about competing perspectives. *Journal of Social Work Education, 31,* 55–66.

Van Soest, D. (1994). Social work education for multicultural practice and social justice advocacy: A field study of how students experience the learning process. *Journal of Multicultural Social Work, 3*(1), 17–27.

Weick, A., & Saleebey, D. (1995). Supporting family strengths: Orienting policy and practice toward the twenty-first century. *Families in Society, 76,* 141–149.

Williams, M., Tutty, L.M., & Grinnell, R.M., Jr. (1995). *Research in social work: An introduction.* Itasca, IL: F.E. Peacock Publishers.

Williams, S.E., & Wright, D.F. (1992). Empowerment: The strengths of Black families revisited. *Journal of Multicultural Social Work, 2*(4), 23–36.

AUTHOR INDEX

A

Abrams, R., 162, 171
Adams, J., 219, 228
Adams, M. J., 179, 195
Adams, J. P., 184, 197
Alberti, P. W., 206, 226
Allen-Mears, P., 4, 12
American Psychiatric Association, 124, 130, 156, 157, 158, 171
American Psychological Association, 308, 326
Anastas, J. W., 127, 131
Anderson, F., 153, 154, 171
Anderson, K., 113, 127, 131
Andrews, J. F., 203, 204, 206, 207, 208, 210, 230
Andrews, S., 188, 195
Angell, R. H., 90, 104
Ansello, E. F., 184, 195
Arnold, C. L., 142, 175
Asch, A., 202, 226
Ashley, J., 204, 226
Atchley, R., 147, 171
Atherton, C. R., 127, 131
Atkinson, D., 100, 102, 107
Attie, I., 124, 131
Atteneave, C., 286, 287, 288, 293
Austin, D. M., 127, 131
Avis, J. M., 126, 131
Axinn, J., 138, 139, 140, 147, 161, 171

B

Babbie, E., 192, 199, 308, 329
Babchuk, N., 144, 172
Bachman, R., 267, 272, 276, 281, 284
Backland, 1975
Baker, B. L., 181, 200
Baker, M., 170, 173

Baldus, D. C., 28, 45
Baldwin, S., 121, 131
Balgopal, P. R., 316, 317, 318, 320, 321, 329
Ban, T. A., 156, 171
Bandura, A., 125, 131
Bane, M. J., 18, 42
Barker, R. G., 217, 226
Barnartt, S. N., 205, 226
Barnes, A., 3, 12
Barnhard, S., 186, 199
Barr, J. K., 146, 175
Barraga, N., 215, 226
Barrett, A., 309, 310, 312, 329
Barrett, G. V., 146, 175
Barter, J., 280, 282
Barton, L., 145, 172
Barusch, A. S., 128, 131
Baruth, L. G., 299, 326
Bassett, 28, 29, 48
Bayer, M. B., 224, 226
Beattie, J. A., 209, 226
Beauvais, F., 60, 76, 85, 278, 293
Beck, J. C., 159, 171
Beck, R. B., 189, 195
Becker, B. E., 27, 45
Beckett, J. O., 8, 12, 304, 327
Beckley, G. D., 37, 45
Begab, M. J., 186, 195
Begly, C., 161, 171
Beifus, J. A., 183, 200
Belcher, J. R., 145, 146, 174
Bell, C., 280, 282, 295
Belsky, J., 141, 142, 152, 154, 155, 156, 157, 159, 165, 166, 168, 171
Ben, R., 95
Bengston, V. L., 143, 144, 173
Bepko, C., 126, 131
Berger, R., 233, 241, 243, 245, 246, 254
Berkman, B., 162, 171

331

Berlin, I. N., 269, 280
Berlin, S., 125, 129, 131
Berman, P., 260
Bernstein, B., 123, 131
Berry, G. L., 31, 43, 47
Besdine, R. W., 141, 171
Betancourt, H., 61, 86
Betel, J., 181, 196
Bertrand, P. T., 186, 195
Bialik-Giland, R., 73, 84
Bigfoot, D. S., 285
Biggerstaff, M. B., 130, 136
Bilken, D., 217, 226
Billingsley, A., 23, 40, 41, 45, 303, 326
Billy, J. O., 234, 254
Birba, L., 149, 174
Birns, B., 126, 136
Blacher, J., 181, 200
Blackwell, J. E., 16, 22, 23, 24, 45
Blanchard, E., 271, 272, 294
Blassingame, J. W., 40, 42, 45
Blau, R. D., 117, 121, 131
Blazyk, S., 162, 171
Bleier, R., 129, 131
Bliatout, B. T., 95, 107
Bliatout, H. P., 95, 107
Blum, R., 274, 284, 294
Blumberg, R. L., 112, 131
Blumstein, P. W., 121, 131
Blythe, B. J., 125, 133
Bobo, J. K., 266, 291, 294
Bogdan, R., 217, 226
Bogo, M., 307, 311, 327
Bonilla, F., 54, 55, 56, 57, 58, 85
Booraem, C. D., 249, 254
Botuck, S., 191, 198
Bowen, 73
Bowers, W. J., 28, 45
Bowles, D., 6, 12, 301, 328
Bowman, P. J., 36, 49
Boyd-Franklin, N., 34, 35, 37, 45, 301, 302, 303, 326
Brammer, L., 219, 226
Brantly, T., 33, 34, 45
Brekke, J. S., 129, 131
Briar, K. H., 127, 131
Bricker-Jenkins, M., 125, 126, 131
Bridges, 26, 28
Brieland, D., 138, 141, 171

Briggs, V., 316, 326
Brisbane, F. L., 301, 302, 304, 326
Brody, 36
Brody, E., 153, 154, 160, 171
Brody, G. H., 181, 199
Brody, S., 153, 154, 160, 171
Brooks-Gunn, J., 124, 131
Browne, A., 122, 132
Brown, E. F., 292, 294
Brown, G., 247, 254
Brown, S., 36, 45
Brown, M., 206, 230
Brown, R. I., 219, 220, 221, 222, 224, 226, 230
Buehler, J. W., 250, 254
Buffum, 316, 327
Burger, R., 219, 221, 230
Burke, J. D., 134, 135
Burke, V., 119, 132
Burt, M. R., 122, 136
Burtner, A. P., 54, 66
Butler, R. N., 141, 171
Bye, L. L., 249, 256
Byl, F., 206, 226

C

Caetano, R., 31, 45
Cahir, S. R., 70, 85
Calderon, J., 52, 53, 83
Call, T. I., 183, 196
Calnek, M., 33, 45
Camacho, T. C., 138, 175
Campbell, V. A., 184, 197
Cambridge Documentary Films, 237, 241, 254
Canavan, M., 162, 171
Canetto, S. S., 167, 172
Cantrell, R. W., 206, 226
Capellan, J. M., 240, 255
Carlton-LaNey, I., 6, 12
Carrillo, D., 7, 12
Carter, C., 304, 325, 326
Carty, L. A., 32, 35, 50
Case, L., 181, 196
Castex, G. M., 8, 12, 52, 53, 66, 72, 83
Catania, J. A., 244, 255
Cazenave, N. A., 40, 46
Cecutti, T., 122, 136
Chamott, A. U., 70, 85
Chao, C. M., 87, 108

Chapman, J. R., 122, 136
Charney, D. A., 122, 132
Chatters, L. M., 37, 50
Chau, K. L., 301, 326, 327
Chavez, V., 63, 84
Cherlin, A., 114, 121, 132
Chesney-Lind, M., 126, 132
Chestang, L. W., 39, 46
Chmiel, J. S., 240, 254
Cholden, M. D., 217, 226
Chou, Y. C., 192, 195
Christensen, A. S., 120, 132
Christensen, C. P., 324, 327
Christiansen, J. B., 205, 226
Chu, S. Y., 250, 254
Chung, D. K., 92, 93, 94, 96, 97, 108
Clark, E., 157, 175
Clements, C., 184, 195
Close, D. W., 225, 227
Coates, T. J., 244, 255
Cochran, 30
Cochran, S. D., 252, 254
Cockerhan, 32
Cobbs, P. 34, 47
Cody, S., 161, 173
Coggins, P. C., 30, 46
Cohen, A. I., 33, 46
Cohen, D. S., 181, 196
Cohen, R. D., 138, 175
Collins, B. G., 125, 132
Coleman, H. L. K., 60, 83
Comas-Diaz, L., 68, 69, 77, 84, 126, 132
Conway, D., 151, 157
Cook, D. T., 291, 294
Coopersmith, E. I., 221, 227
Coppedge, R., 167, 172
Corso, J. F., 206, 227
Corvea, M., 151, 152, 157, 158, 172
Cose, E., 320, 327
Cotton, J., 19, 46
Coudrouglou, A., 304, 325, 326
Council on Social Work Education, 6, 12, 300, 321, 327
Courtney, M. E., 4, 13
Coverman, S., 121, 132
Cowdry, E. V., 139, 172
Cox, E. O., 127, 132
Cox, C., 62, 64, 84
Craig, G. T., 168, 174

Crapps, J. M., 181, 199,
Crestoffel, K. K., 282, 294
Crichton, J., 154, 170, 172
Criswell, E. C., 209, 227
Crocker, A. C., 179, 195
Crutchfield, C. A., 26, 28
Cullen, R. M., 54, 85
Cumming, E., 142, 143, 172
Cunningham, P. J., 264, 285
Curiel, H., 70, 84
Curran, J. W., 250, 254
Czaja, S. J., 146, 175

D

Daley, A., 8, 12, 304, 327
Daly, M., 120, 132
Daly, A., 238, 256
Dana, B., 186, 195
Darity, W. A., 18, 20, 46
Davenport, J., 280, 294
Davenport, J., 280, 294
Davidson, W. R., 149, 150, 172
Davies, M. W., 114, 132
Davis, A., 74, 85
Davis, S. K., 63, 84
Davis, C. H., 181, 199
Davis, J. S., 232, 254
Davis, L. E., 125, 132
Davis, L. E., 302, 327
Davis, L. V., 128, 132
Dawkins, M., 33, 46
DeAnda, D., 63, 84
Deaux, K., 124, 132
Debating the Plight, 21
DeBlassie, R. R., 75, 84
DeFreitas, G., 56, 72, 79, 84
DeVoe, G., 94, 110
De La Cancela, V., 77, 84
De La Garza, R. O., 73, 84
De Lange, J., 325, 327
Delgado, M., 64, 68, 69, 71, 84,
Delgado, G. L., 205, 227
Delk, M. T., 205, 230
Deloria, V., 261, 294
Demographic Portrait, 19
Denmark, J. C., 204, 227
Desipio, 73, 84
Deutsch, H., 183, 196

Devore, W., 300, 309, 314, 321, 322, 329
DeWeaver, K. L., 176, 177, 178, 185, 186, 187, 188, 189, 190, 194, 195, 196, 199
Diamond, T., 164, 172
Dickerson, M. U., 190, 196
Dike, S. T., 28, 46
Do, V. T., 95, 107
Dobelstein, A., 164, 172
Dodson, J., 39, 40, 46
Dohrenwend, B., 36, 46
Domino, G., 76, 84
Donahue, T., 119, 134
Donovan, R., 21, 46
Donovan, M. E., 120, 123, 135
Dover, F., 219, 227
Duignan, P. G., 52, 55, 65, 67, 84
Duke, W. M., 145, 172
Dukes, J. L., 36, 48, 74
Dunn, L. P., 88, 93, 94, 108
Dziegielewski, S. F., 157, 159, 160, 172

E

Easterbook, P. J., 240, 254
Eckstein, F., 272, 294
Edgerton, R. B., 193, 196
Edgerton, R. B., 6, 12
Ehrenreich, B., 127, 132
Eichler, M., 129, 132, 307, 308, 327
Ekerdt, D. J., 149, 172
El-Bassel, N., 240, 255
Elliott, H., 203, 209, 210, 211, 212, 213, 227
Engram, E., 6, 12
Epross, P. H., 3, 12
Escobar, D., 292, 294
Estrada, 56
Estrada, L. F., 70, 84
Etter, R., 223, 232
Evans, S. M., 113, 114, 115, 132
Eyman, R. K., 183, 196
Eysenck, H., 27, 46

F

Falco, K. L., 251, 254
Falcon, A., 73, 84
Faludi, S., 115, 132
Farber, B., 193, 197
Farley, J. E., 20, 46, 57, 84

Farrell, R. A., 27, 50
Fashimpar, G. A., 191, 194, 196
Fay, R., 234, 254
Feldman, M. A., 181, 196
Ferrante, C. L., 120, 132
Figueria-McDonough, J., 194, 196
Figuero, 53
Fineman, H., 318, 327
Fischer, J., 164, 172
Fishbein, M., 206, 227
Fisher, 316, 327
Fitzgerald, R. G., 219, 227
Fleming, C. M., 262, 297
Flesher, 26
Flowers, J. V., 249, 254
Fong, R., 8, 12
Fonseca, J. A., 63, 86
Foreman, G. T., 272, 294
Foreman, C. T., 272, 294
Forthofor, R., 161, 173
Foulke, E., 220, 227
Fradis, M., 206, 229
Frank, L., 139, 140, 172
Fraser, M., 312, 327
Frazier, 75, 84
Freedman, M. L., 128, 132, 159, 171
Freeman, E. M. 22, 42, 47, 312, 328
Freeman, E., 6, 12,
Frieze, I. H., 122, 132, 224, 229
Frost, D., 261, 294
Frumpkin, M., 127, 132
Fuchs, V. R., 118, 133

G

Gabriel, A., 29, 47
Gagnon, J., 234,
Galan, J., 63, 64, 66, 84
Galinsky, M. J., 302, 327
Gambrill, E., 125, 133
Gann, L. H., 52, 55, 65, 67
Gant, L. M., 65, 70, 78, 86
Garcia, F. C., 73, 78, 84
Garland, D. R., 292, 294
Garrett, K. J., 300, 301, 309, 312, 324, 330
Gary, L., 32, 33, 47
Gary, L. E., 16, 31, 43, 47
Garza, J, V., 70, 84
Gaston, M. A., 6, 12, 193, 196

Gebhard, P. H., 233, 255
Gelfand, D. E., 73, 84
General Accounting Office, 73, 84
Gentile, A., 205, 227
Gerstein J. (et al), 36, 47
Gerton, J., 60, 83
Getty, L., 206, 208, 209, 210, 227, 228
Ghali, B. B., 76, 84
Ghelman, M., 271, 294
Giarratana-Oehler, J., 215, 227
Gibeau, J. L., 127, 131
Gilbert, B. J., 309, 329
Gilbert, L. A., 125, 126, 133
Gilchrist, L. D., 278, 294
Gilchrist, L. D., 309, 329
Gilson, S., 180, 196
Gim, R., 100, 107
Ginsberg, L. H., 188, 196
Ginsberg, L., 313, 316, 327
Gitterman, A., 322, 327
Gladstein, M., 301, 325, 328
Glasgow, D., 21, 47
Glass, L. E., 203, 206, 207, 209, 213, 227
Glendinning, C., 121, 131
Glick, P. C., 17, 47
Glidden, C. E., 125, 133
Gochros, H. L., 164, 172
Gochros, J. S., 164, 172
Goddard, R. E., 219, 232
Godfrey, A. C., 98, 103
Goetz, L., 207, 215
Gold, N., 311, 327
Golden, C. J., 178, 186
Goldfield, B. A., 70, 85
Goldsmith, M. F., 123, 133
Gomberg, E. S. L., 123, 126, 133
Gomez, L. E., 52, 53
Gomez, E., 74, 77, 78
Gonick, M. R., 217, 226
Gonsiorek, J. C., 252, 254
Goode, D. A., 225, 227
Goodluck, C., 272, 294
Goodwin, N. J., 30, 47
Gordon, M. T., 122, 133
Gottlieb, N., 126, 131
Gottschalk, S., 129, 137
Gould, K., 317, 318, 326, 327
Gove, W., 35, 47
Graber, H., 128, 133

Grady, W, R., 234, 254
Graham, 19
Graham, J. R., 311, 330
Gramick, J., 235, 246, 253, 255
Graubert, J., 126, 136
Gray-Little, B., 38, 47
Green, J. W., 301, 306, 327
Greenbaum, S., 265, 294
Greenberg, J. S., 182, 196
Greene, B., 126, 132
Greene, R. R., 5, 12
Greene, R. R., 183, 197, 322, 327
Greenley, J. R., 182, 196
Grier, W., 34, 47
Grinnell, R. M., Jr., 308, 330
Grosjean, F., 70, 73, 85
Gross, S. R., 28, 47
Grossman, B., 74, 85
Grossman, A. H., 251, 255
Groze, V. K., 9, 13
Groze, V. K., 253, 256
Gruenberg, E., 124, 135
Guba, E., 312, 328
Gurin, G., 38, 48
Gutierrez, L. M., 305, 327, 328

H

Hahn, H., 178, 197
Hairston, E., 205, 227
Halgin, R. P., 212, 213, 227
Hall, C. M., 126, 133
Hall, R. E., 303, 328
Halpern, A. S., 225, 227
Halseth, J., 128, 133
Hammer, D., 193, 197
Hampton, B., 123, 133
Haney, P., 249, 254
Hanley, B. 191, 194, 197
Hanmer, J., 116, 125, 133
Harkess, S., 120, 133
Harris, T., 36, 45
Harrison, D. F., 159, 172
Harry, B., 191, 197
Hartmann, S., 114, 133
Harvey, A., 23, 47, 302, 202, 328
Hatem, M., 235, 244, 255
Haviland, M., 291, 295

Hawkesworth, M. E., 129, 133
Hayes, S., 289, 297
Haynes, A., 301, 316, 328
Haynes, A. M., 120, 132
Heinemann, M. B., 129, 133
Heller, R., 193, 197
Helms, J., 291, 294
Henderson, G., 5, 12
Henderson, G., 299, 328
Hendricks, O., 301, 325, 328
Henkin, A. B., 89, 93, 97, 108
Henry, W., 142, 143, 172
Hepworth, D. H., 63, 85, 315, 316, 328
Herdt, G. H., 235, 255
Herman, D., 122, 133
Herman, S. E., 191, 197
Hernandez, P., 290, 295
Heschel, S., 120, 133
Hetu, R., 206, 208, 209, 210, 227, 228
Hicks, S., 219, 228
High, D., 169, 172
Hill, R., 23, 41, 39, 47
Hill, W., 27, 47
Hills, S. M., 27, 45
Hippler, A. E., 280, 295
Hirschman, C., 98, 99, 108
HIV/AIDS Task Force Report, 240, 255
Hnat, S. A., 65, 70, 78, 86
Ho, M. K., 94, 104, 108
Hodson, D. S., 164, 165, 172
Hogan, D. D., 29, 48
Hogan, P. T., 292, 295
Hollinger, P., 280, 281, 282, 283, 295
Hollingshead, A., 33, 48
Hollowell, J. G., 179, 195
Holzhalb, C. M., 7, 12
Hoover, D. R., 240, 254
Hooyman, N. R., 125, 131
Hope, R., 160, 175
Hopps, J. G., 127, 133
Hopson, B., 219, 228
Horejsi, C. R., 184, 188, 191, 197
Horowitz, A. V., 35, 48
Howes, C., 181, 199
Hoyt, D. R., 144, 172
Hudson, W. W., 129, 133
Hughes, G. F., 261, 295
Hull, G., 258, 259, 286, 295
Hume, M., 186, 197

Humm-Delgado, 64, 68, 69, 84
Hunt, W. M., 204, 228
Hurley, E. C., 62, 86
Hussian, R., 158, 172
Hyde, J. S., 122, 133

I

Ianello, K. P., 128, 133
Inclan, J., 61, 85
Inouye, D. K., Hon., 281, 283, 285, 295
Ishisaka, H. A., 102, 109
Ivanoff, A., 125, 133
Israelstam, S., 247, 255

J

Jackson, J. S., 36, 38, 48, 49
Jacobs, C., 6, 12, 301, 328
Jaffee, J. A., 54, 55, 85
Janicki, M. P., 179, 184, 199
Jansson, B. S., 315, 316, 328
Jarrett, H. H., 186, 199
Jemmott, L. S., 240, 255
Jennings, J., 8, 12
Jennings, J., 304, 327
Jespen, B., 264, 275, 285, 295
Johnson, L. B., 39, 48, 122, 136
Johnson, B., 164, 172
Johnson, P. J., 188, 189, 196, 199
Johnson, V. E., 165, 166, 173
Jones, L., 25, 48
Jones, O., 25, 48
Jouard, S., 34, 48

K

Kabacoff, R. I., 123, 133
Kader, C., 233, 255
Kaiser, M. A., 144, 172
Kane, R., 123, 131
Kaplan, G. A., 138, 175
Kaplan, H., 210, 211, 228
Kappler, C. L., 272
Kastenbaum, R., 167, 172
Katz, A, H., 185, 197
Katz, P., 258, 259, 277
Kaufman, A. V., 184, 197
Keller, M. J., 184, 200

Kelly, G., 233, 234, 235, 239, 240, 242, 243, 246, 247, 255
Kelly, G. F., 122, 123, 134
Kelly, J. J., 164, 165, 166, 173
Kelly, T. B., 184, 197
Keltner, B., 181, 197
Keopraseuth, K. O., 95, 107
Kertley, D. D., 220, 228
Kessler, F. A., 217, 220, 228
Kew, S., 221, 228
Keys, P. R., 323, 324, 328
Kikumura, A., 88, 96, 109
Kilpatrick, A. C., 302, 304, 328
Kilty, K. M., 313, 314, 329
Kimboko, P. J., 127, 132
King, C.S., 29, 48
King, B. H., 181, 197
Kingdon, J., 315, 328
Kingsley, S. M., 120, 132
Kinsey, A. C., 233, 234, 255
Kinzie, J. D., 90, 103, 104, 109
Kirchner, C., 214, 228
Kitagawa, E. M., 29, 48
Kitano, H. H. L., 88, 96, 109
Klassen, A., 234, 254
Klepinger, D. H., 234, 254
Kobe, F. H., 193, 197
Korr, W., 128, 133
Koss, M. P., 122, 134
Kramer, M. E., 191, 198
Krauss, M. W., 179, 183, 199
Kravetz, D., 124, 125, 129, 131, 134
Kreiger, I., 248, 249, 255
Krieger, 29, 48
Krishef, C., 186, 197
Kropf, N. P., 10, 12, 176, 178, 183, 184, 186, 188, 189, 190, 196, 197
Kryter, K. D., 206, 228
Kubler-Ross, E., 219, 228
Kunze, K., 149, 150, 172

L

LaBoueff, S., 278, 293
LaFromboise, T., 258, 259, 275, 277, 278, 284, 285, 295
LaFromboise, T., 309, 328
Lambert, W. E., 70, 85
Lambert, F. B., 123, 133

Lambert, S., 247, 255
Larsen, J. A., 63, 85
Larsen, J., 315, 316, 328
Larsen, P. J., 127, 131
LaRue, G. A., 169, 173
Lasley, 36
Latting, 316, 327
Leashore, B., 16, 47
Leashore, B., 304, 327
Leashore, B. R., 8, 12
LeBlanc, J. C., 206, 226
Lee, A., 260, 295
Lee, D. T., 95, 107
Lee, E., 161, 173
Lee, J., 303, 328
Lee, M., 210, 211, 212, 227
Leiblum, S. R., 165, 173
Lemon, B. L., 143, 144, 173
LePore, P., 184, 197
Lerner, A. W., 127, 134
Levin, H., 138, 139, 140, 147, 161, 171
Levine, D. L., 186, 197
Levine, E. S., 207, 209, 210, 211, 212, 213, 228
Levy, J. M., 181, 191, 193, 195, 198, 201
Lewis, E. A., 36, 48, 305, 328
Lilienfeld, D. E., 141, 173
Lincoln, Y., 312, 328
Lindblad-Goldberg, 36, 48
Lipman-Blumen, J., 112, 114, 115, 134
Lipsky, M., 128, 134
Lisanky, J., 61, 86
Littrell, J., 291, 295
Littrell, M. A., 291, 295
Lochlear, V. S., 309, 329
Leon, A. M., 75, 85
Loeske, R. D., 224, 229
Logan, 42
Logan, S., 6, 12, 13
Logan, S., 302, 312, 328
Lopez, S., 78, 83
Lopez, S., 290, 295
Lorber, J., 112, 134
Lott, B., 112, 134
Lowenfeld, B., 217, 228
Lowry, L., 140, 167, 173
Lubben, J. E., 160, 174
Luchasson, R., 237, 245
Luey, H. S., 209, 228
Lukoff, I. F., 217, 228

Lundwall, 33, 45
Lurie, N. O., 259, 266, 295
Lusky, R., 164, 173
Lyon, P., 243, 252, 255
Lynsky, J. A., 78, 85

M

Maas, H. S., 219, 228
MacFarlane C., 224,
Machemer, R. H., 178, 199
MacLeod-Gallinger, J., 205, 228
Maddox, G., 143, 173
Maeck, J. P., 170, 173
Maestas Y. Moores, J., 205, 228
Magrab, P. R., 238, 245
Mail, P. D., 277, 278, 295
Maldonado, M., 75, 85
Maldonado, D., 156, 163, 173
Malone, D. M., 178, 190, 198
Manning, M., 299, 326
Manoleas, P., 299, 300, 328
Manson, S., 90, 109
Marin, G., 61, 62, 76, 86
Mark, M., 319, 330
Markwardt, R., 193, 197
Marlow, C., 310, 313, 328
Marshack, E., 301, 325, 328
Martin, J. E., 22, 48
Martin, C. E., 233, 234, 255
Martin, D., 243, 252, 255
Martin, P. Y., 127, 132
Martinez, I. Z., 77, 84
Martinez, J. L., 60, 85
Martinez, 74
Marwit, S. J., 123, 133
Mary, N. L., 193, 198
Massey, S., 71, 81
Masters, W. H., 165, 166, 173
Mattison, A. M., 246, 255
Maurer, J. F., 209, 229
Mauro, R., 28, 47
May, P. A., 277, 279, 291, 295
Mays, V. M., 14, 15, 16, 30, 34, 3848
Mays, V. M., 252, 254
Mazur, R., 75, 85
McAdoo, H. P., 20, 41, 43, 44, 48
McAdoo, H., 127, 135

McAnarney, E. R., 29, 47
McCallion, P., 179, 192, 198
McConchie, S., 63, 86
McCoy, R., 22, 47
McCrea, F. B., 123, 134
McCullough, W. R., 38, 43, 48
McCullough P. K., 161, 173
McDaniel, B. A., 183, 198
McDavis, R. J., 32, 49
McDonald, J. D., 258, 264, 267, 295
McDonald-Wikler, L., 179, 198
McEntee, D. J., 212, 213, 227
McGuiness, K., 119, 134
McHugh, M. C., 224, 229
Mckay, R. B., 277, 295
Mahon, A., 4, 12
McMillam, 30
McMillan, E., 272, 295
McNeece, C. A., 247, 254
McRoy, R., 42, 47
McRoy, R., 6, 12, 13
McRoy, R. G., 312, 328
McWhirter, D. P., 246, 255
Meadow-Orlans, K. P., 204, 207, 209, 210, 213, 229
Medicine, B., 266, 296
Medina, M., 70, 84
Meenaghan, T.M., 313, 314, 329
Meissner, D., 316, 329
Melendez, E., 53, 54, 55, 79
Melendy, H. G., 88, 91, 93, 94, 96, 109
Mena, E. J., 75, 85
Mendoza, R. H., 60, 85
Merton, R. K., 41, 48
Meyerson, L., 176, 198
Meyerson, L., 216, 217, 224, 229
Middleton, L., 244, 255
Milgram, S., 128, 134
Milkman, R., 113, 134
Miller, J. B., 113, 134
Miller, S., 319, 329
Miller, T. E., 249, 254
Milligan, S. W., 37, 49
Mintzer, J. E., 160, 174
Minuchin, S., 40, 49
Mirkin, M. P., 126, 134
Mizio, E., 62, 65, 85
Mokuau, N., 8, 12
Mokuau, N., 100, 102, 109

Monbeck, M. E., 219, 229
Monfils, M. J., 190, 198
Monk, A., 62, 64, 84
Montalvo, E., 75, 85
Montana, P., 150, 173
Montgomery, P. A., 56, 57, 58, 85
Monzon, O. T., 240, 255
Moon, M., 19, 20, 49
Moores, D., 205, 228
Moores, R., 205, 208
Morales, R., 54, 55, 56, 57, 58, 85
Mor-Barak, M. E., 145, 146, 149, 173, 174
Morgan, P. O., 206, 226
Morris, J., 163, 174
Morris, J. K., 192, 198
Morris, R., 140, 173
Morrison, M., 147, 148, 149, 173
Morrow, D. F., 9, 13
Morton, G., 102, 107
Mosby, 34, 39, 49
Mosher-Ashley, P. M., 141, 145, 149, 151, 173
Moss, 14
Mothner, I., 113, 134
Moynihan, D. P., 19, 39, 40
Muhall, L., 248, 255
Murphy, B. S., 191, 198
Mutran, E., 41, 49
Myers, H. F., 6, 13
Myers, S. S. L., 18, 20, 46
Myers, J. K., 124, 134

N

Nagel, W. G., 27, 49
Nah, K., 8, 13
Nakanishi, M., 87, 100, 101, 102, 109
National Association of Social Workers, 134
National Commission on Children, 19
National Council on Aging, 150, 173
NASW National Committee on Gay and Lesbian Issues, 5, 13
National Institute of Mental Health, 32, 49
National Urban League, 26
National Society to Prevent Blindness, 214, 229
Neighbors, H. W., 32, 36, 49
Neligh, G., 258, 275, 276, 279, 281, 283, 284, 287, 288, 293, 296
Nelson, A. H., 113, 137
Nelson, D. J., 225, 227

Nett, E. M., 208, 229
Neukrug, E., 219, 229
Nevels, H., 238, 254
Nevill, R. J., 291, 296
New York Times, 32
Nguyen, L. T., 89, 93, 97, 108
Nguyen, Q. T., 102, 109
Niccols, G. A., 277, 296
Nichols, M., 234, 246, 247, 250, 255
Nichols-Casebolt, A., 18, 49
Nicholson, L., 184, 200
Nirenberg, T. D., 126, 133
Nixon, R., 306, 329
Nolan, K., 169, 173
Nobles, W. W. 24, 49
Norton, D., 302, 329
Novak, A. J., 67

O

O'Brien, J., 184, 198
O'Grady-LeShane, R., 118, 134
O'Neil, M. J., 219, 229
O'Neill, J. J., 206, 229
Oboler, S., 53, 85
Oetting, E. R., 60, 76, 85
Offer, D. R., 280, 282, 295
Ogby, J. V., 24, 49
Okimoto, J. T., 102, 109
Olson, M. M., 126, 134
Orlandi, M. A., 301, 309, 329
Orlans, H., 203, 213, 229
Orlin, M., 10, 13
Orlofsky, J. L., 123, 124, 133
Orr, N., 151, 158, 175
Otero-Sabogal, R., 62, 86
Otto, P. L., 113, 116
Owan, T. C., 89, 97, 110
Ozawa, M. N., 10, 13

P

Padilla, A. M., 75, 79, 80, 85
Page, W. J., 127, 132
Palley, M. L., 115, 134
Pang, L. Q., 206, 229
Panitz, D. R., 63, 86
Pannick, D., 28, 49
Parisi, N., 119, 134, 135

Parker, W. M., 32, 49
Parkinson, C. B., 191, 194, 197
Parlee, M. B., 112, 135
Parsons, R. J., 127, 132
Passel, J., 260, 296
Paterson, S. L., 170, 173
Pearce, D., 127, 135
Pearlman, L. M., 114, 137
Peplau, L. A., 239, 255
Perez-Sable, E. Z., 62, 86
Perkins, K., 156, 167, 168, 174
Perl, D. P., 141, 173
Perlmutter, F. D., 128, 135
Permanet Black Underclass, 19
Pervin, I. A., 165, 173
Petchers, M. K., 37, 49
Peterman, T. A., 250, 254
Peters, G. R., 144, 172
Peterson, J. A., 143, 144, 173
Peterson, J. L., 244, 255
Peterson, M., 151, 174
Peterson, R., 214, 228
Pevar, S., 262, 263, 265, 296
Phillips, M. J., 216, 229
Pinderhughes, E. B., 36, 43, 44, 125, 135, 150, 302, 303, 304, 329
Piper, M. H., 129, 135
Pisapia, M. L., 186, 188, 198
Pitonyak, D., 181, 198
Piven, F. F., 127, 132
Plum, F., 157, 174
Podoshin, L., 206, 229
Pomeroy, W. B., 233, 234, 255
Ponterotto, J., 309, 310, 312, 329
Posnick, W. R., 61, 67
Pratt, C., 163, 174
Proctor, C. D., 9, 13
Proctor, C. D., 253, 256
Proctor, E. K., 125, 132
Public Citizen Health Research Group, 160, 175
Puckett, S. B., 249, 256
Pugh, K., 10, 12
Purdy, J. K., 64, 86

Q

Queralt, 68, 70

R

Ramakrishnan, K. R., 316, 317, 318, 320, 321, 329
Ramirez, R., 66, 67, 86
Rasberry, B. H., 188, 198
Rath, B., 90, 104, 109
Redlick, F., 33, 48
Red Horse, J. G., 259, 267, 269, 287, 296
Reid, W. J., 308, 329
Reidel, M., 27, 51
Reimers, D. M., 317, 329
Reimoneng, A., 238, 256
Reinharz, S., 129, 135
Resnick, R., 217, 229
Reynolds, C. F., 156, 167, 174
Reynolds, L., 123, 135
Rhodes, C., 138, 141, 142, 143, 144, 145, 150, 152, 153, 154, 156, 161, 163, 165, 174
Rhodes, E. R., 284, 296
Rice, S., 164, 165, 166, 173
Richek, H. G., 70, 84
Richmond, M. E., 4, 13
Ridley, C. R., 35, 50
Rieger, B. P., 309, 310, 312, 329
Ries, P. W., 203, 205, 206, 229
Rife, J. C., 145, 146, 174
Riffenburgh, R., 219, 229
Riger, S., 122, 133
Riley, 62
Rimmerman, A., 191, 198
Rittner, B., 87, 100, 101, 102, 109
Rix, S. E., 119, 121, 135
Roberts, A., 217, 229
Robertson, S. E., 219, 221, 229, 230
Robins, L. N., 124, 135
Robinson, E. A. R., 125, 133
Robinson, J. B., 302, 329
Rock, M., 120, 135
Rodrigues, C., 53, 85
Rodriguez, M., 75, 85
Rodriquez, C. E., 61, 86
Rogan, A., 289, 296
Ronan, L., 31, 50
Ronnau, J. P., 299, 329
Roscoe, W., 236, 256
Rose, H., 129, 135
Rose, S. M., 191, 199
Rose, T., 184, 195

Rosenfeld, S., 36, 50
Rosenthal, J. A., 70, 84
Rosenthal, E., 32, 35, 50
Rosenwaike, I., 157, 174
Rost, K., 160, 174
Roter, D., 160, 174
Roth, M., 159, 174
Rothman, 65, 70, 78, 86
Rothman, B. K., 123, 135
Rothman, J., 191, 199
Rubin, L., 115, 135
Rousey, C. L., 209, 230
Rowe, W., 309, 328
Rowitz, L., 193, 197
Ruan, F., 236, 256
Rubin, Z., 35, 50
Rubin, A., 188, 189, 192, 199
Rubin, A., 308, 329
Rubinstein, R. L., 160, 174
Ruchlin, H., 163, 174
Rupp, R. R., 209, 229
Russell, D. E., 122, 135
Russell, R. C., 122, 132
Russo, N. F., 123, 135
Ryan, A. S., 96, 103, 105
Ryan, R., 127, 131
Ryff, C. D., 144, 174
Rynearson, A. M., 94, 110

S

Saah, A. J., 240, 254
Sabogal, F., 62, 86
Sack, W., 90, 104, 109
Safford, F., 154, 159, 174
Sagi, P., 157, 174
Saleeby, D., 303, 304, 329, 330
Salgado de Snyder, V. N., 75, 86
Sanders, M., 120, 135
Sanford, L. T., 120, 123, 135
Sapiro, V., 116, 119, 120, 123, 135
Sauber, R., 63, 86
Sawyer, M. B., 39, 50
Scharf, L., 113, 135
Scharlach, A. E., 149, 174
Scheff, T., 36, 50
Schein, J. D., 205, 230
Scheyett, A., 121, 127, 135
Schiele, J. H., 303, 322, 329

Schiff, M., 206, 230
Schilling, R. F., 240, 255
Schinke, S., 278, 290, 291, 292
Schinke, S. P., 309, 329
Schlesinger, E. G., 300, 309, 314, 321, 322, 329
Schlossberg, N. K., 219, 230
Schmall, V., 163, 174
Schmolling, P., Jr., 219, 221, 230
Schopler, J. H., 302, 327
Schreiber, M., 186, 199
Schultz, G., 102, 104, 105, 110
Schulz, P., 219, 220, 230
Schwartz, L. R., 247, 256
Schwartz, P., 121, 131
Scotch, R. K., 178, 199
Scott, 71
Scott, A. F., 113, 135
Scott, A. M., 113, 135
Scott, R. A., 217, 221, 230
Segrin, C., 138, 174
Seltzer, M. M., 179, 182, 183, 196, 199
Shanks, S. L., 215, 216, 230
Shapiro, A., 217, 226
Shapiro, J., 221, 230
Shapiro, J. P., 10, 13
Sheldon, R. G., 126, 132
Shelley, J., 121, 132
Sherrets, T., 35, 51
Sherwood, S., 163, 174
Shiels, J. W., 210, 230
Shock, N. W., 138, 139, 174
Shontz, F. C., 224, 230
Shotland, R., 319, 330
Siegel, L., 305, 330
Silk, K. L., 206, 231
Sills, J. S., 143, 174
Silver, S. M., 293
Silverstein, C., 251, 255
Simmons, F. B., 206, 230
Singh, R., 301, 328
Singleton, S. M., 323, 324, 330
Skeen, P., 164, 165, 172
Sloan, I., 14, 50
Slotkin, S., 270, 296
Small, G. W., 156, 167, 174
Smallegan, M., 155, 157, 174
Smith, J. M., 37, 50
Smith, B. E., 122, 136
Smith, E., 264, 296

Smith, E. M. J., 112, 135
Smith, G. C., 184, 199
Smith, L., 205, 227
Smith, M., 248, 250, 256
Smith, T., 232, 254
Smith, W. E., 186, 199
Snell, W. R., 123, 133
Snipp, C., 260, 268, 296
Sobel, S. B., 123, 135
Solomon, B., 303, 304, 330
Sorensen, R. C., 239, 256
Sparks, R., 309, 310, 312, 329
Spearman, M., 306, 329
Specht, H., 4, 13
Specht, R., 161, 168, 174
Special Issue on Women, 124, 136
Spelkoman, D., 217, 226
Spencer, M. B., (et al), 38, 50
Spicker, P., 319, 330
Spindler, G., 270, 291, 296
Spindler, L., 270, 291, 296
Stack, C., 41, 50
Stafford, W. W., 20, 50
Stanley, L., 129, 136
Staples, R., 24, 26, 27, 30, 50
Starr, P., 161, 174
Statham, D., 116, 125, 133
Steffensmeier, R., 124, 136
Stein, E. M., 156, 167, 174
Sterns, C. R., 186, 199
Sterns, H. L., 146, 175
Steuer, J., 157, 175
Stewart, D. E., 122, 136
Stock, W., 126, 136
Stocks, J. T., 220, 230
Stoddard, E. R., 215, 216, 230
Stoneman, Z., 181, 199
Storms, M. D., 253, 256
Strawbridge, W. J., 138, 175
Strom, S. H., 113, 136
Stulberg, I., 248, 250, 256
Sue, S., 33, 50
Sue, D., 102, 107
Sue, D. W., 259, 267, 289, 296
Sue, D., 259, 267, 289, 296
Sui, S., 292, 295
Swan, F., 164, 175
Swigert, U. L., 27, 50

T

Taber's cyclopedic medical dictionary, 153, 175
Talbott, J., 163, 164, 175
Tanfer, K., 234, 254
Tangri, S., 122, 136
Taube, C., 161, 173
Tausig, M., 181, 199
Tavris, C. B., 123, 124, 125, 136
Taylor, R. J., 32, 37, 49, 50,
Tennessee Commission on Eldercare, 146, 175
Teri, L., 156, 167, 174
Terrell, R., 33, 50
Terrell, S., 33, 50
Terry, J. A., 33, 46
Thase, M. E., 178, 199
Thomas, A. J., 203, 208, 230
Thomason, T., 258, 297
Thompson, D. C., 40
Thompson, S. D., 291, 297
Thornton, S., 300, 301, 309, 312, 324, 330
Thyer, B. A., 7, 12, 130, 136, 188, 191, 198, 199, 220, 230, 309, 330
Tice, C., 156, 167, 168, 174
Tidwell, B., 6, 13
Tienda, M., 117, 136
Timbrook, R. E., 311, 330
Tippeconnic, J. W., 275, 297
Tobin, S. S., 184, 199
Tomaszewski, E. P., 189, 199
Toseland, R. W., 179, 198
Towns, F., 181, 196
Tracey, T. J., 125, 133
Treatment Team Handbook, 240, 256
Triandis, H., 34, 51, 61, 86
Trimble, J. E., 262, 289, 297, 309, 329
Tsai, Y., 236, 256
Tsui, P., 102, 104, 105, 110
Turk, M. A., 178, 199
Turner, C., 234, 254
Turner, F. J., 219, 230
Tuttle, D. W., 202, 215, 217, 219, 220, 221, 230
Tutty, L. M., 308, 330
Tyler, I. M., 291, 297
Tynan, M., 145, 146, 149, 173

U

Uba, L., 94, 95, 97, 98, 111
Underwood, L., 181, 188, 191, 199
Unger, O., 181, 199
Unz, R. K., 317, 330
U.S. Bureau of Labor Statistics, 19
U.S. Department of Commerce, Bureau of the Census, 262, 264, 265, 275
U.S. Department of Commerce, Bureau of the Census, 114, 136
U.S. Department of Commerce, Bureau of the Census, 123, 136
U.S. Department of Commerce, Bureau of the Census, 117, 121, 136
U.S. Department of Commerce, Bureau of the Census, 118, 136
U.S. Department of Commerce, Bureau of the Census, 117, 118, 121, 136
U.S. Department of Education, 116, 136
U.S. Department of Health, Education, Welfare, 30
U.S. Department of Health and Human Services, Indian Health Service Office of Planning, Evaluation, and Research, 261, 263, 264, 268, 276–283
U.S. Department of Interior, Bureau of Indian Affairs, 260, 265, 273, 297
U.S. Department of Justice, 122, 136
U.S. Department of Labor, 117, 120, 136
U.S. Elections: Some gains for women, 118, 136
U.S. Senate Special Committee on Aging, 153, 175

V

Van Oss, Marin, B., 62, 86
Van Soest, D., 321, 323, 324, 326, 330
Varga-Willis, G., 59, 86
Vaughan, C. E., 215, 216, 217, 218, 220, 221, 222, 230
Ventress, C., 34, 51
Vernon, M., 203, 204, 205, 206, 207, 208, 210, 230

W

Wagner, E. E., 207, 228
Walker, A., 121, 137

Wan, T., 168, 175
Wanat, J., 127, 134
Warshaw, G. A., 159, 171
Washington, A. C., 29, 51
Watts, T. D., 31, 51
Weaver, N. H., (in press), 60, 86
Weibel, J., 277, 297
Weibel-Orlando, J., 276, 288, 297
Weick, A., 304, 330
Weiner, L., 115, 137
Weiss, R. S., 121, 137
Weitz, S., 235, 256
Weitzman, L. J., 121, 137
Weitzman, L. J., 121, 127, 137
Wekker, G., 233, 256
Welke, D., 190, 197
Wells, C., 158, 175
Wells, J. W., 238, 256
Wertheimer, B. M., 113, 137
Wertimer, D. M., 238, 256
Westermeyer, J., 89, 90, 111
White, J. F., 183, 196
Wilhite, B., 184, 200
Williams, B., 153, 154, 171
Williams, M., 308, 330
Williams, S. E., 8, 13
Williams, S. E., 303, 330
Wilson, W. J., 21, 41, 51
Wilson, J., 181, 200
Wilturner, L. T., 180, 196
Wingert, J., 278, 298
Winkler, A. E., 117, 121, 131
Winkler, D. M., 217, 230
Wirt, R., 74, 85
Wise, S., 129, 136
Witkin, S. L., 129, 137
Wodarski, J. S., 27, 51
Wolf-Klein, G. P., 145, 172
Wolfe, S. M., 160, 175
Wolfgang M. E., (et al), 27, 51
Wolinsky, F. D., 142, 175
Womble, M., 301, 302, 304, 326
Women in the states: Governors, Legislators, Candidates, 119, 137
Wong, M., 98, 99, 108
Wood, P., 35, 51
Woodman, N. J., 242, 245, 256
Wool, H., 114, 137
Wright, R., 31, 51

Wright, B. A., 217, 226
Wright, B. C., 212, 230
Wright, D. F., 8, 13
Wright, D. F., 303, 330
Wright, J. W., 206, 231
Wright, S., 163, 174
Wyers, N., 253, 256

Y

Yaffe, N., 157, 174
Yeakey, 16, 21, 25

Yee, S., 192, 200
Youkeles, M., 219, 221, 230
Young, D., 240, 255
Young, M., 205, 212
Young, T., 260, 261, 266, 277, 278, 279, 281,
    298

Z

Zarit, J., 151, 158, 175
Zarit, S., 151, 158, 175
Zastrow, C., 221, 231

SUBJECT INDEX

A

Activity theory, 142–144
Acute condition, 153, 154
Adjustment, 207–209, 219–220
Affirmative action policy, 318–321
Aged
  Characteristics, 140, 142
  Definition, 141, 148
Aging
  Health concerns, 150, 153
  Historical aspects, 138–240
  Hospital care, 161, 162
  Mental health conditions, 163–164, 167
  Myths, 151, 165, 171
  Population trends 138–142, 147, 156, 161, 166
  Sexuality, 164–167
  Study of, 138–139
  Theories of 142–144
AIDS, 30, 240, 245, 248–251
American Association of Mental Deficiency, 185
American Association of Mental Retardation, 191
American Psychiatric Association, 124, 157, 158
Americans with Disabilities Act, 10, 178–182,
Applied behavior analysis, 39
Asian religions, 89, 92–93
Asian socioeconomics, 97–100
Asian World View, 92–95
Assessment methods, 310–312
Assistance and Bill of Rights Act Amendments, 187
Attention-deficit hyperactivity disorder (ADHA), 181

B

Baby boomers, 140, 149
Behavior modification techniques, 61
Bisexual, 250–251
  Definition of, 232, 234, 249
  Legal issues, 242
  Myths, 239
  Prevalence, 234
  Practice issues, 251–253
  Religion, 241
  Coming out, 243
Black Power Movement, 15
Blindness, defining, 214–216
Body language, 212–213

C

Caribbean, Central America, & South America, 55
Characteristics and Demographics, 55–58
Chinese, 88, 91–93
Chronic conditions, 153–154, 159–160, 166
Civil Rights Movement, 15
Communication with the deaf, 209–213
Compadrazgo, 64
Council on Social Work Education, 185, 189, 190, 192, 300
Crime, 26–28
Cubans, 54
Cultural awareness, 25, 43
Cultural competence, 301–303, 305–307, 309–310
Cultural diversity Training, 305–306
Cultural identity, 59–61, 76
Cultural stereotyping, 102
Curanderismo, 69

D

Deafness, 203–214
Death, 169–170
Death, 249
Dementia, 157–159
Depression, 156, 157, 159
Developmental Disabilities Assistance and Bill
    of Rights Act, 177, 179
Disabilities Services and Facilities Construc-
    tion Act, 1970, 177
Discrimination, 217–218
Disengagement theory, 142, 143
Downs syndrome, 90, 99, 183
DRG system, 161, 162
Drugs & alcohol

E

Education, 73, 116, 128
Education of All Handicapped Children, 180
Education, social work, 321–326
Elderly (*see also* aged), 168–171
Elderly Asians, 95
Elderly women, 168
Empirical research, 308–309, 310
Employment, 113, 114, 116, 117, 119, 120,
    127
Empowerment, 303–304
Erectile failure, 165, 166
Espiritismo, 68
Ethnic-sensitivity, 300–303, 307–307
Ethnographic research, 312, 324
Ethnographic studies, 6
Etiology of deafness, 206
Extinction, 44

F

Faggot, 237
Family, 62–66
Family therapy, 104
Family unit, 14, 16–18, 22–24, 39–44
Female headed households, 18
Feminism/feminists, 113, 115, 120, 123–130
Filial piety, 93
Filipinos, 91

G

Gay bars, 247
Gender, 304–305, 325–326
Gerontology, 139
Great Depression, 138, 139

H

Health care, 28–32
Health concerns of aging, 154–157
Health/mental health, 123–126
Hearing aids, 34, 210–211
Hearing impairment/concerns, 154
Heart disease, 154
Help-seeking behaviors, 100–103
Heterosexist, 253
Heterosexuality,
    Definition of, 232, 233, 234
    Prevalence, 234
History, 52
History/changing role of women, 112–114, 117,
    118
Hmong, 90, 91, 97
Homophobia, 243, 246, 248
Homosexuality
    Coming out, 243
    Cultural perspectives, 235
    Definition of, 232
    Incidence of, 234
    Legal, 242
    Medical model, 241
    Myths and stereotypes, 239–240
    Oppression, 237
    Practice implications, 245
Hospice, 170
Hospital care, 161, 162
Human developmental theory, 144

I

Immigration, 72, 140
Immigration policy, 316–318
Intelligence testing, 152
Interpreter, 212–212

J

Japanese, 88

K

Korean, 91, 92

L

Labelling, 214–216
Language, 69
Language, 321–322, 325
Leisure time, 149
Lesbians
  Coming out, 243–244
  Definition of, 232, 233
  Discrimination, 244
  Legal aspects, 242
  Myths and stereotypes, 239–241
  Oppression, 237
  Practice implications, 245
Lipreading, 210–211
Living wills, 170
Long term care facilities, 163

M

Machismo/marianismo, 63–64
Macro practice, 305–307
Marital Counseling, 106, 107
Media, 120
Medical model and homosexuality, 241
Medicare, 161, 170
Medications, 157, 159, 160, 166
Mental health, 32–38
Mental health concerns, 163, 164, 167, 170
Mental Retardation Practice Inventory, 191, 192
Minority, 301, 304, 322
Minority groups, 205
Multicultural, 323, 325
Multi-infarct dementia, 158

N

National Association of Social Workers, 185, 186, 189, 19
National Learning Disabilities Network, 74
Normal aging, 151

O

Old age, 138
Older adults, 206, 209
Older Americans Act, 184
Oldest-old, 10
Oppression/inequality of women 112, 116, 118–121, 123–127
Outcome studies, 309–310

P

People of color, 322
Pink triangle, 237, 238
Policy, 221–223
Political/legal, 113–115, 118, 119, 122, 127
Poverty, 19
Poverty rate, 57
Practice, 299–307, 316
Prevalence of deafness, 205
Principles for practice, 71–72
Principles For research, 80–81
Psychology adjustment, 207–208
Psychopharmacology with elderly, 157, 159, 160, 166
Puerto Ricans, 54

Q

Qualitative methods, 312–313
Quantitative methods, 312–313

R

Race, 302–303, 317
Race/ethnicity, 112, 113, 117, 121
Racism, 302–303, 322
Rehabilitation Act Amendments, 182
Religion, 25, 66, 120
Research, 224, 307–314
Retirement,
  History, 147
  Current perspective, 148
Risk, conceptualization of, 313–314

S

Santeria, 68
Santiquadores, 69

Sappho, 232
Self-esteem, 74–76
Senile, 151
Service delivery, 76–80
Settlement House Movement, 4
Sexuality and aging, 164–167
Sexual orientation, 252, 253
Shame, 96
Sign language, 203, 212
Sign language interpreter, 212–213
Social adjustment, 208
Social policy, 314–321
Social work education, 223
Socialization, 38–39
Socioeconomic status, 116–120, 126
Southeast Asians, 89, 90
Stereotypes, 216–218
Suicide, 167–169

T

Technological advancement, 225

U

Unemployment, 20
Unemployment 139, 145, 148
University affiliated program, 190, 191,

V

Value, 61
Violence/rape, 121, 122
Vision impairment, 154, 155
Visual impairment, 214–225

W

White House Conference, 184
Women, 304–305, 325–326
Work place adjustment, 208–209
World war, 138, 139

Y

Young Adult Institute, 189